Becoming Free in the Cotton South

BECOMING
FREE
IN THE
COTTON
SOUTH

Susan Eva O'Donovan

HARVARD UNIVERSITY PRESS

CAMBRIDGE, MASSACHUSETTS ❀ LONDON, ENGLAND 2007

Library of Congress Cataloging-in-Publication Data

O'Donovan, Susan E.
Becoming free in the cotton South / Susan Eva O'Donovan
p. cm.
Includes bibliographical references and index.
ISBN-13: 978-0-674-02483-0
ISBN-10: 0-674-02483-4
1. Slaves—Georgia—Social conditions—19th century. 2. Freedmen—Georgia—
History—19th century. 3. Slavery—Social aspects—Georgia—History—
19th century. 4. Slaves—Emancipation—United States. 5. Cotton growing—
Social aspects—Georgia—History—19th century. 6. Plantation life—Georgia—
History—19th century. 7. Georgia—Social conditions—19th century.
8. Georgia—History—Civil War, 1861–1865. 9. Georgia—History—1865–
10. Georgia—Race relations—History—19th century. I. Title.

E445.G3 O36 2007
973.7/1140975822   2006052022

For Merle and Marianne

Contents

Acknowledgments

The debts I have accrued in writing this book are abundant. My slothful pace accounts for a number of those obligations. The generosity of the people I've encountered over those years accounts for a good many more. Leading the list are Lee W. Formwalt, who a very long time ago introduced a complete stranger to southwest Georgia, and Steven Hahn, who has nudged me along with equal doses of frankness and friendship. Together they have taught me what it is that the best mentors do. Eight years at the epicenter of emancipation studies—the Freedmen and Southern Society Project at the University of Maryland—gave me a historical perspective no individual could possibly obtain on his or her own. While our collective endeavors focused on the events that unfolded in the wake of the Confederate surrender, my ongoing conversations with Steven Hahn, Anthony E. Kaye, Steven F. Miller, John C. Rodrigue, Leslie S. Rowland, and Stephen A. West, about the conflicts that punctuated the first months of freedom, repeatedly called my attention to the complicated connections between black people's pasts and the futures they envisioned. Ira Berlin had stepped down as director of the project before I arrived, but his influence on my thinking cannot be overstated. Nor can his readiness to support junior scholars. Ira has read every page of this book, offering sage advice at each turn and raising deceptively simple questions—some of which I'm still trying to answer.

Harvard has provided me with the perfect environment to advance and elaborate on the lessons I learned in Maryland. I am particularly indebted to Emmanuel K. Akyeampong, Sven Beckert, Vincent Brown, Caroline Elkins, Henry Louis Gates Jr., Evelyn Brooks Higginbotham, James Kloppenberg, Orlando Patterson, Tommy Shelby, and John Stauffer for making space for me within Harvard's community of scholars, and for their willingness to advise on all matters, large and small. I thank the departments of History and African and African American Studies for the leave that made it possible to accept James C. Scott's offer of a spot at Yale University's Program in Agrarian Studies. There, surrounded by pictures of chickens and a cohort of fellows who quickly came to be friends—Nancy Jacobs, Peter Linder, Dilip Menon, Hugh Raffles, and Leander Schneider—I found myself writing a much different and, I would like to think, much better book, one that reflects a year in which I learned new ways to see and speak of the people I study. Harvard has been generous in other ways as well: awarding me a Clarke/Cook grant that funded a rich and rewarding trip to Georgia; providing a wealth of teaching and research support; and above all, entrusting me with a sequence of very smart students, most of whom have probably heard their fill about southwestern Georgia but all of whom helped make the book a much stronger study. Indeed, it was in working with them that I finally figured out how to write.

Ideas take shape at conferences, seminars, and public presentations, as well as in archives and libraries. Mine have been no exception. I have rehearsed pieces of my research before audiences on both sides of the Atlantic, in four countries, seven states, and twelve universities. There is no way I can possibly thank all of those in attendance for the tough questions they asked, for the evidence they called to my attention, and for corrections gently offered. But rest assured that the welcome they gave me and the insights they shared have not gone unnoticed. I can, however, single out those colleagues and friends who have read and commented on chapter drafts—sometimes more than one and sometimes more than once. These truly good citizens include Christina Adkins, Emmanuel K. Akyeampong, Ira Berlin, Vincent Brown, Jonathan M. Bryant, Vincent Carretta, Paul A. Cimbala, David Brion Davis, Stanley Engerman, Michael W. Fitzgerald, Lee W. Formwalt, Harold Forsythe, Alejandro de la Fuenta, Steven Hahn, Evelyn Brooks Higginbotham, Nancy Jacobs, Brian Kelly, Peter Linder, Mary Ann Mahony, Kay Mansfield, Dilip Menon, Joseph C. Miller, David Montgomery, Katy O'Donovan Peterson, Ami Potter (who also gave me run of her New Haven home), Lawrence N. Powell, Hugh Raffles, Joseph P. Reidy, Leander Schneider, James C. Scott, John Stauffer, Joe William Trotter Jr., Sarah J. G. Wauzynski, and Stephen A. West. Special thanks go to the anonymous readers for Harvard University Press, without whose careful scrutiny this book would be considerably diminished. None of these generous people, of course, bear any responsibility for errors, omissions, faulty assumptions, or lapses of logic. Those belong entirely to me.

Researching, thinking, and writing are only three parts of a much larger process. Granted, they are important, but so is getting a book to press and keeping the author healthy and human. Credit for the first goes to a wonderful team of editors at Harvard University Press. Joyce Seltzer enthusiastically and efficiently brought to a close a project David Lobenstine started, taking my manuscript into her very capable and caring hands when David departed the Press for another career. Without Joyce's timely and wise interventions, as well as those of Elizabeth Gilbert, Wendy Nelson, and the folks whom I only know as "Marketing," this would be much less of a book, and certainly more difficult to read. My siblings Carrie and Sarah contributed a geologist's sense of time and an artist's sense of aesthetics, while Tom and Donna took me for hikes, horseback rides, and exhilarating snowmobile adventures. Katy—who grew up, graduated from college, found John, and launched a career as I puttered along—provided that brand of loving but brutal critique that daughters like to reserve for their mothers. The dogs insisted on regular runs; the cats warmed my lap; the horses offered much-needed distraction; and Lee took care of everything else, even when it meant following me into the mountains of south-central New Hampshire and onto a farm that grows more rocks than it does trees. But most of all, credit in the end goes to my parents, who convinced us as kids that we could be whatever we wanted, and that whatever we wanted was sufficient for them. Thus as one of a family that is best described as joyously eclectic, I give this book to Mom and Dad: a little something to read come winter in Taneum Canyon.

BECOMING

FREE

IN THE

COTTON

SOUTH

Introduction

This book is about a small place and big questions. It is about the southwest corner of Georgia between the second decade of the nineteenth century, when the area opened to white settlement, and the presidential election of 1868, a moment that marked the beginning of the end of regional radical politics. It is about the black men and black women who, torn abruptly and often with little warning from their natal homes to the north, the east, and sometimes the west, came to occupy that place and through their labor, rapidly transformed forest to field. It is about how, on that strange terrain, surrounded by strange faces, and in all too many cases confronted with the unfamiliar but nearly all-consuming demands of cotton's regime, those black men and black women struggled to make their lives anew. It is a story about a Civil War that, held at bay by an accident of geography as much as by the political maneuverings of the region's slaveholders, served more to amplify than to revolutionize antebellum rhythms of slave life and production. It is about a late-arriving, loosely supervised liberation, one that in its initial phases gave the initiative more to old masters than to new freedpeople, a circumstance that when coupled with a federally enforced mandate to planters to purchase the labor power they had once taken by force, galvanized black people—led at a critical juncture by black women—to mobilize in a near-futile defense of their own particular vision of freedom.

What follows is also, in many important respects, a gendered story. Other things mattered, and sometimes they mattered in

ways that eclipsed the social distinctions between men and women. Such was the case of a domestic trade in slaves that selected
primarily for age. But how southwest Georgians thought about
enslaved men and women's social, productive, and political roles
ebbs and flows through this story from beginning to end. Never
a parallel story or a secondary story, gender, which is as much a
historical construct as is place or race or class and arises from a
common set of circumstances, constitutes an integral dimension
of a single story about slavery, about freedom, and about the
passage between them.[1] The gender assumptions embraced by
white slaveholders, for instance, contributed in significant ways
to the gendering of slaves' everyday labor. This was a development with enormous consequences for the communities and
domestic relations that slaves were fashioning under cotton's oppressive reign. Later, as wartime cannons boomed, black men's
understandings about their responsibilities to their wives and
children kept them anchored to antebellum homes rather than
heading in all due haste toward Union lines and an early liberation. When freedom finally arrived and former slaveholders acknowledged that they must henceforth pay for the labor services
they had formerly taken by force, they applied a calculus of gender in evaluating whom to hire and whom to fire. To avoid the
disaster that subsequently loomed, black women, whose value to
planters had declined precipitously since emancipation, adapted
to an economic and political crisis born of free labor, domestic
assumptions born under slavery.

The story of southwest Georgia's transition from bondage to
freedom is a tragic one. Slavery, by all accounts of its black survivors, was horrific. Full freedom, replete with promises of civil
and political equality, was short-lived, felled by a shower of violence that preyed on the vulnerabilities of a people emancipated
with little but the clothes on their backs and the flimsiest of in-

stitutions on which to depend. And black women discovered all too soon that the system of family-based wage labor, which they were instrumental in ushering in, could be used by landowners and planters to bludgeon them down. In the seasons following radical politics' untimely decline, sharecropping, with its well-documented litany of evils, would gradually spread across the region, eating away at black people's lingering hopes that liberation might translate into an economic and political autonomy even as they attempted to expand control over their labor and their lives. As the century drew to a close, and as black people in many other southern communities and locations continued to elect their own to political office, about all that southwest Georgia's black men and black women had left were their dreams. As one historian of nineteenth-century black political life remarked recently of southwest Georgia, the "rack-renting remnants of an older plantation regime" had in the years following freedom "squeeze[ed] everything but the life out of its black denizens."[2] Reconstruction was a revolution that failed, but it failed with shocking speed in a region where slave society arrived fast, ferociously, and late.

The details are grim, especially when viewed from the perspective of the black men and black women who heroically and repeatedly constituted and reconstituted their lives and their selves, only to fall short of their goals in the end. It is a story that breaks away from the tendency among scholars of slavery and emancipation to extol the power of self-determination.[3] Aspirations, we learn from closely examining black southwest Georgians' passages to freedom, are not possibilities. Choices are not limitless. Human reality, their experiences remind us, is contingent, but it is not boundlessly so.[4] In the case of the black men and black women of southwestern Georgia who in the months following liberation labored to once again rebuild their lives, what they managed to create was conditioned by what they had been, what they had done, and what they had endured in the past. Their experience underscores Marx's observation: "Men [and women] make their own history, but they do not make it just as they please; they do not make it under circumstances chosen by themselves, but under circumstances directly found, given and transmitted from [their] past[s]."[5]

Such was the case in the former slaveholding South. There, where the slaveries were many, freedom often assumed numerous and differently gendered shapes. Thus it was that in October 1865, as the nation shrank back from the revolution it had unleashed, black men situated on the South Carolina sea islands voiced desires that emerged out of a past distinctly their own. These men were products of a low-country regime characterized by a relative demographic and social stability, as well as by tasking, a method of labor organization that gave workers considerable control over the pace of their labor. They visualized in a petition a new nation composed of black people in possession of property accumulated in bondage and salvaged from war. "General," pleaded the men who claimed ownership of "Horses, cattle, carriages, & articles of furniture," "we want Homesteads." A few months later and a few miles north, a crowd of female hucksters of Portsmouth, Virginia—longtime entrepreneurial habitants of urban streets and public spaces—envisioned a state as welcoming to black women as to black men. Indeed, they presumed to speak not only for themselves, but for their husbands as well. Then deeper into the south, at the tag end of Georgia's so-called cotton belt, in the rural isolation of the state's late-settled southwestern corner, a still-different version of freedom gradually unfolded as the nation struggled to recover from four years of war. There, where the disruptions of a vast domestic migration were not yet a thing of the past and where most black institutions remained youthful and fragile, freedwomen salvaged themselves and their tiniest children from planters' version of freedom and free labor by invoking one of their own.[6]

In North America, where slavery was first and foremost a system of labor, those multiple configurations of freedom derived to a considerable extent from the services black people had performed for their owners. To be sure, slaves' lives could not be reduced to work. They played, they courted; they married and had babies. They cultivated gardens, raised small flocks of poultry, and sang out at Sabbath-day services. They dressed their hair and their bodies in colorful styles reflective of personal, cultural, and political proclivities. And when the tearful moment arrived, they buried their dead with kindness and dignity. But exceedingly rare were the slave men or women who could for even the briefest of moments step outside the oppressive system of labor that ensnared them. This became especially true as slaveholders tightened their control in the years following the Prosser, Vesey, and Turner rebellions, and as slavery's free critics raised their voices in an ever more strident chorus. Hence, whatever slave men and slave women managed to do for themselves, the scope and constituency of the institutions they formed, even the meanings they ascribed to being a man or a woman, had a good deal to do with the nature and location of the labor their owners demanded and whom they found themselves working alongside.[7]

In the fields of southwest Georgia, cotton's gang regime was the backdrop against which a forcibly recruited army of enslaved men and women struggled to fashion anew their communities, their cultures, their families, their senses of self. Thrust into a system plotted and patrolled by slaveholders intent on recouping their investments, southwest Georgia's black workers found little spare time at their disposal. If opportunities—economic, social, as well as political—beckoned enticingly from places like Richmond, Virginia's shadowy back alleys, riverside dives, and the boardinghouses operated by free people of color and patronized by slaves, they closed down with a snap in that hinterland corner of Georgia where Florida abuts Alabama.[8] What lives slave migrants reconstituted for themselves, they made right under their masters' (and mistresses') noses. Thus it was in the cotton fields, the gin houses, on the wooden seats of the wagons that regularly trundled from one plantation to another, at the wartime salt-making camps located along the Gulf coast, that the region's black men and black women revised understandings about their roles and responsibilities as parents, as producers, as partners. It was in the course of serving their owners that black southwest Georgians etched into the social terrain of their enslavement the basic parameters of the freedom for which they yearned. And so, when the Civil War ended and the sixty-two thousand or so black men, women, and children who occupied the plantations around Albany, Thomasville, and Cuthbert came to be liberated, the freedom they attempted to define as they navigated their way across the postwar terrain bore a considerable allegiance to what they had been and done in the past.

To be sure, America's former slaves in Reconstruction shared many of the same goals. They all knew the value of education, a lesson driven home repeatedly after emancipation as most struggled to defend themselves against employers' dubious accountings and to meet contractual terms that few of them could read on their own. As laborers in an agricultural economy, most believed that land provided the only meaningful foundation for social and political autonomy. Black women, who had been as deeply involved in market production and community building as black men under slavery, never seemed to consider the shaping of freedom wholly a man's business. But black people's notions about how those ends would be achieved, on what terms, to what effect, and especially by whom, were matters of considerable dispute among the freed slaves. When a group of black clergymen, many of whom were free before the Civil War and many of whom were longtime guardians of church property and church wealth, offered their advice on the subject to General William T. Sherman in January 1865, like countless other black southerners they expressed an interest in land, asking the general if they might be placed on it "until we are able to buy it and make it our own." The ministers' belief that the market constituted the primary means by which to obtain propertied independence was not shared, however, by ex-slaves on the South Carolina sea islands, a people who, although they had frequently been owners of other forms of property, argued for land in equity as compensation for their unpaid labors in bondage. Nor was it shared by the vast majority of black southwest Georgians, whose experiences in slavery had virtually foreclosed the possibility of purchasing much of anything in freedom, let alone a parcel of land. Similarly, it is difficult to imagine that those petitioning Portsmouth hucksters, who assumed they held the ear of national officials, or the black women of Richmond who after freedom formed their own marching clubs and joined black men in the city's streets, would exchange places with someone like southwest Georgia's Henrietta, a black woman who shielded herself from freedom's impositions by "promis[ing] and agree[ing]" to a labor agreement drawn up in the name of her husband.[9]

　　Without a doubt, black southerners took more than a few cues from their liberators. This was particularly true of the emancipated men who had shared bivouacs and battlefields with Abraham Lincoln's northern-born soldiers.[10] But America's multiple slaveries played a significant role in begetting what has emerged from scholarly desks over the past few decades as a welter of freedoms.[11] Recognizing the substance and source of that postwar diversity, however, requires a critical shift in perspective. And that is what this book sets out to provide. Rather than taking as its starting point the moment of liberation, a methodological approach that has the effect of neatly—and artificially—dividing black people's lives into unconnected, if serial, narratives, *Becoming Free* opens with the first days of slavery on southwest Georgia's frontier terrain. For it was there, as settlers, traders, merchants, and masters poured in, with their sights firmly fixed on cotton and the profits it promised to bring, that the region's own species of freedom really began.

Southwest Georgia lends itself particularly well to an analysis of this order. Settled late and settled hurriedly, the region's history compresses into four or five decades dynamic processes that in most other corners of the slaveholding South unfolded over much longer stretches of time. This characteristic has the advantage of reducing the analytical "clutter" that obtains as populations change and age, as cities and towns come into being, as economies diversify and expand, and as deepening layers of contingency increase exponentially the number of influences that continuously shape and reshape human experience. Southwest Georgia's location well off the beaten path likewise recommends it to a close examination of the relationship between the rhythms and routines of slavery in the cotton South and the forms freedom took in the years following black liberation. During the Civil War, for instance, no Union armies fought across or occupied any part of the region. This was a phenomenon that not only introduced new players and new sensibilities to large sections of Mississippi, Louisiana, and Virginia, but also abruptly disrupted preexisting social and productive relations between men and women, and masters and slaves. Similarly, southwest

Georgia's geographic location has allowed it to evade scholarly scrutiny. Indeed, the region's historians can almost be counted on one hand, and most of them have focused almost exclusively on the twentieth century or have confined their inquiries to narrowly defined events or moments in time.[12]

This book is not a regional history in the conventional meaning of the term. My interest lies less in coming to know a place than in coming to know how the "socio-ecological order" of a place—any place—infused much larger processes with distinctive and localized dimensions. Nonetheless, *Becoming Free* has the advantage of calling attention to an understudied corner of the cotton South, a component of a much bigger landscape that on the eve of secession contained almost three-quarters of the nation's slaves.[13] In this sense, then, what unfolded in southwestern Georgia in the mid-nineteenth century was at one and the same time universal and particular. It was deeply embedded in and a part of a national and indeed transnational story about the demise of slaveholding systems. It also, and importantly, retained at the same time its own distinctive regional flavor, a combination of the small and the large, the micro and the macro, the specific and the general, that when taken together have much to teach us about the factors and forces that shaped slavery, freedom, and the passages that lay between them.

1

Doing

the Master's

Bidding

The plantation society of southwest Georgia rose quickly, if late, in the development of southern slavery. Long the homeland of the Lower Creeks and hunted across by Seminoles, the region did not see the arrival of any appreciable number of white settlers until well into the second decade of the nineteenth century. But when peoples of European descent came, they came in great numbers, and they came suddenly. Moreover, they came with the Africans and people of African descent whose labor many of them commanded. By the eve of the Civil War, a prosperous slave society had sprung up in the basin that straddled the Flint River. It was to be short-lived. Within two generations, Civil War and Reconstruction would sweep the land, reconfiguring political and social relations. Nonetheless, in that forty-year interval between settlement and emancipation, tens of thousands of black men, women, and children plowed, hoed, chopped, and harvested the land, bringing their owners wealth, power, and privilege.

The services that enslaved men and women performed for their masters and mistresses, and the conditions under which they performed them, left indelible and distinctive marks on their lives in bondage and ultimately on their futures. How the slaves who came to inhabit southwest Georgia thought about themselves as men and women, as producers, and as participants in broader communities—indeed, the parameters of the freedom for which they yearned—would be deeply conditioned by the day-to-day requirements of making their owners' cotton.

Today southwest Georgia is filled with pecan orchards, fields of corn, cotton, and soybeans, factories and towns, but it was a much quieter place at the beginning of the nineteenth century. Back then southwest Georgia was tied to an Atlantic world by a trade in deerskins and cattle, and by the occasional travelers (generally white frontiersmen and slaves on the lam) who passed through the lightly rolling hills, piney woods, and oak thickets—all part of the coastal plain—while en route to Florida and the Gulf coast. Traders and missionaries camped in scattered locations along the rivers and creeks. But the region's permanent residents consisted primarily of the Lower Creeks, an agricultural Native American people whose main towns lay along the Chattahoochee River, and who had only in the previous half century begun establishing subsidiary villages in the Flint River drainage.

Despite long-standing trading relations with Europeans and later Americans, the Lower Creeks found themselves subject to the same federal actions that were clearing Native Americans from regions to the north and west. In a series of treaties signed between 1814 and 1826, they ceded to the United States and Georgia their traditional homelands, most of which lay in the southwest portion of the state. In turn, the state divided the appropriated land into standard-size lots ranging from the 400-some-acre parcels carved from the 1814 cession to the 202.5-acre parcels of the subsequent cessions. A public lottery redistributed the land among the state's citizens, and some (such as men with wives and minor children, military veterans, orphans, and wid-

ows with minor children) received multiple draws. The only payment required was a nominal fee of a few dollars per hundred acres. Government largesse ensured that the several million acres that constituted southwest Georgia quickly made their way into private hands.[1]

The opening of southwest Georgia for settlement coincided with an economic boom fueled in part by a growing national and international demand for cotton. Although most of the migrants who rushed into the newly acquired southern lands headed for Alabama, Louisiana, Mississippi, Arkansas, and even Texas, a portion detoured into the southwestern corner of Georgia. A few arrived by happenstance; but most arrived by design, attracted to a region that was both proximate to their old homes and rich with resources. Bibb County's John B. Lamar was especially excited about the prospects of augmenting the "unprofitable soil" of the family home with fresher (and presumably more fruitful) lands to the south and west. "I have established a large planting interest in Sumpter [County]," Lamar bragged to his friend and fellow Georgian, Howell Cobb, shortly after he had purchased his new estate. "Lord, Lord, Howell you and I have been too used to poor land to know what crops people are making in the rich lands of the new counties. I am just getting my eyes open to the golden view." "I am decidedly in love with Sumpter."[2]

For a good many, the view was golden indeed. Charles Munnerlyn, who immigrated to Decatur County in the 1830s, did not regret his decision. He remarked to a friend in 1839, "I moved, in wretched health, with only money enough to buy necessities the first year . . . and I am now tolerably settled, my land paid for, and own 23 negroes more than I brought to the country." He also had 120 bales of ginned cotton waiting shipment to market. E. D. Huguenin arrived in time to begin preparations for the 1836 crop. In less than ten years, he had tripled his slaveholdings and had traded in his Early County plantation for an even richer and larger estate on the western bank of the Flint River in Sumter County. By the eve of secession twenty years later, Huguenin's assets included 7,400 acres distributed across three plantations, 270 slaves valued at $216,000, and household furniture, provisions, and livestock worth an additional $37,000. The Bond family wealth grew at an even faster pace. When the patriarch Lewis died in 1836, scarcely six years after arriving in southwest Georgia, he left his children an estate of more than twelve thousand acres and an untold number of slaves to work it. By 1859, one son had translated his part of the inheritance into an estate of slaves and land worth in excess of a million dollars. Winborn J. Lawton, who started from what he described as "humble beginnings" as the son of a South Carolina carpenter, amassed by 1861 several thousand acres, over a hundred slaves, and "the necessary appliances to work his negroes in the business of raising cotton." Settlement in southwest Georgia, concluded planter John Banks of Stewart County, had "been a good investment."[3]

Not just planters prospered. So too did the artisans, merchants, lawyers, and physicians who served them. Nelson Tift, an aspiring shopkeeper from Connecticut with a nose for profit, followed the line of settlement westward, stopping first at Augusta and Hawkinsville before finding a permanent home in Baker (later Dougherty) County. There he helped establish Albany as one of southwest Georgia's premier trading hubs, promoted various transportation schemes designed to facilitate the agricultural economy, speculated in land, and regularly extended credit to friends and neighbors. Andrew J. Swinney found employment and eventually financial security as a shopkeeper in Albany, a path taken by Hawthorne Chamberline in Stewart County sixty miles to the north. Business boomed for those who catered to the cotton trade. In one year alone the merchants at Albany (all six of them in 1843) sold "$120,000 worth of Dry goods & groceries," and those located to the west at Fort Gaines were begging the state government eight years later for a "tri-weekly" stage or mail service. "We think we have grown to such an importance in a commercial way that we are entitled" to some service, given that "we ship annually between 8 & 10,000 bales of cotton from this point & sell 250.000 or 300.000 dollars worth of goods."[4]

Prospects such as these were hard to resist. Within a space of twenty years, a surge of fifty-four thousand migrants rocketed southwest Georgia from a forested landscape occupied by indigenous people and the occasional white trader to a full-blown slave society.[5] It remained, however, a rather liminal plantation society. Bands of Creeks and Seminoles could still be seen periodically slipping through the forests, settlers continued right up to the eve of secession to stalk the native bears, and opportunistic gangs of thugs remained at large along the area's roads, taking advantage of a loosely established civil government to prey on unsuspecting travelers. Planters' homes testified to the raw quality of the region. With their attention riveted on the state of their fields rather than on the state of their furnishings, even the wealthiest favored the utilitarian over the ornate. "They take little pride in having things nice," sniffed a northern visitor to Baker County in 1843. Most planters' "Big Houses" were small, single-story affairs: hastily and cheaply constructed from hewed logs, usually unfinished inside except for a blanket or two carefully arranged to distinguish one room from the next, and equipped with the barest minimum of household furnishings. Cover the kitchen floor with "clay," one planter commanded the crew constructing his home. Unlike those who, nearly simultaneously, were settling down around Tallahassee, Florida—people who eagerly acquired the trappings of an "improving class"—the newcomers to southwest Georgia had other priorities. By the early 1840s, the Bonds, Lawtons, Huguenins, and hundreds more like them were well on their way to accomplishing what they had set out to do: plow out their fortunes from the South's latest agricultural craze. Remarking on the heavily laden wagons that rumbled daily past his Stewart County shop, Hawthorne Chamberline observed that it was cotton that drew them, cotton that fueled their dreams, and, when all went according to plan, cotton that lined their pockets.[6]

The settlers' timing was right. Antebellum prices for cotton tended to fluctuate wildly and in general slipped downward over the antebellum period, but that decline in raw price was more than matched by an upward trajectory in world demand, and profits kept on rising as growers raced to keep up with a booming consumption of textiles. Moreover, prices for Georgia cotton broke with national trends by climbing from a low of about 5 cents a pound during the depressions of the late 1830s and early 1840s to 10½ to 12 cents a pound toward the end of the 1850s. Planters took full advantage of that bounce in demand. Between 1850 and 1860, the state's output rose by 250,000 bales, from half a million to nearly three-quarters of a million bales. Southwest Georgia's share of the market more than kept pace. Planters in Early, Baker, Stewart, Thomas, and Decatur counties produced 27,000 bales (of four hundred to five hundred pounds each) in 1839. Ten years later, that number had increased nearly threefold to 73,000 bales—or roughly 15 percent of the state's output that year. By 1860 the region's cotton production had doubled again to reach 154,000 bales, a harvest that this time represented almost a quarter of Georgia's annual crop and matched the annual American crops produced in the first decade of the century. Not surprisingly, planters with an eye to benefiting personally from what appeared to be an elastic supply as well as an elastic demand, continued right up to secession to "rush [forward] in crowds to buy lands in the S.W. counties." A party of four North Carolinian planters cut it particularly close, materializing in Mitchell County nearly the night before Christmas in 1860, bringing with them "50 or 60 Hands" each.[7]

Cotton was, as both contemporaries and later observers insisted, "the ruling monarch" of southwest Georgia, the great staple, "the controlling elemen[t] of civilization." To be sure, planters and farmers sowed annual crops of corn, peas, and potatoes, established small orchards, and raised an assortment of melons, pumpkins, and vegetables. Some experimented with varieties of cane; some kept sheep for their wool. But such products, along with the cattle and hogs that feasted on grasses and mast in the forests, were raised for use at home, not generally for sale abroad. While critical to subsistence, meat and meal did not carry the social cachet of cotton, nor did they dominate the market like cotton. It was the latter, not ground peas or sheep's wool, that sparked informal competitions to see whose crop would mature the earliest or bring the highest yield per acre. It was cotton, not wool, that packed the dozens upon dozens of wagons (and later railroad cars) that rolled out of the region on their way east to the wharves at Savannah and Macon for transshipment to Europe and New England. It was cotton, not pork, that prompted inventive planters to hammer together "cotton boxes" (the local vernacular for glorified rafts) that carried their cargo to the Gulf port at Apalachicola when the rivers ran too shallow to accommodate the deeper drafted steamboats. Neither the passage of time nor the brutality of war could tarnish the shine of cotton. "This is the great cotton region of the State, and, perhaps," enthused a report issued by the national commissioner of agriculture shortly after the Confederate surrender, "the best in the whole South."[8]

Free white migrants may have been responsible for the decision to cultivate cotton, but it was slaves who produced it, and pro-

duction on the scale that prevailed in southwest Georgia required armies of biddable workers. There was no gradual prolif-
eration of slaves. During a period in which close to a million
people were shifted from the older and upper to the newer and
lower South, southwest Georgia's slave population expanded at a
breathtaking rate. From a low of 219 in 1820, their numbers shot
up an astonishing 290-fold over the next forty years. On the eve
of secession, 63,000 enslaved black men, women, and children
resided in southwest Georgia. Their numbers propelled by the
continued arrival of free settlers—many of whom transported
slaves along with their stocks of plows, seed, cattle, and hogs—
and by traders who, like William W. Cheever, speculated "wildly"
in the slave trade, bound men and women constituted an un-
disputed majority of the area's population, representing just shy
of 54 percent of the total number of residents. In two of the
most fertile counties, Dougherty and its neighbor Baker to the
south, slaves came to outnumber white residents by a margin of
two to one. Southwest Georgia became one of the most heavily
slave regions of the cotton South, and it sometimes gave pause
to the people who made it that way. In an 1853 letter to northern relatives, Mary Kendall, the wife of a newly arrived planter,
rather ruefully noted the predominance of slaves in her immediate neighborhood. "There is but one white family within half a
mile from us," she wrote, "but any quantity of negroes."[9]

Cotton on the new ground was a finicky consumer of labor,
with a special appetite for the fit and the fertile: people capable
of both carving plantations from forest and bringing up a next
generation of bound workers. Because of a decided tilt toward
those with the highest capacity to produce and to reproduce,
the antebellum migration selected for slaves between the ages of
15 and 30, a preference that repeatedly shredded black people's
bonds of blood and affection. Upper South slave communities,

the headwaters of that antebellum river of slave migrants, were particularly hard hit. As many as one half of all antebellum slave sales in the Chesapeake area separated parents from children; one-quarter tore husbands from wives. Workers, as Samuel Wight of Baker County understood when he advertised a slave woman as a fine field hand, "*first rate* Cook, Washer, and Ironer," were what sold well to the planters of southwest Georgia, just as they did to those hoping to till fortunes out of the ground in Mississippi, Alabama, and even the panhandle of Florida. Carefully categorizing their human wares—some of whom came from as far away as Kentucky, Maryland, North Carolina, and Virginia— by height, weight, age, sex, and capacity to produce (and reproduce, if the slave was female), itinerate peddlers of slaves disposed of a "good many" as they tacked their way across the countryside. Others set up shop in the corners of local dry-goods emporiums, displaying their stock of slaves alongside stacks of rope, harness, boots, hoes, hats, shoes, and bacon. So confident was Gabriel Sibley that he could turn a profit on the slaves he imported to Albany in the late 1840s, that he opened his own office out of which he shouted an intent to "SELL AND BUY NEGROES."[10]

Moving with their masters, as 30 to 40 percent may have done, diminished but did not erase the rupturing effects of the domestic migration. It was a rare planter who carried the whole of his slave force with him on a westward trek to new lands, for planters, like the traders with whom they shared paths, tended to select among those they owned (buying or selling to fill in any gaps) according to a similar measure of productive and reproductive capacity. As Charles Munnerlyn pointed out to an Abbeville, South Carolina, friend preparing for his own move to Decatur County, workers were of paramount interest. Remember, Munnerlyn wrote, "the first thing to do will be to build camps for the negroes, then put as many men to building a ware house on the River bank on some high spot, as near the center of your intended farm, and as convenient to your settlement as possible . . . this house will always be useful and indispensable, and should be built pretty well." Selecting only those slaves whom they judged the most suitable for relocation to new land meant separating those chosen from their communities, and often their families. When planning his move out of north Georgia, Benjamin C. Yancey sorted his slaves into four groups. He sent one group to a plantation on the Coosa River in Alabama, kept one group at his home in Spalding County, and split the remaining slaves between two plantations he had recently purchased in Dougherty County. Central Georgia planter John B. Lamar did something comparable after acquiring a plantation of forty-three hundred acres just east of Americus. Dividing his labor force by three rather than four, Lamar sent fifty-four of his strongest, most capable slaves south almost immediately. "Another 1/3rd" were eventually instructed to follow. The remainder went nowhere at all, ordered by their master to stay on his Bibb County plantation.[11]

The effect of these moves on the slaves, especially those who made the trip in the hands of a trader, was nothing short of catastrophic. Migrating masters occasionally sent back for their remaining bound workers, as did Lamar, but the damage done to slaves' fragile networks of family and community was extensive. Although a few managed to stay in touch with loved ones left behind ("Wesley told me to tell you that he wanted to come Home very Bad and sends His Best Love to His Wife," a Decatur County overseer relayed back to the absentee owner who had remained on his original estate near Athens, Georgia), traders' transactions and owners' resettlements left a good many of those involuntary migrants with little more than memories of the families from which they had been torn. When asked in 1870 of the whereabouts of his father, Philip Joiner (who had been sent as a teenager from Mecklenberg County, Virginia, to Dougherty County) could only remark, "Never saw him." Anice Weston faintly recalled a father who had "died somewhere in Ga somewhere some years ago," and the last time William Walker's family had been intact had been on their way to the auction block in Richmond, Virginia. William eventually landed in Thomas County, a twelve-year-old, clinging to the names of his kinfolk and the memorized address of the man who had once owned them. But at least Weston and Joiner and Walker had memories and names from which to draw comfort. The youngest migrants rarely had that. Vina Micken (whose migration started in Kentucky when she was but a baby and ended in Lee County the year she turned thirteen) could not recall the names of her father and mother when asked after freedom, "having," as she explained, "been taken from them when small." Indeed, so youthful and bereft of mothers and fathers, sisters and brothers, were some of the slaves who ended up in southwest Georgia that planters sometimes found it necessary to designate proxy parents to watch over the youngsters until they could fend for themselves.[12]

The scene that greeted these young people when they arrived at their new homes could hardly have filled them with hope. What they faced stood in sharp contrast to the worlds from which they had come. The enslaved migrants from the Chesapeake region suffered perhaps the sharpest break, having emerged out of long-settled communities that since the late eighteenth century had been experiencing a steady transformation of economic and social life, changes that often worked to slaves' benefit. There, where tobacco had been in decline for ecological and market reasons since before the Revolution, landowners had been replacing their colonial staple with mixed-crop agriculture, a shift that altered slaves' worlds by releasing them from the demanding regime of the noxious weed that had caused their grandparents and great-grandparents to be carried from their African homes. New opportunities were opening in skilled work, mobile work, and increasingly industrialized and urban work, arrangements that destabilized slaveholder sovereignty by frequently giving to enslaved people an expanding authority over their lives and their labor. Even gang labor had been tempered by decades of ongoing struggle, so that workers commonly labored in small groups under the supervision of another slave, who as often as not was kin to those he directed. The population of free people of color had jumped as well in the years immediately following the Revolution as a significant number of slaveholders, for various moral, ideological, and practical reasons, divested themselves of their property in people. Spread out across the landscape rather than concentrated in urban spaces, as was often the case in the lower South, this population of free "coloured" (which numbered 100,000 in 1830 and 140,000 twenty years later) served as the eyes, the ears, and frequently the partners—in marriage, in labor, in play, and perhaps even in plots—of those still enslaved. So adeptly had Chesapeake slaves turned the post-Revolutionary developments to their own advantage that many had laid claim to half of Saturday as well as the whole of Sunday free from labor; slave women had increasingly joined slave men in rural roads and urban streets, environments that diluted their owners' ability to control and to command; and in Virginia, black Baptists, the majority of whom were women, had won the right to meet in their own churches with their own preachers—at least until Nat Turner and his soldiers shattered the silence one night in Southampton County.[13]

Those who migrated into the southwest from the swamps of

the Atlantic coastline also found a world far different from the one they had come from. Left behind, again, were long-settled communities. But unlike those abandoned by forced migrants out of the Chesapeake, slaves' communities in the low country tended to be insular enclaves presided over in significant ways by those who resided within. There, on the banks of the Savannah, southward along the Georgia coastline to the St. Johns River in Florida, and northward past Charleston and Georgetown toward the Cape Fear region of North Carolina, a unique form of slavery had emerged over the course of more than a century. It was the product of the particular requirements of rice cultivation and of an environment deadly with insects, disease, and meltingly hot summers. There, slaves were under the management of overseers for large portions of the agricultural season (the owners having fled for cooler and less sickly climates). Entrusted with much of the supervision of the day-to-day operations of the plantations they inhabited, and having won over the decades a singular control over the pace at which they worked, enslaved men and women—many of whom could trace their personal ancestry back to the African shore—had fashioned a culture, a society, an economy, a language (Gullah north of the Savannah, Ogeechee to the south), and culinary practices that were peculiarly their own and that frequently afforded slaves some protection against a master's impositions. By the mid-eighteenth century, plantation slaves in the low country were already producing a surplus of foodstuffs and had won the right to sell their labor on Sundays, activities lucrative enough to finance "very gay Wascoat[s]" for men, lengths of fancy fabrics for women, and stoves for their cabins. Although in the decades following the Revolution, low-country slaveholders had taken steps to assert new control over their slaves, sea islanders remained into the nineteenth century a distinct people, one whose

circumstances continued to underwrite a lively informal economy and a thick bulwark of kin.[14]

Even those enslaved migrants who embarked on their journey
to southwest Georgia from the older cotton districts of the South
Carolina and Georgia piedmonts found a world appreciably different from the one they had just left. By the time migrants began arriving around Albany and Thomasville in any significant
numbers, the enslaved people who populated the cotton plantations back to the east and the north (areas settled shortly before
and after the Revolution) had already won, by dint of day-to-day
struggles with slaveholders, the privileges of time, space, and
mobility critical to family formation, economic production, and
the establishment of those cultural and religious institutions that
gave structure and strength to their communities. To varying degrees of success and extent, slaves on up-country cotton plantations enjoyed the right to keep dogs (which were useful as sen-
tries and for hunting), chickens and ducks, and occasionally
other small livestock. Many also kept gardens—which sometimes included rows of cotton as well as a variety of vegetables—
the harvest from which augmented slaves' diets and, if plentiful
enough, made its way into local markets. They attended church,
and occasionally camp meetings. Some, like those who labored
to the north in Maryland and Virginia, had successfully bargained for and won Saturday afternoons off in addition to the
Sabbath that was largely theirs already, privileges that gave slaves
leverage enough to occasionally convince their masters that any
work performed on Sunday deserved some sort of compensatory
reward. Holidays—often the Fourth of July and the week between Christmas and New Year's—had become commonplace as
well, and celebratory rituals had grown up around them.[15]

Black men and black women arrived in southwest Georgia to
find an ominous new variant of slavery. "This land was a little

Hell," a "grave-faced" survivor later recalled. His memory seemed to have served him well, for his assessment was not unique. The region's planters, anxious to recover the enormous expenses they had incurred as they shifted their operations onto fresh ground (liabilities that amounted to thousands of dollars for the land alone, never mind the price of labor, livestock, tools, and seed), wasted little time ratcheting up their demands upon slaves. Arriving often alone, bereft of the cushioning properties of family and friends, and deposited on strange ground, slaves could do little initially to shield themselves from planters' assaults. Favoring, as did most cotton producers, the close supervision of a gang regime—an organizational scheme that placed squarely into the hands of the slaveholder or his agent the authority to determine the length of the workday, the manner in which slaves' labor would be allocated, the pace at which they would work, and the nature of the work to be performed—southwest Georgia's planters drove their enslaved workers hard in their haste to turn forest to field and to replenish wallets made thin by the expenses of moving.[16]

A few transplants hoped to make back those costs by adapting to the new ground the management techniques developed in their previous homes. Those who moved from the low country were often the most insistent on doing this, dragging along in their wake a system of production that had grown up along with their crops of rice and long-staple cotton. Though not entirely averse to the more widely employed gang labor, Savannah native E. D. Huguenin, for instance, advised his overseer right from the beginning that "in all Kinds of work where such a thing can be done I wish my people *tasked*." By this he meant that each of his slaves would be assigned a series of discrete daily chores (a length of rows to hoe, a number of rails to split, a pile of wool to card), the completion of which would mark the end of the slave's workday and release him or her temporarily from the master's service. Such an arrangement, Huguenin believed, "answers more than one good purpose" by prompting slaves to greater industry in order to reap the rewards of expanded time off.[17]

But Huguenin was a rarity among those who flocked to the region to grow rich on cotton. Most of his neighbors were far too interested in harvesting the greatest possible profits from the soil in the shortest possible time. They had little taste for a system that diluted their authority to command. Dismissing tasking as a "deplorable" system, "injurious in every way," southwest Georgia's planters just as quickly abandoned the family-based and slave-directed variation of gang labor that prevailed on many Chesapeake plantations. They, like those who located themselves at other points along the cotton frontier, rejected the use of enslaved drivers and overseers commonly found to the north and the east, relying instead on hired white men ("experts," according to an Early County observer, "in the art of farming and managing negroes"), a management strategy that subjected slaves to unaccustomedly harsher regimes. Planters did not stop there. Convinced that "the maintenance and progress of civilized society" sprang from the obedience and service wrenched from their laborers, those who sought their fortune in the southwestern corner of Georgia left virtually nothing to chance. Demanding that their plantations and the people who worked them "be kept in perfect order and subjection" whether "in or from the fields, well or sick," they (or their overseers) intruded into nearly every dimension of their laborers' lives. Besides directing the minute-by-minute performance of agricultural operations—shifting slaves from job to job to ensure that not a moment of daylight was lost to productive activity, establishing and maintaining (by force, if necessary) the pace at which they labored, selecting even the tools to be used—planters and their agents strove to keep tabs on the clothes their slaves wore, the foods they consumed, the language they used, the conversations they held (and whom they held them with), and the condition of their cabins (inside and out).[18]

It was that particularly steely attention paid to producers and production that earned southwest Georgia's planters a lingering reputation for "pressing [their] workers" excessively. Stories echoed up from contemporaries and survivors of slaves who collapsed into their rows only to be "kicked aside" out of the way of the plows, of people being "worked like cattle," of shortages of food, of packs of dogs specially "train[ed] to trail negroes," and of punishments that even white residents—some of whom considered it "fin[e] sport" to spend their Saturday evenings hunting down slaves from horseback—occasionally found disturbingly cruel. Unworthy of legal action, concluded a Thomas County grand jury, were acts involving the "Beating, whipping & wounding [of] a slave"; but worthy at least of a judicial scolding was the "inhuman treatment inflicted on a negro slave" that involved "singe[ing]" the flesh from the victim's bones. Small wonder, then, that when in the months following freedom a handful of north Georgia black men were told about "high wages" available down around Albany, they recoiled in horror, "universally reply[ing]" to the northern official who had unwittingly made the suggestion that they "would rather die than go there."[19]

The planters' reputation for hard driving was well deserved. Loath to waste a moment of productive time, southwest Georgia's cotton masters seized back not only Saturdays but sometimes Sundays (an act that violated state law) and holidays as well in their haste to make their fortunes. While work routines varied by the season, and from estate to estate, depending on a planter's personal selection of crops and the particularities of the labor force at his command, general patterns emerged. Commencing shortly after January first, the agricultural cycle of plantations that grew short-staple cotton spanned nearly the whole year. While frost still lay on the land and the occasional light snow fell, slaves felled trees, split and hauled rails with which to repair existing fences and construct new ones, cleared brush and briars from established fields, sowed oats, threshed the previous year's oats, raked manure out of the stock pens and barns, broke up new ground (of which there seemed an ample supply), and picked up the always ubiquitous "trash" (sticks, broken tree limbs, dead brush and weeds, and other farm debris that materialized with each gust of wind). As the weather warmed and the soil dried, slave workers spread various fertilizers (initially barnyard manures and seeds discarded from cotton fiber; then eventually guano as their masters experimented with new agricultural technologies) in preparation for sowing crops of cotton, corn, sugar cane, oats, wheat, occasionally rye, tobacco for home use, vegetables, and potatoes, the staples of market and subsistence. Although speed counted in spring planting, transplanting seedlings, interplanting "pindars" (peanuts) with corn (a job slaves performed with hoes on William Dickey's plantation), and distributing seed at optimal intervals in the furrows were tediously slow processes. It was also work, overseer George Davis sighed in a letter to his absentee employer on a spring day in 1855, "that takes about all the force I can start."[20]

John Lester and Daniel Horn, two middling-size Decatur County planters who chronicled each day's work in meticulous detail, would probably have agreed with Davis if asked. An air of urgency infused their accounts of spring planting, as they rushed to put seed into the ground. Wednesday, March 6, 1861 (growing fear of war scarcely rippled the region's well-rehearsed rhythms), found Horn's slaves hard at it, sowing the year's crop. From daybreak to 9 a.m., Mike, Sarah, Charity, Moses, Campbell, Minerva, Honor, Norah, and Daniel planted potatoes. After a one-hour break, Horn ordered his slaves into the Branch field (planters habitually named their fields) to plant corn. Trudging along in a rural ballet not of their own design, the slaves crossed the field in three waves. Taking the lead with their "drills" (homemade tools usually constructed of a board rounded to fit the raised bed or row, "through the center of which a small piece of iron [had been] inserted"), Mike and Moses opened a furrow into which the second wave of workers (adult women Charity and Sarah) carefully dropped the seed. Following along behind came Allen, Minerva, and Honor, whose job it was to cover the seed with soil. They finished the corn at 3 p.m., but their day's work was not yet done. After another one-hour break, Horn sent Mike, Moses, Allen, and Charity along with Peter and Abb (who until then had been plowing with another slave, Sampson, elsewhere on the estate) to the Big Field, where they began to "list," raising rows that would later be planted with cotton. While they plowed, the remainder of Horn's field hands (teenage boys and the less physically fit women) beat down the remnants of the previous year's cotton. Armed with clubs with which they smacked the dead stalks flat, this group, which included Campbell, Norah, Daniel, Sarah, Minerva, and Honor, remained at their work until the sun fell below the horizon shortly before 7 p.m. that night.[21]

John Lester demanded a similar intensity from the slaves he commanded. Sunrise on Wednesday, April 22, 1857, found his bound laborers hard at work planting the year's cotton. In all likelihood having commenced in the twilight that preceded true sunrise, Frank, Mat, Evans, and Peggy finished planting cotton in a field bordered on one side by a new crop of cane and on the other by dryland rice. Frank led the way with his drill, Mat came

next "strew[ing] cotton seed," and Evans and Peggy brought up
the rear with their hoes. Once they had completed the one field,
Lester added them to the gang who had been sowing cotton
since daylight in another. There Henry, Aaron, and Dave, aided
now by Frank, opened up rows with the drills; Rachel and Mat
dropped the seed; and Jim, Sally, Lucy, Vilot, Cely, Evans, and
Peggy followed along with their hoes. "After they all finished
planting[,] Dave went to knocking off cotton stalks in" a thirty-
acre field, "Levi & Dolly replant[ed] corn in the old 50 acre field,"
and "Lucy and Maria finished ploughing out the sugar cane
patch" before joining Aaron, Frank, Henry, Evans, and Peggy to
"finis[h] ploughing out the potato patch"—a chore that carried
them into "the evening."²²

Midsummer brought no relief to the region's slaves, only
endless hours of thinning cotton (a laborious process in which
hoe-wielding slaves imposed one-foot intervals between growing plants), chopping weeds (again with the aid of a hoe), plowing, pulling fodder that would feed the livestock over the winter,
hilling potatoes, pinching suckers from corn, and tending to the
plantation vegetable gardens and orchards, all the while keeping
pace with the regular round of maintenance work and stock
management. Much of this was, as William Dickey noted in a
late-June entry, "verry Tedious work." On Lester's estate, half of
his slaves might spend a summer morning laying by corn while
the rest hoed in the cotton. After their noon break, they would
resume their labor, perhaps "beat[ing] out rice peas &c until
night" (as they all did on Tuesday, July 21, 1857) or "draw[ing] up
potato ridges in the Irish potato patch and set[ting] them out
in vines"—a job that had occupied Maria, Peggy, Rachel, Evans,
Henry, Frank, Sally, Cely, Lindy, and Vilot the whole of the previous afternoon. "I have got nearly all the Logs for my house and
have got Between 6 and 7000 shingles [cut]," George Davis re-

ported a few years earlier in a midsummer letter that masked behind a first-person voice the identities of the nearly one hundred slaves he commanded. "I am pulling fodder—I have got 50 stacks pulled[,] 25 up Last night and I will put up a good many more this evening."[23]

Mid-August heralded the commencement of cotton harvest, even as slaves continued to pull and stack fodder, hoe potatoes, and gather in corn. Workdays grew even longer and more demanding as planters raced to get in their crops before the dropping temperatures and fall storms damaged the fiber and lowered its value. George Davis admitted to his employer in September one year, "Wee Have Had a great Deal of Rain," but then he went on to assure him, "I am picking it out[,] I will get 20,000 pounds picked out By tomorrow night." John Lamar's slaves picked cotton while standing in the mud; so did William Dickey's. It took more than "a right smart shower of rain" to stop harvest on the latter's plantation. Regular autumn visitations of "Billous fever," "chills," "rising[s]," and other laborer-leveling afflictions confirmed the brutal character of the harvest regime. Aside from the hot days of July, Daniel Horn's slaves—like those of John Lester—lost more time in the fields due to sickness during the peak harvest months of September, October, and November than at any other time of the year. In September alone, the five women Horn regularly sent to the fields lost a total of eight and half working days, and the eight male field workers lost nine. The previous January, not one of the same group of workers missed a day's work for ill health. It was a pattern that prevailed more generally. No sooner did "Some come In [than] others go out," reported a Sumter County overseer during a fall plagued by wave after wave of illness. "All of them has Bin Sick & som of them has Bin sick twice & Several of them down the third time." At one point twenty-two slaves had been confined to their beds; significantly, twenty "of that nombr Field hands too." "They hate to work Badly," their overseer concluded.[24]

Toward the last days of November, harvest began to wind down. Most plantations by then were finishing or had completed the customary third picking of their fields. As Christmas—the holiday that signaled the end of the annual agricultural cycle— approached, slaves spent their days processing cotton, boiling cane syrup into sugar, plowing over stubble, shucking and shelling corn, getting in firewood, and generally preparing the plantation for the next cycle of crops. By December 14, 1860, David Barrow's overseer was able to report that all that year's cotton— 160 bales—had been picked, ginned, and packaged in protective bagging. Over the next three weeks, he expected the slaves to process "800 to a 1000 pounds worth of bacon," finish "clearing in the Beech Hammock" (one of the plantation's many fields), sow the ensuing year's oats, and haul the remaining 106 bales to Barrow's factor, the firm of William G. Porter & Co. located in Apalachicola, Florida. (Slaves had already deposited 54 bales with a merchant in Bainbridge.) Not every planter finished up their cotton as quickly. Christmas Eve of the following year found Daniel Horn's Abb hauling rails for a roadside fence and Campbell running the cotton thresher, while everyone else— Mike, Daniel, Norah, Moses, Peter, Allen, Sarah, Sampson, Charity, Minerva, and Honor—picked out the last of the cotton in the "60 acre cut." A week later, however, they were packing and ginning that cotton, hauling more rails, cleaning weeds and dead grass from along the fence lines, and plowing up the Branch field, readying it to be seeded in a matter of weeks.[25]

Departures from the general pattern abounded, but rather than reducing or holding steady the labor expected of slaves, any alterations (including unexpected fluctuations in the weather) tended to complicate and intensify the exploitation they suf-

fered. John Lester and George Davis operated plantation brick-
yards in addition to raising the usual selection of crops. Bricks,
however, do not produce themselves, and the job, as Lester's
careful account reveals, entailed a series of labor-consuming
steps—cleaning the yard and repairing the kiln, "moulding" then
hacking apart what amounted in 1857 to 31,000 bricks, chopping
the wood to fire the kiln in which to "burn them," and finally,
tending the bricks as they hardened—all of which coincided on
Lester's estate with the harvest-time peak in demand on slaves'
labor. Brick making then, much like the tobacco produced by
William Dickey's slaves, repeatedly extended laborers' workdays
into the evenings; on at least one occasion on Lester's estate, this
work consumed the whole of their Sabbath. Despite his gestures
toward tasking, E. D. Huguenin had no qualms about lengthening his slaves' workdays on either end, insisting as he did that
wagon and cartwheels be greased and tarred before every use,
and that horses, mules, and their harnesses be thoroughly
cleaned at the end of every day. Wildfire kept David Barrow's
slaves at work "night and Day for four Days & nights without
eating or Drinking much," and on another occasion a cold and
dreary spring ("the weather Looks Like Fall," complained the
overseer) sent slaves back into the fields repeatedly to sow and
resow the annual crops of corn and cotton.[26]

Time off proved a rare and irregularly awarded prize. With
planters greedily reappropriating the Saturday afternoons, evenings, and even occasionally the Sundays that had been gradually conceded to slaves in older cotton districts, the low country,
and the Chesapeake, free daylight came to slaves largely at their
owners' convenience. Convinced that labor meant profits, planters doled out those gifts of time with a parsimonious hand. Exclusive of the few days commonly given to slaves between Christmas and New Year's, and perhaps—if grass and weeds were not

overrunning the crops—the Fourth of July, the breaks that came slaves' way between sunrise and sunset could be counted in minutes and hours, not days. On Daniel Horn's plantation, for instance, no slaves enjoyed any formally recognized moment to themselves during the six months of the year that were the busiest on the agricultural calendar: January, February, April, May, October, and November. When his field laborers did get a respite from their master's work, it more often than not consisted of an hour's rest between assignments; a slightly truncated workday (such as a Saturday early in July when all but Mike were permitted to "knock off" at 5 p.m.); or a few surprise hours when weather halted activities outdoors and Horn had no indoor employments readily available. Three such hours ("lost" hours to Horn) came to the gin crew Mike, Honor, and Norah one day in September when a band wheel tumbled to the ground, bringing the operation to an abrupt halt until the part could be replaced. Horn was as stingy with the holidays. His slaves celebrated national independence by burning cane, hoeing cotton, and raking straw. Their Christmas break lasted three days. Other planters were just as miserly. In 1858, William Dickey turned his slaves "loose" on seven Saturday afternoons, the last of which fell on July 3; and only three times between January 26 and December 22, 1857, did John Lester give his slaves a whole Saturday afternoon to "work for themselves." One of those afternoons landed on Independence Day. Free time on these estates, as was the case on Horn's, came at sporadic, unpredictable, and usually brief intervals: an hour here, an hour there. Only if fortune smiled, and a mule went lame or a piece of the gin machinery came crashing down, was a fractionally longer respite obtained.[27]

Slaves worked hard in antebellum southwest Georgia, yoked as they were to their owners' productive enterprises six if not seven days a week. But slaves did not all work hard in the same way. Brawn especially counted, not only during the initial wave of construction and clearing that accompanied migration, but later, as planters and slaves settled into their new agricultural routines. It took enormous reserves of physical strength—possessed more generally by men than by women—to fell the region's oaks and pines with axes or crosscut saws, to roll logs, hew boards, split rails (four hundred for every one hundred yards of fence), prepare fertilizer, cut oats and wheat (a chore accomplished with crudely fashioned iron scythes or sickles), heave into place gin and milling machinery, wrestle cattle to the ground for branding and castration, pack cotton, and, on Lester's estate, put up all those bricks.[28] Slave men, likewise, dominated the ranks of teamsters (the drivers loaded and unloaded their cargos as well as held the reins), fishermen, and herders (herding required beating through the region's forests and thickets, rounding up free-ranging cattle and hogs). Slave women's work was no less critical to agricultural production, but it demanded less physical strength or length of arm than many of the chores reserved to slave men. Along with boys too young to do a man's work and any infirm or elderly men, slave women and girls spent their days chopping cotton, hoeing weeds, raking up manure from livestock enclosures to redistribute it on cultivated fields, knocking down cotton stalks, tending piles of burning brush and logs, pulling fodder, digging potatoes, harvesting vegetables, shocking grain, strewing seed, and—when bad weather drove them out of the fields and their masters had no corn waiting to be shucked—sewing, cooking, and washing for the master's family.

Although the boundaries and categories were never absolute, more often than not the distinctions between men's work and women's work held steady. Slave women felled trees, but slaveholders tended to restrict their chopping to small trees (on E. D.

Huguenin's estate, specifically small and already dead pine trees).
Slave men harvested cotton—especially the "middle" crop or
second picking, when the plants generally produced the largest
bolls, of the finest quality, and in the greatest quantity. Indeed,
slave men proved themselves particularly adept at the job, often leading the daily tally of weights picked. (When Lester sent
Levi, Dave, and Aaron into the cotton to assist the women with
the harvest—a month after it commenced—they regularly out-
picked the rest of the gang, registering daily averages around 150
pounds each to the 135 pounds averaged by the adult women,
a phenomenon not restricted to his plantation.) But it was
slave women, particularly those with a compromised capacity
for physical labor—the pregnant, the nursing, the infirm, and
the elderly—who spent the longest sustained periods picking
their way through the rows. Women like William Dickey's Flora
and Peggy regularly commenced their gather as the first bolls began to open in mid-August, and remained in the fields to pick
off the last as the weather turned frosty. George Davis launched
his 1860 harvest on August 6 with a crew that consisted of "suckling women and chaps that could not pull much fodder." Over
the next four weeks, as the rest of the slave force burned brick (a
job usually assigned to slave men) and pulled fodder, this gang
of nursing mothers and middling-size kids (augmented by the
addition of Anna, who had been confined to her bed by illness
until sent out to assist with the harvest) "picked the crib field
twice and started in the pine land field the second time."[29]

Just as slave men filed out periodically to pick cotton, slave
women occasionally filed into the fields in the company of mules
and plows. Horn's Charity and Lester's Peggy, Lucy, and Maria
regularly took their turns along with the slave men behind their
master's plows; so too did William Dickey's slave woman Peggy.
But as was the case with the gathering of ripe cotton, slave wo-

men's plow experiences differed considerably from slave men's, for planters expected the latter to master the full range of plowing equipment. In antebellum southwest Georgia the typical inventory included "shovels," which were heavy, iron, V-shaped plows equipped with swept-back wings and which "pulled broad-side foremost" through the soil (a maneuver one contemporary likened to "dragging a cat by the tail"); "sweeps," specialized cultivators that took the form either of a semicircular board pulled flat between the rows or an iron plow with wings welded on to enable it to cover more ground per pass; and "scooters," a smaller, relatively nimble plow designed to do little more than scratch the surface, uprooting weeds and grasses from between rows of already growing crops. Although slave women occasionally took their turn behind a sweep, their masters more commonly assigned them to the scooter. Thus while slave men plowed in all seasons and under all conditions—breaking new ground in the winter, opening rows in the spring, cultivating the summer's mostly grown crops, and plowing under dead stalks in the fall—slave women rarely plowed except in the late spring and summer months. That was the period of the year when grass threatened to overrun valuable crops, and when the light and shallow-cutting small scooters offered planters any significant advantage.[30]

Planters seldom hesitated to call on slave men to do the jobs slave women performed. Almost never, however, did they put women to work at jobs they understood to be men's. This phenomenon introduced slave men to, and gave them mastery over, nearly the whole range of productive activities. On Daniel Horn's plantation, for instance, slave men performed 195 of the 206 discrete chores their master chronicled over the course of the year in his meticulously kept farm journal. On John Lester's estate, slave men likewise practiced, mastered, and performed

196 out of the 213 jobs recognized by their master in his daily entries. Usually smaller than men in stature, and frequently compromised by the physical and logistical demands of childbearing and rearing, slave women performed a much narrower range of agricultural chores. If slave men, whose masters expected them to do better than 90 percent of all the jobs on (and off of) the plantation—95 percent on Horn's estate, 92 percent on Lester's—assumed the character of jacks of almost all trades, slave women were expected to do less than half of the jobs. On neither Lester's nor Horn's plantation did slaveholders assign their slave women to more than 45 percent of the annual range of agricultural chores. On Horn's estate, Charity, Sarah, Minerva, Norah, and Honor together performed only 93 of those 206 jobs. On Lester's plantation, women's work was confined to 95 of the 213 occupations he described. Like planter Richard Hill of Early County, Lester and Horn made it a practice to "put the women at no work belonging to men."[31]

The asymmetrical nature of slave men's and slave women's work was particularly visible with respect to chores performed away from their owners' estates. Almost without exception, translocal work was masculine work. Slave men monopolized the seats on planters' wagons and oxcarts, hauling baled and bagged cotton to riverside wharves, local merchants and factors, and by the late 1850s, to railroad depots. It was they who transported loads of grain and timber to local mills for grinding into meal and slicing into boards, fetched physicians for the sick, ran to the nearest village to pick up any messages or mail for their owners, and hauled supplies of every description from town and wharf to farm. Slave men built and rebuilt the public roads, often in crews "detailed" from wealthier districts to poorer, "so as to equalize the business of Road working as near as possible." Masters more regularly swapped the labor of slave men than of slave women, dispatching workers to kinfolk and neighbors as need required. Thus it was that while Daniel Horn sent no woman to work on the far side of his plantation boundary, the able-bodied of his enslaved men—Abb, Mike, Peter, Daniel, Moses, Allen, and Sampson—chalked up fifty-eight trips away from their owner's estate in the space of twelve consecutive months. John Lester's slave men traveled nearly as often, going abroad on their owner's command at least thirty-eight times over less than eleven months.[32]

Most of the trips made by slave men on their masters' orders were short in duration and in distance—to the nearest town or village, down the road to the neighbor's estate, off into the woods for timbers. Other excursions, especially those done for the purpose of delivering loads of cotton to merchants and factors or to relay messages to absentee owners, could entail extended miles and multiple days on the road (with "road expenses" of a dollar or two safely tucked into a slave pocket). Starting well before Christmas and continuing through January (unless weather "not fitten" to "Hall" suspended their travels), David Barrow's wagons and enslaved teamsters shuttled between their Blowing Cave home and Bainbridge (a distance of thirty to thirty-five miles by today's roads), carrying away the cotton they had helped to produce. "I Have got Receipts for 171 Bales," the overseer reported in February 1861 of the portion of the 1860 crop he had already deposited in town. "The load I will carry to Day will make 177." Whether out and about for a few minutes or a few miles, or for more of either (one master launched a pair of slave carpenters out of their Oglethorpe County plantation on a mission to his absentee estate in Decatur, nearly three hundred miles and as many as twelve counties apart), slave men were a regular fixture on the public roads, a state of affairs that occasionally disturbed the more timid of white society. But efforts to curb slaves' mobility usually had little lasting effect. Slave men remained at large, hauling, delivering, herding, laboring, and conveying, all on their masters' command.[33]

It was against this backdrop of cotton's distinctive labor regime that the flood of incoming slaves set about restoring a semblance of order to their disjointed lives. No enslaved migrant could possibly hope to replicate in full the life he or she had been compelled to leave behind. Too much had changed to permit that. But those who arrived in the first wave of settlement stood the best chance of casting bondage on cotton's new ground in accordance with terms more to their own liking. When the 216 or so slaves whose presence the federal enumerator noted in the 1820 census entered the region, they found, for instance, more forest than field, and a society composed of just a few hundred white people (563 total). In the short period before the oppressive regime of cotton closed in around them, the earliest arriving slaves moved relatively freely about a countryside dominated by itinerant traders and straggling bands of Creeks. Able to evade the close scrutiny to which their successors would be subjected, this initial population of slaves engaged in a lively trade in cotton, cowhides, liquor, and labor—only a part of which the slaves could claim as their own. But such a world was ephemeral. Within just a few years, its liberal promises had been trampled by the flood of white migrants who, in the interest of production and profits, cracked down as fast as they could on licit and illicit "trafficking" and trade with slaves. Planters organized patrols to keep their workers at home and joined with other white settlers to drive out or destroy the last of the Creeks. "One eye Jim, Bob and Bill Indians of the Hitikalah Town" were among the last to be eliminated from Thomas County, hanged for murder in 1827.[34]

Although unable to partake of the autonomies enjoyed by the very earliest of the region's slaves, those who migrated in familiar company—plantation communities uprooted lock, stock, and barrel by migrating masters—managed to preserve some features of their previous lives. Already embedded in established communities (albeit whose ties to a broader, transplantation community had been severed by their move), such slaves stood a marginally better chance of fending off new assaults on their services and of retaining privileges won in their old homes. Migrants who traveled in the company of friends or close kin were more likely, for instance, to continue working by the task if that is what they had done in the past. Others who migrated under comparable conditions sometimes retained their right to keep little gardens and the use of the time and tools to make them produce. Others demanded, and received, permission to raise their own cotton for sale, or have restored to their ranks loved ones who had been left behind during the initial migration. In the space of nine years, the preexistent community of fifty-three slaves John B. Lamar had transplanted from Bibb County to Sumter County managed to exact all of the above. Not only did a group composed almost wholly of families seize control over a significant portion of plantation resources and win the right to cultivate crops of cotton—the harvest of which earned them hundreds of dollars annually—but they also lobbied successfully to have one of the missing brought down from their previous home. "P.S.," overseer Jonas Smith amended to a report submitted to his absentee employer after the slaves under his supervision had mobilized against him, "Peter Angus Sams anxious to have Catherine home you can attend to that as you Like If S[h]e able to work I have no obdicthans myself nor don't car . . . She can come [down] with old Sip."[35]

But sharing a common language, a common knowledge of

their masters' culture, and to a considerable extent a common religion—attributes and experiences denied to those who had suffered the transatlantic migration—even those who traveled alone gradually settled in and began to build their lives anew. Because of the character of the domestic migration, all of them started, however, from an unusually youthful foundation. As late as 1860 nearly 57 percent of the region's enslaved people were under the age of nineteen, 45 percent under the age of fifteen, and barely 12 percent were fifty years old or older, an age distribution not only distinct from black migrants' former homes, but distinct as well from the more equitable balance found in earlier-settled cotton plantation districts to the east and the west. Still, slaves met, they formed friendships, they married (in their eyes, if not in the law's), and—much to the delight of slaveholders for whom every baby represented a capital gain—they gave birth to a next generation. Forming one of the many loving attachments that slaves repeatedly used to blunt the edges of their masters' regime, Arnold Cater found a wife on the plantation to which he had been sold, replacing—not without regrets—the woman from whom he had been forcibly parted. Roger, property of Decatur County's Alexander Allen, badgered his master into purchasing "of Trulock," another Decatur County planter, "a negro woman & child at seven hundred dollars whom Roger had taken for a wife." Philip Joiner grew up, married a slave woman, Henrietta, with whom he would eventually raise two daughters, Lucy Ann and Mary Jane. Lavinia married Josh; Emeline married John; and Harry Peterson met and married Eliza (who was then the property of another man) "on or about July 1844." So strong, indeed, were the bonds of affection that connected Harry to Eliza that their relationship survived repeated separations, including one that put close to one hundred miles of pine woods and plantations between them. Even little Vina Micken formed a family of her own, marrying at least once and giving birth to four sons, though only one—Charley Waddell—survived to see freedom.[36]

Slaves also managed to begin producing for themselves. But excluding the remarkable activities of Lamar's enterprising slaves and the occasional bound blacksmith willing to extend day into night in order to ply his trade, no one produced very much. Gardens and field crops were especially hard to support. Sundays alone were not enough to make up for the infrequent, unpredictable, and irregularly scattered hours slaves might otherwise escape their masters' work. The prerogatives of staple production meant that slaves' crops, if sown at all, seldom went into the ground at the optimum season or during spells of good weather. Subsequent cultivation was similarly wedged inefficaciously around daily schedules dictated by and for the master's convenience. Under such circumstances, accident, not design, usually determined the fate of slaves' crops. Black men and black women were somewhat more successful raising small flocks of chickens for their meat and eggs, brewing beer, foraging for wild fruit, and cutting firewood for sale—productive activities that called for no special tools, designated spaces, or claims to the time that slaveholders were always loath to relinquish. Some of these items, along with the labor a few enterprising slaves managed to convert into cash during their infrequent holidays, made their way into the local marketplace, earning their producers ten cents here, a dollar there, sums that over the course of the year might add up to enough to pay for a plug of tobacco, a length of colorful ribbon, or a new pair of shoes. But with the exception of the few individuals in possession of tools, talents, and the time to use them, the region's enslaved people accumulated too little to finance their freedom.[37]

Although a puny subaltern economy hampered their development, a handful of black churches also eventually came into being. Largely of evangelical persuasion, under slavery these churches remained very small and widely scattered. A single church, for instance, served the rural black Baptists in Dougherty County, and as late as 1860 its congregation of 54 formally enrolled members represented just nine-tenths of 1 percent of the county's total slave population. Still, enslaved Christians worked hard to import their spiritual sensibilities into cotton's new country. Those who had held formal membership in an organized church in their previous home, and who had been given enough advance warning to make the necessary arrangements, often arrived, as did Eliza, James, and Titus—migrants who arrived out of the low country sometime before 1840—bearing letters that gained them admittance into new Christian communities. In other cases, churches came courting the slaves. Taking seriously an evangelical impulse to broadcast Christ's message widely, Protestant proselytizers steadily pushed their missions into the countryside. By the eve of secession the Baptists especially had managed to establish, with slaveholders' permission, what amounted to ecclesiastical beachheads on some of the region's outlying plantations, drawing small groups of slaves into formal, if physically distant, associations with usually town-based churches. Other slaves worshipped more or less on their own, gathering informally and outside of established ecclesiastical channels to listen, as did the enslaved men and women on John B. Lamar's Domino Branch plantation in Sumter County, to homilies presented by one of their own. Old Scipio did the Sabbath-day honors there. Fredrick Grist, "slave of the Grist family," offered similar services to some of Early County's enslaved men and women, and by the eve of secession the Albany Presbyterian and Baptist churches had followed suit, bestowing approval on a free man of color, John Maxwell, and the "servant

boy" Davy Hines to preside over the black portions of their respective spiritual flocks.[38]

Southwest Georgia's slaves fought hard for these small gains.
The right to sell a cake in the Albany market, to till up a few
yards of soil, to attend a Sabbath-day service, to marry another
man's slave, or to bury with dignity the body of a dead child (as
Lester's slave Dave did for the infant Sam on a Saturday afternoon at the peak of cotton harvest) all required the careful rewriting of whatever unspoken, and usually uneasy, accord existed
between themselves and their masters. It was a process slaveholders preferred to avoid. Every moment slaves diverted toward
their own needs represented a loss of the same to their owners, a
dilution of sovereignty most masters found especially repug-
nant. Thus while slaves' determination to suture together a domestic and social contentment was not necessarily oppositional
in intent, it often was in effect. The ensuing contests took all
manner of forms: from chronic skirmishes that ebbed and flowed,
day after day, as masters and slaves jockeyed for position on a
steeply unequal terrain, to less frequent but explosive and often
deadly encounters between heavily armed combatants. Sometimes
slaves selected from tactics rehearsed and fine-tuned in former
homes, expressing their assessment of a slaveholder's orders by
slowing the line, feigning sick, or laying out. Other times they
improvised, fashioning new strategies extemporaneously to meet
specific and immediate circumstances. It was not necessarily by
happenstance that the boiler attended by slave Sam exploded for
having run dry. Nor was it accidental that when Wade, "a negro man
Slave," snatched up an axe and lit into an overseer, he amplified
his intentions—as well as new sense of self—by bellowing at the
top of his lungs that the man on whom he whaled ought to think
twice about "fooling with any of his little Georgia Negroes."[39]

But rebuilding their lives in the wake of cotton's migration involved more than simply opening up space between themselves
and their hard-driving masters. Just as new circumstances of de-
mography, labor, and place converged to condition and constrain the scale of slaves' productive activities and the size and
location of their church congregations, those same underlying
historical features prompted new understandings about themselves as men and as women and the social and political terrain
they properly occupied. Thus what slave men and slave women
managed to make not only for, but of, themselves on southwest Georgia's cotton plantations had a good deal to do with
what they did—and how they did it—for their masters. Or, in
other words, survivors of the domestic trade in slaves were compelled to "reinterpret the lessons of the past in the context of the
present."[40]

This process was especially visible with respect to the region's black women. Drawn primarily from the upper and older
South, as were the majority of cotton's forced migrants, most
had emerged out of a diversifying society in which, over time,
women had gradually pushed beyond the boundaries of their
masters' estates, slipping out from under slaveholders' noses and
into new roles, infiltrating and occupying a vast and richly populated translocal political and social terrain. By the early decades
of the nineteenth century, black women had become a common
feature of public life. Those located in or near urban centers embedded themselves in market exchanges, handling strangers and
money with equal aplomb and operating small shops that often
served double duty as forums for civic and subaltern exchanges.
Others won the right to hire out their own time, an arrangement
that, depending on the terms struck with their owners, could
permit enslaved women to "receive," as Yarico did, "principally, if
not entirely" all the money they were able to make. Some lived

on their own, renting rooms apart from their owners; and many rubbed shoulders with—and frequently married into—a steadily expanding population of free people of color. In Richmond, Virginia, slave women constituted a small but obvious part of a new industrial labor force that included free workers and white workers as well as enslaved men; and on Sundays, attired in fine muslin and silk gowns financed with their earnings, they joined a polyglot population on promenades through the streets. Enslaved women also flocked in disproportionate numbers to the evangelical churches that had been multiplying in the upper and seaboard South since before the American Revolution. By the first years of cotton's expansion, women constituted a solid majority in upper South and low-country black congregations and could be found taking a lead in spiritual and moral matters. According to the antebellum minutes of the black Gillfield Baptist Church located in Petersburg, Virginia, some could even be found holding ecclesiastical offices traditionally considered the province of men.[41]

Such experiences powerfully affected and gradually transformed the ways in which slaves related, not only to their owners, but also to one another as women and men. They were also experiences that rarely, or barely, survived the peopling of Deep South plantations. In newly settled territory, such as that of southwestern Georgia, locations where the few towns in existence were scarcely more than hamlets, black women's public appearances slowed to a crawl. Certainly they did not disappear entirely from view. Though a good many of the region's slaveholders apparently never permitted any female slave to step away from their plantations, it was not entirely unheard of for others to occasionally send a woman to serve a neighbor in need or to let a female slave venture across plantation boundaries for a brief evening visit with nearby close kin. Other slaveholders sometimes allowed black women to attend church services or, if the distances were not very great, to trade on village streets. Flora, for example, received leave from her master to visit her mother, who was located on a nearby plantation. Nelson Tift permitted Silvey to sell homemade cakes in Albany's Sunday market, though this practice eventually cost her the goodwill and support of her church congregation. Planters with too many workers and too little work, as well as the men who served as executors or guardians of a dead slaveholder's estate, also occasionally hired out women, along with surplus slave men. Betsy, for instance, had a string of temporary owners following the death of her old master in the late 1840s. Similarly a woman named Minerva was hired out to five different people before eventually coming to rest in the possession of one of her dead owner's daughters; these transactions invariably exposed her and her baby to public view during the annual January hiring fairs. But even on those exceedingly infrequent occasions when a slaveholder permitted a slave woman to leave the estate, the woman was seldom allowed to go very far or, more important, to go on her own. Just as Jonas Smith did when he finally relented to requests from the quarters that he allow Catherine to be brought from central to southwestern Georgia, most owners of black women allowed them to go out and about only under the close supervision of a black or a white man.[42]

This is not to say that female slaves' arrival on cotton's frontier cost them all contact with and knowledge of the world that lay beyond slaveholders' gates. The epicenters of everyday life as well as the locus of rural production, antebellum plantations—even those as remotely situated as the estates that sprang up in southwest Georgia—were anything but private locations. As both work place and home place, they attracted endless streams of varied guests, for with the exception of enslaved women, everybody seemed to have business at one time or another on someone else's plantation. Peddlers trooped through with their packs on their backs. So too did patrollers, teamsters with their wagons, friends of the slaveholder and his family, preachers on proselytizing missions, tax collectors, census enumerators, candidates for political offices, enslaved men running their owners' errands, and people who wanted nothing more than a drink of water. Visiting planters were also a regular feature, given the practice of measuring their own crops by personally comparing them against those made by their neighbors. Plantation blacksmith shops drew steady successions of customers, as did the gristmills, sawmills, and gins their owners often made available to "the neighborhood"; and in a region where "hospitality [was] considered a virtue," out-of-town, and at least until the eve of secession, out-of-state visitors usually found warm welcomes from the region's slaveholders. Indeed, such was the pace of comings and goings, especially along the region's navigable rivers where steamboats arrived on a regularly scheduled basis, that a week could not pass without one person or another dropping in on someone else's plantation. Not even the chilliest or wettest of weather could keep visitors at bay, and close to two hundred people descended on William Dickey's landlocked estate between the first and last days of 1858. Nearly that many visited John Lester, in a procession that started in February, ended in December, and included family, friends, paying overnight guests, "William the horse drovier," hired workmen up from east Florida, and on at least one occasion an itinerate trader down from New York.[43]

Almost always on hand, enslaved women could scarcely have missed such a colorful pageant of people. But as the visited more than the visitors, a phenomenon that often left them dependent on knowledge distorted for having been obtained indirectly, few were able to replicate on cotton's terrain the social and political lives they had previously known. Thus while they continued to occupy critical positions at the center of their owners' estates—a location that among other things enabled them to monitor and manipulate slaveholders' law—black women had little choice but to reconstitute their lives within the borders of their owners' estates. Not only did cotton's uneven regime encourage female slaves to rely more on their wits than on their feet when they attempted to deflect slaveholders' excesses, but their cabins quickly came to serve as the locus of slaves' reordered communities. It was in the shelter of those cabins, for instance, that the region's bound workers fell into the habit of storing their meager possessions. As was the practice on other Deep South plantations, Rachel, who belonged to a Dougherty County slaveholder, surrounded her home with a flock of highly prized fowl—or did until *"they all died"*—while Lydia, whose master lived just north of the Florida border, came to be known locally as a woman who owned and occasionally loaned to the black people around her the "one dollar axe" that she kept in her cabin. Others, such as Maria on one place and Nancy on another, not only headquartered at their homes the flocks of cackling hens or the occasional spare change of clothes, they also sponsored many of those orphaned by cotton's migrations, those an Early County slaveholder blandly described as the "young negroes . . . without [resident] relatives."[44]

While rearing children—theirs or those who arrived in the hands of traders—vested in black women the power to shape their charges in ways more pleasing to slaves than perhaps to their owners, other women showed themselves and the dreams and beliefs that animated their lives in the garments they designed and created for one another. Although sewing was a tedious chore that frequently intensified the demands made on black women's time and required doing battle with the coarse, canvaslike cloth favored by masters for slaves, clothing, especially that enlivened by small scraps of ribbon and bits of bright colors, lent itself to aesthetic and arguably subaltern expressions. That certainly seemed to be the prevailing belief of at least one group of Sumter County's slaves, a group attracted, or so claimed their owner, to "neckties" of multiple colors, "calico dresses of gaudy patterns, and other et ceteras to[o] numerous" (or dissident) for their master "to mention."[45]

Nowhere, however, were the contracted dimensions of black women's lives more visible than in the composition and constituencies of southwest Georgia's small rural churches. Christianity was no stranger to the South's female forced migrants. As was the case with enslaved men, enslaved women also often arrived having already borne witness to Christ in their previous homes, or succumbed to his teachings in their new ones. Some of them entered into formal membership in one or another of the region's new churches, while others expressed their faith in those informal religious celebrations of the quarters, gatherings that often drew scoffs from their owners. Indeed, such was the interest of southwest Georgia's female slaves in their own spiritual well-being that they commonly matched and occasionally surpassed the number of enslaved men who enrolled in the churches that sprang up in the region's towns and villages. In Americus, for instance, twelve of the twenty-one slaves who belonged to the Friendship Baptist Church in October 1842 were women. Though the Americus black Baptist women would lose their numerical edge over black men, when two years later the latter outnumbered the former by one, the Macedonia Church in Blakely was clearly a female space, for there in 1860, black women constituted nearly two-thirds of a slave congregation of 150. Similarly, at the Albany Baptist Church, which drew its congregation from within the town or from nearby plantations, fifty-three slave women worshipped in the company of fifty-four slave men.[46]

Something altogether different unfolded, however, outside of southwest Georgia's small towns. There, in a surprising inversion of black Christianity as it had unfolded to the east and the north, membership tilted steeply in the favor of men. Take the "Tarver Arm" of the Albany Baptist Church, for example. Tucked in the corner of one of Dougherty County's most productive plantations and surrounded by high concentrations of slaves, the church was dominated by men who commuted as many as three or more miles to hear the Sabbath-day preaching. Fully three-quarters of the female congregants, by contrast, lived on the plantation that sponsored the church or on the one located immediately next door. Reflecting the new—and narrower—scope and constituency of black women's communities, only six of the little church's female members lived any farther afield, and all of them attended in the company of three or more men.[47]

As black women reconstituted their lives within the recesses of their owners' estates, it fell almost exclusively to black men to serve as the public eyes and ears of southwest Georgia's slave population. Rattling along in their two-horse, four-horse, and six-horse wagons, they mapped in their heads the locations of plantations and towns, rivers and swamps, and the networks of trails and roads that connected them. They shared those roadways and forested paths with itinerant peddlers (many of them recently arrived German Jews, no strangers to oppression themselves), patrollers, the occasional highwayman (a gang of which preyed along the border with Florida), newly arrived white settlers, next-door neighbors, and sometimes visitors from much farther away, overlaying their maps of the land with another that marked the people upon it. They also shared that interstitial terrain—country roads, village streets, and uncut forests—with multitudes of other slave men, building trust and forming friendships as they labored together to patch the public's roads, waited their turns at a mill, and rounded up foraging cattle. Together these out-and-about slave men identified which shopkeepers and purveyors of "spirituous liquors" welcomed slaves' trade, where to find the ubiquitous games of chance ("three up," "chuckluck," and "brag" were among the more popular), and whose storerooms went unguarded. Slave men also weighed slaveholders' capacity for war when they delivered their masters to regimental reviews, an opportunity that came the way of a Baker County slave named Abe in January 1842.[48]

Slave men especially kept track of their owners and the white people around them. Achieving a level of surveillance that owners and patrollers could match only in their dreams, black men developed extensive, if unwritten, files on those who commanded slaves' labor. They shadowed masters' and mistresses' movements about the countryside, spied on their friends, uncovered their foes, and documented their everyday habits. Thus it was that "Rackleys boy" came to know through a series of hazy, subaltern connections precisely the night white teenager Delilah Ward planned to spend with her friends, and the hour she planned to depart from their home. He knew which path she would take, how far she would walk, which creek she would cross, and where on that route a secret trail cut off toward a swamp. Most especially, "Rackleys boy" had particular knowledge of Delilah's licentious past—a detail she had kept from her mother but could not keep from the slaves.[49]

Black men occupied a world of knowledge and experience that black women were rarely able to tap into. It was also a world that spilled out of the countryside, down the rivers, into the sea, and often beyond. Conversations struck up with deckhands and steamboat pilots—frequently black and enslaved—connected hinterland to seaport, opening the way for landlocked teamsters and field hands to inject their voices into a centuries-old discourse of Atlantic proportions. Stealth visits by northern advocates of freedom (visits that became increasingly dangerous as sectional tensions intensified)—such as William Nuel's closely guarded stop at the home of Aunt Hagar, one of a handful of free people of color—brought slaves into personal contact with a national debate then raging about slavery and the future of the Union, reminding them (as did public tirades by unwitting political candidates) of the presence of valuable, if distant, allies. Such conversations with sympathetic friends from the North, and perhaps some of those riverside talks, revealed as well the particular knowledge the region's slaves had of a nation under the governance of black men: San Domingue. Indeed, San Domingue—and how best to get there—was the featured topic of discussion between Nuel and the slaves who queried him closely the evening he spent at Aunt Hagar's. Other slaves, like the twenty or so who witnessed an 1843 strike waged by Irish railroad hands against an enterprise financed by planters' capital, tucked away into their collective memories not so much potent examples of how high black people could rise once liberated, but of how far, given the right combination of pressures, slaveholders could be made to fall.[50]

All slaves took part in the active defense of the communities and lives they were so carefully reassembling in southwest Georgia. But while black women tended to conduct their operations within the boundaries of their owners' estates, black men launched theirs on a much broader terrain. Thus it was that when demands on slaves' labor reached intolerable levels, slave men far more frequently than slave women took to the surrounding woods, spending a few days or weeks hiding out in the swamps and thickets that filled the spaces between the region's plantations. Most never bothered going much farther, "laying out" only long enough to make the necessary point with those who drove them. But occasionally slave men banked on their knowledge of a larger political and social terrain to keep on moving. Clinging to forged passes that in at least one case was the handiwork of a local peddler, some of those fugitives aimed to reunite with families they had been taken from by sale or migration. Others contemplated leaving the nation altogether, directing their gaze toward places where slavery was a thing of the past and black people enjoyed the privileges of citizenship. Indeed, whispered a handful of hopeful black men to northerner Nuel when he visited Aunt Hagar's Thomasville cabin, how soon could he carry them and their children to San Domingue?[51] Most slave men elected, however, to stay put, especially as families grew up around them. For example, a group of slave men belonging to an absentee Sumter County planter opted not to run, but to talk, wielding the mobility that came their way through work against an overseer with a brutal passion for physical punishment. Out and about on legitimate business, the men dropped hints here and there about the "rite Ruff" treatment to which they and their colleagues had been subjected, and especially about a wave of miscarriages that had been one of the more baneful results. News about the loss of those babies eventually reached the slaves' absentee owner at his home in Bibb County, then ricocheted back to strike their target as precisely as the black men had intended. "Dear Sir," began the overseer when called upon by his boss to explain the reports of abuses that had trickled off the plantation and into his ears half a state away. "I received your letter yesterday ev'ng and was vary sorry to hear that you had heard that I was treating your Negroes so cruely."[52]

If the Sumter slaves played off chronic tensions between masters and overseers, it was a keen appreciation for heightening sectional tensions and a confidence born of countless encounters with strange white men that provided enslaved mill mechanic Sam both sword and shield when the planter next door discovered one of his slave women huddled in Sam's cabin. She was not there for him, Sam declared in the presence of both the woman's pugnacious owner and James Filey (mill manager, overseer, and employee of one of the region's most substantial slaveholders). She was there for Filey, said Sam, and she had been coming for him on a regular basis. The accusation was carefully tuned for the time and derailed any confrontation between planter and slave by hurling the conflict off in a whole different direction. "I did not hear the conversation myself," a third party reported in a tone approaching something of awe, "but I heard [the woman's owner] tell it publickly" that Filey "was a strong abolitionist" who deserved to suffer the full weight of the law.[53]

Slave men's master-made access to distant places and people lent a particular cast to their efforts not only to protect but to provide. To be sure, it was in slaveholders' best interest to furnish their workers with the bare minimum required to keep body and soul intact. But theirs was a generally utilitarian aesthetic, taking the form of cornmeal and pork, ill-fitting shoes and garments constructed of heavy, coarse, and canvas-like fabric. It was a colorless and bland domestic existence, and one that slave fathers and husbands, like slave mothers and wives, took great pride in relieving. But whereas black women brought color and comfort to the quarters by wielding a needle or raising chickens for meat and eggs, black men applied what they knew or obtained from off the plantation. Those who managed to earn a little cash in moments snatched from cotton's routine, might, for instance, invest their small wages in a few "little luxuries"—purchasing lengths of ribbon, a plug of tobacco, a new pair of shoes,

or a piece of fresh beef to take back to the quarters. Others occasionally obtained supplemental provisions by more surreptitious
means, trading on their knowledge of the people and places that
lay beyond their owners' estates to ransack unguarded barns,
corncribs, and warehouses, hauling home to their cabins and
families prizes that had until recently been someone else's possessions. That is what Monday McRea had been doing when he
was caught slipping home before dawn carrying a bag of bacon,
and what Sam and George had been doing until their owner
found them out and brought to a halt a series of midnight raids
the men had been making on a neighbor's plantation. But however enslaved men came to acquire what one husband and father
described as "such substantials of life as a person of Color, could
then have & obtain," in delivering those items to their loved ones
they not only gave public confirmation to the matrimonial and
parental bonds no slaveholders' law was willing to acknowledge;
they also expressed for themselves and for others what it meant
to be a good man, and a good father. Indeed, it was this act of
providing—"freely, willingly, and voluntarily"—for the wants of
his family over the space of twenty-some years and several
changes of ownership in slavery, on which Harry Peterson would
rest, and eventually win, legal claim to his children after Eliza, his
wife, flounced out of their lives after emancipation.[54]

By the eve of secession, southwest Georgia's enslaved men and
women had made significant progress in restoring structure and
strength to lives badly wrenched by the settlement process. Families had formed, couples raised babies, and chickens scratched
in the yards surrounding black people's quarters. Networks of
friendship had begun to spill across plantation boundaries, re-
versing the alienation of forced migration. But on cotton's new
ground—where time was dear and the master's demands never

ending—what black men and black women managed to make for themselves was a dim and distorted reflection of what most of them had known in their previous homes. Grandparents remained in exceedingly short supply, as did the aunts and uncles and cousins who collectively constituted those extensive networks of kin that in other locations shielded enslaved men and women from some of the worst of slaveholders' blows. Productive activities produced nearly nothing, and the few churches that had come into existence were shadows—and masculine shadows at that—of what they might have become under different conditions. Most especially, black men and black women's postmigration experiences seemed to have altered the day-to-day dynamics of their domestic relations and, as a result, gave rise to new ways to measure what it meant to them to be good parents, good partners, and even good people. These transformations not only distinguished in varying degrees the experiences of slavery in this corner of Georgia from those that unfolded in other places and in other times, but in very important and lingering ways they would condition the lives black southwest Georgians would make for themselves in freedom.

2

Civil War
in the Land
of Goshen

Before freedom, however, came war. As was the case elsewhere across the Confederate nation, the removal of men and materials to the battlefields disrupted and often transformed the lives of those left at home, thrusting women into roles long considered the province of men, and rupturing relations between rich people and poor. But revolutions can be incomplete.[1] For reasons arising as much from an accident of geography as from slaveholders' masterful ability to hold the war at arm's reach, the same struggle in southwest Georgia allowed the antebellum rhythms of slave life and production to remain largely intact. To be sure, new slaves arrived from points north, east, and occasionally west, deposited on regional estates by refugee owners desperate to salvage a part of their valuable property from oncoming armies; fields of cotton gave way unevenly and incompletely to fields of corn or wheat; and a scattering of wartime industries introduced slave men and slave women to new patterns of production. But more generally and for most of the war, life for those who dwelled in the slave quarters unfolded along trajectories that predated secession. The phenomenon preserved much of what slaves had so painstakingly contrived in the years following migration and meant that in the last months of the war, when black men and black women accelerated their efforts to dismantle the institution that entrapped them, they did so in accordance with habits of action and alliance they had developed and practiced under cotton's slaveholding regime.

White southwest Georgians' preparations for secession began long before the presidential election of 1860. Emerging first in the early 1830s during the nullification crisis, talk of disunion among free citizens grew more vigorous as the antislavery movement gained momentum, and reached heated levels in 1850 as the nation considered the terms under which new slave states would be admitted into the Union. Despite some talk in 1850 of evicting forcibly individuals who failed to exhibit appropriate levels of sectional loyalty, cooler heads—many belonging to southwest Georgia's large slaveholders—prevailed, and the region as a whole deemed it inadvisable that year to fracture the Union. But a slave population that nearly doubled between 1850 and 1860 (rising from 36,000 to 63,000) and whose proportion of the total population rose from 45 to 54 percent provided a daily reminder of the issues at stake. As the national debate over slavery and freedom grew fiercer through the decade of the 1850s, and as southern support for secession gathered momentum, southwest Georgia's planters and their allies began to examine their defenses and plug the holes they found. Anxious guardians of slaveholding society discouraged masters from allowing their slaves to accompany them to political rallies. They counseled newspaper editors not to reprint "the proceedings of some Abolition, Woman-rights, or other fanatical meeting." And in case any doubts lingered, they extolled the benefits of bondage to enslaved and enslaver alike. "Already," wrote one champion of slavery as Kansas and the national Senate erupted in violence in May 1856, "strikes and combinations abound [in Europe and northern communities], and riots are seen and felt. The sure, unalterable, and rapid tendency of free society is through anarchy to despotism . . . From these errors and from this fate, the South is preserved by the institution of slavery." No longer wholly convinced that antebellum patrols were sufficient to ensure the survival of the favored institution, communities formed and uniformed new militias to help. But until John Brown and his party of black and white rebels launched their assault on the arsenal at Harpers Ferry, turnout was lackadaisical among both militiamen and patrollers.[2]

Provoked by the terrifying images of an abolitionist-led slave insurrection, southwest Georgia's beneficiaries of bondage instigated in Brown's wake a series of preemptive strikes against anyone positioned to act against slavery. Strangers, especially those like the Jewish pack peddlers who trafficked directly with slaves and who had long been suspected of furnishing black runaways with illegitimate passes, along with the region's bare handful of free people of color (a population that in 1860 amounted to 125) came under particularly close scrutiny. Dougherty County's grand jury, at its December 1859 session, called on state lawmakers to impose a thousand-dollar tax on "pedlars[,] Book agents, and all transient traders whose character is not well known." Such a tax, the jurists anticipated, would "amount to a prohibition and will effectively free ourselves of a dangerous profession" that could be used "as a mighty engine against our institutions." Local officials enforced with more vigor laws that governed the lives of free people of color, rounding up and re-registering those whose papers were not in complete order. White people suspected of being "abolitionist spies" were run out of Dougherty, Thomas, and Worth counties; when they balked, their pursuers uncoiled their whips. "In some cases" vigilantes laid on as many "as two hundred and seventy-five lashes," a punishment one man considered still too timid. "Hang these villains to the

first tree, and they, at least, can do no more harm," wrote a correspondent to an Albany paper. Reinforced by the ongoing mobilization of "volunteer corps" and efforts to intimidate any whose
political proclivities seemed dubious ("foreigners" were especially worrisome), slaveholders hoped to permanently secure the
"peace and property of our country, and the obedience and hap-
piness of our slave population."[3]

Not every free white man linked arms with the movement its
advocates dubbed "Southern Rights." Indeed, not every slaveholding planter tossed his hat into a ring occupied by secessionists. Ambivalence and conflict abounded. Jurist and Dougherty
County absentee planter Andrew Garnett stubbornly reserved
his loyalties for the Union, as did a slim majority of Thomasville
men whose political allegiances lay with Constitutional Unionist
John Bell. Stewart and Randolph counties may even have sheltered a few Republicans. But those who favored immediate secession pulled out all stops and by one means or another rallied a
slim majority of southwest Georgia's voters to their cause in time
for the 1860 presidential election. Convinced, perhaps by "great
mass barbecues" of the sort held in Albany just days before the
election or by the less subtle exhibition of whips, white southwest Georgians followed the statewide pattern by tipping the
election to John C. Breckinridge, the southern Democrats' candidate for president.[4]

Secessionists accelerated efforts to fend off their enemies,
internal and external, in the wake of the November election.
Equating submission to the Union with slavery, and slavery (at
least of white men) with political death, men who styled themselves the Southern Rights Party combed the countryside rooting out any person or publication suspected of lackluster loyalty
to slaveholders and their cherished institution. On learning of a
discarded pro-Republican northern newspaper, the editor of the

Albany paper suggested its former owner ought to find justice at the end of a rope. When bricklayer William Stewart confessed to voting for John Bell, he was run out of town by one of the county's largest planters and his overseer. Hoping to avoid the same fate, northern-born merchant L. E. Welch proclaimed his loyalty by burning an armload of *Harper's* magazines in the middle of an Albany street and the mayor of Thomasville appointed a "Vigilance Committee." Some of the previously squeamish came around too. Scarcely two weeks after Thomas County voters narrowly chose John Bell's Constitutionalist Union Party over Breckinridge and the secessionists in the presidential contest, they changed their minds. At a well-attended public meeting, the county's white citizens resolved that, given Abraham Lincoln's victory, "the preservation of this Union as it now exists, is of far less moment with us, than the preservation of our honor and our rights."[5]

When the polls closed on the January 2 election for candidates to the state disunion convention, a majority of southwest Georgia's voters made clear that they agreed in principle with the Thomas County resolutions. Eleven of the region's nineteen counties voted overwhelmingly in favor of secession. Only two (Webster and Thomas counties) voted in favor of remaining in the union. Headlines in the Albany newspaper trumpeted most planters' delight: "The Secessionist Ticket Triumphant!" Three weeks later, and despite questions about the actual depth of popular support for disunion, secessionists again emerged victorious.[6]

Once Georgia determined to withdraw from the Union, communities throughout the region intensified preparations to defend their collective decision. Amid much fanfare and in a carnival-like atmosphere that privileged uniforms and parades over tactical proficiency, white men rushed forward to offer their services to the new nation, and freshly minted military units sprouted from every crossroads and village. By late spring, it seemed as if every neighborhood of size had organized an infantry or cavalry, and sometimes more than one. Dougherty County's eager young men could choose from the Guards, the Grays, the Hussars, or the Invincibles. Stewart County mounted out six companies, including Rawson's Rangers. Cuthbert sent the Rifles and Dragoons. From Bainbridge came the Independents and Volunteers. Enthusiasm for the Confederate cause ran high. Only Virginia mobilized more soldiers than Georgia during the first half of 1861.[7]

But unanimity remained elusive. Despite Confederate efforts to stifle such talk, die-hard Unionists continued to mourn the fracturing of the nation, with some predicting dire and bloody results. Presciently commenting from his vantage point near the Florida line, D. J. Brandon warned that in the space of months the South would be "reduced to abject want, and the verry institution of slavery for which we have been labouring" destroyed. Newspaper columnists, convinced of the "existence of *spies* and *abolitionists* among us," encouraged heightened surveillance and urged their readers to be on the lookout for "persons tampering with the negroes." Vigilante committees canvassed the countryside, rooting out the politically suspicious, the purportedly treasonous, "loafers," "Deserters," and "outlaws." One such gang tore Baker County's Waltwen Kelley away from his plowing. Accused of uttering a few stray "abolitionist sentences," Kelley was accosted by a dozen or so well-armed men. After enduring a series of secretive hearings conducted by a self-appointed citizens' committee, Kelley was released and the charges dropped. Others were not so fortunate. Almost simultaneous to Kelley's arrest, another vigilante committee swept through a Mitchell County neighborhood, ousting a handful of poor white men from their farms on trumped-up charges that they were plotting a servile revolt. The affair exposed "the cloven foot," as one observer noted, but it did not belong to rebellious slaves as originally rumored. Rather, that devil's foot belonged to "speculators" and large planters eager to capitalize on erupting tensions between white southerners to "make Som thing out of these men."[8]

If signs of a fraying social fabric were drawing into sharp focus under the force of secession and military mobilization, the threadbare sections belonged to white southwest Georgians, not black. Plantation quarters, from all accounts, were peaceful. Indeed, if planters' own words and their continued commitment to patterns of antebellum production offer any indication, the outbreak of war barely stirred relations between the region's masters and slaves. With two brief exceptions, neither political nor battle news interrupted Daniel Horn's careful record keeping for 1861. No mention was made of Georgia's January secession convention or its outcome. No mention was made of Jefferson Davis's ascendance to the presidency of the Confederacy in February. The firing on Fort Sumter and the commencement of war likewise went without remark, as did the first hints of a changing Union policy regarding slaves and slavery. Even the June rumors of insurrection in Mitchell County, an uprising that purportedly had been primed to sweep his neighborhood as well as those around Camilla to the north, passed unnoticed. Only once, in a year that from a national perspective could arguably be described as revolutionary, a year that echoed with complaints from slaveholders in Maryland, Virginia, and other locations proximate to Union lines about unusual "difficulties [in] retaining their Slaves at home," did events on the warfront invade the quiet backwater of Horn's Decatur County. And even then the interruption was minimal. On a Sunday in late July, Horn's minister dedicated the day's service to the Confederate victory at Manassas. But as Horn took care to note, the choice of homily had not been a local choice: it had been imposed on them by the Confederate Congress.[9]

Horn was not alone in his apparent obliviousness to the tumult of an expanding war. Once the first wave of volunteers had been organized, provisioned, and sent on their way, planters and overseers across the region turned back to the daily business of growing cotton. Secure in the physical distance yawning between frontline and field, as well as comfortable with the existing ratio of white men to black slaves, routine, not revolution, characterized life on the area's plantations. On David Crenshaw Barrow's Decatur County plantation, overseer George Davis sowed the usual corn, cotton, peas, and potatoes in the usual quantities and usual proportions the spring of 1861 while the plantation's hogs feasted themselves fat on the mast they rooted from the surrounding forests. Although Davis could hardly avoid mentioning the June insurrection scare (since several of his employer's slaves were implicated and at least two were taken in for questioning), it was a momentary diversion. His attention reverted speedily to enemies of a more common sort. "Rust," "lice," and "cut worms," Davis reported through the spring and summer, were ruining the cotton. Too much rain fell in August. Too little fell in September. The "caterpillar" showed up in early fall to gnaw the youngest boles off the cotton plants. Nature, not war or slaves, conspired to frustrate the overseer, a circumstance that allowed him to unhesitatingly dispatch his slave men as usual around the countryside on business. So unimpressed had he been by the June "uprising" and so little concerned about the possibility that he might inadvertently assist disgruntled slaves by facilitating the communication of rebellious sentiment, that Davis calmly swapped workers with the manager of Barrow's

Mitchell County mill, the other center of the purported June revolt. Come November, Davis was wrapping up work on the 1861 crop. One hundred twenty-nine bales of cotton sat awaiting a buyer, and the plantation slaves had begun preparations for the ensuing season. As Stewart County shopkeeper Hawthorne Chamberline remarked, it was "business as usual" during the first year of war.[10]

The same could be said of much of the next year. Despite the passage in April of the Confederate government's first enrollment act, the booming of far-distant cannon hardly broke the planters' rhythm for the first half or so of 1862. Indeed, many believed that the security of slavery required a rigorous maintenance of familiar and labor-intensive routine. Idle slaves had been long understood to be mischievous and potentially rebellious. What better than the demanding regime of cotton to stave off the trouble that might arise from hands with too little productive work to keep them safely occupied six and, before the war concluded, seven days a week.[11] "It is manifestly Expedient in order to preserve such property," and not incidentally slaveholder power, opined a Dougherty County court, "to render it productive and to keep the same togeather that such property should be employed in agriculture." Better that bound men and women continue to perform the "monotonous & unexciting but regular & strict work of the farm." Fearful of rocking what amounted to a precarious but still balanced boat, and heedless of a growing conversation across the Confederacy about shrinking food supplies ("You cannot eat cotton," cautioned one writer, speculating on the future availability of critical resources), the area's planters insisted on sowing hundreds of acres with their antebellum staple, cotton, in the spring of 1862. According to one sharp-tongued critic, who would have preferred to see the region's soil sprouting edible grains, the planters' sole motivation was greed—for benefits they would enjoy either immediately or at some future date after the Confederate nation lifted restrictions on sale abroad. "One planter is pitching 900 acres of cotton, the overseer of another . . . is going to plant 300 acres, another (with ten stumps of hands,) 90 acres, another [with] fifteen hand[s] 90 acres, another 300 acres, and two others with full crops of cotton!" An unabashed Dougherty County planter, Richard Hines, agreed. The countryside, he admitted in a letter to a disapproving Governor Joseph E. Brown, was "full of cotton."[12]

Brown's censure made little impression on southwest Georgia's cotton producers. They were likewise undeterred by legislation passed by the state legislature in December 1862 that "prohibit[ed] the cultivation of more than three acres of cotton to the hand." More concerned with unruly slaves than unfed soldiers and citizens, planters sowed their fields to meet personal, not public, needs. Some did expand their crops of corn, but not necessarily at the expense of cotton. The proprietor of a Randolph County plantation, Leila Calloway, put in a full crop of the staple in the spring of 1863. So did Robert Toombs, a Sumter County absentee planter and fierce Confederate defender. Somewhat more conscious of the political implications of cotton, David Barrow made a pretense of following the rules; but just barely. In reference to government inspectors, he insisted, "I do not want them coming to survey my crop. I do not want meetings held on my conduct. I will not have my patriotism brought into question." Barrow kept his cotton crop well within the legal limits on the two plantations closest to the state capital. He made up the difference by planting a greater proportion of cotton to corn at his more remote Blowing Cave estate in Decatur County. "I shall plant no more than 5 to 10 acres at any of my places up here," he wrote from Athens, Georgia, "and with

250 at Blowing Cave, the aggregate of my crop will not vary much the next." And it likely did not vary much the ensuing year, when J. P. M. Epping submitted a surreptitious report to a member of Lincoln's cabinet. Southwest Georgia, he informed Salmon P. Chase, secretary of the treasury, in May 1864 was "one vast Cotton field."[13]

Overflowing warehouses silently confirmed Epping's report. With scarcely any chance of slipping their crops out of the Confederacy and to European buyers until the war ended, planters stashed their relatively nonperishable bales under any available roof. By the last years of the war, storage facilities were overflowing with what amounted to capital-in-waiting. B. J. Smith had packed thirty-three hundred bales into his Cuthbert warehouse by the spring of 1864; fifty-three hundred bales had accumulated in a Thomasville warehouse a year later. Inundated by an avalanche of cotton, the managers of a storage facility in Columbus, Georgia, eventually had to ask customers to take their business elsewhere "until further notice." They had run out of space. But rather than forgo their annual crops of cotton, which would have meant disrupting plantation routines, agriculturalists simply built warehouses of their own, and the stores of finished cotton grew. Union naval personnel, who by the last years of the conflict maintained a steady presence along the Gulf coast south of Thomasville, remarked regularly on the determination of southwest Georgia planters to keep up their cotton. Northern journalist Sidney Andrews confirmed such reports when he embarked on a postwar tour of the former Confederacy. Georgia had produced more wartime cotton than any other rebel state, he learned as he made his way south through the Carolinas, and the "great bulk of that amount" had been grown in the southwest corner of the state. According to Andrews's observations and the information he gathered during his tour, the counties in that quarter had ended the war with approximately two hundred thousand bales on hand and expected another ten thousand bales each from the crop planted in the last weeks of the war.[14]

Maintaining a familiar productive regime promised to keep slave society intact and to protect the sovereignty of masters. But nagging doubts lingered. Always on guard against disturbances that might alter the balance of southern power, scattered skeptics began early to question domestic security and the extent to which mobilization and political excitement might provoke unwanted responses among the region's slaves. The "very vast preponderance of negroes" surrounding them worried more than one white resident of Dougherty County, especially when "in these alarming times of excitement and danger . . . we frequently observe groups of slaves congregating together contrary to law." "Be watchful," cautioned the editor of the county's main newspaper in 1861. "You know not when the incendiary may be at your door." In November of the first year of the war, a Worth County grand jury urged the state government to consider capital punishment for any white person caught selling, buying, or procuring "for a slave, any gun, pistol, dirk or bone knife, or other like instrument." While professing himself unconcerned that the slaves might rise in the night to murder their masters and mistresses, a Randolph County white man relayed to the Georgia governor his neighbors' request for muskets and the authority to organize a "home guard." "I know & so advised them that such an application is unusual, but in days of revolution, every precaution should be taken both at home and abroad."[15]

Such pleas could be read as a mechanism for leveraging munitions and weapons from the state and Confederate government, but slaves had always given their owners reason to worry. Bound men and women were no more oblivious to the larger currents of a national conflict over slavery and freedom than they were to the frantic activities of their owners. The exigencies of war had not yet disrupted or forced fundamental transformations of everyday plantation routine, but in other respects the war infused everyday life, that of the quarters included. Indeed, the same grinding labor regime that owners hoped would stave off domestic upheaval served to keep slaves apprised of national events. Each trip to town for farming supplies, each stint of work performed in the company of talkative white people, and each encounter with slaves from other plantations offered bound workers potential opportunity to eavesdrop on or, if circumstances permitted, to converse among themselves about Yankee advances, Confederate fortunes, and the impact of war on slavery itself. Lee County planter C. B. Calloway leveled special complaint against the railway that bordered his estate. "I live right next to the station," he complained in a letter to the state governor, "where my negroes are subject to all sorts of advice." But the slaves who served in some of Thomasville's stores were also positioned to swap news of the war along with the goods they stocked, and they were not alone. A "*black band,* discoursing animating music . . . serenaded" exuberant celebrations of secession in Albany; slave "musitions" sounded the accompaniment for military drill. When Confederate casualties began to trickle home after the first great battle at Manassas, Virginia, in July 1861, slaves were on hand to witness the dreary homecomings: digging graves for the dead, tending the wounds of the living, and repairing tattered and bloodstained uniforms for reissue or reuse. As southwest Georgia's ex-slaves explained to visiting northern nurse Clara Barton shortly after the Confederate defeat, missing the war had been out of the question. They had been "mity fraid," admitted the dozens who descended on her Andersonville camp, but they had also been mighty informed from the very beginning; "repeatedly so," they assured her.[16]

A few, in the early months of the war, took advantage of that

carefully compiled intelligence and shifts in the white population to probe more forcefully at the interstices of the system
that bound them. When picked up for "clost" questioning by the
regulators who patrolled Mitchell County for enemies of slavery
in the weeks following the commencement of war, Israel, Boy
Green, Wesley, and others quickly fingered as accomplices and
ringleaders the white farmers who owned the property their
masters coveted. Having deflected attention away from themselves by aggravating already existing tensions between rich people and poor, the slaves returned to their homes intact. More
commonly, though not yet on the scale that would character-
ize the last months of the war, slaves—men and women—took
slowly increasing advantage of white men's departure for war to
test the sovereignty of slaveholders. C. B. Calloway's slaves, their
ears seemingly glued to the rails that ran past their plantation
home, acted in the fall of 1861 on the "advise" they received via
the road. It required the assistance, Calloway complained, of his
white neighbors "to subject" the slaves once again to his will and
service.[17]

On Duncan Curry's Thomas County plantation, it took an
uncle's help to reduce newly unruly slaves to obedience. Curry
had left the place in the care of his fifteen-year-old son when he
had accepted a commission and departed for war. The slaves recognized immediately that young Perry was not up to the job.
Squeamish about applying the whip, Perry commanded neither
obedience nor respect, and discipline unraveled. Suky started the
process by ignoring her young master's commands, but it was
Jake who took it up a notch, determining—or so Perry's uncle
Archibald contended—to "become a man of his own accord."
When ordered to feed the livestock and "attend to the lot," Jake
balked. He was hoeing, he retorted, and "when he was hoeing
he did not go to the lott." Not satisfied with exerting new author-

ity over his own labor, Jake extended it into his personal life, "go[ing] off in the neighborhood" without leave, sometimes taking his wife along with him. Jake's insubordination proved infectious. Allen soon followed suit, likewise refusing to feed the horses on the grounds he was busy with a hoe. Observing the decaying of discipline on his brother's plantation, Archibald finally stepped in to set matters right. The first to be "take[n] . . . down" were the slaves Jake and Allen, who each received a "pretty round of flaggelation." Next in line was Perry: not to be whipped, but to learn to whip. Determined that the teenager should assume the manner of mastery to go along with the position he held for his father, Archibald handed Perry a lash and supervised its application. By the time Archibald retreated, returning the plantation to his nephew's control, Jake had been "compressed" back into "the size of his own breeches" and the labor force as a whole had returned to work with renewed energy and industry.[18]

Other owners had begun by the second season of war to report similar problems with slaves who were finding in the frictions of war new social space in which to slack off, talk back, and sometimes slip away on trips of their own. In November 1862 a Thomas County "vigilance committee" accused Narcissa Melissa Lawton's slaves of furnishing the paper on which an unknown author scribbled a warning about a pending slave insurrection. At the gristmill David Barrow operated near Camilla, the notoriously mobile slave Sam gave his overseer new aggravation by taking leave of the quarters on Saturdays and rarely returning before work commenced on Mondays. Punishment, complained James Filey in a report to his boss, had done nothing to discourage Sam from his weekly and unauthorized rounds. "I have whipped Him time & again but all to no purpose last Saturday night he went off and never returned till Monday morning Half Hour after Sunrise with Collins dogs on His track." Filey told

how he had tied up Sam "and give Him the most Severe whipping that He evir did git Starting the Hide in Several places, and
He promised me & Collins to never to go again." But to no avail.
"It is now one week," Filey reported, "and He is off again and I
don't Expect to See Him till in the morning." At least Sam kept
coming back. S. W. Patterson discovered one morning that three
of his slaves had gone missing for good. According to a neighbor,
Patterson's slaves had taken their master by surprise. He "did not
know they had any intentions of leaving till he found they were
gone."[19]

But the whispers of discontent detected by Patterson, Curry,
and others remained largely that during the first year and a half
or two of the war. Most southwest Georgian slaveholders were
confident enough in their mastery to refrain from making dras-
tic changes in slave management or calling for a strengthening of
police powers. The sight of slave men out and about on country
roads, trading in village shops, and gathered with slave women
on Sundays for worship raised some concerns among the more
timid, but rarely did those fears translate into any systematic
plan to reduce the slaves' mobility or redeploy their labor, at
least not until the last months of the war. Instead, no sooner had
the wounds inflicted by the whip healed on the backs of the
Curry plantation slaves than their master hustled nine of them
(including the ambitious Jake) south to make salt on the Florida
shore, a work site situated right under the noses of the Union
vessels that patrolled the coast.[20] Others pronounced their slaves
"cheerful and industrious," and plantations continued to sell,
bought up by newcomers eager to make their own fortunes
from cotton. Indeed, signs of confidence in slaveholding society
appeared nearly everywhere, including the courthouse in
Thomasville, where Confederates staged dancing parties,
"Soires," and "other festivities."[21]

Religious services likewise proceeded as usual, including those involving the slaves. Dougherty County authorities were so indifferent to the insurrectionary potential of regular gatherings of slave congregations, even those consisting more of black men than black women, that they not only granted enslaved Baptist Davy Hines a license to preach to other slaves three days before the state resolved to leave the Union, but renewed his license like clockwork every six months at least through the end of 1862. The First Baptist Church in Cuthbert had the year before faced a similar question. Church authorities dithered for a few weeks, then after a month's deliberation concluded in June 1861 to "resume the afternoon services for the blacks subject to such restrictions as the civil law impose." In nearby Early County, the "colored" Methodists continued at least through the fall of 1863 to meet in the presence of their own minister, a man they hired and supported out of their own pockets. Few slaveholders, it seems, even as late as the summer and fall of 1862, had reason to disagree with an assessment voiced with considerable confidence by Dougherty planter David A. Vason the first summer of the war. "Our slave population is large, but never have we felt more safe, and never have the slaves felt more happy."[22]

It was an air of tranquility reflected in the local courts of law. Southwest Georgia's judges and jurists saw little reason to follow southern judicial practice and stiffen penalties against slaves during times of crisis.[23] The region's judicial bodies continued to extend to enslaved defendants a number of the same privileges and rights enjoyed by free people. Murder and attempted murder of white men was not enough, for instance, to send southwest Georgia slaves to the gallows even after the outbreak of war. Despite hours of testimony from slave and free witnesses detailing a bloody encounter between slave Jacob and his overseer during which brawl Jacob pummeled the overseer with fists and a fence rail, choked "the breath out of him," chopped at him with a knife, knocked him down, stomped on his belly and head, and finally finished off by bellowing across the field to all who could hear that he sincerely hoped that he had "Killed the damed Son of a bitch," the Thomas County superior court sentenced Jacob to a public whipping. It was a punishment more commonly administered by masters to slaves who slacked or sassed. But to the men who sat in judgment that day, whipping was sufficient for a slave they considered to be "a cut above a very good boy," and who had had the misfortune to tangle with a man the community knew as a habitual brute. Monday McRae received a similar result when he found himself hauled in front of the Sumter County Superior Court to answer a charge of assault with intent to murder. Tried in April 1861 for an early-morning scuffle with a white man, Monday eventually went free, released by a lower court that refused to define his crime as insurrection, and then by the state supreme court when it ruled on appeal that testimony that would have aided the slave's case had been wrongly withheld from the jury. Not even the arrival of black strangers could shake white citizens' confidence that all continued to remain mostly right in their proximate world. Thus, despite chronic concerns about the toxic effect free people of color could have on slave society, the Dougherty County Superior Court accepted Bill's claim that he was recognized "as a free negro by the citizens of Waidsborough North Carolina" and on August 21, 1863, ordered "Ben alias Bill" to be released from the jail in which he had been held for nearly a year.[24]

Complacency on this scale was contingent on maintaining a healthy and well-patrolled buffer between their slaves and what slaveholders deemed influences of evil. Although Thomas County citizens conspired in the summer of 1862 to evict from their community the Jewish pack peddlers who had roamed the antebellum roads, the most pernicious of the supposed threats to slave society were, as always, Yankees and their antislavery forces. Devising plans to halt invasion up the Chattahoochee and Flint rivers preoccupied southwest Georgia's slaveholders from the beginning of the war. Not only were they determined to safeguard their stores of cotton and corn, as well as a number of small manufacturing firms that produced everything from hardtack to Confederate naval vessels; they also wanted to keep any "*spies* and *abolitionists*" away from their slave quarters. Evidently hoping to preempt any alliance between the slaves and potential liberators, Albany authorities pondered instituting a police system by which slaves would be liberally rewarded for ferreting out and reporting the presence of such baneful influences. But most of these proposals involved erecting obstructions along the rivers to block passage by Union vessels or arming "home guards" and militias to fend off invading foot soldiers. According to one resident planter, a battery of ten guns placed at the junction of the two rivers would "effectively prevent trouble."[25]

Distance from the main lines of battle gave southwest Georgia's slaveholders an advantage they were not willing to squander. Slave society, they knew from war dispatches, newspaper reports, and personal correspondence, was eroding quickly in, around, and especially behind theaters of battle. Even as David Vason was extolling the equilibrium of plantation order in Dougherty County in June 1861, a steadily rising stream of Virginia slaves was flocking to the Union forces at Fortress Monroe, capitalizing on their proximity to federal General Benjamin Butler's army to secure their freedom. Two months later, Union commander John C. Frémont invoked martial law in Missouri and declared free the slaves of all disloyal owners. President Lincoln hastily countermanded the order, but a few months later the arrival of federal naval forces near Port Royal, South Carolina, shook the foundations of slavery up and down the south Atlantic coast with nearly as much force as had Frémont's premature emancipation to the west. When Union forces made landfall in Georgia on Tybee and Wassabaw islands in late 1861 and early 1862, their arrival spurred the collapse of low-country slavery. Planters scattered, and according to the commander of a naval landing party, the slaves they left behind went "perfectly wild, breaking into evry building and destroying or carrying off all portable property." By spring 1862, former slaves in coastal South Carolina and southward along the coast of Georgia were the sole occupants of some of the most productive plantations in the American South. Having exploited the chaos of war to turn plantation society inside out, they began the process of defining a new social order by appropriating the symbols and objects of privilege. Fine clothing, featherbeds, even a piano ended up in the slaves' quarters along with common plantation supplies, as black men and black women invented a world without masters and mistresses.[26]

This was hardly the future envisioned by southwest Georgia's slaveholders. Considering themselves successful at stalling a Yankee invasion up the Chattahoochee and routing from their midst domestic and foreign enemies, they had all the more reason to bristle when the state and national governments began looking to their slaves to meet the Confederacy's labor needs. Finding it nearly impossible by the second year of war to recruit enough free white volunteers to fill the regiments, build defenses, and meet the needs of wartime industry, Confederate authorities turned to conscription; they also began eyeing the South's slaves. It was relatively easy to recruit such enslaved workers from areas under immediate Yankee threat. Savannah's slaveholders, for instance, volunteered their slaves to assist in the construction of city defenses. By the summer of 1862, however, it became clear that more slaves, in larger numbers, were required to perform war work. What had initially been polite requests for the temporary, and voluntary, loan of slaves transmuted into strident demands. In Georgia, the first impressment order came from General Hugh W. Mercer, commander of the Confederate forces responsible for defenses at Savannah, who in mid-July 1862 sent agents into the countryside to gather up all male free people of color and 20 percent "of all able bodied negro men and boys over 13." The order, which applied to all slaveholders owning more than four such slaves, gave slaveowners until August 3 to comply voluntarily. After that date, Mercer would fill in gaps by dispatching "sub agents" into the plantation districts to "commence impressing the negroes."[27]

The order, which many southwest Georgia planters claimed ignorance of until it appeared suddenly in the newspapers, met with derision and in some instances outright hostility. Part of their concern stemmed from practical considerations. Impressment, slaveholders argued in county meetings and public letters, would deprive them of critical supplies of labor. Who would pull fodder, one of them asked, if Mercer were allowed to pull workers away from the plantations? What would be the effect, queried a number of others, of taking "unacclimated hands" out of the fields of southwest Georgia and sending them to toil for strangers in Savannah's damp summer air? In the planters' view, it was slaves' wartime duty to raise the provisions needed to "support and sustain [the Confederate] armies," perhaps even to build fortifications if done closer to home. It was not slaves' role to travel across the state to perform a job better suited to soldiers or to free workers. General Mercer, growled the region's planters, had neither right nor reason to take their slaves by force.[28]

Worse, however, was what would happen when their slaves were returned to their homes. Impressment, planters fretted, would expose their bondsmen to dangerous liaisons and incendiary ideas. Mercer's plan, they complained, would launch "slaves from every plantation of the interior to the seat of war, there to commingle with a large number of" other black people, both free and slave. Imagine the outcome, asked Dougherty planter Richard F. Lyon of Georgia's governor Joseph E. Brown in an explicit recognition of the efficacy and power of the networks of subterranean communication that linked quarter to field to workshop. "A negro or negroes from any part of the state particularly from the Middle & South Western parts of the state where they are so numerous, will meet in Savannah, where the negroes & traitorous white men are in constant communication with the enemy, as everybody in the state believes, whether true or not, & if not true in fact the negroes there are as fully informed on the subject as we are—an opportunity will thus be afforded to them of talking with one another of their wants & wishes & their situations—their minds will be inflamed by the vicious with false & mischevious notions." Thoroughly "instructed & charged with mischief," each slave would return to the routine of agricultural work "with reluctance & dissatisfaction—If he is not vicious himself he will inform those who are of what he has seen & heard—and incalculable mischief & [misery] will follow." Were Mercer's plan allowed to go forward, Lyon predicted, it would result in "a regular convention in which all the negroes in the state will be ably & fully represented." Enforcement, he concluded, "would be full of peril to the whole Country." If General Mercer came for his slaves, vowed Lyon, he should expect to be met by bayonet.[29]

An overwhelming majority of southwest Georgia's planters stood with Lyon. Concluding that any proposal to send their slaves across the state and out of their control was a "diabolical scheme," they resisted Confederate efforts to recruit from their quarters. Some followed Lyon's example and met government agents at the front gate with pistols drawn. Even when planters conceded to impressment, they complied grudgingly and with restrictions. Baker County's slaveowners, for instance, accepted the policy in principle, but rather than supplying the requested 20 percent for a period to be determined by military need they "cheerfully" sent "one or more of our negroes for two months." Other slaveholders were scarcely more generous. Sumter County, with an 1860 slave population of nearly 5,000, produced 50 slaves (including several belonging to Howell Cobb) for Mercer's agents between August and November 1862. Calhoun, Lee, Terrell, and Stewart counties parted with a combined total of 58, out of a slave population of more than 18,400.[30]

Later levies fared as poorly. While Sumter County's slaveholders were more forthcoming when it came time to dispatch slave workers to the prisoner-of-war camp at Andersonville, providing some nine hundred laborers over the course of the war, planters remained dubious about removing slaves from familiar routine. Despite local concerns about Yankee invasion up the Chattahoochee, Confederate authorities struggled to acquire the labor necessary to construct those defenses. Not even the offer of a dollar a day in addition to "medical care, rations, &C," produced the one hundred slaves W. R. Boggs, the chief engineer, needed to begin the project, never mind the estimated two hundred needed to bring it to completion. While a few river obstructions were eventually built with slave labor, Confederate authorities struggled to the closing days of the war to pry slaves away from southwest Georgia's planters. The besieged commander of Atlanta's defenses found himself resorting to the bully's tactics when, in a last-ditch effort to round up laborers enough to build breastworks around the city, he threatened the planters of southern and southwestern Georgia with military service if they did not deliver up every available "able-bodied negro man." And so it went. Better the Confederacy go down than slaves be "Lond" out, most planters seemed to agree. In January 1865, the post commander at Albany reported his inability to keep the roads between that place and Thomasville in good repair, the "citizens refusing to allow their negroes to work on the road." When the officer attempted to recruit workers by force, the superior court stopped him. "Nothing more can be done," his report concluded, "without some further authority from the Genl Commanding."[31]

Slaveholders may have been remarkably successful at keeping their slaves removed from the war, but they could not prevent the effects of the war from coming to them. Indeed, their remarkable ability to preserve a sense of antebellum order in the face of civil war ultimately backfired. Southwest Georgia, like areas of south-central Alabama and portions of eastern Texas, soon began to beckon as "a Land of Goshen" to slaveholders desperate to preserve their property and their pasts from the uproar of war. Generally, those to the west of the Mississippi headed farther west as armies bore down, and those in Virginia, the upper South border states, and along the Atlantic seaboard headed south and west. Some sought refuge in the up-country districts of North and South Carolina, but a good many aimed straight for southwestern Georgia, attracted by the region's isolation from theaters of battle, a low cost of living (estimated by one refugee to be one-fourth of the price of survival in Mobile, Alabama), and the continued availability of fresh land and affordable plantations. The movement of the dispossessed began as a trickle, but as the war progressed and the danger to slaveholding became more acute, that trickle turned into a flood as slaveholders hurriedly packed up prized belongings and bolted for what they hoped was a safe haven.[32]

Among the first to arrive were those fleeing the Gulf and Atlantic coasts where Union naval forces hove into sight in the earliest months of the war. Refugees stole north from Florida, hiding themselves in secluded camps along the Apalachicola and Chattahoochee rivers where, under cover of brush and surrounded by swamps, they hoped to avoid encounters with the enemy. Others drifted in from Mobile and New Orleans. Larger numbers, traveling more openly, arrived from the east. Immediately after Port Royal, South Carolina, fell to Union forces in the fall of 1861, James Hamilton's widow evacuated more than fifty of her slaves from the family home at Bluffton and carried them to her brother's plantation near Albany in Dougherty County. She was but one of a steady stream of coastal refugees. Late in 1862 a Georgia low-country planter identified nearly thirty families who had "removed" from his neighborhood. A third of the displaced, he estimated, had gone north to the seemingly safe streets of Savannah. The remainder—twenty white families who, if they followed the general pattern, carried with them slaves, livestock, valuables, and portable household goods—had decamped westward, intending to wait out the war in southwest Georgia.[33]

Confederate losses in the summer of 1863 at Gettysburg, Vicksburg, and Port Hudson sparked a new flurry of movement into southwest Georgia that fall and winter. Anticipating the Union's next major theater of operation, Confederate forces had begun to assemble northwest of Atlanta, preparing to block Yankee advancement out of Tennessee. Slaveholders may have welcomed the arrival of General Braxton Bragg's rebel army in north Georgia, but it became clear quickly that the price of protection was the disruption of slavery. Plantation discipline and plantation production were impossible to maintain, explained northwest Georgian William Henry Stiles, when the countryside was overrun with soldiers. Even the friendliest of military men were "good for nothing" when they procured their dinners from civilian smokehouses, corncribs, and gardens. Taking advantage of the winter lull in fighting, Stiles and many of his neighbors went shopping for a safer harbor. Several thought they found it in southwest Georgia, where land prices remained reasonable and prospects for peace appeared good. Forming part of a new wave of migration out of what would become, in a matter of months, a corridor of death and destruction, Stiles and many acquaintances resettled in Terrell County. "Dr Leah purchased a place at $30 pr acre but a mile from me . . . Dr Felton another about 3 miles off. Mr Crowell about one mile—Gen Rice adjoins me," Stiles reported to his son on Christmas Eve of 1863.[34]

The arrivals of refugees accelerated in the spring of 1864. Untold numbers of north and central Georgia slaveholders hastened out of the paths of contending armies and into southwest Georgia the last full year of the war. When General William T. Sherman's army advanced on Atlanta, Hillary C. Mundy and Colin Thrasher packed up their families and slaves to shelter in Thomas and Dougherty counties. The battle for the city itself launched Jane Crews, P. M. Hilton, and Hattie Warren out of Pike and Fulton counties and into Dougherty. Governor Joseph Brown used state resources to ease the process of wartime relocation, pushing through legislation in November 1864 to enlarge an existing refugee camp in Terrell County, a place known locally as Fosterville or the Exile camp. Within a month, somewhere between seventy-five and a hundred families had moved in, followed by still more as Sherman turned his massive army east. Merrill P. Calloway's family, along with the daughter of Wilkes County lawyer Garnett Andrews, and various members of the extended Cobb and Lamar families abandoned Athens and Washington, Georgia, for estates they already owned in Sumter, Dougherty, Early, Decatur, and Baker counties. By the winter of

1864, the displaced—slave and free—were once again arriving from Savannah and other coastal communities. Among them was planter Edwin H. Bacon, who found in Sherman's imminent arrival ample excuse to complete a move to the Mitchell County estate he had been operating as an absentee owner since sometime in the 1850s.[35]

Dispossessed Confederates filled southwest Georgia with slaves, tugging them along with their other valuable possessions, bumping an already majority black population even higher. Observers, both during and immediately following the war, described the influx of enslaved in terms of thousands. Fifteen hundred black men and black women, at least, estimated a Freedmen's Bureau agent shortly after arriving at his Albany post in 1865, were newcomers, brought away "from the coast, and the Carolina[s]." Planter J. P. Stevens thought "a large majority" of the black men and black women resident in Baker County "and adjacent Counties" at the close of the war had come from Liberty County alone. Which is saying a good deal, since Baker County's 1860 population was 70 percent enslaved. Population figures gathered in Early and Thomas counties in the third year of the war testify to the wartime expansion of slavery in southwest Georgia, suggesting that Stevens and Gideon Hastings, the Bureau officer, were not far wrong in their reckoning. According to local officials, Early County's slave population increased by more than 25 percent between 1860, the year of the last federal enumeration, and August 1864 when they conducted a census. Thomas County's slave population jumped even faster, climbing by nearly 30 percent in the same period. These changes, if accurate, meant that Early County's slave majority expanded from an already impressive 66 percent of the county's population in 1860 to 83 percent four years later, while Thomas County's climbed from 57 to 67 percent, a demographic shift that placed both counties squarely among the most densely enslaved areas in the American South. Moreover, if these two counties were representative of what was unfolding across southwest Georgia more generally, the region's slave population increased by as much as twenty thousand between secession and the Confederate surrender. But whatever the exact numbers, by 1864 the changing complexion of the countryside had begun to give slaveholders pause. The influx, observed more than one disquieted witness, had begun to transform their isolated wartime oasis into a "vast negro Quarter."[36]

The steady departure of soldiers for the war further tipped the population figures in black people's direction. Though lengthening casualty lists quickly extinguished the eager volunteerism of the initial Confederate mobilization, Jefferson Davis struggled to keep his armies at fighting strength by signing the nation's first conscription law in the spring of 1862. It was a forced recruitment effort that struck hardest at the South's poorer citizens, and especially those who relied for their living on the capable hands of a husband, a father, or an almost grown son. But wealthy planters complained bitterly as well about Davis's response to shockingly high rates of battlefield attrition. Rather, however, than fret as the wives of yeomen soldiers often did about the difficulty of making ends meet in the absence of men, planters growled about conscription's effect on labor discipline and plantation production. To lose overseers, planters, or planters' adult sons to the war put the whole slaveholding nation at significant risk. And in southwest Georgia, where the number of white people was steadily declining and the number of slaves was shooting up, conscription appeared to invite the eruption of servile insurrection. C. B. Calloway was one of the many slaveholding planters who feared the impact of too heavy a draft. "My overseer the overseers & young men generally that has no ties, are leaving the country attaching themselves to other companys leaving those that cannot get away to stand the draft . . . leaving but very few only to control the negroes," he wrote in distress to Georgia's governor. "I am in the midst of a dence population of negroes & it is as essential to keep up organization here as well as in the Army."[37]

Calloway's was an argument that captured the attention of the secessionists' government, and especially that of Georgia slaveholders' staunchest ally, Governor Joseph E. Brown. By the fall of 1862, yielding to the logic of slaveowning constituents, the Confederacy made provision to exempt enough masters, or men designated in their stead, to police the countryside and manage southern plantations. Planters applied for and received exemptions, which under the first act released one white man for every twenty slaves. Later, when the Confederate government tightened exemption restrictions, they were enforced with less vigor in "some sections of southwest Georgia, where the slave population was very large and the white population relatively sparse." The remainder, if personal resources permitted, availed themselves of the new rules by paying "annually into the public Treasury" five hundred dollars for the privilege of keeping an overseer at home. Still, the shifting ratio of free white men to slaves made local authorities increasingly uneasy, eroding the confidence most had shared in the early months of the war. As Christmas of 1862 approached, Thomas County officials turned their attention to the slaves, calling on the citizens to increase their vigilance as well as the size and number of slave patrols. Authorities specifically instructed owners and overseers of slaves to provide the captains of those beefed-up patrols with "a full list of the negroes under their respective charges."[38]

White southwest Georgians had reason to fret. As evacuation uprooted and transplanted plantation communities from across several states and into the region, and as the Confederate nation siphoned away adult white men, slave society began to show signs of decay. Though the pace of erosion in southwest Georgia lagged considerably behind what was unfolding throughout the Mississippi Valley, or on the Virginia peninsula, masters' carefully crafted image of invincibility fell with their bodies at Manassas, Antietam, Gettysburg, and eventually Atlanta—in numbers recorded in casualty lists that for some southwest Georgia units purportedly exceeded 90 percent. The Dougherty Greys began the war with 125 men and ended it with 10, having lost nearly everyone else to death or disability.[39] White men's power to command fell victim to a Confederate government driven to usurp prerogatives that had once been prized possessions of individual slaveholders. Every time a Confederate agent or officer strode onto a plantation to recruit black workers over the protest of an owner, carried away corn that had been reserved for wintertime subsistence, appropriated a hog or a ham; with every passage of a new dictum on crop mix, increase in taxes, or impressment of tools, all actions the Confederacy deemed necessary to keep their military machine in good repair, planters' authority was reduced. Poised to capitalize on these shifts in the balance of antebellum order, few of which escaped their attention, and with numbers increasingly on their side, slaves grew more assertive.

Hurried departures from antebellum homes presented a good many of the region's slaves both opportunity and motive to reconfigure relationships with their masters. Evacuation once again meant the shredding of painstakingly woven networks of family and community, for masters tended to move only the most valuable of their slaves out of the path of advancing armies. Often left behind were those whose capacity for labor or whose value to plantation production had declined due to age or infirmity or, in the case of small children, lay in a too distant future. As had been the case in the settlement of the cotton frontier, slaveholding migrants favored carrying with them the fittest and the most fertile, abandoning the rest to the "tender mercies of the Yankees." Even in instances where owners could afford to resettle their entire quarters, they sometimes moved their slaves in stages, prolonging and complicating an inherently disruptive process. Disheartened by the prospect of once again being separated from loved ones (as Ben was from Maria), even if masters assured them it was only a temporary situation, slaves might try to sabotage their owner's plans. On occasion, they succeeded. Thus a Dalton planter stayed the war in north Georgia, dodging armies of both nations, anchored in place by slaves who refused to "go down country"; and Betsey's husband (whose master carried her the length of a state away from her partner) did all in his power to "frustrate" their owner's plan for evacuation.[40]

So it went on William Henry Stiles's Cass County plantation when he organized an evacuation south to Terrell County. The first to go, he proposed, would be the "prime men & women," whom he dispatched south in December 1863 to construct cabins and clear ground. Nineteen slaves followed late in February, another twelve in May. To be moved in one of the later groups were the "women with children" whom Stiles had left behind in December. Even then, not all of the slaves went south. Nor did they go in such directions that families might be reunited. Still in possession of several town lots in Savannah and several hundred acres located nearby to that city, Stiles ordered several of his slave men to Savannah and his coastal estates, a decision that separated Maria from Ben, Paddy from Elcy, and Sinai and her three young children (Bark, Abram, and Jennet) from her husband and their father. Somewhere along the line, Little March lost touch altogether with Moses, his father. "He is an orphan" now, Stiles explained later in a letter to his own wife.[41]

Giving the lie to their master's sunny announcement that "the negroes all now seem anxious to go," none of Stiles's slaves hurried to dismember their quarters near Etowah Cliffs. When ordered to begin preparations to move, a chore that made it immediately apparent that they would neither travel all together nor head for the same destination, they stalled. Encouraged by Adam—the "principal one in frustrating our plans," Stiles later complained—the slaves set out to spoil their owner's evacuation. In what appeared to be a carefully choreographed sequence of chaos, they dawdled, they stalled, they made a mess of the packing, or refused to pack anything at all, and Paul ran away. Come departure day, the horses that were meant to haul the wagons were missing their shoes and the corn that had been earmarked to accompany the travelers to Terrell County sat on the far side of the Etowah River, the boat the slaves were ordered to fetch it with having been run aground and put out of commission.[42]

With the exception of Paul, who was surmised to have stayed with his friends in Cass County, Stiles eventually succeeded in moving his slaves to southwestern Georgia. Other owners were not quite as lucky. Flight, many refugee slaveholders discovered, often begot flight as slaves availed themselves of their masters' wartime migrations to set off in often different directions. The number of slaves in H. Whitaker's charge steadily dwindled the farther he got from home. The first to go was Ned, who with a team of his owner's mules happened to disappear from the Tallahassee railroad station where he had hauled a portion of the property bound for North Carolina. Another slave jumped ship at Augusta. "The signal was given for departure & Old Wisdom," who "had left the car & walked off with Kintchen unbeknowing to me as I was with the boys." Wisdom "remarked to some of the women that he *reckoned* he could get back in time, but did not & of course we left the old fellow." The same strategy almost worked for Reuben, who managed to not make the train when it pulled out of a South Carolina station. Unfortunately, his liberty was deferred when an alert stationmaster collared him and ushered him back into Whitaker's care.[43]

Immediate emancipation eluded most slaves sent to work out the war on southwest Georgia plantations. But they found on their arrival that slavery, and slave property, was not as secure as their owners had imagined. News of the Confederacy's dwindling fortunes had been percolating through the quarters (conveyed, perhaps, by black refugees newly arrived from locations closer to front lines, as well as by indiscrete slaveholders), infusing the region's slaves with hopes of liberation. A small number had already succeeded in gaining their freedom. Two enterprising slave men had headed north, hoping to return to their former homes in Atlanta or perhaps northern Alabama, both not incidentally flooded by Union soldiers at the time of their departure. A shorter route to liberty lay to the south, along the Gulf coast, where the Confederacy's near-insatiable demand for salt exposed hundreds of slaves to patrolling vessels of the Union navy. Driven by an appetite for profits as well as for safely preserved meats and vegetables, white southerners from as far away as Tennessee had begun flocking to Florida's panhandle coast in 1862 where, in shanty camps bearing descriptive names like "Salt City," they put hundreds of slaves to work condensing seawater to salt. Exposed as they were to the coast, and as critical as their product was to rebel survival, salt makers attracted Yankee attention. Union patrol boats would swoop down at regular intervals, ripping apart tent villages, breaking apart kettles, gunning down resistant Confederates, and confiscating provisions, livestock, tools, and slaves. With each attack, Yankee sailors plucked another small handful of southwest Georgians from bondage. The Navy took aboard eleven "able-bodied contraband" during an 1862 raid on a saltworks in St. Joseph's Bay, just west of Apalachicola. Sailors "rescu[d]" another dozen or so during a July 1863 operation to destroy saltworks along the Ocklockonee River to the east of Apalachicola. Later raids cost Sumter County planter John A. Cobb at least two slaves, and Decatur County's David Barrow lost "Four . . . Shurly" of those he had dispatched to the coast to make salt. Some of those so emancipated perhaps followed the example of ex-slave Henry Davis. "Captured" by the federal gunboat *Ft. Henry* in 1864, the Decatur County native made his way to the U.S. refitting station at Key West where he enlisted in the Union navy.[44]

Davis was an exception. On the whole, the actual numbers of those who exited bondage between secession and surrender was infinitesimal. But although the system of bondage appeared on the surface intact, even strengthened if measured solely in terms of gross population, it was, by the middle months of the war, an institution rotting away from inside. In piling slave on slave, masters (and mistresses) unwittingly altered the ground beneath their feet, conceding, in an effort to save themselves, powerful advantages to the people they thought of as property. The forced migrations, with the attendant shredding of networks of kin and community, reembittered black men and black women, many of whom had also suffered in the earlier expansion of slavery westward. New productive demands that grew out of the region's efforts to meet its own needs as well as a gargantuan Confederate appetite for grain, meat, clothing, shoes, hardtack, and salt intensified an already burdensome labor regime and its dependency on slaves' labor. Thus enslaved black men and black women found themselves occasionally occupying new roles, assuming responsibilities traditionally reserved for the free and the white as the supply of white men dwindled. These seismic subversions were not lost on the slaves who increasingly dominated the region. Confrontations became more open and threats of violence more explicit as the war ground on. Little by little, the sovereignty of masters—and mistresses—eroded, falling victim to slaves who discovered in the war new spaces within and new means by which to conduct their lives on terms of their own making.

Soaring prices and shrinking supplies of food and other subsistence goods narrowed much of the distance between master and slave, reconfiguring the relations of power and dependency that lay at the center of the antebellum social order. The pinch of war was not particularly a problem on the largest plantations, where legions of able-bodied workers spent their days not only cultivating their masters' cotton but producing enough corn, beef, and textiles to meet their own needs as well as those of the rebel army. (Southwest Georgia was, as W. E. B. Du Bois reminded readers at the turn of the twentieth century, the "Egypt of the Confederacy.") But small slaveholders, who lacked a comparable portfolio of resources—in land, in labor, in seed and supplies— found it difficult to keep up their farms in war. They and refugees, who often arrived out of sync with the agricultural cycle and who might sow nothing more than vegetables on their arrival, often resorted to the antebellum practice of hiring out otherwise idle slaves. Leila Calloway, for instance, who found it difficult to achieve her husband's dreams of starting their own plantation, hired out a number of the family's slaves. By mid-1862, she had arranged for Georgia Ann to earn her keep by spinning. Sandy, a black man, jobbed about for a dollar a day, then landed a steadier position tending fires for a Cuthbert church congregation, while Susannah, a midwife, nursed the neighborhood sick. Arriving in time to put in sweet potatoes, peanuts, and sugar cane—crops that required less daily attention than cotton—William Henry Stiles likewise hired out a number of the slaves he "refugeed" out of north Georgia, finding them temporary employment cutting oats, plowing fields, splitting rails, building structures, and working iron for others. Many were fairly lucrative agreements, netting Stiles as much as fifty dollars per month for the hire of the more highly skilled of his slaves and covering at least the cost of feeding, clothing, and medicating the remainder.[45]

Hiring out worked for a time, but it soon became apparent that it was not a permanent solution. Despite the development of a few small wartime industries—such as ongoing projects to obstruct upriver traffic on the Chattahoochee River and a Confederate boatworks near Blakely—by the second autumn of the war it was becoming apparent that the demand for hired slaves would soon reach its local limit. Having already struggled to find suitable employment for the slaves left in her care, and indeed, having resorted already to the nearly unthinkable—hiring out one of her slave women to a free person of color—Leila Calloway saw no positive prospects on her horizon. "I fear there will be some difficulty in hiring out the negroes," she admitted in a letter to her husband. "Mr Wood says they will not hire half as well [in 1863] as they have this year." Mr. Wood, though claiming not to know for certain, anticipated accurately. By the following summer, the market for slave hire in southwest Georgia had reached a point of saturation, and unable to find positions for their slaves locally, a few owners had begun to ship their excess workers away, hoping that they might find suitable employment elsewhere. It was a chancy solution, as William Stiles discovered. Unable to find anyone in his Terrell County neighborhood to take on an elderly but apparently clever slave woman, eager himself to be "rid of her support," and hoping that she in fact might earn something above a subsistence, Stiles packed Clarissa and her handful of worldly possessions aboard a train for Savannah. "With me," the master explained to the mistress, the slave woman "was not earning her salt." As it turned out, Clarissa did not do much better for him on her arrival in Savannah, parlaying the proximity of Union forces into an autonomy that closely approached full freedom. "It would not do" to press Clarissa on the matter of payment, her master admitted to his wife in what amounted to an admission of defeat after the slave woman refused to share her urban earnings with her owners as they had intended. "She might runaway & go to the Yankees."[46]

Few southwest Georgia planters attempted to follow Stiles's example. Besides, deliberately dismantling the slave quarters through wholesale hire was not to most slaveholders' taste. But when they became unable to feed their slaves, as was increasingly the case as the enslaved population began to exceed the region's capacity to support them, slaves took to feeding themselves. Theft escalated as the war dragged on. Corncribs, smokehouses, root cellars, vegetable gardens, chicken roosts, and hog pens fell victim to slaves' raids. Slaves helped themselves to scraps of leather and to the sacking used to wrap the bales of ginned cotton, presumably appropriating the former for shoes and the latter for clothing. Cattle began mysteriously disappearing from David Barrow's Decatur County plantation along with several sheep, and Big Sam killed one of his master's shoats. Ground peas vanished from planters' fields in Early County only to reappear in the possession of slaves, and Leila Calloway's husband cautioned her to guard the cut cane with care. "Great temptation will be before the negroes to appropriate it," he warned, especially on its trip to the mill. Though at first they took things surreptitiously and under the cover of darkness, slaves acted more boldly in the declining months of the war. Beginning in the summer of 1864, reports circulated among white citizens about growing populations of slaves with "thievish propensities" and newly acquired habits of "running at large." By the following spring, as Ulysses S. Grant's army advanced on Richmond, those propensities had, in southwest Georgia's northernmost neighborhoods—neighborhoods generally characterized by smaller plantations more often than large—became commonplace. The slaves, announced a panicked mistress from near Stewart County, were killing the stock and stealing "every thing they can put there hands on."[47]

Whether hiring slaves out or abandoning them to fend for themselves, slaveholders abrogated authority whenever they abrogated obligation. Masters' and mistresses' efforts to survive a wildly inflationary economy opened cracks through which slaves began to wriggle out from under the region's crushing cotton regime. Those hired out perhaps stood the best chance of subverting the social order. John, for instance, discovered in that interlude between masters—when he was supposed to be conveying himself from owner to hirer—an opportunity to escape for a few days from both. But it was the nighttime raiders who whittled away more quickly slaveholders' power. Slaves' increasingly conspicuous assaults on plantation storerooms, and their propensity to extend into the war years their antebellum practice of exchanging whatever small dabs of surplus (or ill-gotten) gains came to hand with "mean, trifling, low-down white persons," forced slaveholders to rearrange their own lives to accommodate those they thought they commanded. At its most extreme, this accommodation meant abandoning hearth, home, and rural estates for the ostensibly safer environment of one of southwest Georgia's small towns. Yielding to her husband's field workers, who in her words had grown "intractable" by the summer of 1864, the wife of Randolph County planter H. C. Thornton packed up her daughters and headed for Cuthbert. "I am convinced it is not safe for me to remain [on the plantation] without protection," she explained. "On the whole I am rendered extremely nervous." Having ushered his household south in an effort to preserve its coherence, Oliver Prince watched as it crumbled apart. Trying to explain to the wife and daughters whom he had left in the path of an onrushing army why he could not ride to their defense, Prince virtually conceded defeat—as a slaveholder as well as a parent and partner. Only "by my staying constantly on my place day & night" could he protect what remained from the "hordes of negroes [now] running at large." Better, he concluded, to sacrifice his own family than the edifice on which his position and power rested.[48]

Letting slaves dictate the terms of rural life was, as most slaveholders acknowledged, a risky and potentially subversive business. Observing from afar the gradual inversion of productive and social order on his family's Randolph County plantation, Confederate soldier Morgan Calloway cautioned his wife against coming to depend too heavily on their slaves (who had become adept enough at fending for themselves that they were proprietors of healthy and productive gardens) for her meals. Freely offered subsistence, when the hands that served up the offer were bound, was too radical a departure from accustomed relations of power to give the master much comfort. Do not purchase any fruit or vegetables from the slave man Rule or any of the others, Morgan scolded his wife, not even a watermelon. "If they wont grow you some they ought not to have their own. You make yourself the slave!" Indeed, he would prefer that Leila dispensed with the slaves altogether and use any proceeds from their sale to "buy a cow buy a cow," hoping, evidently, that the repetition would convey his growing conviction that slavery on the terms being offered by the family's black workers was no slavery at all.[49]

Planters who managed to retain their bound workers at

home and at work fared little better. Keeping the economy afloat nearly wholly with slaves shifted in subtle, and sometimes not so subtle, ways the balance of rural power even on the largest and seemingly most stable of southwest Georgia's cotton estates. As the war ground on, masters redeployed their agricultural laborers, transforming plow hands into tanners, shoemakers, weavers, ship builders, and in one probable case, a brew master. Latching on to an aching Confederate hunger for salt—a vital ingredient for food preservation—planters from across southwest Georgia threw their slaves by the hundreds onto the Florida coast. There, in the company of others (some drawn from plantations as far away as north-central Georgia) and for weeks at a time— usually whenever the crops permitted their absence—southwest Georgia's bound workers toiled over hot kettles, reducing seawater to salt.[50]

As war depleted the ranks of white men, slaves (such as a handful of those who clerked in Thomasville shops) filled positions traditionally not theirs, keeping alive established businesses and public services by dismantling the strictures of bondage. Thus when the regular mail service was shut down between Apalachicola and the interior for fear that northern spies were using it to eavesdrop on Confederate operations in the Chattahoochee drainage, slave men filled in the gap. Dispatched hundreds of miles from home, on horseback and in wagons, they became a critical, and often the only, mechanism of communication between free citizens. Lending new meaning to the "grapevine telegraph," enslaved men conveyed messages from salt camps to plantations, from town to country, and everywhere in between. Thus when Mary Jane Curry craved information from her son encamped on the Florida coast, she turned to slave Jackson. James Filey regularly relayed messages through slaves between mill and outlying plantations, and between mill and its absentee owner in Athens. No longer willing to trust "the mails" after Sherman had swept through the state, Howell Cobb's extended family likewise resorted to relaying messages by slave. "If you write to Howell by this boy Scipio," Lucy (near Americus) advised Mary (near Blakely), "we will forward it [to Macon]." But it was a dangerous game slaveholders were playing. For when the messages were verbal, as was often the case, slaves not only conveyed them but stood in a position to rearrange them, manipulating, with the words they had been instructed to share, relations between themselves and their owners. It was a possibility that did not pass unnoticed the day Sam rushed into his overseer's yard brimming with word that a "hurricane" had reduced one of their mills to matchsticks. Although not altogether confident in Sam's rendition (the storm "must Have Been awful if it was Like he said it was"), George Davis had no real alternative but to take the slave at his word and organize a party to search for survivors.[51]

The mobility of salt making, the postal service of slaves, as well as the countless responsibilities that came their way as white men disappeared to the front and hunger and inflation stalked the land, extended slaves' own networks of communication and action and provided new mechanisms by which to chip away at the system that ensnared them. But as black southwest Georgians fashioned strategies of action from wartime developments, they did so within the framework of the social and productive lives they had configured for themselves before secession. In short, while class relations eroded across the Confederacy, while white women pondered the propriety of a war that stripped them of their men and thrust them into new roles with both slaves and state, and while the sinews of slavery began to dissolve, life in the quarters—between the black men and black women who inhabited them—retained much of its antebellum texture and rhythm. It was a development strikingly at odds to what was unfolding behind or near Union lines. There, the recruitment—sometimes voluntary, sometimes not—of black men into military service was turning life in the slave quarters topsy-turvy, compelling a reworking of social and domestic roles as black men disappeared and black women found themselves generally alone in the fields with their children or huddled in an overflowing "contraband" camp anxiously awaiting war's end.[52] To be sure, as war opened new breaches to exploit, southwest Georgia's black men and black women ratcheted up their efforts to fashion lives on their own terms, and not on the master's. But as they surveyed their battlefields and considered their strategies, they took their cues from roles and relations they had called into being on cotton's frontier.

Certainly southwest Georgia's slave women shouldered their share of new, war-induced labor burdens, but those that fell to them conformed to, rather than broke with, old patterns. In a region where masters were accustomed to confining slave women to home plantations, mobility remained the purview of men. To be sure, refugee slaveholders transported slave women along with slave men. William Stiles transported slightly more women (thirty-eight of all ages and capacities as compared to the thirty men and boys who composed the rest of the party) when he shifted his property out of the path of onrushing armies. Besides the irascible and creative Clarissa, his party of women included Violet, the wife of Isiah the driver, and their daughters Louisa and Rosanna; elderly Helen and her daughters Hannah and Abby; Betsy the cook (following whose name Stiles carefully amended: "not in field") and her daughter Elcy; Bark, Sophy, Daphne, Caroline (married to July the carpenter); Patience (blacksmith Joe's wife) and their daughters. But when it came time to find something for all those slaves to do, Stiles and others like him conformed to the gendered patterns of antebellum employment. Slave men, to the near exclusion of slave women, were dispatched abroad to work in the fields and workshops of white neighbors, to labor at the saltworks, and in Sumter County, to help maintain the prisoner-of-war camp at Andersonville. A few slave women followed slave men off the plantation, but usually with durable strings attached. Unlike their husbands and brothers and sons, who in the course of doing their masters' bidding spent hours out of white sight ranging often wholly alone across the spaces that lay beyond plantation gates, slave women remained close to home and under close supervision, loaned or hired out for short stints at a time, usually as nurses (as was the case with Susannah) or cooks, or deposited directly into the care of an owner's close kin. Of all the slaves Stiles hired out, and he hired out a good many, only once did he send a woman to labor in someone else's field, and even then he did it with great care. Carolina stayed away just five days. Clarissa, of course, made it to Savannah, but her excursion had been premised on the expectation that she would make her home in the company and care of her master's wife. John Cobb was even more reluctant to part with the women he owned. It took the threat of losing his salt—a commodity that grew more lucrative the longer the war dragged on—to pry one loose from his immediate care. Unless their master sent down "a woman" to cook for them at the shore (along with fresh supplies of "bacon, molasses meal & corn"), his disgruntled masculine salt makers warned, they had every intention of staging a strike.[53]

More commonly, slave women were made to stay put, their lives and immediate communities bounded to considerable extent by the borders of their owners' estates. That is not to say, however, that their routines remained wholly unchanged. Slave women's usual round of agricultural labors—pulling fodder, hoeing crops, shucking corn, picking cotton—kept coming their way so long as their owners remained committed to the production of cotton. But as shortages of food and clothing became increasingly acute, slave women assumed growing responsibility for the subsistence of owners, soldiers, and slaves alike, elaborating as war crushed down on roles traditionally their own. Carding, spinning, weaving, and making up clothes for domestic use were not qualitatively new tasks, but slave women produced with increasing intensity during the war years, and some, like Susannah, whose owner proposed to "teach her to spin," produced where they had never done so before. By the second season of war, home manufactures had grown in importance. No longer able to buy the fabric necessary to clothe the "Hundred Head of Negroes" in his charge (an extravagance he had come to enjoy in the late antebellum years), George Davis began holding back enough cotton from each crop to "mak[e] up" the clothes from scratch. It was a job that required the manufacture of at least four hundred yards of cloth and a considerable amount of female labor, for come fall, black women disappeared from Barrow's fields and "chaps" (young boys) filled the places they vacated. He was hardly alone in turning slave women out of the fields and into the weaving room. The same year, John Lamar, son-in-law to Howell Cobb and proprietor of at least three southwest Georgia plantations, admitted that the future of fabric gave him considerable concern as well. "We make plenty of bread and meat," he reported, but the prospects for slipping cloth and clothing through the Union's blockade "makes me hold my breath." By the fall of 1864, Mary Jane Curry, who with her son struggled to manage her soldiering husband's plantation, had put every one of the Curry Hill slave women to spin-

ning and weaving, producing in the space of one six-month period 264 yards of fabric. It was an expanse of warp and weft that
included twenty yards of woolens (the fiber of which likely originated on the sheep the Curry Hill slave men herded and
sheared) intended for uniforms for Confederate soldiers. It was
also an experience that introduced those whose lives had previously belonged to cotton's dusty red fields to the "mathematical
and mechanical" mysteries of a highly prized art.[54]

Other productive practices that had been commonly associated with black women before secession also took on new importance as the war dragged on. Owners, for instance, actively
directed their slave women toward the plantation gardens and
barnyards where they put them to work raising vegetables and
fowl to feed free and slave alike. Daphne, one of Oliver Hillhouse
Prince's slaves, specialized in the husbandry of fowl. In one
season, she raised a magnificent flock of eighteen ducks, four
turkeys, two guinea hens, and as many as a hundred chickens.
Her bemused owner noted that the only species Daphne failed
to nurture to harvestable maturity were peahens, the female of
the large terrestrial pheasants more commonly known as pea-
cocks.[55]

These wartime shifts in routine guaranteed that slave women,
no less than slave men, understood the strength of northerners'
assault on the Confederacy and its slaveholders. They also understood the implications for slave society. But when black
women acted to turn the situation to their own advantage, using
the war to pry open more social and political space for slaves, the
campaigns they waged exposed once again the particular place
they occupied in cotton's plantation regime. Largely denied access to the army of partisans and the flood of firsthand knowledge of the larger, translocal community—resources that more
easily came black men's way—women, for instance, tended to act

on their own, or in alliance only with the slaves with whom they shared the plantation quarters. Tactics and weaponry likewise reflected the constraints that operated on black women's lives. Few accounts told of women holding pistols, dirks, or knives, items that usually would have been acquired from itinerant peddlers met on the road, cardsharps, and keepers of the small shops where slave men traded. For similar reasons, black women were just as unlikely to mobilize geographically expansive, transplantation rebellions, tending instead to rely on spur-of-the-moment and individualized acts of subaltern expression. Female slaves sassed, they loafed, they engaged in various sorts of sabotage, and according to increasingly frustrated owners—one of whom fumed that female slaves were simply "a plague"—more than a few turned inexplicably and suddenly deaf. Though women's defiance was small in scale, and almost always confined to their owners' estates, nonetheless it was highly effective and capable of destroying plantation order. Women's unruliness and deliberate noncompliance were also often highly contagious. As a Decatur County slaveholding family quickly discovered, what black women began, black men could be quick to exploit. Thus within days of Suky's decision to withhold her services from her youthful owner—refusing, in effect, to follow his orders—several of her male counterparts followed suit, walking off their jobs in what amounted to a general strike.[56]

Although just as likely as slave women to dawdle, equivocate, and let loose with angry words within the confines of their owners' estates, slave men additionally continued to dominate the public face of slaves' campaigns. Translating the services they performed on command—as couriers, salt makers, and laborers on Confederate defenses as well as their customary chores as agricultural workers—into instruments of protest and protection, black men's efforts repeatedly transcended the social and physical boundaries of their masters' plantations. Drawing on those far-flung networks of friendship and the firsthand intelligence accumulated in the course of their everyday work, slave men increasingly conspired together, fled together, and as the war spilled into its fourth year, launched collective strikes against slaveholders and slavery. Drumming up convincing and collaborative self-serving tales was easy to do, given, for instance, the new weight owners attached to slaves' words: "Strange dogs" had devoured their master's young sheep, claimed Norton and Jim as slaves began to suffer from growing shortages of food; "wolves" had eaten the calves. Sam, a mill hand, likewise did a good deal of talking, "concoct[ing] plans with negros that come to the mill through the week that lives 18 to 20 miles" away, then "pay[ing] them a visit on the Saturday night following." No one knows what transpired between Sam and his collection of friends, but rumors ascribed purpose to other such masculine meetings. Salt workers—who frequently numbered as high as five hundred— were accused, for example, of hatching a plan involving a collective escape, perhaps into the hands of the Union sailors whose vessels hugged the Florida coast. As Atlanta came under federal attack, it was Thomas County black men who "laid [a] plan of insurrection." The plotters purportedly were headquartered on Mitchell Jones's plantation, and every "negro man on the place" fell under immediate suspicion. From there, the trail spun outward, spilling into surrounding counties and deep into Florida. Two months earlier, roving bands of black men had confronted and cowed into submission the feeble and elderly white men who composed the local patrols in Decatur County. "[You will] let thss fellows alone," slaves warned their own masters and mistresses, "if you know what Best for your Self." Such demonstrations horrified white witnesses, who wrote fretfully to beg the state's governor for formal assistance. But while white women especially worried about being "ranover by the Negroes," black men's collaborative acts conveyed a much different message to the wider slave population. As one man explained to the woman who owned him: We "will Be free few days more."[57]

Alarmed by the growing assertiveness of their slaves, and especially that of the black men who openly taunted their oppressors and who rode as they wished in the night, southwest Georgia's courts rallied on the side of slaveholders. By 1864 it was no longer sufficient to whip a recalcitrant or even murdering slave. Punishments became harsher, and the protections of the law less certain. In Thomas County, where court-ordered hangings generally had been private, thinly attended affairs, executions became public events, staged at suitably "convenient location[s]" and open to anyone who wished to attend. Elsewhere, frazzled and frightened white citizens abandoned the law and its practices altogether. Murder, or anything that resembled a capital crime, required no court's intervention. Thus it was that Wallace, who had been arrested for nothing more than swinging a stick at a white woman, died at the hands of a mob. It was done, participants later explained, not to save the citizens the cost of a trial but to issue a warning to all other slaves. The law, they and others publicly proclaimed, was too much of a "slow coach" for such times "and in such cases."[58]

Despite the wild rumors of conspiracies, rebellions, and deeds too ghastly to mention that had begun to circulate through the region in the last year of the war, the destruction slaves wrought on bondage could be, and often was, more incidental than intentional. Each arriving group of tattered war refugees reminded black people of the vulnerabilities and fragilities of their families, and many of the slaves' actions that so bothered their masters were less about revolution or outright rebellion than about love, affection, and domestic connections. To be sure, much of what the region's black people did in the name of their families—from feeding them to keeping them safely intact—had a corrosive effect on slaveholders' order. Each small act, whether it was the theft of a chicken or a collective appeal to the master when rations began to run low, nudged the balance of power in black people's direction. But while the wage Sandy earned for "work[ing] out every day" and the message about hunger that Sam in his capacity as "principle complainant" conveyed from the slaves to their master provoked subtle shifts in the relations of slavery, especially when viewed from the owners' perspective, the slaves seemed to have understood their actions somewhat differently. In Sandy's view, he was not rewriting plantation order so much as doing what his mistress could not: clothing and feeding his very large family of very small children. The imminent destruction of slavery also was not necessarily the force that animated and guided another slave when he captured, killed, and began to carve up for an evening meal one of his owner's young shoats. Subsistence, not subversion, was what drove the man to purloin that pig.[59]

Nowhere, however, was the tension between family and freedom as clearly in evidence as in the routes southwest Georgia's slaves tended to take when circumstances allowed them to choose their direction of travel. Much to the astonishment, and occasionally amusement, of their masters and mistresses, home and the lives they had created on the region's plantations beckoned to the slaves with an intensity that liberty was hard-pressed to match. Time after time on the Florida coast, overseers and owners found themselves posting guards not between their slaves and the sea but between those slaves and their inland plantations. Turning their backs on Union vessels that were only too willing to ferry slaves away to an immediate freedom, nearly all of the dozens of men Howell Cobb sent down to the coast from his Sumter County plantation "run away and come home" at their first opportunity. They were hardly alone in feeling that particular directional pull. Slave men gravitated repeatedly back toward their cabins and the people who waited within. Only threats of harsh punishment kept William Braswell's "boys" on the beach. "They are anxious to go home," their overseer wrote, though the one named Tillman "want[ed] to go Home worse than anything else." Slaves who had been dispatched by their masters to build fortifications, to work in Confederate factories, or to lay obstructions in the region's rivers, also wanted to go home in the worst way. Fed up with the distance that yawned between them and their inland kin, those who had been impressed into service on the Chattahoochee River likewise took their leave as soon as they could. "So great was the desire" of one party of "negroes to get home" that four of them took off in advance of the rest, electing to "*walk* back instead of waiting" to catch a ride north on a boat. Isham, too, yearned to go home. Sent by his owner to work at a Confederate factory in Macon, the Sumter County slave fretted continuously for his faraway family. He "has a wife and is very anxious to see her," his master cautioned those who managed the slave's labor. "In fact, I fear he may run away if not permitted to do so." Alex Lawton certainly did. Rather than bide his time and await his master's permission, he simply helped himself to one of the mules and commuted between his master's Dougherty County plantation and the Florida home of his wife.[60]

Though Alex's owner fretted that his slave might simply keep on going and seek refuge with those Union patrol boats, freedom did not exert the powerful draw that Lawton imagined. Sandy, for instance, could not be pried away from his plantation home, not even to serve his master who repeatedly asked the slave to join him on the Confederate front. The slave's family, Morgan

Calloway eventually admitted, was a "great barrier to his coming." A black man named George had gone "off with [his master] in service," but was back at home before the war was scarcely half over, surprising his friends with an unannounced, late-night arrival. Commenting on seeing him as he passed by on his way from the station "betwixt nine and ten o'clock," an acquaintance observed that George "was going home . . . to his wife's house" on a Mr. Wilder's plantation. Family, in George's opinion, as well as in the opinion of so many others, took unquestioned priority over personal freedom. Thus it was that Bill, when engaged in his own struggle to keep his family intact, would ask and then answer most emphatically in the negative the question that seemed on the minds of a good many. "Don't that seem mighty hard," Bill inquired of a friend when faced with the prospect of losing his own wife, "that a man should be cowed off" from his own flesh and blood?[61]

By the spring of 1865, deep fissures had begun to yawn open in a place hopeful white refugees had called Goshen. Rich and poor white men snapped and snarled at one another over impressment, conscription, and the mix of crops true patriots ought to plant. Citizens berated their governments; wives, sisters, and mothers of Confederate soldiers reluctantly and with much grumbling, stepped into roles once considered the province of men; and slaveholders' control over slaves began to visibly slip, eroded by a war that stripped white men and materials from a once sheltered countryside. Yet, unfolding as these changes did, in a place where enslaved men and women stayed close to home, where Yankees stayed away, and where cotton remained king, much of slavery's antebellum routines and relations lingered on, outlasting or nearly outlasting the Confederate nation. It was an asymmetrical and incomplete revolution, a phenomenon of no small consequence to black southwest Georgians as they passed into freedom. For it was on this uneven ground, where the war had never been fully realized, that the region's former slaves would strive to call into being a new social and political order.

3

Finding

Freedom's

Edges

The end of the Civil War must not be confused with the end of slavery. Nor should emancipation be understood as imbuing freedom with meaning. It would take many people many weeks to enforce emancipation. It would take many more people a good deal longer to work out the terms of freedom. But before the first year was out, it would become abundantly clear to the South's former slaves that the freedoms they sought could not be untangled from the lives that lay behind them. What they had been, what they had done, and what they had made of and for themselves under slavery conditioned the futures that unfolded before them. Liberty, as ex-slaves across the former Confederacy quickly discovered, came with strings firmly attached.[1] As black people strove through the summer and fall to put their lives on new footings, as presidential policies tipped political power back into the hands of the South's former masters, and as planters tallied up the cost of conducting old business on a free-labor basis, it became clear that, in critical ways and at critical junctures, these strings attached differently to black women than to black men. This was especially the case on cotton's expansive terrain. By year's end, those former slaves who had once been prized as much for the babies they bore as for the pounds they could pick of the South's reigning staple found themselves forcibly banished to liberty's furthermost edges by the planters who had previously owned them. Steeply discounted by a past that hounded their heels, the region's former slaves discovered as Christmas approached that a gendered enslavement had begotten a differently gendered freedom.

The year 1865 opened in southwest Georgia in much the same manner as previous years. Despite an upsurge in complaints from white people about rifled corncribs, missing pigs, and a more generalized restlessness in the slave quarters, the new year found black men and black women—particularly those tied to the larger estates—hard at their usual routines. As Abraham Lincoln's government reflected on the impending Thirteenth Amendment, southwest Georgia's slaves plowed out new ground, felled trees, rolled logs, repaired fences, and finished turning the previous year's crop of hogs into bacon and hams. As nearly two hundred "companies" of ex-slaves prepared to put a thousand acres of land at Davis Bend, Mississippi, to the plow, and as Ulysses S. Grant's enormous, if exhausted, army bore down in late March on Richmond, Virginia, southwest Georgia's black men and black women continued to do their masters' bidding. Under the watchful gaze of owners and overseers—many of whom had, in an effort to maintain old levels of discipline, extended the workweek to include the whole of the Sabbath—the region's slaves planted corn, peas, potatoes, and cane. Howell Cobb's son proposed turning the estate's slaves into soldiers and the overseer into their captain. "Barwick," John Cobb remarked, "will make a good officer for the negroes." A few weeks later, during the week of President Lincoln's murder and days after black soldiers under Grant's command led a jubilant procession through the streets of the former Confederate capital, enslaved southwest Georgians bedded up fields, opened furrows for seed, and planted their masters' cotton. The same distance that had kept war at arm's reach for so long, kept freedom at bay as well. The laborers, a black man recalled later that year, "work[ed] on the same way" through that turbulent spring as they had in the past. "All the people thought they were slaves."[2]

But not forever: news of Union victory eventually filtered into even the most remote enclaves of the Confederates' now defunct nation. Rumors circulated through the usual channels, newspapers exchanged hands, paroled soldiers straggled home from the field; and aided by private correspondence, the residents and refugees of southwest Georgia gradually became aware of the revolutionary turn of events. John Banks, who kept a plantation in Stewart County, heard of Lee's surrender, Lincoln's death, and the war's end when he received a letter to that effect in the last days of April. A. J. Swinney, an Albany shopkeeper, got the news at about the same time. Such secondhand accounts could be, and easily were, dismissed by slaveholders unwilling to concede defeat immediately or voluntarily to a federal government they deeply despised. More difficult to ignore, however, was the federal cavalry that finally appeared over the horizon in mid-May, shattering at last the isolation that in war had made southwest Georgia such a haven for slaveholders. Dispatched from their headquarters in Macon, the soldiers made their first stop in Dougherty County, then swept south into Florida, leaving in their wake a series of widely scattered and thinly manned garrisons. Enforcing emancipation was not, however, the soldiers' primary duty. They rode under instructions not to end slavery, but rather to finalize the end of the Confederacy: snooping out fugitives from Jefferson Davis's government, accepting the surrender of any remaining Confederate soldiers, attaching the thousands of bales of cotton that by then clogged the region's warehouses, and confiscating leftover stashes of rebel supplies.

Having been "issued but few formal orders touching on" the matter of freedom, whatever acts of liberation resulted from the cavalry's whirlwind tour were more incidental than intentional.[3]

Indeed, the soldiers' passage served more often to provoke planters to bear down even harder on black labor than to let up altogether. Determined to squeeze everything possible out of their workers before the inevitable overtook them, planters drove them harder by day and locked them into their cabins by night. Hissing, as one planter did, that they would rather see their slaves dead from overexertion than risk losing them or the year's crops, slaveholders and their minions applied their whips more frequently, swung them harder, and reached for them with shockingly less cause—even by the standards of a class already notorious for their malevolent brutality. All it took for one slaveholder to turn on a pregnant black woman—"bucking and gagging" then whipping great gouges of flesh from her back (large enough to contain the length and width of a grown person's finger, one witness reported)—was a single skein or "knot" of yarn. That was the amount she fell short of producing two days in a row. Elsewhere, the dust from fast-riding Yankees had scarcely settled when both driver and overseer laid into Hannah. She had left the field without authorization for less than half an hour. Willis got something of the same, he having let a horse out of the barn. Aleck committed a considerably greater crime— he had, in full view of his master, borne witness to a party of Yankees he had encountered near Thomasville—and he disappeared altogether, led away by a gang of white men, never to be heard from again. Emblematic of a mounting desperation, planters hurled words as well, hoping to stave off freedom by deflating their slaves' expectations. When Lincoln died, went one of the more popular of planters' tall tales, so too did black people's freedom. Numbers of ex-Confederate slaveholders sputtered that emancipation was only a wartime measure, issued for military purposes and sure to expire in peace. Others assured their slaves—and themselves—that "slavery in some form will again be established by the Government," or held out hope that bound labor of some other form would take slavery's place. Reinforcing fast words with fast whips worked for a time, dismaying a federal inspector who made his rounds of the region in late June. Only the immediate and widespread deployment of "bureau" officials—one for every hamlet and village—he advised, could induce planters to give up their slaves once and for all.[4]

"Something should be done," other federal observers concurred. But that something would not transpire anytime soon. The rest of the summer and much of the fall would pass before the first Freedmen's Bureau official set foot in southwestern Georgia. Six months would pass before there were more than two, but not for any locally rooted reason. When Congress created the Bureau of Refugees, Freedmen, and Abandoned Lands in March 1865, it gave it "control of all subjects relating to refugees and freedmen from rebel states." But the Freedmen's Bureau, as the agency was commonly known, remained unfunded and did not even begin to take institutional shape until May, when General Oliver Otis Howard assumed command of it. Further organization at the state and subordinate levels dragged on unevenly. In some states, notably those with a significant Union presence before the surrender and where federal authorities had already assumed responsibility for the former slaves, the process unfolded fairly quickly. The Bureau was crippled, however, not only by limited means but by a shortage of personnel as well (for it relied on personnel recruited from a rapidly demobilizing army), and months sometimes elapsed before Howard could arrange the appointment of assistant commissioners elsewhere in the former Confederacy. Texas, for instance, did not receive its first assistant commissioner until October, delaying the appointment of the legions of subordinate officers who would shoulder much of the day-to-day work of enforcing freedom, serving the needs of refugees, and reordering relations between ex-masters and ex-slaves. To expedite organization, and to install at least a skeleton staff across a jurisdiction that swept from the upper reaches of the Chesapeake to what is today Oklahoma, Howard resorted to bundling multiple and contiguous states under the oversight of a single assistant commissioner. Kentucky, Tennessee, and a portion of northern Alabama thus fell initially under the oversight of Nashville-based Clinton B. Fisk; and J. W. Sprague administered Bureau affairs in Arkansas and Missouri, a jurisdiction that reached from Quincy, Illinois, westward to Fort Scott in Kansas.[5]

The Bureau arrived as haltingly in Georgia. Until the appointment of Davis Tillson as the state's assistant commissioner in late September, Georgia fell under the command of South Carolina–based Rufus Saxton, who also had charge of Florida. Plagued by the same problems bedeviling his superior and responsible for a landmass of more than 140,000 square miles, Saxton succeeded in assigning only a half-dozen agents to Georgia during the summer of 1865, nearly all of whom he posted along the coast with instructions to oversee the settlement of black people on the Sherman reserve. For most of the summer most of the state (an area that constituted roughly a third of Saxton's jurisdiction) came under the direction of just two Bureau officials: ex-soldier and Maine native John Emory Bryant, and the mercurial General Edward A. Wild, both of whom shared a headquarters at Augusta until the latter's antics cost him his job in September. The inadequacy of agency oversight did not go unremarked. General Howard's adjutant observed after a midsummer tour of the former Confederacy that "the affairs of the Bureau have been very badly managed in Georgia—or rather have not been managed at all." A statewide problem—"god Deliver us" from the post commander at Savannah, groaned a black minister who hoped in late May that the deity would step in to lend the Bureau a hand—it was especially acute in the furthermost hinterlands of Georgia. And so things would remain for some months to come. Until Davis Tillson assigned officers to Albany and Thomasville (one to each town) in November, southwest Georgians would encounter the Bureau on much the same terms as they encountered the army: indirectly and from a distance, largely by word of mouth and through printed circulars and orders that only occasionally made their way into the region.[6]

Enslaved southerners refused to allow Howard's problems to become their problems. Lingering in bondage, while awaiting the full organization of the agency established to guide them to freedom, was not to most black people's taste. Acting on what often amounted to second- and thirdhand information, those who knew their geography—generally men and particularly the teamsters and others whose occupations often carried them away from their home plantations—set course for the northerners who were too shorthanded to come out to them. Picking their way across rebel-infested terrain, pursued by dogs put on their heels by erstwhile masters, and sliding past plantations of people who had no knowledge of freedom, liberty's male scouts often covered tens and even hundreds of miles in their quest for "instruction." Turning his back on the Kentucky soldiers who occupied the few federal outposts in southwestern Georgia and whose sympathies lay more with slaveholders than with slaves, George King walked east for a week. "I heard the Yankees were here," he explained after his eventual arrival in Savannah. So too had Frank Frazier and Tal Boid, who likewise followed the railroad east toward firm word about freedom. Northern nurse

Clara Barton had scarcely arrived in Sumter County on a summertime mission to catalogue the Union soldiers who had died in the Confederate prison at Andersonville, when black visitors began appearing by the hundreds to see her. "They had all heard" about freedom, she later recounted to a congressional committee. Some knew "it from one another." Those at work on Benjamin Walters's plantation heard about it from "four or five men" who arrived after dark on a Friday evening. "A few knew it from their masters." But when it came to black people's attention that "a settlement of Yankees [was] forming" at the abandoned prisoner-of-war camp, and that one of the Yankees, moreover, was a "lady," they "commenced to gather around . . . for the facts."[7]

Authenticating black liberty was the first order of business, but it was hardly the only motive for closing the distance between slavery's plantations and the Union's outposts. Crowds whose composition varied every day quizzed Yankee interlocutors about the contents of those official and usually printed pronouncements regarding slavery's end and freedom's birth, orders too often read aloud—and edited extemporaneously—by self-interested masters. Was it true, those who visited the Andersonville camp repeatedly asked, that the government of Lincoln expected the former slaves to work six and a half days of the week for no pay? Assuredly not, replied Barton, who turned over to colleagues the task of counting corpses in order to read those orders aloud—day in, day out—until her departure in August. Others came bearing mute, and sometimes not so mute, testimony to slavery's awful cruelties. People whose lives had been framed by the trade in black flesh chronicled a genealogical disaster—of lost children, of broken marriages, and of parents left in the past. This, recounted Barton when she testified later before Congress, was a common refrain. The black southwest

Georgians with whom she conversed "all seemed to apologize when they were asked where they came from. They would say, 'We were not raised here.'" Others exhibited wounds of a more corporal sort, lifting shirts and, in the case of women, the hems of their skirts, to reveal bellies made gaunt by short rations and bodies hatched with old scars, half-healed gashes, and some not healed at all. When the congressional committee expressed doubts about Barton's descriptions of the wounds she witnessed as ex-slaves paraded their pasts through her camp, she refused to recant. "I believed what I saw. I knew what I saw."[8]

Once satisfied that they understood some of the facts about freedom and that northerners understood some of the facts about slavery, freedpeople usually returned to their old masters' estates. Despite loud declarations by former slaveholders throughout the former Confederacy—including the occasional shrill yelp out of southwest Georgia—that "the universal impulse of negroes was to leave the plantation & flock to the cities," no great exodus attached to freedom's heels. To be sure, war had swept a good many black people out of their cabins and away from their masters' plantations. This was particularly true throughout the Mississippi Valley and the upper South, and along the path of Sherman's hard-marching army. Other black people had been forcibly expelled by spiteful ex-masters "enraged at the loss of their miscalled property." Thousands more had left on their own accord, seizing on a case-by-case basis freedom under cover of combat and the movement of troops. But as military and northern officials gazed intently across the remnants of the Confederate nation, they realized that, planters' assertions aside, the vast majority of the nation's former slaves remained in "their old homes, quietly working." "In fact," noted one of Howard's lieutenants after a midsummer tour through Florida, Georgia, and both Carolinas, "this is almost universally the case."[9]

Black people stayed put for good reason. Cutting loose too quickly from the sites of their enslavement cost more than most recently freed slaves were willing—or able—to pay. To leave too quickly would re-rupture families scarcely recovered from the shattering effects of the cotton revolution, and sunder those communities that had lent structure and strength to their lives under slavery. A too-hasty departure could sever as well access to sources of subsistence that few of the recently freed could possibly obtain on their own: cabins to live in, wood to burn, clothes to wear, gardens for vegetables, pastures for hogs, dirt for chickens to scratch. Even more critical, to leave prematurely would be to lose the advantage of the crop in the ground, the seed of which they had been sowing as Grant swung his army on Richmond, and the harvest of which represented their future subsistence as much as that of their ex-masters. Abandoning their spring labor and its consumable fruits was a price ex-slaves repeatedly judged too high to pay lightly. Thus it was that rather than going, most former slaves—particularly those who ended the war on cotton's ground—opted to stay, biding their time in their old homes. Movement, much to the relief of a good many northern officials, who also feared a wintertime famine, would be deferred to the future.[10]

This rootedness was especially apparent in southwestern Georgia, where slavery's particular regime had bequeathed its survivors a legacy of such pitiful proportions as to preclude a hasty departure. Oppressively long workdays that had stretched too often into the night, fledgling communities, and youthful families endowed former slaves with flimsy foundations on which to establish new lives far apart from old masters. No Edisto Islanders here, denizens of the South Carolina low country who exited slavery with caches of "property in Horses, cattle, carriages, & articles of furniture," amassed under rice's distinctive regime.

Most of southwest Georgia's ex-slaves owned nothing more than the shirts on their backs, and perhaps, if their masters had mounted a successful defense against Confederate agents, a spare change of clothes. A few had, by dint of extending those already long days further into their nights, or by mastering skills prized by free neighbors, managed to accumulate small lots of property: a flock of chickens, a pig, a few articles of clothing, and perhaps a trunk in which to stow them. Sumter County's Arnold Cater, a blacksmith by trade, owned a little of each when slavery collapsed, carrying away from his former master's estate "chickens, furniture, bed and bedding," as well as his sorely abused wife and a small babe. It was sufficient for Cater and his wife to establish an autonomous foothold in freedom. By midsummer, the Caters had found a house of their own in which she bore a baby that had been conceived under slavery, and Arnold practiced his craft for a dollar a day. The majority of black southwest Georgians, however, could only dream of such early autonomy. Liberated "without lands, without money, without provisions," what most of southwest Georgia's eighty thousand or so former slaves owned, if they owned anything at all, was a stake in the crop in the ground. Thus rather than observing slavery's death by hitting the roads, a decision that would cost them corn, community, and cabins in which to reside, they, like a good many other heirs to the South's many slave regimes, marked it by sticking close to old homes.[11]

As the oppressively hot summer days closed in, the institution that had survived the war largely intact finally collapsed, pushed to its death as much by black people claiming their liberty as by military officials and the orders they published. The number of masters and mistresses still clinging to fanciful delusions that the nation's high court would find emancipation unconstitutional, or plotting removal to a place where slavery remained legal, dropped by the day. In most cases, pragmatism of pocket and politics won out. Even the truest champions of secession were coming to admit that slavery was done and that their best opportunity for making a full recovery lay in their southern estates. With alternatives fading away, southwest Georgia's planters finally conceded defeat. Sometime in early July, David Barrow "declared freedom" to a hundred or so black people who probably already considered themselves free. Benjamin Yancey followed suit on his Dougherty County plantations a week or two later. Before the end of the month, former Confederate general Howell Cobb issued his own emancipatory announcement to the black men and black women sequestered on his Sumter County estates. Even diehard rebels like William Stiles, who had shepherded his property out of north Georgia in the last year of the war and who continued to nurture a fierce grudge against the victorious North, could not escape what was now inevitable. After much grumbling and prevarication, Stiles yielded sometime in August, giving up on an ambition to hold his workers in rhetorical, if not bona fide, bondage at least through the end of the year. As Stewart County diarist and former slaveholder John Banks noted, the "effects of emancipation" were at last beginning "to be felt" in the place Confederates had previously known as Goshen.[12]

Those effects were not felt as sharply as they might have been. Shifts in the national political climate cushioned slaveholders' fall. Rumors had abounded that a vengeful, victorious Union planned to strip secessionists of all forms of property, of civil and political rights, and perhaps even more—defeating the rebellious South not only on fields of battle but in every dimension of everyday life. Andrew Johnson's ascension to Lincoln's old office in April intensified those fears. After all, it was Johnson who, as Lincoln's vice president, had pledged to punish all rebels as the traitors he believed them to be. "Treason must be made infamous and traitors must be impoverished," southerners remembered the new president declaring only a few months before. Some worried that they might be made to pay for secession and the subsequent war with their lives. Such a prospect looked all too possible to white southwest Georgians after the May 1865 arrest by federal authorities of Henry Wirz, the rebel major who had presided over the carnage at Andersonville prison. Indeed, the prospect of further arrests for the deaths of thousands of captive soldiers prompted delegations of Sumter County's white women to stifle their distaste for everything Yankee and submit a bid for clemency. Shortly after Barton's arrival, they began to approach her encampment, "very neighborly, very bland," on self-appointed missions to wipe the living clean of all crime by casting the wrongdoing onto the backs of the dead. "They wanted to screen Wirz," Barton explained before Congress, "because if they could get the matter to stop [with] him, that was the last would be heard of it—there was no going over that; but if it went over him, there was no knowing how far it would go. So they screened everybody but [General John] Winder," Wirz's immediate, but conveniently deceased, boss.[13]

Those white women need not have labored so hard. Further arrests were not forthcoming. The new national president, ex-Confederates were coming to realize, was more bark than bite. Indeed, Johnson's bluster subsided considerably in the weeks following his promotion, and then stilled almost entirely when he proposed a scheme for restoring the rebellious states to the Union. Left to his own devices, for both houses of Congress were in recess and would remain so until December, Lincoln's successor drew up a surprisingly magnanimous plan, offering to return to ex-rebels control over their lives, their laws, their land, and, with one significant adjustment, their labor as well, demanding in return only the most minimal concessions. Under the direction of provisional governors, the first of whom Johnson appointed on the day he issued his amnesty proclamation, each state need only organize new governments of "republican form" and repudiate secession, slavery, and the Confederate debt in order to regain their positions within the Union. Individuals fared similarly under the president's plan for Reconstruction. According to the terms Johnson laid out, most former Confederates could be restored to full citizenship and to "all rights of property, except as to slaves," simply by swearing an oath of loyalty to the national government. The remainder—generally people who had resigned positions in the federal government in order to serve the slaveholders' rebellion, held high political and military offices in the Confederacy, or had owned significant amounts of property—could resume their places in the Union by "making special application to the President for pardon."[14]

More than a few ex-rebels bristled at the prospect of pledging allegiance so soon after their defeat at the hands of "the Northern Vandall." But recognizing the practical advantage of accepting the president's offer, most contained their contempt long enough to swear fealty to a nation they continued to despise and, if personal circumstances necessitated, to submit and win presidential pardon. By July the reorganization of the former rebel states was in full swing, and by August requests for amnesty streamed out of the former Confederacy and into Washington D.C., including at least eighty that originated in southwest Georgia. Not that their authors necessarily meant what they said in their appeals. "I have my pardon in my pocket and have taken the oath three times," declared one of Albany's applicants, "but I'll be d—d if I ain't as big a Rebel as I ever was!" Still, those sacrifices of personal pride appeared to pay off. Within three months of the somber salutes that had marked the end of the war, Georgia once again had a civilian governor—James Johnson—and preparations were under way for the election of delegates to a constitutional convention scheduled for October. By the end of the summer, courts and town councils—institutions whose operations had been suspended in the last months of the war or the first weeks of peace—had already resumed or were in the process of resuming regular business. Thomas County's lower court reconvened on the first of July, albeit with justices handselected by federal officials. In Early County, the judge of the probate court oversaw the selection of the court's first postwar jury on September 11. Incrementally, semiweekly mail service, triweekly stage service, and once-weekly rail service reconnected southwest Georgians to one another and to the world at large. Perhaps best of all from the perspective of the region's producers, the first load of new cotton headed downriver from Albany to Apalachicola in early September. Although the shipment left a month later than usual (planters traditionally dispatched their first bales to market in August), its departure seemed to herald a return to familiar rhythms.[15]

As the president's policies shifted the initiative from victor to vanquished, planters' moods brightened. Emancipation, especially, no longer seemed quite as menacing as it had in the spring. With the enforcement of contract, along with all other questions pertaining to citizenship, productive arrangements, and political rights soon to be secure in white southerners' hands, planters opened their eyes to the coercive potentials at the heart of the system the Yankees were foisting upon them. Slavery was gone, but Johnson's reluctance to extend the power of the national government into areas traditionally reserved to the states gave former slaveholders considerable optimism as well as critical room to maneuver. To be sure, they continued to voice doubts about the efficacy of free labor, and especially about the practicalities of replacing the compulsions of bondage with the carrot of wages. As a Virginia ex-slaveholder remarked, he and most of his peers considered the "love of *reward*" an "[*in*]*sufficient inducement*." But increasingly confident that they themselves, not northern free-labor meddlers or (worse) laborers, would be calling the shots, planters—even those in the most remote corners of the former Confederacy, places scarcely touched by Union occupation—began dropping their objections to free labor and its companion, the contract. "They know they must have [black labor]," observed a senior Bureau official in July, "or their plantations will be uncultivated and they will be ruined."[16]

Thus it was with very little prodding from the very few soldiers on duty that southwest Georgia's former slaveholders began to engage their customary laborers on a contractual basis. And at first glance the terms they espoused were a significant break with the past. Acknowledging, if unenthusiastically, the principle that labor services could no longer be taken by force, almost all guaranteed remuneration of one sort or another. With "no gold or silver worth mentioning in the hands of the people, and but very little national currency," the form of that compensation bore a striking resemblance to the support formerly provided by master to slave: cabins to live in and the wood to warm them, a part of the vegetables then in the ground, a suit of clothing or a comparable length of fabric, perhaps a blanket, a hat, or a pair of new shoes, and less frequently, medicines and medical care for the sick. Rarely did a planter promise to deliver the whole of that list. Far more often they spoke or wrote of provisioning their former slaves with portions: giving them, for instance, the use of their former quarters, or perhaps promising to furnish rudimentary allotments of "vituals & clothes." Other employers considered a few bushels of corn, a gallon or two of sorghum syrup, a pair of shoes—distributed after the potatoes had been dug, corn shucked, grain threshed, and cotton baled— sufficient reward for a year's worth of labor. Tom Barrow followed that parsimonious pattern when he told the one hundred or so former slaves on his father's Decatur County estate that the Barrow men would give them "everything for a support" and *"one tenth of the corn crop."* James Whitehead offered even less. When making the shift from owner of slaves to manager of free labor, he promised to pay corn only, at the rate of ten to twenty-five bushels per person to those he supervised on a plantation for which he served as executor.[17]

A few planters did commit themselves to providing somewhat more. As contracting and its corollary, competition, accelerated during the summer, those most fearful of losing their workers sweetened the rewards they offered. Signifying the severance, at least in the abstract, of labor from laborer, such planters loosened their grip on black people's bodies, ceding them regular periods of time to themselves. One granted his ex-slaves the right to "attend Church." A Randolph County planter retained his former slaves on his place by permitting them "one Day in each and every week" for their own purposes as well as access to the plantation woodlot and wagons and permission to cart in the latter what they cut from the former to customers in Cuthbert. In some instances, planters went further, parting with small amounts—usually "1/10 to 1/20th" but rarely more than one-sixth—of the year's crop of cotton. David Johnston of Early County told his former slaves—forty-two men, women, and children—that he would divvy among them on a "pro rata" basis whatever remained of the year's harvest after plantation expenses had been met. Even less frequently, planters showed themselves willing to pay their workers with limited amounts of their very scarce cash. Such generous gestures were usually reserved for laborers whose contribution to productive activities would be the most difficult to replace: carpenters, mechanics, and craftsmen generally. Taking the first tentative steps forward in a process by which former slaves would reconstitute themselves as a new laboring class, "Jack (foreman)" and "Jerry (blacksmith)" received assurances from their old master, McQueen McIntosh, that they would receive in return for their services "fifteen dollars per month" in "money." They "prefer the same," acknowledged the man who had once owned them and endeavored now to keep them.[18]

Planters acknowledged as well a new temporality. Slavery had been for life, wage labor was not, and nothing symbolized as clearly the absolute end of enslavement as the termination dates embedded in those inaugural contracts. Because planters wanted to ensure that they had sufficient laborers at hand during the critical weeks of fall harvest, contracts and crops usually wrapped up at roughly the same time. Most former slaveholders stuck to antebellum slave-hire tradition, releasing their laborers from employment the night before Christmas, or on Christmas Day. Others, hoping perhaps to get a jump on the next season, kept their workers fully engaged until New Year's Day. Then there were those like Benjamin Yancey, who hired his former slaves back for the somewhat ambiguous "balance of the year." But if termination dates reflected an explicit acknowledgment of slavery's demise, commencement dates spoke of planters' regrets. None seemed to have started their contractual clocks ticking with either the fall of Richmond or Lee's surrender. A few began counting forward from the day the first federal soldiers arrived on the scene; a small number of others keyed the commencement of contract to the date they first read one or another government order regarding freedom and free labor. Nancy Davis's owner agreed to start paying her on May first, the day the freedwoman recalled being "told freedom commenced." The vast majority of planters did nothing, however, until June, well after President Johnson had launched his benign policy of reunion. McQueen McIntosh dated the commencement of wage labor on the twelfth of that month; David Johnston, two weeks later. The contract William Wilkinson drew up took effect the second week of August. Others delayed even longer. Despite urgent reminders from his Sumter County overseer, John Cobb had not drawn up a contract as late as the last week of August. A good many more failed to ever commit their new arrangements to writing. They preferred "agreement[s] verbal," a practice that secured them a good deal of interpretive room. But by admitting to the new realities of productive relations in practice, if not in print, even those who relied on oral agreements departed significantly from a past that had required no agreement whatsoever.[19]

For former slaveholders, that was concession enough. Auction blocks stood vacant, slavery for life was an acknowledged thing of the past, and black laborers, they realized, must henceforth be paid for services performed. But the revolution stopped right about there. In most planters' minds, managers, not workers, would be the sole and final arbiters of productive relations. Theirs was a unilateralism that expressed itself early, for it was the rare former slaveholder who freely admitted any ex-slave into the contracting process. Dismissing as utterly nonsensical both northerners' belief in a harmony of capital and labor, and what one observer derisively dismissed as black people's "'airs' about 'freedom and equality,'" planters monopolized the bargaining process. Negotiation, as James Harrison understood when he dealt directly with the man who had once owned the woman he intended to hire, was a white person's prerogative. Some exercised that right informally, "interchanging opinions" with their landowning neighbors, arriving occasionally at a community consensus about what constituted a fair wage, and in what form to pay it. Others convened countywide cartels to serve as regulatory bodies, pledging, as did the one formed by Dougherty County planters, to "take into service [no] negro without a written recommendation" from his or her former owner. Differing only in detail from the measures adopted at the same time by cartels elsewhere in the former Confederacy, such resolutions represented an effort to preserve landowners' exclusive access to their own former slaves, to keep down the cost of production by containing competition between planters, and to keep laborers out of the process altogether.[20]

Planters' insistence that former slaves must "know their proper sphere and not attempt to turn to the right or the left" extended beyond the moment of contract and into the fields. Brooking no further challenge to the authority that had served them so well in the past, former masters anticipated "wield[ing] the bone and muscle of the negro" in freedom as had been their habit in slavery. Picking up where they left off, planters took for granted that they and their agents would determine the disposal of labor. Clamoring bells would launch ex-slaves out of their cabins, signal mealtime breaks, and sound the end of the laboring day. The very same overseers who had driven black people in slavery would continue to drive them in freedom, appoint workers to their daily assignments, distribute tools and livestock by morning, inspect them for damage by night, and ensure that laborers maintained a profitable pace in between. Black people's personal lives, their cabins (and the contents thereof), the number of dogs they supported, the number and name of the visitors they entertained, the hours they kept, the food they consumed, even the quantity of wood they burned, would, most planters presumed, remain similarly subject to an ex-master's will. And what a will: McQueen McIntosh required his seventy-two former slaves, transformed with the stroke of a pen into wage workers on July 8, to "remain as laborers . . . from this time henceforward *continuously* until the first day of January next." William Wilkinson ordered his erstwhile slaves to remain on his farm until Christmas, "render[ing] good & faithful service as they had done heretofore, at any business that may be deemed necessary, under and by" his "direction and control." Former slaves, these men and most of their peers presumed, would work "as they did before they were freed."[21]

Planters rarely stopped there. Unable, or unwilling, to differentiate between obedience and obsequiousness, former slaveholders-turned-employers demanded both. Civility and respectful demeanor, or more commonly "language and manner" and "character," vied with service for primacy of place in the order planters projected in drawing up their first set of labor agreements. Former slaves, most assumed, would comport themselves in freedom as they had under slavery, reproducing with every deferential tip of a hat or honorific prefixed to a white person's name, the subordination certified by landowners as a fundamental component of the South's productive and political recovery. For similar reasons, former slaveholders continued to wage in freedom the crusade against liquor that they had conducted under slavery. Booze, they knew from experience, threatened their interests in numerous ways, especially in its capacity to embolden imbibers to speak their own minds. Not even the death of valuable farm stock could provoke a planter as fast as the whiff of whiskey on a black worker's breath. Ruffin Mitchell was made to pay cash for the mule whose death he hastened by leaving the animal unattended while hitched to a plow. Ex-slaves caught drunk in the quarters on Benjamin Yancey's plantation paid a good deal more. Liquor cost them immediate, unpaid, and uncontestable dismissal.[22]

Often these expectations jumbled together, stubbornly entangled by their landowning authors in contractual texts. Defiant of all efforts to pull them apart, this recurrent trope of industry, sobriety, respect, and slavish obedience exposed the outermost edges of planters' vision of freedom and free labor. They spoke and wrote in the vernacular of impersonal contract, consenting even to terminal clauses and promises of payment, although usually deferred, but they aspired to a system that reeked of the regime that defeat had forced them to abandon. They were not purchasing labor power alone; they were purchasing the labor of people who would, with every gesture, figure of speech, and appeal for their weekly allotments of meal and meat, sustain the deferential face of the raw exploitation that had enriched their owners in slavery. Servility counted as much as, and occasionally more than, service, justifying at least in the minds of former slaveholders their ongoing rough usage of black laborers. Thus it was that William Stiles advised his grown son to send packing the "impudent" but otherwise highly skilled Adam for omitting—just once—the requisite *"Mr."* when addressing his erstwhile owner, and David S. Johnston anticipated in his inaugural contract that the five dozen black men, women, and children—"Negroes once owned by him and now controlled by him"—would continue to look to and "implicitly rely upon him" for the whole of their support and security.[23] Outright ownership might be a thing of the past, but if ex-slaveholders were to have their way, the spirit of slavery would outlast the institution from which it had arisen.

Ex-slaveholders presumed too much. All attempts to renew that vaunted control backfired almost immediately. From the perspective of the former slaves, it was one thing to remain on a former master's estate in order to have the advantage of friends, family, and the crop in the ground. It was another to remain in a state scarcely distinguishable from the odious bondage receding behind them. As landowners' designs registered among the former slaves, many of whom first learned about the new terms of engagement as they were put into effect, black men and black women acted to derail their former masters' attempts to resuscitate a now outdated system. Joining figurative forces with ex-slaves throughout cotton's Confederate kingdom, people sharing a stake in forging a freedom unmarked by the inequities of the past, black southwest Georgians translated labor routines into terms that better accorded with their own version of freedom. The pace of labor declined, lines slowed, workdays shortened, bells went unheeded, dinner breaks lengthened, holidays proliferated, machinery failed through no fault of its own, workweeks shrank from seven to six to five and a half days, and the most degrading and distasteful chores went unattended. "'I'll clean no streets for poor white folks' uses,' is the general cry," complained one disgruntled white Albany resident. Some former slaves consented to undertake such chores but demanded high prices in return. Fifty cents became the going rate demanded by black men before they would agree to tote a fifty-pound parcel. Others simply stopped working at all, or for large parts of the day. Dolly did. So did Ben Mitchell and most of those employed on David Barrow's estate who extended the time they had for themselves by subtracting from the time they gave to their old masters. By such means, and despite planters' most strenuous efforts, the finely tuned labor regime of slavery and war at last began to unravel. Rather than doing for their ex-masters as they had in the past, freedpeople spent more of their daylight hours doing for themselves: fishing, foraging, chopping firewood; gathering honey from the forests, green corn from the fields, and the fruit from landowners' orchards. Some of these products they consumed, some they retailed to customers exhausted by wartime fare at wartime prices. Cornmeal and firewood sold particularly well, earning its vendors a "tolerably good profit"—enough, indeed, that one planter lost his best workers, who made more selling kindling than they could from tending his crops. "Oh What a Change!" headlines screamed from the Albany press as midsummer passed. "A few months ago our negroes were a guileless, contented and happy people. What are they to-day, at least the greater portion of them?" "Arrogant and lazy," the author answered himself. "Freedom sick," sneered an overseer from east of Americus.[24]

Ex-slaves were also litigious. Hardly strangers to the law—as slaves they had been regularly paraded through antebellum courts as both property and people—and fully aware of the role judges and juries played in governing relations between free men and free women, they anticipated laying claim to similar privileges immediately on freedom. Indeed, the right to seek protection from and take disputes before an impartial tribunal captured for many former slaves the essence of black liberation. Laying a case before a jury or judge appeared in their minds as both the symbol and the substance of a new political and productive order, one that leveled old inequities of power and privilege by breaking the back of slaveholder sovereignty. It was a right few black people took lightly. As a senior Bureau official recounted after conducting a midsummer tour of Florida, Georgia, and South Carolina, whenever he paused to ask former slaves' opinions of "their present condition, the common reply is 'we have no massa now—we is come to the law now.'" "Meaning," the officer translated for those who might have missed the salient point, "that they now wish to live under, and be subject to the law as other people." And go to the law they did. Taking for granted what few northerners had yet come to consider—that freedom conferred the right to seek legal solutions for what a group of black Tennesseans called "grievances felt and feared"—ex-slaves across the former Confederacy hastened to bring their cases to court, overwhelming Freedmen's Bureau officials, provost marshals, and military tribunals with complaints about employers who insisted on acting like masters. Reeling under the weight of the cases thrust onto his shoulders by freedpeople in the counties under his supervision, the Bureau's lone agent at Albany petitioned within days of his arrival for administrative assistance. "It is impossible for me to do all that should be done in the whole of these Counties. I am engaged here from sunrise until 9 o'clock in the evening," performing the work of at least two men. The burden, Gideon Hastings learned, would grow heavier as contracts expired and workers called on him not only for protection but for help in securing their wages.[25]

As black southwest Georgians discovered, the summertime substitution of federal for slaveholder authority guaranteed neither warm welcome nor fair hearing. More often than not, the black men who spearheaded the rush for justice found themselves escorted roughly and rudely back to their workplaces by the soldiers who were first on the scene, many of whom "having lived amongst Negroes all of their lives," habitually discounted laborers' complaints. But as the Kentucky-born cavalrymen rotated out in July and as new soldiers—many of them natives of Maine, Illinois, and low-country South Carolina—rotated in, the scales tilted in freedpeople's favor. Able at last to confront their ex-masters on more neutral terrain and before more impartial tribunals, black men, followed by small but increasing numbers of black women, came forward to seek resolution for all manner of cases. Some sought to change their place of employment. Some wanted their pay. Some brought complaints of tiresome long days and exceptionally oppressive workloads.

Some brought complaints against one another. Felix Massey carried his case to the Freedmen's Bureau office at Thomasville after Sidney Burden ambushed him along a country road, attempted to gouge out his eyes, and then fired a pistol his way "contrary to the laws of the United States." Samuel Green, Frank McElvey, and William Culpepper just wanted the right to play an uninterrupted game of cards during nonworking hours. Another man named Green was fed up with the curses and blows rained down on him by his old owner's agent. Although federal officials hesitated to tamper excessively with existing contractual arrangements, revoking only the patently fraudulent or abusive out of a conviction that wage work fully performed best instilled in ex-slaves the habits of industry and thrift appropriate to a free people, they acted with alacrity in most other cases: calling witnesses, taking statements, summoning defendants, passing judgments, and levying fines on those they found guilty. "Madam," C. C. Richardson wrote on November 13 to one of Thomas County's former slaveholding mistresses, "Maria, a colored woman has shown me that she is capable of supporting her child, and further states that the child is in your possession. Pleas deliver the child over to her charge, well clothed and oblidge."[26]

Northern authorities especially wanted planters to abandon the physical compulsions most Yankees associated with the worst abuses of bondage. Freedpeople, they generally agreed, must learn to abide by the terms of their contracts. But they must not be made to obey by physical force. Corporal punishment had no place in a free-labor system, and as Davis Tillson advised white Georgians shortly after his arrival in the state, their continued reliance on whips and fists would only make wage workers "unsettled, suspicious, restless, and unprofitable." Insisting instead that the "freedpeople must be made to feel safe" and that the law rather than the lash provided the most appropriate means for resolving workplace disputes, Bureau agents cracked down on planters and their agents who continued to crack down on black workers. In southwest Georgia, that meant hauling them in on charges of kicking, beating, knifing, whipping, shooting, and otherwise harming their former slaves. The Bureau's agent at Thomasville, C. C. Richardson, had scarcely established his office when complaints began to pour in, and he opened his register with an account of T. J. Lightfoot's assault on "Richard (freedman)" for refusing to fetch "a gun to shoot one Dangerfield, 'Freedman.'" A few days later, Henry Stringer, "a Freedman who being duly sworn" recounted how his former owner had "made a violent assault upon him, and then [and] there did Stab him with a knife." In less than a month at his post, Richardson collected one hundred dollars in fines and jailed at least one former slaveholder—all, he reported, for "cruelties practiced on freed[people]."[27]

Going to the law, especially law enforced by federal officials, paid off. Although such actions were risky (planters took a dim view of workers who sought assistance from Bureau officials) and never entirely successful (violence or the threat of violence would remain a feature of everyday life), the level of abuse of exslaves by ex-slaveholders declined precipitously. Repulsed by the thought of "being arrested by the 'd—d Yankees'" on charges brought by those one white woman dismissed as "nig[s]," employers with a penchant for the more coercive forms of plantation discipline began to think twice before landing a blow, pulling a knife or stinting on laborers' rations. Even those who had been recruited specifically for their expertise "in the art of farming and managing negroes," who competed to see who "produce[d] the most corn and cotton to the acre," and who were long accustomed to serving as "both judge and jury" in deciding workplace disputes, scaled back the punishments they had traditionally meted out. Indeed, Nathan Barwick, the Sumter County overseer who had been identified in the last days of the war by his boss as an ideal candidate to lead an army of slaves into battle, and who had once been the object of neighborhood gossip for treating his slaves "rite Ruff," had by the middle of August laid aside his whip. Beating, he sighed to his absentee employer after recounting a worrying rise in recalcitrance and of people inclined to work "mity badly," was a thing of the past. Too bad, he confessed with callous nostalgia. If permitted to whip, he said, "I would know what to do."[28]

As black men and black women edged their old masters out of their lives, they accelerated the process of social and domestic reconstitution begun in the years before freedom. To be sure, other items figured into freedom's agendas: the acquisition of property in land, education for themselves and their children, securing the independence of institutions—especially churches— that had been formed under slavery and under the oversight of white people. But for former slaves whose domestic and personal lives had been buffeted roughly and repeatedly by migration to the cotton frontier and its corollary trade in black labor, suturing together domestic and affective connections tended to top their plans for the immediate future. Family reconstitution took on urgency as well for those whose lives had been further disrupted by the wartime flights of fugitive slaveholders, many of whom began "bothering" their former owners by midsummer for permission to "visi[t] their kin afar off when the crop [was] laid by." Sinai, however, was satisfied to make do with a less corporal connection. A survivor of both patterns of movement, she relayed a request through her former master to her former (and absentee) mistress for the latter "to send her her age." Sinai had lost during the course of her forced migrations the Bible that had contained the date and location of her birth. It was more than age, however, that Sinai was seeking. In misplacing the Bible, she had misplaced textual ties to a family she perhaps no longer knew in person. To restore the where and when of her birth was to begin restoring her place among kin.[29]

Sinai was hardly alone in wanting to locate herself within a lineage of her own flesh and blood. As black southwest Georgians carefully lifted the oppressive weight of cotton's antebellum regime, they began to reach out for those faraway and long-ago families. Combing the past for loved ones and then repairing the ruptures that had resulted from bondage was no easy task, and there were no assurances of success. Time, travel, and travail had distorted the faces and places involuntary migrants had kept carefully stored in their heads. Memories were fungible, Esquire Sherman discovered. "There is no place called Orange Court House, and no man named *Archibald Dixon*," Bureau officials explained after the Dougherty County freedman launched an attempt to retrieve his son by first locating the man who had last owned him. For those whose recollections were sharper, fresher, and better mapped onto the physical landscape, mending domestic relations came somewhat easier. This was especially the case with those who had been brought into the region during the war. With clear recollections of where they had come from and how to get back, wartime refugees had become by year's end a regular fixture out on the roads as whole plantations of black men and black women packed up their belongings and departed for the places they knew as home. A party of eleven embarked in December for South Carolina. Fourteen left at about the same time for North Carolina, hoping, they told Sidney Andrews, to arrive in time for Christmas. Another one hundred embarked shortly thereafter for their old homes in "Middle Georgia." Most traveled in large parties, and as had been the case under slavery, women rarely traveled alone. Indeed, although Adam dearly wished to be reunited with his wife (she ended the war in south Georgia, he in the north), and Sinai's husband yearned to have her join him in Savannah, both urged the women to wait where they were until the men could arrange safe passage. None, however, intended to wait very long; going home was much too important to postpone any longer. By early December, refugee planters stood helpless as the property they had struggled to save from the war turned and headed in the other direction. "It is estimated that in this Section of the State," J. P. Stevens, late of Liberty County, lamented from near Newton, that "there are not less than 1200 to 1500 Negroes who have Signified their determination to return" to the coast. Nothing he or other former owners said, nothing they threatened—including a winter of want and starvation for those who vacated their plantations—and nothing they promised, such as hearty assurances of "ample subsistence" and high wages to any who stayed where they were, could stem the outbound migration. "They are ignorant, impulsive, destitute of foresight, & deaf to reason," Stevens complained of restless ex-slaves in an eleventh-hour plea for assistance from a federal official. "I have endeavored patiently to explain to those on my plantation, the folly of their contemplated course of action but they seem to be inflexible in their purposes & plans."[30]

Stephens and his ilk fretted too much. Travel on the scale they witnessed was largely confined to those whose lives had been disrupted by wartime migration. The vast majority of the region's former slaves, people who had been carried into the region by traders and slaveholders in the years between settlement and secession, tended to stay put, as reluctant at the end of the year as they had been in the days following freedom to abandon what they had made for themselves under slavery. Unlike the refugees, they already occupied the places they now knew as home.

For them, breaking free of their ex-masters' orbits opened up opportunities, not to embark on new lives in new locations, but to develop, without dislodging, the families, friendships, and communities they had tenderly assembled in slavery. Some couples took advantage of their newfound access to courts of law and federal officials to formalize existing marital unions or to enter "Solemnly, duly & legally" into wholly new ones, as did Harry, who met Mary in the late days of the war. Others divorced, liberating themselves from unions that had formed, then fractured, under the pressures of slavery, as the Petersons did after a marriage of twenty-some years, four children, and multiple masters. Parents embarked upon frequently lengthy and contentious missions to recover children from former masters, some of whom refused to extend freedom to the youngest of their property, or boasted that black mothers and fathers should expect to "sweat" before they saw their children again. Churches that had been established under slavery began the equally tedious process of creeping out from under white oversight. Hampered by old laws still on the books that denied Georgia's former slaves the right to buy property in their own names, by a thicket of denominational requirements, and by a dearth of the material means necessary to create and maintain church structures and staffs, these churches struggled to their feet. Like emergent black churches more generally, years would pass before they stood firmly on their own. But before the end of the year, black congregations in Thomasville, Americus, Albany, Blakely, and elsewhere had put those processes into motion. Slowly but surely, black women drifted back into church spaces, filling up with their bodies and voices sanctuaries that had been closed to most of them by cotton's gendered demands. This is our church, we "payed for" it, a group of female black Baptists near Cuthbert would shout six years later in a dispute that not only resulted in the dismissal of a black male teacher but signaled women's return to what had been under slavery the special prefecture of southwest Georgia's black men.[31]

New institutions also gradually took form, and few of these were more important in freedpeople's minds than schools for themselves and their children. Acutely aware of the advantages that came to those who could read, write, add, and subtract—skills critical to making and enforcing the labor agreements under which almost all of them labored—ex-slaves eagerly and "intence[ly]" scraped together their scarce pennies to rent ramshackle rooms, purchase supplies, and support what was, in the first year of their freedom, a homegrown cadre of black teachers. Although their pedagogical efforts paled considerably when compared to those that had been launched in cities like Savannah—where a much more richly endowed population of urban-based ex-slaves had earlier that year established a system of schools for hundreds of students, conducted by nineteen black teachers, and funded by thousands of dollars—black southwest Georgians took considerable pride in the few institutions they brought into existence. By the end of November, Thomasville boasted of three small schools devoted to the education of freedpeople's children. Another forty recently freed scholars ranging in ages from 5 to 32 (two-thirds of whom were male) attended ex-slave Peter R. Hines's modest academy in Albany. Small though their numbers might be, the whole of the Albany contingent—from Mamie the youngest to Robert the oldest—were, as their teacher proudly observed, exceedingly "anxious to learn." Enthusiasm was not enough to sustain early and indigenous efforts at black education in southwest Georgia, however. As strapped for resources as were the churches, all four schools shut their doors for good before the close of the year.[32]

Nothing demonstrated black people's freedom from bondage

as much as freedom from physical dependence on their former masters. It was not enough to simply lay claim to a greater portion of their day-to-day lives by reducing the labor they allowed their old owners, or to have "the privilege of buying their [own] supplies, *without being allowanced*," as a group of Early County ex-slaves demanded of their astonished ex-master later that fall. Most former slaves aspired to outright possession of the means of production and to live, as a black Charlestonian patiently explained, "on our own hook." These efforts could take the form of independently owned and operated groceries, blacksmith shops, taverns, livery stables, or, as was the choice of a handful of freedwomen in Portsmouth, Virginia, small cookshops from which to serve the appetites of an urban clientele. But those whose pasts belonged to the fields—and these were by far the largest contingent of the South's former slaves—looked to the land for an autonomous future. Indeed, this was the message conveyed by a group of black ministers when asked by one of the Union's most feared generals to advise how best the nation's former slaves could take care of themselves, and how they might "assist the Government in maintaining [their] freedom." "The way we can best take care of ourselves," the ministers answered, "is to have land, and turn it and till it by our own labor." Although the ministers went on to suggest at that January 1865 meeting that black people should be required to "buy it and make it their own," the general to whom they spoke made land appreciably easier for ex-slaves to acquire. Within days of that memorable meeting, William T. Sherman set aside a large stretch of the Atlantic coastline for the exclusive settlement of the Confederacy's former slaves. By early April, Union authorities had already settled something on the order of thirty-five thousand black men and black women on what came to be popularly known as the Sherman Reserve—a thirty-mile-wide strip that extended from

Charleston, South Carolina, to the St. John's River in north Florida—and thousands more filled up coastal cities and abandoned estates, eager to partake in one of the most radical of wartime developments.[33]

With the cessation of hostilities, word of Sherman's gift of land as well as of other federal settlements of ex-slaves percolated into the interior. Conveyed by a chorus of mobile voices—from sympathetic Union soldiers and refugees making their way home, to planters who continued to talk as if their servants entered life hard of hearing—such news traveled at considerable speed, often arriving hot on the heels of (and occasionally in advance of) more general announcements of freedom. Indeed, Rufus Saxton, who oversaw the low-country resettlement project and served as the first assistant commissioner of Georgia, suspected that a good many black people had learned of Sherman's reserve well before the end of the war, getting the word probably "from those in rebellion." Certainly by midsummer such information had reached southwest Georgia, where it first surfaced on plantations whose owners and workers had been deeply involved in making and moving Confederate supplies as well as much of white people's mail. Speaking of the one hundred black people who ended the war under his care, many of whom had spent long hours on the roads carrying salt from the Florida coast, an astonished George Davis announced to his absentee boss that "they have Been under the impression they would" not only "Draw an equal portion of the crop" with their old master, but that his "Land[s] would Be equally Divided Among them." Such rumors and increasingly firsthand accounts withstood planters' best efforts to quash them and by fall, talk about land could be heard just about everywhere. Excited voices conveyed it along the Florida border; others talked openly about it on some of the richest plantations adjacent to Dougherty County, and on

William Stiles's estate rumors about coastal settlements of black settlers induced a small-scale exodus of freedpeople eager to lay their own claim to a piece of an old slaveholder's estate.[34]

It is unlikely, however, that the seven freedmen and one freedwoman who slipped away from Stiles's plantation on the pretext of heading for church ever found the utopia they sought. By the time they heard of, let alone acted on, that whispered promise of land, it had been effectively revoked by Lincoln's successor. When Andrew Johnson had signaled in May his intent to return to former Confederates all their property, exclusive of slaves, he meant it. In Johnson's view, Reconstruction was more about reunion than about a radical remaking of the American state. It was enough that Union victory had liquidated ex-Confederates' property in slaves. It was too much to liquidate anything else—a move considered as threatening to landowners in the North as to those in the South. Drawing support from moderate Republicans, many of whom shared his reticence about allowing the revolutionary impulses unleashed by war to spread nationwide in peace, Johnson overrode protests from the more radical Republicans and hastened to return abandoned and confiscated plantations to their previous owners. By midsummer, that transfer was well under way, but at too slow a pace for the president's liking. Annoyed by the ongoing efforts of high-ranking Bureau officials, including the agency's chief officer General O. O. Howard, to hold large sections of southern land in reserve for the benefit of the former slaves (the land represented not only the material substructure of black freedom but the primary source for agency funding), the president sped up the exchange. On September 12, just twelve days before that party of eight aspiring black farmers set course for the coast from southwestern Georgia, Johnson made it even easier for planters to reclaim their estates. With nothing more than a land title, an amnesty oath, and if necessary, one of the president's pardons, dispossessed former Confederates could be reinstated to land they had lost during the war. Only those black settlers with viable titles of their own stood any chance of staying in place beyond the end of the year. As General Howard explained to heartbroken audiences on Edisto Island, South Carolina, and elsewhere that fall, everyone else who occupied plots on the Sherman Reserve or similar land under federal control must make arrangements to vacate their homesteads or to enter into wage-labor agreements. The soil, he told them, would soon revert to its previous owners.[35]

As prospects for a large-scale redistribution of property grew dimmer, so did the possibility that southwest Georgia's ex-slaves might secure their freedom in land. A few tried, cutting pragmatic deals with war-weary small farmers and yeomen ready to turn part, if not all, of their operations over to the "exclusive" control of black farmers. A few simply squatted in place, refusing, one planter howled, "to surrender their houses or leave the plantations." But such efforts were doomed from the start. As settlers on the Sherman Reserve had already discovered, digging freedom out of the soil (however one came to occupy it) required significant capital investment that few former slaves could immediately afford. This was especially true for those whose slavery had bequeathed them a material legacy of puny proportions. The few lengths of ribbon, plugs of tobacco, or changes of clothes that accompanied black southwest Georgians out of bondage did not go far toward making a farm, and crops do not grow well by themselves. Even the hardiest require some form of capital and technological assistance. William Wells managed to finagle access to five hundred acres of good land, but failed in the end for the want of a mule. The agricultural enterprise launched collectively by thirty or so freedpeople in Decatur County failed for the want of everything else. Entering into their experiment without the tools needed to work up the soil, the seed to drill into it, or even the rations to live on until the crops started to ripen, the farmers were forced almost immediately to abandon their own fields to take up wage-paying positions on land belonging to others. Perhaps "if these Freedmen had a sufficiency of Food and Stock to run the farm," a Bureau official reported after conducting a close investigation of the aborted affair, "they could make a living but under the circumstances I see no way for them to feed themselves without subsisting almost Entirely upon their neighbors."[36]

One group of black farmers did manage to put seed in the ground and feed themselves without depending upon the goodwill (or employment) of their neighbors. Well organized, well funded, and backed by layers of federal authority, they came to stand out for the success of their farming experiment. They also stood out because they were newcomers to postwar southwestern Georgia, the first of them arriving out of the northeast from Wilkes County toward the end of November. Heirs to a past shaped on the leading rather than the lagging edge of the state's cotton revolution, the Wilkes County colonists (as they were popularly known) were able to convert social and material gains made under a much older slavery into a freedom of remarkable and propertied proportions. By late September, their project was well under way. As southwest Georgia's indigenous black people fought for the right to labor a less taxing day, more than two thousand former slaves "of which the larger portion were males" gathered together in Wilkes County to discuss setting up entirely free of their old masters' control. Located on lands long past their agricultural prime (the county had been settled before the American Revolution and put to cotton shortly thereafter), still reeling from General Sherman's march through their midst, and bedeviled by "bushwhackers" and "jayhawkers" who delighted in "*burning* and beating negroes to get money," "many yea thousand[s]" of the county's ex-slaves concluded that their interests were better served by moving away than by staying. Reaching into pockets fattened by years of investment in resources of time, mobility, and materials they, as slaves, had won—individually, collectively, and carefully—from their owners, the Wilkes County freedpeople contributed "different Sums of Money varying from four to Seventy Dollars" to one of the most impressive cooperative settlement schemes put into place by the South's former slaves. Within two months, their kitty held close to seven thousand dollars, and its guardians expected the level to climb by at least three thousand dollars more. It was money enough to purchase or lease a fully appointed, ready-to-plow plantation, the supplies to make it productive, and a year's worth of rations for those who would farm it.[37]

At first the colonists considered locating close to their known homes. But after discussing the matter with a senior Bureau official who reminded them that the far eastern end of the state's cotton kingdom had little to offer beyond "worn out" soil and surly white occupants, the colonists shifted their gaze toward Albany. Even after four years of war, southwest Georgia continued to attract aspiring agriculturalists. Its land remained fertile and thinly populated enough that the best of it could still be bought for less than three or four dollars per acre. Following a path carved into the ground by thousands of bound workers, migrating planters, and those who had made their livings catering to cotton's demands, the colonists sent two representatives shopping for a settlement site. It took a few weeks and much touring of potential locations and careful inspection of several locations, but the point men, Lawrence Speed and Wallace Sherman, eventually found what they wanted in Dougherty County: a five-hundred-acre established estate situated in comforting proximity to the Bureau office recently opened in Albany. Davis Tillson believed that the former slaveholders of southwest Georgia would make decent neighbors, or at least would make "no objections" to their presence. Sherman and Speed were not quite as sure. They liked being within a half-dozen miles of a federal agent. Leaving the latter, a former provost marshal by the name of Gideon Hastings, to look after their interests, the two colonists were soon on their way back to Wilkes County, eager to begin preparing and packing for their pending migration. The plan, which they ultimately realized, was to be back on the Dougherty plantation in time to put in a full complement of cotton and corn for the upcoming agricultural season.[38]

All this initiative on the part of their former slaves was simply too much for most of southwest Georgia's former slaveholders. Declaring themselves bedeviled and "out Done" by freedmen and freedwomen who not only refused to serve them like slaves but showed themselves altogether too eager to treat white people like equals in matters pertaining to etiquette, landowning, and law, planters' moods grew progressively darker. This was not the productive and political order they had intended to nurse into being. Rather than restoring the substance of a slaveholder's system, they felt its remaining foundations giving way under their feet, eroded by those they had hoped to contain and constrain by means of unilateral labor agreements and a continued recourse to whips. "Freedom," one sighed to another in early October as it became apparent that planters' dominion was slipping, "runs badly down this way."[39]

Indeed, freedom ran so badly in some white people's minds that a few resumed earlier discussions about cashing in, selling off, or at the very least diversifying their productive portfolios in order to reduce their reliance on people who refused to jump at

every command. But given the condition of their own war-rav-
aged pockets, talk of flight or a wholesale retooling of productive
practices was as impractical in October as it had been in June. So
too was a notion that had been gaining some currency in limited
circles about recruiting new workers from Europe, Asia, and
even the North to replace some of the old. But at the miserly "$4
to $6 per month and four suits of clothes a year" that planters
proposed awarding Chinese laborers in return for their services,
or the $15 per month considered adequate for Irish men lured
down from New York, that was unlikely to happen. Far better
wages were available outside of the former slaveholding South.
In hiring for the upcoming year, Pennsylvania farmers, for instance, were offering double that sum, California close to triple,
and in Colorado, farmworkers could expect to earn $67 a month.
Better conditions were available elsewhere as well. Few immigrants with alternative options were likely to stake their futures
on employers who insisted in public that none of their great
staples could be "profitably cultivated" without "some strong assurance, something approaching at least a certainty, that the labor can be commanded and controlled for the season or the
crop." The prospect of dining on a slave's ration, living in a
slave's cabin, and performing a slave's work for what most of the
nation's free laborers considered not much more than a slave's
wage discouraged all but the most desperate of immigrant workers from taking ex-slaveholders up on their offers. As a former
slaveholding mistress would later observe from her family's
Dougherty County estate, planters' best chance for recouping
spent fortunes lay in sticking to what they knew best: cotton,
corn, and the labor force most accustomed to the everyday
rhythms and requirements of plantation production. "Sometimes I wish we were off the plantation," William Smith's wife
admitted, but "that is the only way for us to make a living."[40]

As the summer of 1865 gave way to an increasingly contentious fall, the majority of Smith's agrarian neighbors had still
not resigned themselves to throwing in the towel. But without a
doubt, from the planters' perspectives, prospects looked ominous. They were especially anxious about the pending expiration
of the current year's contracts. In many respects, Christmas
would mark the majority of southerners' first experience with
full freedom. After all, black people's earlier tendencies to stay
close to, if not actually in, their former homes had relieved former masters of much of the process by which employers commonly recruit new workers. Most southern planters had simply
captured in contract those whom they had the day before owned,
regardless of their age, their condition, or even their capacity to
labor. When agreements began to expire toward the end of the
year, however, those who had once been their slaves would be
legitimately loosed on the land, affording planters only a few
weeks to replace a labor force most had spent a lifetime accruing.
Coinciding with a holiday associated traditionally with the rituals of social inversion—when the bottom rail momentarily, if
symbolically, displaced the top—it was a predicament that posed
a novel and unnerving challenge to the South's former slaveholders. As a people far more accustomed to acquiring their laborers through purchase or birth and then holding on to them
for life, hiring in a hurry was anything but a routine affair. "My
great fear," admitted a planter who had charge of two Early
County plantations, is "that [the ex-slaves] will refuse to contract until too late to make a cotton crop—a crop . . . now
need[ed] above all others, for the sake of the gold it will bring us
from Europe."[41]

The reestablishment of civil government, a process that had
commenced systematically with the election of delegates to state
constitutional conventions (Georgians elected theirs on October

4), imbued planters with renewed hope. After all, the restoration of state and local authority afforded former slaveholders and planters two significant advantages. First, and most obvious, the reorganization of the state's lawmaking and law-enforcing apparatus would render federal involvement redundant, giving southern citizens ample excuse to edge the national government and its increasingly annoying Bureau officials out of their lives and away from their estates. Indeed, planters across the South had been servicing this point every time they alluded to their particular gift for knowing black people's "wants" and "the best mode, and manner" for exploiting their labor. Second, with the state courts, legislatures, and police powers back in their hands—or at least in those of people born on the free side of a slaveholding system—planters anticipated being able to replicate through those structures much of the personal and productive authority they had lost along with the war. In the right hands, they believed, the law could be made to stand in for the brutal and now thoroughly proscribed machineries of chattel slavery. As a perceptive Bureau official pithily observed from Mississippi in early November, former slaveholders had "an ulterior motive" in their rush to restore their state and local governments. "If they can once get free of all [federal] control," Samuel Thomas warned General Howard, "they know they can do as they please with the negro."[42]

Thomas's caution came a little too late, if Johnson's administration felt inclined to heed it at all. The seven former Confederate states that fell under the provisions of the president's Reconstruction were already well on their way to shaking off that federal control by the time the general set his pen to paper. South Carolina and Mississippi had been especially quick off the mark and would finish much of their work before recessing for Christmas, but Georgia was not far behind. By the first week of

December, the state's general assembly had sat down to business in Milledgeville, where they promptly took up the problem of free labor by taking in hand an "Act to authorize and regulate contracts between master and servant," the creation of a committee appointed in early November by the president of the constitutional convention. Chillingly similar to the "black codes" under construction in Mississippi and South Carolina—legislation that sharply restricted black people's ability to direct their own lives and control their own labor—the authors of Georgia's proposal elevated planters' self-serving vision of free labor to the level of state law. Leaving little but the choice of employers to workers' discretion, the act secured for planters what they had given themselves in the contracts drafted the preceding summer: workdays that stretched from daylight to dark, unquestioned obedience, and an uncontestable authority to determine all causes for dismissal. A "master," wrote the authors of a law that with the governor's signature would have put the state at planters' private disposal, "may discharge his servant" for negligence, indolence, intemperance, absence without leave, and the "want of respect and civility for himself, his family," his guests, or his agents.[43]

Even if the legislature were to complete its business before the holiday recess, the law applied only if laborers remained in the fields. That was not yet enough for southwest Georgia's anxious former masters, who had convinced themselves that the former slaves intended "to quit at Christmas & go up the Country some here & some there," a situation guaranteed, they believed, to "ruin themselves & the entire planting interest—if some measure is not adopted to *Keep them where they are*." Not trusting the state to act quickly enough, and doubtful that federal officials could or would do any better, planters stepped into action. Availing themselves of a political reorganization that extended from statehouse to courthouse to the smallest town

councils, planters in southwest Georgia participated in a wave of
year-end assaults against black workers: lashing out at those who
spoke too freely of striking bilateral bargains when their old ones
ran out, who attempted to go it alone, or who dared to muse
aloud, as did a black man named Jack, of impending changes
that would "make them 'more free.'" Although town councils
and grand jurors lent considerable assistance by passing new
laws that sharply restricted black people's options and prose-
cuted black men on dubious charges, it was the newly reinforced police forces and a reorganized system of civil militias
that took the most noticeable lead. Armed with ample supplies
of rifles and rope, galvanized by rumors of servile insurrection
then sweeping the South, and operating under "the color of law"
(and frequently under the cover of night), posses scarcely distinguishable from antebellum patrols prowled their way through
the region's plantations, pried into black people's cabins,
roughed up unauthorized visitors, seized whatever weapons they
happened to find, and brutally savaged those who stood in their
way. "Oh Lord, Master don't kill me," a witness remembered
hearing Wesley scream after a gang of five tricked him away from
his house and into the woods. Although civil officials defended
the militias as legitimate keepers of community peace and on occasion patrolled in their ranks, both militiamen and their victims knew a good deal better. They rode to restore relations of
labor, sputtering openly, as did the party who caught a white
man on his way from Sumter County to Savannah, that unless
former slaves returned to work on planters' terms, the woods
would soon reek from the stench of rotting black bodies.[44]

Despite the impression left in the wake of the Yuletide terror,
cotton planters were not conducting an indiscriminate or wholesale enclosure of ex-slaves. Freedom and free labor had broken

them of that particular bad habit. With slavery abolished and Bureau officials zealously enforcing the payment of wages, planters were no longer interested in accumulating both the fit and the fertile. Nor were they interested any longer in supporting those whose productive years lay far in the future or back in the past. Both were habits of plantation management that had been common in slavery, but whose logic had collapsed along with the Confederacy. What planters wanted were the "young and sturdy," people able to work hard, work steadily, work at whatever task they were assigned, and above all to work at the lowest possible price. Planters wanted, in other words, what most employers usually want under a free-labor system: to keep the costs of production down and the level of productivity (and profits) up.[45]

Some of the South's former masters found such a free-labor force in the not-so-free labor of black adolescents, scooping up under apprenticeship codes leftover from slavery or reworked under freedom, armloads of teenagers and preteens. Maryland landowners were especially enamored of juvenile labor and the ways indenture could be deployed to circumscribe black liberty, but other former masters caught on almost as fast. Indeed, within six weeks of calling the local lower court back into session, Thomas County officials shifted thirty-five working-age kids out of the guardianship of parents declared by justices to be invisible, incompetent, or immoral and into the hands of applicant planters. Other southwest Georgians likewise expressed (and would continue to express) an appreciation for apprenticed farm labor. Convinced that black youth lacked the "run away & fortune-making natures of [grown] men," they plotted to flesh out the ranks of their workforces by "try[ing] to get the best of the children." Thomas Willingham was particularly keen to displace his ex-slaves with a youthful contingent, submitting a bid in early December for an army of children to cultivate his eleven-thousand-acre Dougherty County plantation. "I will take from 25 to 200 boys & girls Between the ages of 10 & 14," he wrote a senior Bureau official in the first week of December, bumping the number up by one hundred a couple of weeks later. He volunteered to pay what amounted to a finding and binding fee of ten dollars a head in addition to "mak[ing of the children] all that can be made anything of." "I don't feele at all diposed to let every thing go as I see some people doing &, give up," he unctuously wrote of a plan that would deliver to him on fruition as many as thirty-three hundred years of black labor for less than the price of a small herd of hogs. "We can all get along if we try."[46]

Too many problems attached to juvenile labor for most planters' tastes, however. Children fell ill; they got hurt; and they were novices, at best, in the art and science of making the South's staple crops. The youngest especially remained as inadequate to meet planters' taxing demands in freedom as they had been in slavery, under which owners had often waited until children were ten, eleven, or twelve before assigning them to gangs of suckling women and old men, a status most would hold until their early teen years. Moreover, as angry parents began to avail themselves of a thickening Bureau presence to recover children bound out without their permission, apprenticeship lost much of its luster. S. W. Brooks most likely thought so when, after a long and fiercely fought battle with Margaret, the mother of several of his eight youthful workers, he lost two at the height of spring planting. The recruitment of adult workers, while presenting planters with the distasteful prospect of bargaining directly with people they had recently owned, at least removed the problem of parents and the possible loss of labor at an inopportune time.[47]

One adult was not the same as another, however. Cotton

planters remained as selective in freedom as they had been in slavery, only now they based their decisions on different criteria. Workers were about all they wanted. Determined to rebuild the South's fortunes, and their own, planters hoped to confine to their estates not only those capable of harvesting high daily weights of cotton, rebuilding fences, and chopping down weeds—labor traditionally performed by women as well as by men. They also wanted employees capable of felling trees, raising rafters, commanding the meanest of mules, and muscling five-hundred-pound bales of cotton from wagon to wharf. They wanted workers who could plow out new ground as well as turn up the old, who could sweep through acres of ripe grain with a scythe, split three hundred to four hundred rails between daylight and dark, and perform such services day after dependable day. They wanted, in short, the same class of workers who had performed the same types of labor in slavery, people whom they had esteemed for a capacity to produce significantly more than the cost of their keep, people not distracted from their duties by reason of age, infirmity, or, especially fertility—the people whom slaveholders once prized as *"Prime Hands,"* as jacks of all possible trades. They wanted, in other words, what one former slaveholding Georgian called "operatives" and what many others described as "No. 1" hands.[48]

Planters began fairly early to reconfigure workforces composed under slavery to accommodate the novel demands of free labor. Defiant of northerners' pleas that they retain and maintain on their estates "the old, decriped, worn out &c." until civil authorities made provision to support them, and insistent that the obligation to hire conferred the right to fire, former slaveholders evicted on dubious grounds or no grounds at all those whose labor they doubted would turn a measurable profit. They started out somewhat tentatively, launching their first assaults during the late-summer lull in agricultural routine known as the lay-by. But planters soon picked up the pace, deliberately shortening the payroll before wages came due. Condemned as "superfluous 'help,'" those reckoned incapable of producing to their old master's standards—the very old, very young, the feeble, and the infirm—were sent packing, usually with nothing to go on and nowhere to go. "Make [your] livin' on . . . freedom," a Dougherty planter sneered when he dumped seven men and six women on an Albany street in November. He, at least, gave each of the party $3.50 for the services they had rendered him since freedom; most did not bother. It was, a northern official concluded as he observed in July a process that expanded exponentially as settlement day crept closer, "a striking commentary on the old pretences of a strong & intense affection subsisting between the planter on the one hand & his negroes on the other." "The rough barbarism of war has torn off the vail that covered the radical barbarism of Slavery." As a measure of the depth of that barbarism, both military and civil officials calculated that roughly half of the South's rural ex-slaves stood at risk of eviction before the end of the year; in southwest Georgia that figure came to more than thirty-one thousand.[49]

Planters took special pains to rid their estates of black women, especially those with small children. Once prized by their owners—women for their capacity to bear babies, and infants for their prospective contributions to slaveholders' fortunes—their value to landowners tumbled to near nothing in freedom. Neither made sense to employers under a free-labor system. Wage-paying planters had no interest in recruiting, unless absolutely necessary, jills of something less than half of all trades, and even less interest in supporting babies who consumed but could not produce. They wanted employees who could put in a full day's work immediately, not at some undetermined point in the future. They wanted "working hands." They wanted them now, and they especially wanted them devoid of all external distractions. "Hire no women, who have children," recommended Dougherty County's Benjamin Yancey, especially those the other planters dismissed as "*sucklers.*" They "stay in too much & jeopard[ize] the crop." Occasionally planters honored what one of them called the "dictates of humanity" by retaining the female and pint-size elements of their dismantled slave forces. Most did not. Whether they carved out their living on the plains of east Texas, in southside Virginia, on lush Delta estates, or on one of the plantations that sprawled along the banks of the Flint, planters generally took as their own some version of Yancey's hard-nosed advice. Out of patience with the pregnant, the recently pregnant, the potentially pregnant, and the very young— people who had been reckoned "a heavy Expense" in bondage but tolerated for the value they had added to a slaveholder's purse—planters turned their backs on the distaff and diminutive portions of their former slaves. In their view, mothers of youngsters, people incapable of "work[ing] well and regularly," would simply not do in the new order of things. Reported a senior Bureau official from Alabama, such individuals were "every where regarded and treated as an incubus." Be gone by Monday, Dolly's former master ordered the twenty-nine-year-old mother of eight-year-old Abby and six-year-old Jane on a day in September. Agnes's ex-master drove her away in November. Susan's turn came in December. So too did Adeline's, when her old master abandoned her and her children to shift for themselves on a chilly and translocal terrain that up until then had been the special domain of black men. "Starvation," mourned one of free labor's female victims, "seems at length to be the price I & my helpless children must pay for freedom, a bargain I had no hand in making."[50]

The demographic imbalances of southwest Georgia's ex-slave population threw into relief the special disdain with which ex-masters beheld black women and their offspring in freedom. Scarcely allotted time enough since settlement to overcome the youthful character of slavery on the cotton frontier, less than 6 percent of the region's black people were forty-nine years old or older on the eve of secession. Five years later, that proportion had dropped even further, pushed downward by the arrival of refugee rebels who insisted on bringing only those slaves deemed most critical to recovering their fortunes after the war, a population sharing characteristics of age and capacity with those who had been favored in previous migrations. Thus black women and their children in southwestern Georgia bore the brunt of planters' postemancipation productive recalculations. Cast aside in numbers that both swelled the rate of local indigence out of all previous proportion and gave poverty a youthful and feminine face, freedwomen struggled to salvage themselves and their children from a freedom that had suddenly turned sour. Lending a distinctive gendered dimension to the frantic last weeks of 1865, when contracts expired, wages came due, and rumors of insurrection swirled through plantation communities, "colonies" composed almost entirely of unemployed black "women of sound constitution" began to take shape in and between southwest Georgia's small towns. By the time Christmas passed, which it did peacefully in spite of planters' impassioned predictions, black women found themselves thrust outside familiar surroundings, huddled among strangers in tumble-down shacks— or out in the open—without furnishings or fuel, and, ominously as winter approached, without much to eat.[51]

No former slaves obtained the whole of what they wanted as they steered their ways across the fast-changing landscape of the first year of freedom. Slavery, over and above the fickle and contingent advances of federal interests or former masters with decisive plans of their own, still stood in their paths. The peculiarities of cotton's frontier regime had foreclosed well in advance on black southwest Georgians' prospects for attaining immediate education, developing their own churches, and cutting loose completely from the sites of their enslavement. The rhythms and relations established under one of cotton's older regimes likewise but dissimilarly set up the Wilkes County colonists as targets of white men who wanted their money. Most especially, slavery blocked black women differently than it did black men. Once cherished for their ability to provide what liberty negated—lifetime supplies of perpetually bound labor—black women stumbled especially hard as they attempted to cross freedom's irregular and seemingly capricious surfaces. By late fall, those who had passed out of slavery on cotton's terrain teetered at the edge of a precipice, scorned and denounced by ex-masters in a free-labor system that under their touch unapologetically privileged the fit over the fertile. But as scholars of the nation's passage from slavery to freedom have taken considerable and recent pains to point out, slavery bequeathed to its victims significant gains as well as crippling losses. And rather than cling to their babies in ramshackle huts, attempting to make what living they could off of the land and former slaveholders' leavings, the black women of King Cotton's domain would find their salvation in what they already knew: the gendered lives and ideas that they and black men had made for themselves under slavery's antebellum regime.

4

Black Women
and the Domestication
of Free Labor

Freedwomen could not long survive as vagabonds. The material deprivation that resulted from the conditions of their previous enslavement made certain of that. So too did the youthful and unfinished character of the communities and families to which they remained deeply committed. But in flatly rejecting former slaveholders' scheme of a thoroughly regendered plantation order—an ambition one dispossessed former slave woman bitterly denounced as a "bargain I had no hand in making"— black women could not replace it with the futures they and black men had imagined and held dear in the first days of freedom. Nor would they internalize and enact the free-labor ideas that prevailed among the federal authorities who preached their own gospel of political economy. Instead, under cover of a largely masculine political mobilization that in a matter of months would pry Reconstruction from the president's hands, the black women of the cotton South conjured their own form of free labor, piecing it together from the circumstances of their day-to-day situations. Little would have as profound, as troubling, or as lingering an effect, however, as the processes they would put into motion. For in attempting to improve on that one-sided bargain—a unilateral agreement that threatened to affix a crushingly high price on their freedom and that of their small children—black women unintentionally helped to inscribe onto cotton's postwar terrain the domestic foundations of what would eventually evolve into one of the plantation South's most distinguishing new features: an agricultural wage-labor system composed of family-based units.[1]

The winter of 1866 was an extraordinarily difficult time to be female, black, and unemployed in the former Confederacy. Like northern states more generally, since the 1830s the states of the slaveholding South had been steadily expanding the scale and scope of their public relief programs. By the eve of secession, state-funded asylums sheltered persons who were entirely incapable of supporting themselves: the deaf, the dumb, the blind, and the insane. County authorities distributed food, clothing, and occasionally cash to those who needed only irregular infusions of assistance; and locally managed and maintained systems of poorhouses, poor farms, and child apprenticeships took care of most of the rest. As the Civil War sent prices and tempers soaring, southern governments hastily and exponentially expanded the amount of public revenue they invested in pauper relief, committing enormous proportions of their state budgets to the support of a fast-growing population of Confederate poor. Georgia, for instance, obligated more than half of its 1864 state revenue to the poor. Theirs was, however, like that of the remainder of the slaveholding states, an especially selective public contribution; for with very few and infrequent exceptions, white people were the only recipients. In the years before secession, a few free people of color were occasionally admitted to state-run asylums or, as happened once in a while in pre–Civil War Georgia, provided a cell in a state penitentiary. But slaves who declined due to age, disease, or catastrophic injury almost always withered away on their masters' plantations, their care residing by law and by custom in the hands of the people who owned them.[2]

It was a policy of preferential public expenditure that few former rebels had any interest in changing. Embittered by the loss of the war, staggering under mountains of debt, and facing enormous numbers of white refugees—people broken and displaced by the war and clamoring for continued assistance—civil authorities bristled when federal officials insisted that "each county, parish, township or city" must "care and provide for" the entirety of its own poor. Adding black paupers to an already strained system, they growled, was a burden no "humane Government" should expect its citizens to bear. Sharing a white Tennessean's conviction that if "slavery had been destroyed for the good" of the nation, then the nation "ought bear the expense," the best most southern lawmakers could bring themselves to do was deflect the problem of black poverty onto black people themselves. Relieving ex-slaveholders of what had been their traditional duty, Mississippi, for instance, levied a capitation tax on all black residents, whether freeborn or former slave, between the ages of eighteen and sixty, the funds from which would go to support "all colored paupers." South Carolina's first Reconstruction government enacted something similar when it charged the support of indigent freedpeople to "the father and grandfathers, mother and grandmothers, child and grandchild, brother and sister" of such persons, demanding that black kinfolk assume responsibility for what had previously been the slaveholder's duty. Others, if they gave recently freed paupers any thought at all, simply recast them as vagrants, a semantic shift that granted county and parish authorities the power to arrest, try, and fine or confine the deprived as well as the delinquent.[3]

Georgia's lawmakers were scarcely more generous in their treatment of the state's homeless and hungry ex-slaves. After first considering, then dismissing, a measure comparable to Mississippi's black pauper tax, the legislature elected to update old laws to meet the new situation. Similar to its antebellum precursor, the revised statute vested the supervision of all poor people—former slaves as well as former Confederates—in the state's county-level system of inferior courts. Legislators endowed judicial officials with the authority to do whatever they thought necessary to care for and support the indigent, a power that extended from collecting taxes to build and maintain poorhouses and poor farms to determining who did or did not qualify for public relief. In principle, Georgia's revised poor law looked remarkably impartial. In practice, it was anything but. Enforced by justices who generally shared former slaveholders' and, as it happened, the governor's conviction that state institutions bore no legal or moral obligation to meet the material needs of dependent former slaves, years would pass in many locations before black Georgians joined white people on locally composed lists of authorized paupers. Ignoring entreaties from local Freedmen's Bureau officials to act with more speed, Early County authorities, for example, refused to admit the first freedperson to the local relief system until four years after the end of the war. Sumter County officials stalled even longer. Other counties accepted black people somewhat sooner. But as Patience, a single mother of five, discovered, enrollment conferred no assurance of public support. Added to the list of authorized indigent applicants by the judges of Thomas County's inferior court in late 1868, the freedwoman likely saw little or nothing of the money they tagged to assist her in the support of her small flock of fatherless children. Patience, the justices instructed, must wait her turn at the end of a long line of people to whom the county owed funding. The list of people who would receive their government benefits before her included the man who made his living directing the chain gang, the man who repaired the prisoners' tools, the merchant who provided their meals, the sheriff who provided them shelter, and an existing roster of white paupers. Her five dollars, the judges advised from the bench, would be paid out of funds not otherwise spent.[4]

The national government hardly served black paupers any better. Like mid-nineteenth-century middle-class northerners more generally, a population from which the military drew most of its commissioned officers, the military and Bureau officials who conducted much of the nation's business in the post–Civil War South were wary of giving too much too freely to indigent people. Excessive philanthropy, they feared, particularly outdoor relief—a practice notorious for its loose system of controls—produced rather than prevented the moral depravity and personal shortcomings from which they believed poverty emerged. Charity's potentially baneful effects multiplied, moreover, in the case of ex-slaves. In the minds of many northern authorities (and ex-slaveholders as well), public relief threatened to perpetuate habits of indolence, intemperance, and immorality that supposedly were learned under slavery when whips drove black people to work and when black people received food to eat, clothes to wear, and beds to sleep in regardless of the quality or quantity of the labor they performed. Convinced that the South's prospects for economic and political recovery rested in large part on former slaves' fast acquisition of the habits of self-reliance, self-motivation, integrity, and thrift esteemed by most northerners as fundamental components of a free-market system, federal officials moved immediately to cease the government relief programs that had been put into place to cope with wartime displacements. Men like the Freedmen's Bureau's top official in Virginia thought it would be better for black people to feel the "spur of necessity" than to be spoiled for freedom by misguided acts of philanthropy. Others, including the Bureau's commissioner, General Oliver O. Howard, emphatically agreed. "You do not own a cent's worth but yourselves," the military commander in South Carolina told the former slaves under his charge as he explained their new obligations as a free people. "The plantation you live on is not yours, nor the houses, nor the cattle, mules and horses; the seed you planted is not yours, and the ploughs and hoes do not belong to you." "How can you get these things?" he asked before offering up the answer he wanted: "By hard work—and nothing else." Paid labor, particularly lengthy stints of contractual labor, held the key to former slaves' futures and their ability to become contributing members of civil, and perhaps political, life. "Labor is ennobling to the character," observed Rufus Saxton, Georgia's first assistant commissioner. But its obverse was not. "Bear in mind," Saxton continued in one of his first sets of instructions to the former slaves under his command, "a man who will not work should not be allowed to eat."[5]

By the time southwest Georgia's planters began expelling black women and their babies from their fields and quarters in late 1865, federal philanthropy was all but a dead letter. Determined that former slaves should assume immediate responsibility for their own subsistence (and men in particular for that of their wives and young children), military and Bureau authorities had been, since the Confederate surrender, slashing rations, closing down the government camps that had sheltered black men and black women during the war, and in some instances halting the flow of government relief altogether. Few enforced federal policy as enthusiastically as Clinton B. Fisk, the Bureau's assistant commissioner for Tennessee, Kentucky, and parts of northern Alabama, a man who drove the project forward with pithy aphorisms about the need for "tubs" to learn to "stand on [their] own bottom[s]." But the officer who replaced Rufus Saxton as the Freedmen's Bureau assistant commissioner for Georgia, Davis Tillson, easily kept pace. No slouch himself when it came to advocating the therapeutic properties of a free-labor system, and fully convinced that paid labor contained within it a mystical capacity for elevating ex-slaves on the "scale of civilization," Tillson launched a vigorous campaign against black Georgians who did not earn their own keep. "All homes, asylums, hospitals or other modes of furnishing relief will be regarded as subsidiary and for temporary use only," he announced shortly after his September 1865 arrival.[6]

Despite the rearguard action of a small handful of agents who recognized that the decision to enter into wage-paying employment did not reside entirely with the former slaves, and who understood that in some instances poverty arose from conditions beyond an individual's control, federal relief expenditures in Georgia began an immediate and unrecoverable tumble. Making good on his belief that public assistance should be provisional at best, Tillson reduced the number of government rations issued to Savannah's black poor by more than half in less than a month, serving up a sour second course to the thousands of land-hungry ex-slaves who had crowded the city in the last days of the war in the vain expectation that they too might benefit from Sherman's distribution of low-country estates. Nor did Tillson stop there. By early December, Bureau agents were busily sweeping out of the state's cities and up-country neighborhoods any black people with no visible means of employment. Doubling as labor brokers on behalf of planters to the south and the west, regions suffering a relative shortage in wage laborers, they forcibly transported hundreds of out-of-work former slaves to Mississippi, Alabama, and elsewhere; the remainder received a stern ultimatum. Find paying employment by January 10, 1866,

Tillson ordered in a Christmastime circular, or his agents would make it their "duty to make contracts for them." General Howard quickly scotched the plan as an unwarranted form of "compulsory labor" and demanded that Tillson revoke it, but federal support for the state's former slaves continued its headlong collapse. By the time Tillson issued his first annual report, he and his staff had scaled back relief contributions to a fraction of their original number, in October 1866 issuing just one-seventh the number of rations as had been delivered into the hands of Georgia's destitute black people in the weeks immediately following the Confederate surrender.[7]

Over the course of subsequent seasons, Georgia's Bureau officials, like their counterparts in other corners of the former slaveholding South, gave up for good the business of regular relief. Acting only to relieve the most critical cases, they would eventually restrict themselves to handing out occasional suits of secondhand clothes to the near naked, medicine and medical care to the most desperately sick, and small allotments of food to people who had absolutely none. Strangling public and federal philanthropy did not, however, have the effect its authors envisioned. While black men usually found employment of one sort or another, the same could not be said of those deemed by ex-slaveholding planters as too old, too young, too infirm, and above all too fertile to pay. As one former Confederate explained patiently, employers "naturally want[ed] able bodied labor only." Thus no matter how draconian the means applied by Bureau officers and agents, no matter how stubbornly civil authorities and lawmakers kept their backs turned to the whole matter, the state's population of black paupers refused to go completely away. Black women with children, along with the sick, the injured, and the elderly, would remain a constant feature of the state's postemancipation terrain, an emblem of freedom's deficiencies and a source of frustration to the Bureau officials to whom they applied repeatedly for some small amount of assistance. "Every day," reported the subassistant commissioner at Albany two years almost to the day after the end of the war, former slaves approach "me with starvation" etched into "their faces, and I am obliged to send them away empty handed."[8]

With no government agency willing to lend them a hand, southwest Georgia's former slaves did what they could to assist those among them whom planters so emphatically no longer wanted. But the fruits of the first season of free labor ensured that most of them could rarely do much. Wages, which hovered too often between slightly above nothing and a negative number, did little to relieve the region's ex-slaves of the material shortcomings that were slavery's endowment. Occasionally a few freedpeople who were unusually skilled or held supervisory positions on their old masters' plantations would conclude the year with something tangible to show for their efforts. A freedman named Ed earned sixty dollars for his services as a carpenter on his old master's estate. Peter Jackson, a mechanic, earned nearly that much; so did Bob Dickens, who appeared on his employer's 1865 account book as the "Foreman" of a large and well-populated Dougherty County plantation. Such men, however, were the exception, never the rule. Compensation, as the vast majority of southwest Georgia's former slaves discovered on settlement day, more commonly took the form of a few dozen bushels of corn, perhaps twice that number in pounds of fresh slaughtered pork, and a gallon or two of syrup. If converted to money, such payments in kind translated into wages of two, three, or at the most lavish, four dollars per month for even the most accomplished agricultural workers. But ex-slaveholding employers took considerable pains to ensure that most did not see even that much. Taking shelter behind newly restored civil tribunals, protected by laws former slaves played no part in enacting or enforcing, and subject only to the control of what in southwest Georgia amounted to a skeletal staff of two overworked Bureau officials, planters routinely absconded, defaulted, and cheated their way free of any previous agreement to pay. Employers who had refused to reduce their agreements to writing, and those who artfully balanced their books on black workers' backs—docking their ex-slave employees for everything from lost tools to lost time—numbered among the worse of offenders, leaving their former slaves no better off at the end of the season than they had been at its beginning, and often for a lot longer. For it was highly unlikely that those who were swindled ever saw much of anything of their overdue pay. Parties scattered, memories were distorted, and account books had a dreary habit of coming up missing. "I feel my heart sink," admitted an agent several years later when unsettled 1865 claims materialized before him. It was difficult enough to resolve conflicts involving more recent agreements. He held out no hope in the case of the old ones. "I wish they would not go back of [18]67." [9]

Yet despite their own gloomy prospects, the region's former slaves heroically did what they could to help those who were clearly incapable of helping themselves. Replicating on a considerably more limited scale the black-founded and -funded charitable societies that had surfaced in better-endowed regions during the war, southwest Georgia's former slaves opened their purses, their pantries, and occasionally their cabins to the poorest among them. Most contributions were by necessity small and short-term in nature: a few emergency meals for a friend or acquaintance put out of work by reason of illness or injury; clothing, such as the garments a black man gave to Cherry McGlotney for the use of her four fatherless small children; or a safe place to sleep, like the bed Peter made available for nearly a year to an elderly black woman named Cuba. Less frequently, the compassionate acted collectively. Mobilizing in some cases as church congregations, in others as fellow employees on one of the region's plantations, groups of benevolent-minded former slaves pitched in to bury the dead, feed the living, and put roofs over the heads of people who otherwise had none. Indeed, a pair of elderly black women in Albany owed to a local church congregation the access they enjoyed to the floorless room they called home. Unable to cover more than half of the ten dollars needed for a single month's rent, their brothers and sisters in Christ had emptied their pockets to pay the remainder. But few former slaves could sustain such generous gestures indefinitely. Even the most richly endowed of black people's mutual aid societies and asylums—most of which were located in the South's cities— faltered in the face of the postwar explosion of impoverished and deeply needy ex-slaves. Worn out by the demands that had been placed upon them during four years of war, unable to convince northern philanthropists to continue providing support at wartime rates, and unable to locate alternative sponsors, many found themselves forced to evict their tenants, give up their habits of gifting the poor, and close their doors altogether. In southwest Georgia, poverty weighed so heavily that county commissioners abandoned the antebellum tradition of assigning black men to maintain the public roads. "It is almost impossible to work [them]," declared one such body from Early County, "from the fact that many of the freedmen have no tools." True, there would remain "a determination on the part of the Colored people to take care of their own," but philanthropy on the scale demanded by federal reluctance and civil disinterest lay far beyond the ability of even the most generous of southwest Georgia's former slaves.[10]

Black women knew this. As the first winter of freedom closed down around them, southwest Georgia's former enslaved women understood acutely that the responsibility for their material security, and that of their children, had defaulted onto their own shoulders. Left with little choice but to do for themselves what others would not or could not do for them, some attempted to fall back on jobs that had been derivatives of, or subordinate to, the South's principal economy. Housewives, after all, and despite their petulant threats to hire none but Irish or northern-born servants, remained deeply dependent on black women's services. So did hotel keepers, dairymen, and former slaveholding mistresses. The sick, the aged, and the infirm continued to require personal nursing; gardens and lawns wanted weeding; and M. L. Fort, mother-in-law to Sumter County's ex-slaveholding planter E. D. Huguenin, believed it absolutely essential after emancipation that she acquire some person immediately "to wait on [her] table." Jobs of this nature did not, however, account for a significant part of southwest Georgia's postwar economy. Indeed, in a region that five years after the war would be able to boast of just seventeen towns—nine of which contained fewer than three hundred people and only six of which had more than a thousand—domestic and nonagricultural employments constituted only a fraction of the wage-labor positions available to former slaves. Manufacturing jobs were particularly scarce. The few in existence were generally small operations that relied predominantly on the labor of men: gristmills, sawmills, and blacksmith shops. But black women who had been booted out of plantation homes took whatever wage-paying posts they could find: milking cows, churning butter, tending chickens, hauling firewood to feed kitchen stoves, and then stirring the pots that simmered on top. They bent their backs over washtubs, burned their fingers on hot irons, carded wool, spun thread, wove fabric, and sewed—some with talent enough to qualify for the title of seamstress, a handful of others at a small Albany clothing manufactory that had been recently converted from the hardtack factory it had been during the war. Other black women scoured floors, tended the dying, cleared boardinghouse tables, washed dishes, and beat the dust out of white people's rugs. Women located closer to towns and military encampments, or posted along the region's recovering railways, made piecemeal livings peddling fruit, eggs, cakes, fish, and sexual services to a variety of customers. A few peddled the labor of their nearly grown kids; that is, if they could keep them free of illegal indentures and out of the grasping hands of disaffected fathers, problems that would plague single black mothers through and beyond Reconstruction. Some even discovered that while ex-slaveholding planters cast general aspersions on female laborers, there were some who were willing to take back black women on a part-time and seasonal basis. Perhaps small farmers who had never owned any slaves, or men who had lost most of their fortunes during the war, put the occasional black woman to work performing the same range of chores that had fallen to women in slavery: sowing, hoeing, harvesting, fixing fences, tending vegetables, mucking barns, chopping weeds from summertime fields, running farmers' small plows, and most especially, picking out in August and September the year's crop of ripening cotton.[11]

But these were practices and employments that rarely resolved black women's postwar dilemma. As marginal to cotton's economy as the people who usually performed them, nonagricultural jobs in particular tended to be impermanent, irregular, and poorly rewarded. They also often exacted painfully high personal costs. Domestic positions were nearly the worst. Characterized by dismally low wages (which commonly took the form of a modest subsistence augmented infrequently by a dollar or two in monthly cash wages), exhaustingly long days, and the constant and close supervision of employers who favored employees with "no freedom" in them, black women viewed domestic positions as ports of last resort. Live-in arrangements were the most distasteful, particularly to those who, like the black women of southwestern Georgia, passed into freedom far out of view of anything that could pass for a town. At a time when urban locations offered the best opportunities for domestic employment, accepting a position within a white family usually required housemaids and servants to move away from family, friends, and familiar terrain to Macon, Athens, or Atlanta. Some, of course, did, scouting out routes that in later years would convey disproportionate numbers of black women out of the countryside and into the South's cities. But the decision or need to leave came at considerable cost, compelling black women to rupture the families and domestic connections that they had fashioned in slavery and salvaged from war. So loathsome were the prospects of sacrificing affective relations for material security, and so deeply did black women pine for faraway family, that domestic employers increasingly vowed to hire no servant encumbered with kin. Black women with small children, hissed an especially vexed former slaveholding mistress, were the worst: the mothers were "annoyances" and the infants and toddlers to whom they wanted to give the whole of their time were intolerable "pests." The ideal candidate, sniffed another woman after she had failed to staff her home with suitably submissive cooks and nurses, were "orphan[s]," people she defined as lacking any countervailing social or familial ties that might pose a challenge to an employer's command.[12]

Other forms of part-time or nonagricultural employment were more locally plentiful than household service positions. They also tended to accord black women marginally more control over their time and their labor, and under some circumstances promised to pay a little better than the pittance usually reserved for housekeeping help. This was particularly true of skilled work. For instance, in the early years of black freedom an experienced midwife could expect to be paid four to five dollars for each baby she ushered out of the womb and into the world. Competent spinners, who regularly commanded fifty cents for every pound of wool they spun into yarn and who could process as many as ten pounds of previously cleaned and carded fleece in a day, could hypothetically earn almost as much as could women who knew their warp from their weft and who managed to retain in freedom the value planters had attached to their talents when wartime embargoes had interrupted imports of finished fabric from the north and Europe.[13] But other jobs available to recently freed black women—gardening, washing, ironing, dressmaking, milking, churning, and nursing the victims of contagious diseases—paid significantly less. Seamstresses, for instance, earned just seventy-five cents for laying out, cutting out, and sewing up an adult woman's everyday dress, a project that required yards of fabric and days of labor, to say nothing of keen eyesight and ample light to stitch by. Laundresses earned all of two dollars per month for tending to one person's wash; on this income, a washerwoman would need a minimum of five clients to be able to afford a single month's use of a one-room apartment. Martha Ann Turner probably found it difficult to do even that. A dairymaid who made her living serving a herd of twenty-six cows, she received her wages in kind rather than cash, a strategy that meant she had to convert milk into money even before purchasing her own meager living. Still, the potential existed for black women to achieve a minimal subsistence by stringing together a series of short-term and part-time positions, working "a few days here" and a few days "there." That is how Malinda, a single mother of ten, managed to get by. She ran errands and performed various odd jobs for the people of Cuthbert, bringing in fifty to sixty cents a day on those days she managed to land enough little jobs. Amy, a laundress, accomplished something comparable, making a peripatetic living washing and ironing for the boarders who passed through Albany's Stubblefield Hotel. So long as occupancy rates remained stable and the rooms filled to capacity, Amy could earn enough to afford her own room and board.[14]

At least that was the general idea. But cows must produce calves in order to produce milk, wool is a finite commodity, and both infants and travelers generally kept their own schedules. Such contingencies could cost black women critical sources of very scarce income. Moreover, as derivatives of, rather than pivotal to, the staple economy, many of the arrangements women depended on to escape their postwar predicament were notoriously hard to enforce. Not only did employers refuse to put into writing their agreements with laundresses, cooks, and dairymaids—a choice encouraged by state contract laws that required only long-term agreements to take textual form—but nonagricultural work tended to fall beyond Bureau officials' field of vision. It is not that federal authorities did not care whether nurses, midwives, and the like received fair treatment and just compensation. They did care, and more than a few Bureau agents took nonagricultural workers' complaints seriously: tracking down defaulting employers, pressing criminal charges against those who refused to relinquish old habits of physical coercion, and guiding female black plaintiffs through often hostile civil judicial systems. Indeed, without the intervention of O. H. Howard, who was assigned to the Albany Bureau post in May 1867, Harriet Jackson and Ellen Gibson would have been robbed of the $6 and $2.50 they had respectively earned scrubbing white people's dirty linens. But being chronically shorthanded, and convinced that long-term agricultural wage labor better prepared former slaves for full freedom than did piecework, "jobbing," and other forms of itinerant and nonagricultural labor, most agents focused their attention on those workers who produced the South's great staples. This preference had the unintended effect of encouraging employers to openly bully, beat, and deceive the women who cleaned their homes, nursed their babies, and waited their tables. It also had the additional and equally unfortunate effect of elevating the interests of year-long agricultural laborers over the interests of those who occupied the edges of cotton's economy. The latter became especially visible at settlement time, when Bureau agents found themselves forced to divvy up too little money or too little harvest among too many workers. For when push came to shove, part-time employees tended to be the first sent away empty-handed. As a Bureau agent would later observe from his Lee County office, "Some had to lose," and it was better if the loser was a jobber rather than any of the regularly engaged "year hands."[15]

This message was not lost on the women who had been so recently and rudely condemned by their former masters as "heavy Expense[s]." Moreover, they knew full well, from having lost them, that there were other advantages attached to making a living by making corn and cotton. Full-time employment on a farm or plantation almost always assured workers a cabin to sleep in, wood to warm them, and food for their tables, amenities of critical importance to women who otherwise wandered the roads by day and slept out of doors by night. Although most of the handful of black women who successfully talked their way back into the fields worked like Marianne did—"for no pay"—a small number managed to hold out for promises of a little bit more. These women, almost always younger and childless, or women who applied to planters and farmers with whom they were personally acquainted, might additionally receive a new suit of clothes, a hat to cover a bare head, a fractional share of the crop, or less frequently a few dollars "extra," usually made payable at the end of the year. John Jones, for example, pledged Martha Harris one-thirteenth of one-sixth of the crop, two dollars per month, and two suits of clothing in exchange for her labor on his Early County plantation. Ailsey, who pled her case before the man who had owned her in slavery and with whom she lived for many years after freedom, traded twelve months of continuous labor for a calico dress, two aprons, and the promise of forty post-harvest dollars. The assistance of newly arriving Bureau officials, particularly those the assistant commissioner for Georgia recruited out of civilian populations, additionally and ironically eased black women's passage back onto southwest Georgia's plantations. As longtime constituents of the communities they served, and sometimes as landowners and planters themselves, the hundreds of civilians Tillson hired statewide were far better posted than northerners to assess and exploit the local demand for black people's labor, an expertise that facilitated matching black women to those farmers willing to hire them. "There are few women with children, in my county I cannot get homes for," one such civilian agent bragged after reporting he had already obtained "a good home" for one woman: "she to be Boarded, Clothed Physiced & $2 or $3 Dollars per month."[16]

Rarely, however, did the black women who returned on their own to local plantations collect even a fraction of the promised wage. Landowners, they discovered, remained deeply committed to "No. 1 hands"—laborers capable of working uninterrupted, six days of the week, fifty-one or fifty-two weeks of the year. Women who, for reasons of inclination as well as physical incapacity, failed to perform, in effect, like men, found their wages docked repeatedly and deeply. Planters were especially impatient of female employees who attempted to put the needs of their families ahead of the needs of the fields. Nursing, an activity that had been actively promoted so long as black women's babies were received as capital gains, became under planters' scheme of free labor exceptionally offensive. Heedless of the resultant spike in infant mortalities, especially among "children born to mothers not married," planters who hired back black women made employment contingent on what amounted to daily acts of child abandonment. They likewise took a dim view of women who lost time in the fields due to pregnancies, postpartum recoveries, and bouts of what one planter dubbed "delicate health"; planters slashed wages, levied fines, and ejected repeat offenders with an enthusiasm born of new market and class relations. Illness, for instance, cost Delia her job and all of her belongings after her employer drove her away unpaid and with no chance to pack. Planters also expected black women, like black men, to pay out of their wages for the care and keeping of any nonworkers. Such deductions consumed inordinate and often what one federal observer judged "excessive" portions of even the highest-paid black workers' wages, but they almost always exhausted the whole of women's already negligible pay. Whereas men occasionally and, as Bureau supervision thickened and spread, increasingly ended the season in possession of measurable wages, black women who brokered their own labor usually closed out their contracts mired deeply in debt. As a result, even the best of black women's wages tended to be pitifully small: a few articles of hand-me-down clothing, a few bags of potatoes, or something on the order of the forty-five ears of corn "Old Auntie" received in exchange for making her employer a "good crop of corn."[17]

It was an unstable place that black women occupied in the early free-labor order. Even those who managed to trade their own labor in a market that heavily favored black men knew that the least miscalculation or poorly planned step could ruin their lives overnight, stripping them of shelter, subsistence, and sometimes their children, the youngest of whom seemed constantly to be in ex-slaveholders' way. This was a threat all black women knew. But few knew it as well as a former slave named Rachel. Rachel represented everything planters swore they detested about the women they had prized and possessed under bondage, and on a late January day in 1868 freedom and free labor converged to nearly destroy her. Sharing a surname with several of Thomas County's more prominent white families, Rachel had been since the end of the war scratching out an itinerant living from a small plantation community located just north of the Florida border. Although Rachel worked among and for people who had apparently known her in slavery, and remained in the general vicinity of Duncansville, the hamlet that gave the larger community its name, she never seemed to stay in any one place for long. Drifting from one plantation to the next, she would spend only a few months in one man's employ before departing to take a new job in a new location. In 1867 Rachel labored on at least two different plantations, before concluding the season on yet another. Finding work, if not keeping it, was evidently something Rachel had become fairly adept at. But in January 1868, landing a job had suddenly become much more of a challenge. For starters, Vernon, Rachel's son, had grown up too much. Born immediately before or shortly after secession, he was still too small to be of much use in the fields, but at a time when planters customarily charged as much as forty-four dollars to board a child older than five and younger than ten, Vernon had become too expensive to tag along in his mother's wake. Whatever small wage planters agreed to give her would be immediately consumed by the price of Vernon's board. How to dispose of a boy was not Rachel's only challenge in January 1868. She was pregnant. It was a development she had been keeping to herself, and with good reason. Few planters were eager to hire a woman soon to be distracted by a suckling-size child, even if the woman was someone they knew and had employed in previous seasons. As long as Rachel could successfully conceal her fast-changing status, she stood a chance of landing a job; but with the baby due to arrive in late spring, time was definitely not on her side.[18]

Rachel, however, found a home for herself in fairly short order. Drawing most likely on her extensive knowledge of the Duncansville community and the people who called it home, by the middle of January she had arranged to begin the season on Henry Wyche's plantation. But before moving into her new home, an event scheduled for the second or third week of the month, she needed to dispose of her son. When no one responded positively to an increasingly desperate series of appeals for someone, anyone, to take Vernon off of her hands, Rachel consigned him temporarily to the care of a former employer, a man known only by his surname Powell. Perhaps Rachel talked the man into taking her child by assuring him Vernon would not stay very long. Or maybe she convinced him that Vernon could perform enough small, light chores to cover the cost of his keep. But whatever she said, or Vernon did, was evidently insufficient: Powell almost immediately reneged on the agreement and demanded that Rachel return and take the boy away. What happened next—the blows Rachel rained down on Vernon for lagging behind as they walked along the road at the end of the day, her panicky efforts to stifle his cries, the grave she dug in the clay—and the fears that crowded her mind about Wyche's response if she arrived on his place with Vernon in tow and the unlikely prospects of finding a new home with a belly growing larger with each passing day—came pouring out at the court-ordered hearing and subsequent trial. Not that any of Rachel's concerns mattered to the jury of white men who eventually decided her case. Nor did they matter to the Thomasville journalist who forgot to note in the article he wrote that the defendant was a mother who had come up hard against the gendered inequities of former slaveholders' free-labor order. All they saw was a murderer who deserved to sit out her life in a cell.[19]

Even with the strength of the reorganized state at their command, planters failed once again to get things entirely their way. Married women, and women who could otherwise command the allegiance of men, would not let them. Planters could bully the domestically and affectively deracinated—women who, like Rachel, lacked the protective advantages of familial ties—subjecting them to new forms of exploitation that came close to matching those they had served up daily in slavery: denying them the right to function as mothers, engaging their services for less than they had given their slaves, and dismissing with no warning those who stepped the least out of line. But planters met their match when they attempted to treat in the same way women who could call on the assistance of men. These women were a formidable force. Dead set against any action that might jeopardize the small but significant social and material gains they had made for themselves under slavery, nieces called on their uncles, sisters their brothers, daughters their fathers, and above all, wives their husbands, to make their own access to cotton's plantations, as well as that of their children, a condition of black men's employment. Part of a much wider phenomenon that swept the former Confederacy in the wake of the first Christmas of full freedom, when planters pitched freedwomen out of their cabins while terrorizing freedmen into staying, southwest Georgia's black women refigured free labor by demanding that black men render the family the most basic unit of staple production.[20]

And so most of them did. Black men rarely flinched away from the duty black women had thrust suddenly upon them, hastening to ratify what had been enacted and "author[ized]" by their daughters and wives. Freedwomen, of course, were not entirely absent from the contracting process. Single mothers who were able to command the labor of teenagers, for instance, continued to put them to work earning much-needed support for themselves, their mothers, and any nonworking sisters and brothers. When their personal circumstances demanded, grandmothers, aunts, and other female kin did likewise. Fifteen-year-old Robert, for instance, was "brought in by" his mother, Caroline; thirteen-year-old Little George was "brought in by" his older sister, Eliza; and Judy Holt went to work on a large Terrell County plantation in the company of sons Wilson and Sam. But it was men, more than anyone else, who mediated the new season's agreements, who monopolized laborers' seats at landowners' bargaining tables, and who demolished the previous year's contractual practices by insisting that labor recruitment be conducted on a wholly new basis. Surprising northern observers, most of whom believed that workplaces were masculine spaces and that women belonged in the home—a sentiment shared by military officials who in their early instructions repeatedly advised former slaves that it was a man's obligation to produce his family's subsistence—black Southerners demanded that "contracting be done in a very different manner" than had been the case the previous year. As a Freedmen's Bureau official observed from Mississippi on the eve of the new year, "The older people are trying to get their families together" and "employers will have to contract with the heads of [freed] families." Participants in a much larger process, one that swept much of the former Confederacy, southwest Georgia's black fathers spoke for their daughters, brothers for sisters, uncles for nieces, and most especially husbands for their wives and minor children, arranging for all of them to return to the plantations together. Isaac Squash of Arkansas approved a contract that included himself, his wife, and their seven minor children; William entered into one for himself and his wife; Peter approved one for Virginia and Jane; Toby did the same for Georgiana; and Henry approved the terms of an agreement he had made in his name, the name of his wife, and those of their fifteen-year-old daughter and two tiny babies.[21]

Having collectively called into being a unique scheme of free labor, most, and in some cases all, of the region's ex-slaves returned to work in the company of very close kin. To be sure, single men and single women would continue to be a visible feature on southern plantations, striking bargains for themselves and nobody else to chop weeds, clear fields, repair fences, and pick the crops for the South's former masters. Moreover, made perhaps somewhat more flexible by the absence of affective connections, people who brokered only their own labor tended to do so in much larger numbers outside of the peak hiring season: dominating the names attached to contracts drawn up in May, June, July, and sometimes later. But as Bureau officials observed in the opening weeks of the new agricultural season, freedpeople who arrived on their own on the cotton plantations, or who engaged to labor in groups of unrelated individuals, composed only a small part of the workforces planters mobilized at the start of the season. On the vast plantations of the Mississippi Delta, for instance, estates that during the Civil War had been cultivated primarily by flexible combinations of women, children, the elderly, and the infirm—people who had been dismissed as unfit for military employment—more than half of the contracts for the 1866 season were drawn up by able-bodied black men for themselves and for the families they had come home to after the war.

In southwest Georgia, where slavery had left black women with depressingly few means of survival that did not involve ex-slave-holders' plantations, the proportion of unaccompanied employees dropped even lower, rarely adding up to more than 15 to 20 percent of those who entered into a year-long agricultural agreement in early 1866, and sometimes falling well below that. Indeed, on many of the small- and medium-size estates, those that operated on the scale of A. T. MacIntyre's Thomas County plantation with its workforce of approximately two dozen former slaves—ten couples, their children, and a man named Sam—families tended to entirely displace unattached workers or workers who attempted to go it alone.[22]

Men, as women knew, brought more to the table than the strong backs, capable hands, and deep wells of endurance much sought after by wage-paying planters. They also brought a keen awareness of the larger social and political landscape, a body of knowledge and experience that fitted them particularly well for the task women set them. No longer subject to the constraints of passes and patrols, and protected in their new right to travel by northerners who considered mobility a prerogative of freedom and free labor, black men, moreover, could move farther, faster, and more frequently than they had been permitted by their owners in the past. Teamsters became especially ubiquitous in the months following freedom. Better able to take paths of their own choosing, to pause to speak with whomever they pleased, and to spend their nights in the transient camps that materialized along their more heavily used routes, the men who drove the wagons brought into full view the subaltern communities they had helped to forge in slavery. Matt Brown, Thom Rhodes, Ned Tomlin, Let Johnson, and George Ford—the ringleaders of a gang of black teamsters who ran afoul of Dougherty County authorities for the clandestine trade in highly prized mules they conducted in conjunction with their more legitimate business—represented only a tiny part of a growing population of men who "hired their wagon[s]" for a small fee. Elias Duncan and Toby Daniel were two of the other men who in freedom crisscrossed the landscape as whim and business took them, covering routes that stretched from well north of Americus to deep into Florida, and from Alabama to the east side of Georgia.[23]

But other men were also out and about, and in much larger numbers than previously, particularly as the 1865 contracts expired. Besides those who simply took to the woods and roads on personal business—hunting fresh game for the table or honey to sweeten their meals—or who continued their painful attempts to reconstitute broken-up families, steamboats and cotton boxes with their crews of black men quickly resumed their regularly scheduled runs and then some. As technological innovations improved the safety and speed of steam-powered vessels, and as laborers cleared Confederate obstructions from the rivers, boat traffic quickened and companies expanded their fleets from the single boats they had commonly operated in slavery to lines of as many as seven or eight ships, each of which carried a crew that included a dozen or more employees, most of them black. Indeed, the region's postwar expansion of railroads—systems that depended heavily on the labor of large gangs of recently freed men and that increasingly served black passengers as well as white—hastened the growth of steamboat lines as planters realized that using both technologies, they could move their crops even more efficiently out of the field and into the factory. At Bainbridge, for instance, planters in allegiance with merchants, steamboat companies, and the Atlantic and Gulf Railroad—which reached Thomasville by the eve of the war and shortly after the surrender commenced laying tracks farther westward—had constructed by 1868 a single facility that functioned as both depot and wharf, directly connecting the port of Savannah to the vessels that served the Flint River. Not long after, an optimistic combination of entrepreneurs and planters constructed a similar depot-wharf installation on the banks of the Chattahoochee. Galvanized by what one historian of the region's rivers calls the "age of commercialization" and planters' insistence that the revival of the South's battered fortunes rested on the rapid revival of cotton, steamboats became regular visitors to no less than thirteen private and public wharfs along the Flint River below Albany and more than one hundred along that portion of the Chattahoochee that flowed south of Columbus.[24]

As black men walked, rode, or traveled by rail, they continued to talk as they had in the past. Linking together a still largely illiterate population of rural ex-slaves, these men-on-the-move remained the backbone of an informal but highly effective system of communication, conveying all manner of personal and community gossip, and local and national news. As it became clear to them that, if left to their own devices, planters would call into being a freedom only marginally more liberal than slavery had been, black men's talk turned increasingly and insistently to the problems and prospects of free labor. Deeply dissatisfied with their experiences of the previous season, some listened intently and attempted to act on a continuous, if low-key, hum about land, refusing to "leave the plantations or hire themselves," an opinion one frustrated planter attributed to "the idea that at least a [moiety] of the land stock &c is to be theirs." Others paid close attention to reports circulating in from outside the region—and sometimes from out of state—about planters who "offer[ed] to *feed* & *clothe*—give every hand a good overcoat— and ($180) one hundred & eighty dollars a year!!" In Early County, it was the arrival of "some freedmen down from Atlanta" that stirred black people's interest, whereas in Randolph

County it was the arrival of white men from nearby plantations sent to "decoy" away potential workers that set black men to talking. They also eagerly exchanged more local information, telling of personal encounters with planters who were too quick to whip or too slow to pay. But most of all the former slaves learned from one another how to distinguish good offers from bad, and how much was too much to ask. Thus it was that when Howell Cobb's son attempted to recruit a new workforce for the 1866 season, he came face-to-face with black men who had established their own understanding of what composed a minimum wage. "Henry," sputtered Howell Cobb Jr. of the landowners and agents against whom he found himself bidding for labor, "says *none* offer less than a hundred and fifty—some include—food *and clothing*—others food only." The former slaves, he reported in a letter littered with angry punctuation, wanted it all: cash wages, rations, plus new dresses and suits. "None" of them will "listen [to anything] less."[25]

Massaging this body of carefully accumulated knowledge into a new frame of reference, and banking on planters' need for their labor, black men forcibly inserted themselves into the bargaining process. Competition was the fiercest and bargaining the most contentious in those locations where talk among workers had flowed the most freely. But everywhere, planters found themselves working hard to hire an adequate number of workers. Complaining bitterly about once-submissive ex-slaves who had suddenly turned "ignorant, impulsive, destitute of foresight, & deaf to all reason," and eyeing with suspicion landowning neighbors with whom they were engaged in an unanticipated race, planters consented to terms few had previously considered. Obliterating both the unilateral and homogeneous agreements that had characterized the previous season, as well as the free-labor system they had hoped to encode into law, planters found

themselves in the unhappy and, as one put it, "annoying" position of appealing to the interests and needs of workers who were
no longer slaves. Some, such as Thomas Steele, who hoped to acquire the services of "ten able bodied field hands," extended offers of fine fields, warm cabins, advances on the year's rations,
suits of new clothes, access to land for gardens, and occasionally
pastures for cattle and hogs. Not infrequently, planters offered to
make available larger lots of land, the right to grow staple crops,
and the mules and tools to work them. Others dangled promises
of schools for black children and the teachers to conduct them,
in hopes that they might attract sufficient numbers of workers
by catering to black people's dreams for their kids. William Kay,
the agent of the English-owned Georgia Land & Cotton Company, not only offered a schoolhouse but announced himself
fully prepared to equip it with books for the students and to
feed and house the teacher. Many also found themselves compelled to abandon the "heretofore" language that had been
a prominent feature of the 1865 agreements, replacing it with
exhaustively detailed descriptions of the chores they expected
workers to accomplish in the upcoming season. Freedpeople,
they realized, had run out of patience with ex-slaveholders' relentless and unending grip on their labor. Other planters gave up
as well their old but cherished command over time, guaranteeing, as Benjamin Yancey did, workers their Sundays and the right
to use them as they pleased. "They may have religious meetings,
once in the week, on each place," Yancey grudgingly conceded after nearly two weeks of dickering, "so long" as they do "not continue beyond [their] ordinary bed time."[26]

Former slaves may have shared a general dislike of planters'
productive and political plans for the future, but the solutions
they conceived of were anything but uniform. Confounding easy
assumptions about community, collectivity, identity, and even

race, the men who drove their old masters wild by driving very hard bargains used the agreements they produced to simultaneously reorder their lives on a much more personal basis.[27] Breaking free of the plantation societies into which they had been thrust often unwillingly in slavery, the freedpeople used the interlude between agricultural seasons to sort themselves by age, by aspiration, by friendship, by kinship, and in at least one case, by "colou[r]." Some agreed to work by the day, some by the month, some by the year, some by the task. Some accepted as compensation "1/4 of what is raised," some "1/2 of the net profits," some "$100 to $125 per year" along with "a piece of land, and the time to cultivate it, and the privilege of keeping and raising hogs, poultry &c." Many entered into agreements that guaranteed clothes, food, and cabins in addition to various combinations of cash or crop shares, or used them as a man named John did to reunite a family that had been scattered over much of the state. Others used their agreements to put distance between themselves and old enemies, not all of whom occupied the plantation "big houses." Take George, for example. Remembered by his old master as a "great coward" and convinced that "his enemies would . . . kill him," George fled the site of his enslavement—and the people who populated the quarters—for what he hoped would be safer employment on a neighbor's estate. Lewis and Julia did too, having held "their heads above the rest" in slavery, a habit that had earned them considerable unpopularity. It was the introduction of strangers who prompted others to take off or "work separate," though on one Sumter County estate, a relieved planter reported that with enough "high [money] & hard prying" he managed to keep the "old negroes" from leaving when the "'New' nigger[s]" arrived.[28]

The multitude of arrangements Daniel Horn made with his workers for the 1867 season stand as an example of the near-infinite variety of conditions and concerns former slaves brought to the bargaining table. Horn fielded a full complement of laborers, but the terms under which they agreed to work represented a broad, though hardly exhaustive, range of possibilities. They labored as sharecroppers and for share wages, as jobbers and month-hands for cash, as families, and as singles. Felix Rus, Jack Owens, and Simon Winn—who brought his wife with him into the contract—were the first to sign agreements with Horn, accepting a share-wage arrangement that gave them one-third of the year's crop along with a year's supply of "Bread & Wheat." Henry Cowan and his family, who arrived shortly thereafter, came onto the place in the capacity of sharecroppers— early pioneers of a system that would come to dominate the region in later years—taking as their compensation a part of what they raised on the New Ground field, remaining at the same time subject to Horn's beck and call for service anywhere else on the plantation. Crosby and his family (or "crowd," which was Horn's designation for kin who contracted together) came in on similar terms, but raised their compensation on a different corner of the place. Henry Ball worked for a combination of cash and free time: ten dollars and a half-Saturday off each month. Sally worked for "no pay but rations." Irene, who likewise seemed to bargain on her own behalf, commenced work for a relatively generous ten dollars a month and board. James Bryant, who joined the plantation fairly late in the spring, agreed to perform any work Horn assigned him in exchange for "1 suit of clothes," food to eat, a bed to sleep in, a hat for his head, shoes for his feet, and a year-end payment of seventy-five dollars. Still others came and went on a more irregular basis, working and earning as crops, seasons, and personal proclivities demanded.[29]

Without question, black women risked prying open a Pandora's box of problems when they vested their husbands, fathers, and brothers with contractual authority over their labor. As many came to discover, backing out of one form of oppression does not preclude backing into a wholly new one.[30] It was not partners, however, but planters who posed black women's most immediate problem. Alert to any measure that promised to restore to their plantations a part of slavery's old order, landowners quickly recognized the advantages that accrued to them under black women's free-labor scheme, for in affixing their marks to the documents they made for themselves and their families, black men found themselves conscripted into a role once reserved for overseers and plantation agents: "Regulat[ing] and Control[ling]" the day-to-day behavior of those for whom they had spoken and wrote. Thus it was that the freedmen who did freedwomen's bidding came to assume, however unwittingly, a legal and actionable obligation to ensure the full execution of the bargains that were returning their families to cotton's plantations. Most of these expectations lay half-hidden in agreements men accepted, revealing themselves only in the event of a dispute or a purported violation. But as planters became increasingly aware of the uses to which they could put the new system, they bound black men to their new duties with more definitive language, demanding, as did Daniel Palmer in the contract he made for the 1866 season, that the men who signed for "self & Family" govern the comportment and conduct of all who lived and labored aboard the region's plantations. "We the undersigned labors," promised Mathew Allin and Peter Gibson, "binds him self & family to commence work at Daigh Light, to remain on the plantation at all times, to take care of the stock, to render "Sutch service as the accasions & weather may require," and above all, to enforce and maintain "oderly quiet" whether at work in the fields or at home in the quarters.[31]

More planters came to see similar benefits in a system of family-based labor. Within just a few months, white Georgians who had respected the marriages of black people in slavery only to the extent that such unions had advanced slaveholders' interests, and who had previously talked about making marriage between former slaves a privilege to be conferred only on formal application, abruptly changed their minds. In the eyes of men who also thought it advisable to "establish the sir names of freedmen" as a means of identifying people who were no longer legally tied to an owner, the marriages of black people had suddenly become worth promoting. Rejecting a proposition that, when it was proffered in October 1865, would have prohibited former slaves from marrying before reaching their majorities and would have required prospective couples to obtain permission from "some religious society or minister of the gospel," state lawmakers roughly dismissed black people's own understandings about what constituted a legitimate marriage when they approved, and the governor put into law on March 9, 1866, a measure that declared legally wed all black Georgians then cohabiting as husband and wife. The only couples exempt from instant compliance were those who could prove the existence of multiple spouses. But theirs was the briefest reprieve. According to further clauses of a law that was part of a bundle designated the "Freedmen's Code," the man in such situations must "immediately select one of his reputed wives, with her consent, or the woman one of her reputed husbands, with his consent, and the ceremony of marriage between them will be performed." In an era still committed to the legal idea of *coverture*, the marriage code served former slaveholders' interests by reinforcing black men's authority over their wives and minor children. A measure designed to control as much as "civilize" the former slaves, its advantages were not likely lost on an Early County planter, who four days before the law went into effect entered into a contract that made the black men who signed it fully accountable for the productive and private behavior of their wives and children. "We agree to govern our families as well as possible," vowed Peter Blocker and several others, "aid[ing] our employer or agent to do so, to keep peace among ourselves," to "be promptly at our places at the hours of work," and "to help to have good order on the plantation."[32]

More than a few black men took those instructions too literally. Encouraged by planters and civilian Freedmen's Bureau agents who called on the male part of the labor force to make their wives mind, as well as by military officials who likewise let it be known that "husbands have the right and privilege to control their wives and fathers their minor children," freedmen who had been deeply steeped in slavery's brutalities occasionally lit into their children and wives with a gusto that alarmed even the most battle-hardened Yankee observers. Staking claims to their families in language brought forward from bondage, freedmen beat, kicked, cheated, punched, knifed, and sometimes murdered with gruesome impunity those whom they declared were the "only nigger[s]" they owned. In southwest Georgia, Elizabeth's husband knocked her repeatedly off of her feet; Ellen's threatened to kill her; Rhody's came close to putting out her eye; while Caroline's "ran up accounts" that consumed not only the entirety of his annual wage but the whole of hers too. Other husbands and fathers simply took off, responding to what one distressed Bureau official bemoaned as "the new order of affairs" by abandoning older wives, pregnant wives, and wives "with 3–4–6 children" to take up with "young women 'who are able to work.'"[33]

While desertion usually left none of the bruises of a physical beating, its impact on black women's lives was no less catastrophic. As abandoned wives and children discovered in short order, employers usually took a very dim view of black men's premature and unilateral departure from the workplace and considered black men's absence an actionable offense. Moreover, having lost the prized portion of a laboring family, few former slaveholders saw any reason to keep the remainder on their payrolls. Indeed, so convinced were most rural employers that the right to hire by the family conferred the right to fire by the family, only timely intervention on the part of a Bureau official could save a fugitive's wife and small children from immediate and uncompensated dismissal. Through such intervention, Mima Reid and the wives of Hamp Adams and James Jones managed to retain access to plantation resources and the fruits of their labor when their husbands took off on their own. Other freedwomen were not quite as lucky. No one, for instance, stepped forward to assist the wife of John Dawson, who lost not only her husband but her home on Middleton Phipps's plantation and the eight dollars per month she had expected to collect in wages at the end of the year. But when hauled before federal authorities to answer for infractions that were at once domestic and contractual, absconding husbands such as John Dawson and Hamp Adams usually bristled with self-righteousness, retorting, as did Joshua Cook when called upon to explain why he sent his wife reeling with what he described as "a slap for her impudent chat," that the women to whom they were wed, as well as the children they had fathered, constituted nothing more than a man's "own wrights and property" to use and discard as they pleased.[34]

Freedwomen refused to put up with such rubbish. Nor were they interested in losing their homes to black men's infractions. Trapped in a world in which planters continued to snub the labor of those who had often been slaveholders' first purchases, they vigorously defended themselves and their children from black men's assaults. Carving out their own civic and political space, one almost wholly devoted to patrolling the internal and gendered dynamics of the families on which so much depended, black women bombarded Bureau authorities with demands that the husbands, fathers, stepfathers, and uncles to whom they had bequeathed control of their labor repay them in full by "tak[ing] care of [them]" and their children. Pressing private and personal cases fifteen times more frequently than did black men, and positive that the privileges of marriage and family begot specific obligations, freedwomen relentlessly pursued the men who reneged on what women considered a reciprocal relation. With the assistance of Bureau agents who continued to prefer that husbands rather than the nation support wives and nonworking children, and availing themselves of the marriage codes that exslaveholders had enacted for significantly different purposes, angry women brought to heel the men who had let them down. They rousted husbands out of strangers' beds, brought charges against parents who took but failed to give, paraded battered bodies and torn dresses in front of horrified federal officials, and bitterly complained when male parents or guardians failed to "find [them] in clothes." Few escaped black women's wrath. Missouri pressed charges against the woman she caught "trifling" with her husband; Hely Ann took after her stepfather when he refused to supply her with blankets to put on her bed; and Dinah went to Edmund and simply deposited their child in his yard, telling the two-timing father to "take care of it." When conditions warranted, freedwomen also laid their cases before civil tribunals, all of which were composed entirely of white men. Lavinia did so after her husband drank up their wages and then threw her out of their house. Patsy Kendrick did too, though in her case the man she carried before the Dougherty County grand jury had once owned her and their three young children. Indeed, so completely did former slaves such as Mary, Maria, and Eveline corner the market on black people's domestic disputes, that Tom Arnet and John Saunders, the only two men across five Bureau jurisdictions who sought relief from misbehaving wives, stood out in a sea of complaining women who steadfastly insisted that men must "be made to help support" the families so many had formed before freedom.[35]

But while the occasional older son or daughter protested the right of a parent to broker and control his or her labor, impatient like teenagers Charles and Jefferson to be the masters of their own lives, married women stubbornly clung to the system to which they pinned their hopes in freedom. Their devotion hardly stemmed from any reservations about carrying personal and private disputes before courts of federal or civil law. Besides availing themselves of all legal means to bring wayward partners to heel—actions that revealed the most intimate details of their domestic lives—women wrangled repeatedly with estranged husbands over the custody of children. They complained about unpaid debts and about white men who beat them for no apparent reason. They reported rapes and attempted rapes, and spoke out against neighbors who broke down their doors and barged into their cabins. They fought hard to break counterfeit indentures and to recover stolen or destroyed property. Later, as electoral excitement swept across the region's plantations, inciting former slaveholders to new heights of violence, black women bore formal witness to a terror that more than matched that of their slave pasts: producing affidavits such as the one Mary Ballard dictated for the governor's benefit in July 1868 that detailed late-night assaults and identified for federal prosecution the disguised white men who mobbed and murdered Republican men. But women never spoke up in the open about any objections they may have privately harbored about the free-labor system they had collectively called into being. Of the nearly six hundred complaints registered by freedpeople with the Bureau officials stationed at the five busiest offices in southwest Geor-

gia—Albany, Thomasville, Bainbridge, Newton, and Cuthbert—
not one involved a freedwoman who rejected in principle the
right of a husband or parent to assign her labor to another.[36]

Women had good reason to hold their tongues. Unlike the older
teenagers, whose labor ex-slaveholders relished, black women
did significantly better with the assistance of black men. Wages
especially took a turn for the better when husbands and fathers
got involved. Whereas even childless and otherwise healthy young
women rarely coaxed more than a dollar or two or three a month
from their former masters when they contracted on their own
behalf, husbands and fathers repeatedly converted their own
productive capacity into wages for their wives and older children
that matched, or nearly matched, those commonly drawn by single men. Certainly Shadrach Williams did that, wangling a remarkable "three full shares" for himself, his wife, and their son
from ex-slaveholding planter Richard Davis. Henrietta Holmes
likewise had good reason to "promise and agree" to "cook wash
and Iron and render such other service as may be reasonably
required of her" for a Worth County white widow. In accordance
with the terms of the 1867 agreement hammered out in her
name by her husband Ben, Henrietta stood to receive a lavish $10
per month along with her rations, a wage no domestic could
hope to garner when she bargained alone. Lizzie received something comparable when her husband Levi took both her and
their daughter Eliza into a contract with a Baker County planter.
Together, the family anticipated collecting close to $250 at the
end of the season: $120 and $72 for Levi and Eliza, respectively,
and another $10 per month for Lizzie. Frank Adhame did even
better, snaring wages of $150 for himself, $120 for his wife, and
$80 for their son from William Moughan, an absentee land-
owner who operated a large estate in Dougherty County.[37]

Men's intervention was especially critical for women whose

health, age, or maternal situations prevented them from performing full-time labor. For the first of the former female slaves
to be flung aside by their old masters, nothing but a husband or
father or older brother or uncle stood between them and the fate
of Rachel, or Violet, who spent months "living in the woods . . .
in a miserable condition." Indeed, Juda Bond bore more than a
passing resemblance to the women whom planters decried. Juda
was a mother of four and expecting a fifth when planters began
recruiting new workers for the 1866 season, and it was obvious to
those who knew her that "owing principally to her peculiar state
of health or condition," Juda would not be able to work the entire season. Yet with her husband's assistance, Juda spent the year
in a cabin on a Dougherty County plantation, her young brood
received all the food they needed, and she earned fifty dollars
and three suits of clothes for the work she managed to wedge in
around maternal demands. Henry Thomas effected a similar
magic when he struck a bargain for a family composed of a wife
hampered by pregnancy and chronic ill-health, a fifteen-year-old
daughter capable of "work[ing] in the field [but] does half as
much work as a grown up person ought to do," and "two small
infant children—unable to do any work." Despite representing a
family the planter who hired them described as an "expense and
annoyance," Henry traded his own labor and that of his wife and
their older daughter for all "the produce raised on one acre of
good new land," a cash wage of $75 to $135 depending on the
price of cotton "on or before 15 Dec. next," and "4 or 5 hours
each day for" the care of their own little brood.[38]

The flexible terms under which Henry's wife returned to cotton's plantations became increasingly commonplace as families
returned to slavery's old quarters. Although employers remained
reluctant to engage women as regular, year hands, particularly
those whose capacity to labor was compromised by age, fertility,

and maternal commitments, they welcomed the opportunity to employ the female and youthful kin of their full-time workers on a seasonal or part-time basis. Adapting to free labor what had been in effect a general pattern of labor deployment practice in slavery, planters regarded the wives and middling-size children of their laboring men as a useful and easily accessible pool of exceedingly cheap surplus labor, "hir[ing] them by the week or the day" to perform in exchange for small, usually cash wages the same sort of seasonal work they had been put to as slaves. Thus it was that "Laura (John's wife)," the "female portion of Sheppard Waddels, colored, family," Betsy "and her Boy," and Henry Anderson's daughter Athy came to compose a significant part of a reconfigured rural workforce, dipping in and out of paid employment as their needs and those of their husbands or fathers' employers demanded. They operated the small plows, tended vegetable gardens, herded livestock, chopped weeds, shucked corn, assembled fences, milked cows, cooked meals, washed clothes, and ran endless errands. Above all, they picked each season's cotton, comprising as they had in the past the larger part of planters' harvesting crews. The wages married women earned through part-time employment rarely amounted to much, and seldom more than those commonly earned by their unmarried counterparts. But the $6.50 that Maria earned picking cotton on Perry Duncan's plantation, and the ten cents Sis collected for every load of straw she raked up for Daniel Horn, were doubly welcome additions to family incomes that rarely exceeded more than a few hundred dollars per year at most.[39]

Women and children benefited in other ways when men spoke up in their behalf at the bargaining table. Besides guaranteeing *"good board,"* housing, and frequently *"medicine* and *medical* attention" to the laboring parts of their families, the contracts brokered by men almost always included benefits that extended to those who worked part of the time or none of the time. Many freedmen, for instance, talked employers into furnishing rations and other supplies to the nonworking members of their families, as well as access to garden plots and woodlots and, not infrequently, guarantees of medical care. Some families received gratis allotments of shoes, hats, and, in at least one case, a new handkerchief—items enjoyed by workers and nonworkers alike. The terms varied tremendously from farm to farm, and between laboring families, depending on the size of the plantation, the quality of the land, the price projected for that season's cotton, and the number and capacities of the workers each family brought into the agreement. Thus in some instances employers might offer advancements of food, fuel, garden space, and medical care to one part of their crews of laboring kin, guaranteeing, as A. C. Turner did for the 1866 season, what amounted to a whole new wardrobe to one of the families in his employ along with their rations, while requiring others to feed and clothe themselves out of their own wages. Similarly, some planters provided rations to those who worked, while making garden space available for those who did not, and where small children and other nonworkers or part-time workers threatened to outnumber those who went to the fields each day, landowners generally expected the laboring part to pitch in and pay all or some of the support for those unable to pay for their own. But no matter how the details unfolded, and no matter whether women and children were fully employed, partially employed, or unemployed, those who returned to the plantations under the auspices of family-based labor agreements enjoyed at the absolute minimum "Houses to live in, [and] wood to burn," necessities few women could dream of obtaining if left to their own devices.[40]

Perhaps most important from the perspective of black women whose worlds had generally been encircled by plantation boundaries, men's obligations did not end at the bargaining table. What they sealed, they went on to enforce. Thus while women generally confined their formal complaints and civil disputes to the domestic side of the new plantation order, they insisted, as Patsy did when she demanded "in the name of her husband Squire" that her former employer relinquish her overdue wages, that it fell to black men to hold their old masters to contractual clauses. Positioning themselves often literally between the families for whom they had bargained and those who had purchased their labor, freedmen spilled off the plantations and into the region's small towns and military encampments to protest against planters who failed to honor their part of labor's agreements. Outnumbering female complainants by three to one, aggrieved husbands and fathers bore witness to planters' continuing use of eviction to discipline and control their former slave forces, of workloads that exceeded contractual limits, and of planters who deployed workers in ways that once again threatened the integrity of black people's families. Black men complained as well of bosses who issued inadequate tools and who provided mules that were too old or slow to keep up with the crop. James Alexander sought Bureau intervention when his family's employer reneged on a contractual promise to permit the workers to grow melons in the sugar cane field; while countless others complained about poor provisions or planters who charged usurious prices for syrup and bacon, or simply helped themselves to unguarded pigs and produce in an effort to see their families fed. Men defended their families from other forms of abuse as well: bitterly objecting when planters presumed to usurp what black men and black women considered their parental rights; shielding sisters, daughters, and wives from former slaveholders' blows; and protecting the pregnant, the nursing, and the "afflicted" from excessive demands on their labor. These defensive maneuvers carried considerable risk, as Jessie discovered when he burst in and broke up an altercation involving his wife and the white man who occupied the same plantation. He would have come to report the incident himself, a friend reported days later to the federal commander at Starkville, but "he taking the part of his wife Culpepper shot him."[41]

Most of all black men fought to collect for their families the wages they had dickered so vigorously to get. Settlement disputes were the single largest category of complaints brought before southwest Georgia's Bureau officials by former slaves, and they were also the single largest category of complaints made by black men, constituting more than 46 percent of the cases they called to federal attention. Going to bat for their wives and children, for sisters and brothers, and occasionally for an elderly parent or a parcel of grandkids—which is what Charles Perry Sr. did the spring of 1867 when he confronted his family's former employer on behalf of thirty-two adults, teens, and toddlers—black men were as relentless in their pursuit of defaulting bosses as women were of fugitive men. Effectively carving the state into two differently gendered dimensions, black men came forward in droves to demand that planters be made to pay in full for the services of "Self & wife" or "Self & family." It was a daunting project, as those who closed out the 1865 season empty-handed had already discovered. Memories would continue to distort, parties would continue to scatter as jobs pulled people in different directions, and account books would continue to come up missing critical pages. Nonetheless black men descended daily on Bureau offices to seek federal assistance in resolving claims to long-overdue wages. Indeed, such was the pressure black men brought to bear on the region's Bureau officials that by May 1866, at least one official—the agent who had charge of the office at Smithville, Lee County—decided to throw in the towel and give up his commission. "It would take 40 agencies in every district, yea an agent for every negro," he groaned in what amounted to his resignation letter, to keep up with the litany of complaints that poured into his office from workers who wanted their pay.[42]

But rather than improving, as black people advanced their own claims on freedom and free labor, the problems of settlement grew steadily more daunting. In Georgia, where lawmakers apparently were not satisfied with tampering with black people's marriages, the state widened its gaze to include contractual relations. Concealed within what appeared to be a straightforward plan to organize a system of county courts, the proposal captured the intent, if not the identical language, of the by-then defunct "Freedmen's Code," that unratified body of 1865 law that would have put the state at landowners' disposal. Constituting a deliberate, if veiled, attempt to derail black workers' growing insurgency and to prevent federal authorities from "prying into" what many ex-slaveholders declared were private—not public—affairs, lawmakers defined the courts and their operation in a way that conferred on locally elected judges and all-white juries near-exclusive authority over any labor agreement that fell under their jurisdiction. Not all planters availed themselves of an act that effectively restored to landowners and their judicial confederates the right to exploit their workers much as they had in the past. But numbers of them did, filing their 1866 contracts with judges who, along with their juries, had been vested by state legislators with the authority to decide and enforce "all issues of fact," and who were not particularly well known for unbiased neutrality when it came to cases that involved former slaves. Indeed, reported one unhappy observer, most of those who occupied seats in the local judiciary routinely showered favor on ex-slaveholding planters, refusing repeatedly to "adjust or remove even the grossest of inequities" and allowing to stand labor agreements that were notorious for their excessively low wages, exhaustive demands, and rations inadequate to meet workers' most basic needs. Bureau agents did what they could to mitigate the more baneful effects of what came to be known as "Court contracts," attempting in many cases to adjudicate them just as they would those that had been registered with federal officials: issuing summonses, examining witnesses, checking the math in planters' accounts, seizing crops to force payment, and occasionally tossing defaulters into jail. Some considered calling out federal soldiers, hoping that a show of force might convince former slaveholders to treat black workers with a much-needed degree of justice. E. F. Kirksey in Stewart County did not bother to enforce the more egregious contracts at all, choosing instead to nullify agreements that lacked Bureau approval and advising black workers that they could leave to seek new employment at any time.[43]

Freedmen's Bureau officials would continue to badger planters in the name of ex-slaves until the agency ceased operations two years later. But by the time plows began to turn up the ground in preparation for planting the 1866 crop, it was growing clear that the black men who struggled to patrol the employment relation, and the black women who held them tightly on task, had seen quite enough. Deeply dissatisfied with the turn freedom had taken since they had dominated the bargaining tables so effectively at the first of the year, and fully convinced that they "would not be dealt fairly with" in any encounter with the new county courts, southwest Georgia's former slaves turned their gaze outward, joining forces first figuratively, then literally, with a vast political mobilization that had already begun to move the nation in an unexpectedly radical direction. Thus even as planters schemed to restore old forms of power in the guise of a bilateral agreement, and as Bureau authorities rallied to workers' defense, those who had waited until weeks after the Confederate surrender for their first taste of freedom fixed their attention on a much larger prize. Fully confirmed in their initial conviction that to carry a case before an impartial jury or judge constituted a key feature of freedom, one that effaced the inequities of slavery, southwest Georgia's black men and black women now understood that laws were themselves the products of people. And so long as the people who wrote and enforced those laws were ideological kith and kin to the people who had once owned them, the nation's ex-slaves would remain caught somewhere short of the dreams they still kept alive in their minds.

5

To Make

a Laborers'

State

Political movements, like race and place and other human creations, have their own histories. As the circumstances that give rise to various constellations of people, ideas, and practices change, so too do the processes, principles, and purposes of collective mobilization. Inherently unstable, politics is seldom a linear matter. Rarely is it a broadly homogeneous matter. And nowhere were both characteristics more visible than in the era of black Reconstruction. Just as nearly all former slaves celebrated emancipation as an opportunity to build schools, organize churches, reconstitute badly damaged families, and accumulate the foundations of a material autonomy, they also celebrated the collapse of their old masters' power. But there the commonalities come to a halt: sharing an opponent cannot be understood as sharing a solution. For the nation's former slaves did not share a singular vision of the state they yearned so badly to call their own, nor did they agree on their relative positions within it. They were especially divided—as women, as men, as workers, as property owners, as producers of the South's great staples, as people with their own distinctive histories—about the purposes to which they aspired to put their freshly minted civil and political institutions.[1] Thus it was in the aftermath of enslavement on cotton's newer ground, where the rhythms and routines of a peculiarly gendered and excessively oppressive regime—one that rose in a hurry and collapsed in the space of a few generations—had held sway, that black men and black women fashioned their own unique body of political dreams. Hardly respectful enthusiasts of a free-labor system their old masters too eagerly wielded against them, schooled long enough in freedom's hard knocks to know the elusive nature of a landed independence, and drawing on the skeletal material and institutional resources that their history had bequeathed them, southwest Georgia's black men and black women would project, and nearly produce, their own variation of a wage workers' state.

Even before the end of the Civil War, former slaves had begun meeting in community and statewide conventions to declare their belief that freedom ought to bestow upon them the same civil and political rights enjoyed by white Americans. As southern state governments reorganized under the auspices of Andrew Johnson's plan for Reconstruction, the black call for institutional action took on new urgency. The president had required that the reconstituted governments be composed of men capable of meeting the terms of his amnesty proclamation, and that they "put into force all laws of the United States." All other decisions, including what constituted a citizen and the spectrum of rights such an individual could exercise, were matters best left to the states themselves. "The said convention[s], when convened, or the legislature[s] that may be thereafter assembled" retained the right to "prescribe the qualification of electors, and the eligibility of persons to hold office under the constitution and law of the state,—a power," Johnson reminded his national audience, that "the people of the several states composing the Federal Union have rightfully exercised from the origin of the government to the present time." It was a power the newly restored southern governments exercised with unsavory and often brutal enthusi-asm. Indeed, if the first discriminatory "black codes" passed in late 1865 by white lawmakers in Mississippi and South Carolina were any indication, former slaves could expect little more from the Johnson-sponsored state governments than the few and sharply constrained rights that had been extended to free people of color under slavery, and a future confined to the fields they had cultivated in bondage, under terms dictated if not by their employers, then by the state itself.[2]

Meeting in the wake of the national uproar that greeted the publication of Mississippi's and South Carolina's openly asym-metrical constitutions, Georgia's lawmakers toyed with similar measures but acted with greater restraint. Still, the codes they drafted were hardly less discriminatory in practice, construed as they were by men wed to the notion that capital must control labor. Rather than specifying in exhaustive detail the social and economic place former slaves would occupy in the free South, Georgia simply assigned black men and black women to the margins of civil life. No "negros, mulattoes, mestizoes, and their descendants, having one-eighth negro or African blood in their veins," regardless of prior status or condition of birth, would rise beyond a third-class citizenship, the new constitution an-nounced. "Citizens" and "Aliens" exercised greater ranges of civil and legal privileges than "Persons of Color." Black Georgians might make contracts, sue and be sued, inherit, purchase, lease, sell, hold and convey real and personal property—privileges that had been categorically denied to slaves and held only par-tially by free people of color in the years before secession. They won the right to marry before the law (or in their churches), and their children would stand in relation to them as white children did to their parents. Those rights, however, marked the extent of their privileges. Black people might bear witness in civil cases "whereto a person of color is a party, and in all criminal cases wherein a person of color is defendant," but they could not bear witness in cases involving only white people, or hold elective office. Most important, black Georgians would not be able to vote. White men continued to command the heights of civil order: they held the judgeships, made the arrests, and as jurors, interpreted and applied the laws they wrote. In the space of a few legislative pages, the Georgians who took their seats under Johnson's Reconstruction plan conveyed what had been the master's sovereignty directly into the hands of a state they controlled.[3]

Black Georgians, like their counterparts across the former Confederacy, expected something else. The law, they believed, should operate impersonally, not as the handmaiden of former masters and current employers. Even before white legislators concluded their deliberations, black delegates began gathering in Augusta to debate an alternative vision of citizenship and black rights. Scarcely nine months after the Confederate surrender, former free people of color and ex-slaves convened from across the state to discuss their futures as free people and as citizens. Guided by a handful of Savannah-area ministers (many of whom had obtained their freedom by birth or by purchase long before the Civil War) as well as a smaller number of white northerners (most notably John Emory Bryant, a Maine-born Republican who had served a short stint as a Freedmen's Bureau official in Augusta, and General Davis Tillson, the Freedmen's Bureau assistant commissioner for Georgia), more than one hundred delegates representing eighteen counties threaded their way cautiously into an arena hitherto reserved wholly for white men.[4]

The delegates spent the next four days devising a freedom— and a citizenship—more to their liking. Largely propertied men in their own right, they were ambivalent if not outright hostile to schemes of land confiscation and redistribution. This conservative tendency prompted them to plot a course that avoided deliberate engagement with the problems confronting black workers, emphasizing economic advancement, education, and the limited expansion of the civil and political rights already conferred rather than the balance of power in the fields around them. "We had not come to hold a *Secession* convention," the delegates assured one another and attentive white reporters, "but as free men, we have met to ask for free laws, [and] we mean to seek justice for men irrespective of color, or condition." Addressing a state legislature that was due to resume, the delegates noted pointedly that "the laws which now govern us, [are] oppressive and cruel, [and] we want them changed."[5]

Reminding white lawmakers of black Georgians' moderation during the war years, the delegates pleaded for the enactment of laws designed not simply to meet present needs but also to promote the future prosperity of both the formerly enslaved and the former enslavers, though not in a way that necessarily privileged the more radical of freedpeople's demands. Having already revealed a healthy respect for the rights of property, their words reassured, if not pleased, the white men who made up their audience. For what the black delegates had in mind resonated more clearly with the aspirations of the landowners than with those of ex-slaves. In language that recalled the unilateral contracts of 1865, the January delegates condemned idleness, vagrancy, and pauperism, and asserted that industrious, diligent labor, not sloth or even gifts of land, was the "talismanic of power." Former slaves, they insisted, were eager to work "as heretofore," resuming on the basis of wages familiar places in the state's fields, workshops, kitchens, and laundries. Those who balked would be compelled, if not by agents of the Freedmen's Bureau, then by the black delegates themselves. All that the convention participants asked in return was "clemency and kind treatment" for black labor, representation on juries deciding cases involving former slaves, a "conditional suffrage" that would give educated black men the "privilege to vote in all cases where our interest is at stake," and color-blind accommodations on the state's railways.[6]

Hardly advocates of a full-scale assault on the categories of citizenship proffered by white legislators, the delegates at least announced themselves determined to win for their constituents the privileges they proposed. Naming themselves somewhat misleadingly the Georgia Equal Rights Association (GERA), the delegates vowed to expand their organization across the state, establishing county and subcounty chapters replete with presidents, vice presidents, treasurers, chaplains, secretaries, and "Examining Committee[s]" whose primary duty would be to evaluate applicants for admission, sorting the worthy from the unworthy. At an April meeting of the executive council, the delegates admitted that obtaining a "reciprocal right of representation" would be difficult. While they could do all they could by "precept and example," they decided that, simultaneously, "[we must] avail ourselves of all the means, such as organization, petitioning, sending a delegate to congress, &c., whereby our condition and claims as a people may be kept before the country and its rulers." Not even violence was out of the question. If white southerners refused to volunteer political space for their black neighbors, the latter would take it outright.[7]

The GERA spread rapidly. Transported beyond the Augusta meeting hall by delegates as they returned to home communities, by traveling emissaries selected for that purpose by the state committee, and by white newspaper reporters eager to share with their readers the audacity of the recently freed, news of the organization and the purposes it served captured the attention of former slaves and free people of color. Joining informally in some communities with chapters of the Union League of America, a secretive political club organized in the North during the Civil War to advance the Republican cause, local GERAs appeared by April in Macon, Savannah, Augusta, and the counties around them. The association advanced westward and southward, showing up by October 1866 in more than a third of Georgia's 131 counties.[8]

The GERA, along with the Union League that caught a ride in its wake, found a receptive audience among southwest Georgia's former slaves. A year that had begun on an auspicious note had soured steadily as the weeks passed and crops sprouted. Workers and planters who had anticipated that the new generation of contracts, with their more specific and tailored terms and with the protections they extended to black women, would resolve many of the disputes and tensions of the previous year found themselves proved wrong. Former slaves and ex-masters continued to fumble as they felt their way into their new roles as wage laborers and employers. Ex-slaves who had exercised a novel say in the making of the agreements under which they labored chafed at the subordination and dependency inherent in wage work. It bore too much resemblance to slavery. Planters gave them good reasons to believe so. Almost to a man (and the employing woman), employers scoffed at the possibility that the reward of wages could replace the sting of a lash, and laughed away as a northern fiction the notion that a harmony of interests linked capital and labor together in cooperative alliance. Violence, freely and personally applied, not plentiful and promptly paid wages, was the surest method of making laborers work, they contended. Contracts secured landowners the necessary labor, but once signed, hired workers were theirs to use, abuse, and punish as they had their slaves. Selling the most recalcitrant was no longer possible, they sourly admitted, but most clung to other forms of coercion. "A negro is like a mule," an Early County man explained patiently to a Bureau official. He "will not do anything except being wipped." Another planter, aggrieved by the extent to which black men and black women had imposed their own sensibilities on the year's contracts, expressed similar sentiments when he groused that laborers had for the briefest of moments controlled capital, but predicted that soon, when capital regained its natural ascendancy over labor, the world would return to rights. Workers disagreed. Sparks flew and blood sometimes flowed as laborers stalled, fell mysteriously ill, fought back, or quit altogether when called upon to perform services not spelled out in their contracts, and when planters attempted to extend their authority beyond the workplace. They were "determined," remarked a frustrated planter, "to have their own way irrespective of their or mine interest."[9]

Tensions built. Planters who at the beginning of the year had expressed their satisfaction with the terms they had struck, the general prospects for the coming crop, and their laborers for "aworking verry well" began to speak within weeks of a creeping "demoralization." Workers, they moaned, were becoming recalcitrant, reluctant to obey orders, slower to go to the fields, and quicker to leave them. Scarcely two months into the new year, Malachai Timmerman, overseer on one of Benjamin Yancey's Dougherty County plantations, launched into a steadily intensifying litany of grievance. The crops were looking well, and the planting progressing as planned, but, he said, "I have some little complaint to State to you in reference to the freedm[e]n." "The Boy Larkin," he commenced in a report to his boss, "is the triflingest boy that I Ever had any thing to do with." When assigned to the plow, Larkin abused the mule. Transferred to the trash gang, he worked only when watched. And he was not the only thorn in Timmerman's side. "The Boy Green was verry careless" with his work. "The Boy Bennett Mallory" performed scarcely any labor at all. The infection deepened. By mid-March, Timmerman admitted that "all or moast" of the workers were "hard down on me." "They don't like me atall nor they wont like any person that want them to do there duty." Old Ben, part of the "Mallory set . . . a rough set," had by then transitioned from torpor to trouble, a development that provoked Timmerman to write him off as "a contrary old buger."[10]

Other planters shared Timmerman's growing dismay. The workers under the charge of Thomas Cooper, another Dougherty County overseer, feigned illnesses that tended to take turns for the worse the more disagreeable the work assignments became. "Some of them fownd Monday," he recorded in a springtime report, "that I was going to shelling corn & they lade up & as soon as we was done they came out," magically cured by the cessation of shelling. Others quibbled about rations. "Some [want] all meat & no syrup & others want it mixet." Some simply helped themselves, or so Cooper suspected, as he documented a diminishing return on the corn he sent to be milled. "We are having corn stold," he owned up to his employer, "either at the mill nor on the road." "[I] mist out of the last milling 6 Bushels of meale cant tell ho got it" despite measuring it into and then out of the wagon. To top it off, "oald Easter Sam" was driving Cooper to distraction, "no man can pleas him & he is always ready for a fuss." "Begging and hiring cannot make them do better," opined a mid-May correspondent to the *Dawson Weekly Journal*. "Some are quitting their employers, and we fear many more will follow their example." "The freedmen," the writer concluded in language that could just as easily have issued from Malachai Timmerman's pen, "do not work as well as they have been."[11]

Verbal sparring escalated into shooting frays as planters, frustrated by freedpeople who refused to be treated as slaves, turned back once again to management techniques perfected on slavery's plantations. Flaunting Freedmen's Bureau orders forbidding the use of violence, they uncoiled their whips, cocked their pistols, and hauled out their trace chains—heavy iron links designed to hitch teams to wagons but proven suitable by past experiment for hitching black men (and sometimes black women) to trees for beatings. Skeptical that the state and local governments they controlled could replace the personal sovereignty of a master, white men took it upon themselves individually and collectively to discipline black workers much as they had in the past. Timmerman "slaped one of old man Bens gals afew times," and gave thought to using the shotgun he had been toting to the fields since January. Fists, feet, and sticks flew on Sam Field's Terrell County plantation, all aimed at the black employees. A Stewart County employer broke an employee's jaw not once, but twice; a Randolph County planter whipped one of his female employees before hanging her by her thumbs; and John Jones flung an axe into Louisa Parom's back after he caught her using the wrong bridle on one of the plantation mules. "It is considered a wonder she was not killed," mused the Bureau official before whom Louisa presented her bleeding body.[12]

When individual acts fell short of intended goals, "secret clans," self-styled "cavalries," and roving bands of thugs did the work for them. Reminiscent of the somewhat more legitimate militias that had terrorized workers the previous December, mobs of "regulators" swept through the springtime countryside, usually by night, frequently disguised. One suspected nightrider was caught skulking around with a woman's dress draped over his arm; others blackened their faces. Bordering on the mercenary, they sometimes sold their talents for terror for the going rate of forty or fifty dollars per ride. The more magnanimous offered their services gratis. While most operated in the communities they called home, doing the dirty work of neighbors and kin, at least one gang commuted in from Alabama, crossing the Chattahoochee to wreak havoc on the Georgia side of the river. Some, such as the "Black Horse" cavalry that patrolled the plantations in Stewart County, were fairly stable organizations that conducted ride after regular ride. Others were more ad hoc, assembling on a case-by-case basis to conduct onetime assaults. Often these practices were mixed and matched, tailored to meet specific needs. Such was the case on a Randolph County plantation when a simple slapping failed to bring the workers into line. Taking her cues from neighborhood practices, the owner— a widow—recruited outside muscle to do the job in her stead. Two hours after midnight, on the first Monday in June, a mob of thinly disguised male white neighbors burst into Caroline and William Perrin's cabin, dragged them from their beds, stripped them of clothes, and then whipped them with lengths of cowhide. Pregnant Caroline received 350 lashes on her bare back and legs. William said he was warned that if he reported the whippings he "would be taken where nobody would hear of me."[13]

Going to the law did remarkably little to stem the violence that swept the plantations in the spring and summer of 1866. Black victims who sought justice in civil courts discovered quickly just how limited in effect were the rights conferred on them by the late constitutional convention, especially after Andrew Johnson vetoed a congressional bill to extend the life of the Freedmen's Bureau and Davis Tillson returned jurisdiction over all but the most petty cases to civil tribunals. It was a sequence of events that further tipped the balance of civil power into white Georgians' hands. In an environment where the solicitor general of the southwest Georgia circuit shot holes in one of his own employees in lieu of registering a formal complaint, case after case withered and died. White prisoners "escaped" (a particular problem along the Chattahoochee River, given the proximity of Alabama), witnesses recanted their stories, plaintiffs turned up dead, and judges empowered grand juries to evaluate on their own the validity of the "Colored testimony" brought forth. Civil officials violated military orders by releasing white prisoners, often on the grounds that no provision had been made to feed them, and violated them again by chaining black men to jail floors, leaving them in that position for months awaiting trials that might never occur. Sheriffs passed sentences against black people on their own authority, courts ignored bills of indictment, and black defendants when asking permission to bring witnesses on their behalf were instructed by civil authorities "to 'hush up.'" If black people did by some happy chance gain entrance to courtrooms, judges regularly turned bruised and bloody defendants into victims, and plaintiffs into aggressors. It was a juridical sleight of hand that in one instance transformed the slightly built female victim of a knife attack by her employer into an attempted murderer. Though how the small cook could have managed to flip her employer's wife out a window defeated the imagination of the Bureau official who related the case to his superiors.[14]

Prospects for fair hearings and evenhanded justice became even more elusive in communities where civil officials spent their nights riding with the mobs and "black horse cavalries." The gang commanded by Stewart County judge Robert Walton left a bloody wake as it crisscrossed the landscape, enforcing plantation discipline more generally, lining its own pockets specifically. His particular outfit would descend on plantation quarters to raid black homes of pigs and poultry, shooting down anyone who stood in their way, then mutilate the bodies to drive

their point home. Walton acted with special venom. On one occasion, under cover of performing legitimately as a member of
a sheriff's posse investigating a plantation shooting affair, the
judge held a bound black prisoner by the collar with one hand
and fired five shots into the defenseless man's body with the
other. One of his colleagues used a ramrod to drag the entrails of
another freedman through the dirt. Walton eventually fled for
Texas and was replaced by a man who while serving as prosecut-
ing attorney had limited his arrests to former slaves. By April
1866, black corpses were piling up at a rate of two to three a
week. Numbers of other freedpeople simply vanished—either
dead or fugitives from what one Bureau agent described as a
"hellish spirit of murder and robbery." Hardly surprising, former
slaves' confidence in the legal system they had inherited in freedom plummeted, monopolized as it was by men they believed
were bent on their oppression.[15]

Former slaves thought scarcely better of many of the local
Freedmen's Bureau officials. Some like the subassistant commissioners at Thomasville and Cuthbert—officers in the Union
army until assigned to duty with the Freedmen's Bureau—kept
their constituents' trust. More problematic, however, were those
recruited from the civilian population. From the outset, the
Freedmen's Bureau had been hampered by a lack of funding and
insufficient personnel. These were problems exacerbated by the
president's policy of land restoration and by the rapid demobilization of the Union army, problems felt across the former Confederacy. Though the original plan had been to borrow officers
from the Union army, a speedy postwar demobilization not only
cost the Bureau serving agents—including C. C. Richardson and
Gideon Hastings, the first two agents assigned to southwest
Georgia—it also depleted the ranks from which replacements
would have been drawn. In an attempt to deal with what was fast

becoming a critical shortfall in staff, Georgia's assistant commissioner, along with his counterpart in Florida, turned to the civilian population for assistance. In an October 1865 speech before the state constitutional convention, Tillson urged the delegates to nominate likely candidates to fill what were more than two hundred empty posts across the state. What he got were 244 men whose interests generally lay more with the planters than with the ex-slaves, and more with the South than with the North. Grand juries and citizens' committees frequently nominated those "having a thorough knowledge of the character and disposition of the freedman," which when translated usually meant large landowners and former slaveholders or those sympathetic to both. Others chose the utterly inept—drunkards, the convicted "Horsethief," and the dull of mind—hoping evidently that an incompetent agent would reward planters with more freedom to act. Whatever their qualifications, most shared the Lee County (civilian) agent's belief that Tillson had appointed them "to keep [all freedpeople] straight."[16]

Complaints surfaced immediately. Native-born agents, argued freedpeople, wanted nothing less than to reduce black men and black women to old positions of "crouching servility." "Pander[ing] to the exacting whims of our employers," or so contended later spokesmen for black southwest Georgians, civilian agents used coercive means to entrap them into exploitative contracts, including hiring out or apprenticing children without parents' permission and turning a blind eye to, if not openly advocating, the use of corporal punishments. Some used their posts to overcharge freedpeople "from *Five* to *twenty dollars*" for services rendered or to manufacture new fees with which to pad their pockets. The assistant commissioner's office refused to approve inequitable contracts or those that paid a dismally low wage, regularly returning for revision those brought to their attention, but it was impossible for Tillson's small staff to review every decision reached by the new corps of civilian agents. Thus Joseph Taylor of Randolph County took advantage of his office to advance his family's fortunes by hiring out freedpeople at bargain-basement prices to his brother and father and then beating any worker who objected. When freedpeople brought reports of contract violations and white aggression, civilian agents sometimes stalled, holding cases over for weeks on end—that is, if they reported them at all. Others turned questions of punishment back over to the very men (and women) of whom the black people complained. Taking the opposite tack, civilian agents such as S. A. McClendon took it upon themselves to serve as judge, jury, and executioner, handing out corporal punishments that involved long stints of hanging by thumbs, bucking and gagging, and whipping. They profited from the fines they imposed, and not infrequently used their posts to secure labor for their own plantations. W. B. Walker, one of three civilian agents in Terrell County, offended even his colleagues by pulling a knife on another civilian agent when the man questioned him about the low wages he sent a young freedwoman out to work for.[17]

One of the worst offenders in southwest Georgia was J. C. DeGraffenried of Miller County. A self-proclaimed enemy of those white men who had refused to elect him to a lieutenant's post in the Confederate army, he accepted a position with the Freedmen's Bureau precisely to watch old enemies squirm before his new power, and to "make [as] big [a] cotton crop with the freedmen" that his office allowed him to command. The rule of law fell by the wayside. All a hapless freedperson needed do to bring the wrath of DeGraffenried down upon his or her head was to "make [the agent] mad."[18]

Freedpeople who flatly refused to be subjected either to "the overseer's cudgel" or the "'bureau's' ball and chain," talked back, fought back, and, with increasing frequency as it became clear that they were their own best advocates, shot back. Plantation quarters fairly bristled with weapons. Freedpeople purchased some from peddlers; others transformed everyday tools into defensive arms. Nearly always, those weapons of war were wielded by men. Dandridge "got [himself] . . . a double Bbl gunn." Frank Baley equipped himself with a musket. Jim favored knives. Allen Calhoun preferred fire, fashioning a torch from a stick and, not the least bit ironically, scraps of fabric from his dead wife's dress. They used them, too. Big Harris sank an axe into the head of a robber. Jim stabbed the Clay County sheriff to death rather than submit to the "buck[ing]" the officer had come to inflict. Allen Calhoun crept up to the barn of his wife's last employer, intent on burning out the man who had killed her. According to one admittedly biased observer, freedpeople had come into the habit of "Shooting their guns, and Pistols promiscuously day and night."[19]

Open warfare is more effective when conducted in groups, and with gangs of ruffians marauding and murdering their way through the countryside, former slaves wasted little time organizing among themselves more systematic and collective responses to white violence. They started on the plantation, redeploying by night cooperative relationships perfected in the fields and workshops by day, often organizing around men who, like the "principal contractor" on a Thomas County plantation, put a workplace authority to community good. So it was on the Rood plantation in eastern Stewart County late one February night, 1866, when a black man from a neighboring estate arrived in a hurry, bearing warning of a gang of robbers on the prowl and on their way. Word circulated quickly through the quarters, and the freedmen armed themselves before slipping back into the darkness of their cabins. All that is, but Big Harris. He stood alone in the yard, greeting the gang when it rushed into the yard on horseback. When asked by the leader "what he was doing out with his ax in his hand so late out," Harris explained he was guarding against robbers. "And when asked what he would do when a Robber came to his house? Answered 'I would kill him.'" With that, the interrogator cocked his pistol menacingly in the direction of Harris's head, and the other black men, hearing the ominous click of steel on steel, rushed to their friend's defense. A shouting match suddenly gave way to a shooting, shoving, striking match. Within moments, the leader lay dying, felled by Harris's axe. Another robber was mortally wounded, his "scull" cracked open. The third, caught by his coattails as he tried to scamper to safety, was beaten to a survivable pulp.[20]

Mobilization for the good of community was no more susceptible to confinement at home than were rumors of high wages and bad bosses. Black men's efforts to launch a collective defense of themselves and their families breached the boundaries of home plantations. Armed with any manner of items— clubs, muskets, pistols, shotguns, sticks—freedmen rose up, as one critical white man observed in a not so subtle attempt to obscure a problem of class under the veil of race, "to defend their color against whites." In Thomasville, the arrest of a group of freedwomen on charges of stealing a few pigs triggered a masculine response that sent the town sheriff racing for shelter. Before the armed men were through for the day, they had halted the arrest and backed the sheriff into the office of the local Freedmen's Bureau authority, where the freedmen forced him to account for his conduct. Not long after, a body of black men came to the defense of July, a field hand, after his employer accosted him for purportedly beating a mule. Tired of the constant harangues, July had turned on Henry Hardee, daring the man to whip him.

Not willing to tangle one-on-one with the slightly built but demonstrably fierce July, Hardee rode off to scrounge up reinforcements. But as he made his rounds of white homes, word of July's predicament preceded him. Zeal, the aforementioned "principal contractor," had overheard Hardee's complaint and with a speed the white man could not hope to match, dispatched couriers across the neighborhood, into quarters and through fields, recruiting a workers' army that far outmatched the puny "two or three" white men who heeded the call of Hardee.[21]

It was with reason that the GERA, and the Union Leagues that shadowed it into the Georgia countryside, found fertile soil among the former slaves when the two organizations launched their drives across the southwest corner of the state. Deeply invested in what often took the form of a life-and-death battle with former slaveholders over the balance of power between labor and capital, black men and black women had already found wanting the impartial law they thought came with freedom. They had also begun mobilizing on their own, adopting patterns of organization rehearsed and refined in the fields to an escalating contest about the meaning of government and the problems of equity. But on their own, southwest Georgia's former slaves could wage only a holding action. Battlefield victory was no guarantee the war might be won. After all, Big Harris, the catalyst of action and wielder of axes, landed on death row, convicted of murder rather than acquitted for reasons of self-defense.[22] Success, former slaves realized, hinged on carrying their struggle out of their neighborhoods, beyond their communities, and into the spaces of state. Until just men, unbiased men, men willing to take the perspective of laborers as well as that of landowners, pinned on the sheriff's badge, sat on the juries, and decided the cases before them, black workers would stumble under the weight of capital. Making cotton on freedpeople's terms required making a new state.

Their chance came with the arrival of external, statewide, and nationwide organizations. Committed to correcting at least a portion of the civil imbalances imposed by the late constitutional convention, the "traveling emissaries" whom the GERA launched out of Augusta—and the more radical Union League representatives who traveled in near tandem—found eager recruits in the fields. As spring edged into summer, rumors began to circulate among southwest Georgia's black and white residents of a freedmen's association devoted to the cause of equal rights, civil rights, and, to the dismay of former masters, political rights. Former slaves were overheard by nervous white people murmuring in Newton, Albany, Cuthbert, Dawson, and the plantation districts surrounding them, about the newly arriving societies and their implications for freedom. In Thomasville, the county's "sable population" convened a meeting on a Monday evening in late May to elect a delegate to represent their interests at an upcoming council meeting of the GERA. Rejecting the candidacy of a blacksmithing former free person of color who had purportedly given money to the Confederate cause, they elected a man who promised to solve the problems of civil (in)justice.[23]

The locus of activity seemed centered, however, on the Whitlock plantation near Albany. It was there, six miles south of town, that 150 black colonists from Wilkes County had resettled in mid-January, bringing with them babies, household furniture, farm tools, supplies of seed and tools, and, to the horror of their new (white) neighbors, a formal affiliation with the GERA. One of their leaders, indeed one of the two men who had scouted the colonists' path the previous fall, Wallace S. W. Sherman, had been a delegate to the January convention and would return in April to meet with the GERA's governing council. When the colonists organized their own chapter of the state association shortly after arriving in Dougherty County, they elevated another of their original leaders, Lawrence Speed, to the presidency. News of their activities, which included raising funds for the support of the indigent and aged, the establishment of a school for their children, and the cultivation of flourishing crops of cotton and corn, captured attention from as far away as Thomas County, fifty-some miles to the south. New members joined by the score. When John Griffin paid his fifty-cent initiation fee "sometime the spring of 1866," he added his name to a list some nine hundred long.[24]

Membership transformed and emboldened black workers. Acceptance into the GERA or a chapter of the Union League made available to former slaves an infrastructure that transcended the fields and quarters, enabling them to mount a more effective challenge to planters' constrained variation of freedom. For those who had sat out the war on their owners' estates, enlisting in one of the new political organizations did for them what military service had done for thousands of others: it confirmed their place as citizens of a nation. But when black men enrolled their names, swore their oaths, paid their fees, and gathered under the sheltering symbol of the federal stars and stripes, they did not accept uncritically the politics and goals of the associations—or by extension, the nation—they embraced. Instead, what they adopted, they adapted, tailoring the aims of their various organizations to meet the needs of their everyday lives and the aspirations they held for their futures. Just what those needs precisely were in southwest Georgia, and how black men and black women intended to achieve them, had begun to crystallize by midsummer, when rumors began to circulate outward from the Whitlock plantation about justice, parity, and above all the rights of black workers.

Not much was known about the meetings that were staged the summer of 1866 on the Whitlock estate. Oaths of secrecy, armed guards (whose task was to keep out anyone "who does not belong"), careful screening of potential participants by an "Examining Committee of three," and undoubtedly a healthy sense of self-preservation on the part of those who had been admitted prevented much information from filtering off the plantation and into waiting ears. But enough seeped beyond the boundaries of the Whitlock plantation to indicate that the society's "teachings [had swept] far & wide" of a simple quest for a limited suffrage. Instead, during its regular menu of Sunday discourse and drill, the Dougherty chapter promoted a vision of freedom that, if put into effect, would right the wrongs of the spring. Having judged both civil and Bureau authority inadequate for the task emancipation had put in front of them, the society advised the avoidance of both. Let black men—and workers—govern themselves, the communities in which they lived, and last but not least, the spokesmen purportedly urged, the agreements under which they and their families were laboring.[25]

These were heretical ideas to planters, and nearly so to the black and white men who had met in Augusta and who would in October swear off all pretense of political debate. But it was a vision warmly embraced by people who had too long suffered under the stifling authority of their old masters. Workers' discontent, which had been on a steady upward trajectory since the beginning of the year, intensified in midsummer—fueled, planters contended, by the shadowy activities taking place on the Whitlock plantation. Captivated by the notion of a state of their own and encouraged by the example in Dougherty, former slaves across southwest Georgia accelerated their assault against exploitative bosses, oppressive terms of work, and the violent reprisals to which many were subjected. Contending that they were "at liberty to use what language they please[d]," vocabularies grew more raw and tones more menacing, and even the previously mute had begun to speak up, "talk[ing] back" in a chorus of frustration. When not talking, they walked, or at least laid down their tools. To the growing dismay of their employers, employees stayed out longer at night, came in later in the morning, and left more and more frequently "when & for what causes they" wanted. Threats of fines, dismissal, and physical coercion elicited scoffs of derision and retorts that white men's authority had been supplanted by that of the societies the workers had formed. Others announced to their employers that committees of "collored men"—selected by those over whom they would sit in judgment—not Bureau agents, civil officials, or even distant federal authorities, would henceforth serve as the keepers of peace and arbiters of employment relations. Government, a new brand of rural black radical made explicitly clear, ought to and would reside entirely in the hands of the governed. Former slaves were coming to the law, but by the summer of 1866 the law to which those who lived and labored in southwest Georgia were turning was a law of their own creation.[26]

Turning their backs on civil and federal systems that tended in their different ways to favor planters over ex-slaves, southwest Georgia's black men began to assemble alternative institutions. Formal drilling clubs, military companies, neighborhood posses, and as fall approached, a rush of new chapters of the GERA, sprang up. At least 450 men in tiny Calhoun County, a place that on the eve of the war contained fewer than 580 black men over the age of twenty, paid their initiation fees and entered their names in Bryant's association, while numbers of others joined up from Quitman, Webster, and Sumter counties. Seven delegates from southwest Georgia attended the fall convention of the GERA, a sevenfold increase in representation since the previous meeting. Union League chapters sprouted and spread as well. One of the first was headquartered on the relatively safe terrain of the Whitlock plantation; other chapters would be forthcoming by summer. Alarming white onlookers, armed black men commenced drilling nightly at twilight on the outskirts of Bainbridge and on rural roads close by to Albany, and, at the behest of a traveling black agent, a series of meetings was convened in Dawson to consider doing the same. "The negroes," grumped a Baker County correspondent to a Macon newspaper that fall, "are more engaged in forming 'Loyal(?) Leagues' than anything else."[27]

While the Dawson men gathered together for the express purpose of preparing "to strike for [their] rights" (a plan that chilled the hearts of planters and northern agents alike), others put their associations to different uses, monitoring and sometimes replacing entirely existing institutions that failed to measure up to black people's ideas of equity. A self-appointed committee of three "leading black men," for instance, spoke out publicly against the Albany agent of the Freedmen's Bureau, Lieutenant H. C. Strong. Appointed to replace a man who had exhibited a decided preference for employers by repeatedly citing Lawrence Speed, the first president of the Dougherty County chapter of the GERA, Strong apparently was cut from the same mold and within weeks of his appointment came under fire for his biases against the people he had been assigned to assist. According to those "leading black men," Strong had been spending too much time tending to his paperwork and too little time tending to the needs of the county's former slaves. Particularly grievous was his habit of leaving black defendants to fend for themselves before all-white juries.[28]

On the Whitlock plantation, residents applied the advice they had been circulating at GERA meetings. Money troubles had plagued the Wilkes experiment from the very beginning. Accusations ranging from mismanagement to theft had hounded their heels as they migrated south, and continued to haunt them at their Dougherty home. Repeated appeals to various levels of Bureau authorities to help clear up the various matters, as well as their good name, brought the colonists no relief. By late summer, pinched for funds that had mysteriously disappeared but reluctant to present their difficulties to civil authorities, the colonists took matters into their own hands: arresting, trying, and sentencing "to hard labor on the society's plantation" one of their own, Lawrence Speed, for the embezzlement of four hundred dollars. Resolute in their decision, it was not until Speed had been stripped of his privileges and his presidency (of their "society") and put to work in the fields that the colonists spared a moment to report their actions to the assistant commissioner. They did so not to seek the general's approval (which they did not get, for Tillson emphatically rejected the society's right to exercise an autonomous legal or juridical authority). They wrote solely to ensure that moneys owed the society from another source be directed to the new president and not to the deposed.[29]

By late fall, southwest Georgia's planters were panicked. A year that had started peacefully enough, 1866 was ending in a way they had never imagined. Rather than reasserting their authority over labor and law by means of force and fraud—and, commencing in midsummer, a wave of evictions—the opposite appeared to have happened. Undaunted, mobilized black men were taking numerous steps to better protect themselves, their families, and their communities from their old masters, murderous white judges, and biased white juries. Some refused to register new labor agreements with local courts, doubtful of the ability or willingness of justices to hold all parties equally accountable.

Some—including a number of the Wilkes colonists—looked to the recently passed Southern Homestead Act, hoping to ground that autonomy on plots of public land. Others contemplated throwing their lots in with the thousands who were leaving Georgia for the higher, and sometimes cash, wages that workers were earning on the cotton plantations of the Mississippi Valley, east Texas, and parts of Louisiana. Acting more locally, every one of the freedpeople Howell Cobb employed on his Sumter County plantations staged an impromptu strike, helping drive up the local price of labor. Whether black people were contemplating staying or going, their complaints, along with those of uniformed agents, had already prompted Davis Tillson to begin cleansing his organization of the most objectionable of the civilian agents. Among the first to lose their posts were Terrell County's Daniel S. McCoy and William B. Walker, both relieved in April. Dougherty County's Winborn J. Lawton followed them out in October, and the remainder vacated their offices (by choice or design) over the next few months. These were developments that, when taken together, a pair of black leaders later recalled, "at once brightened the hopes of our people."[30]

Federal authorities further brightened black people's hopes. Reports of violence continued to flow out of the South—tales of terror and fraud conveyed in part by a host of sympathetic black and white newspapers, including John Emory Bryant's *Loyal Georgian*, a short-lived sheet that reported on both Union League and GERA activities, as well as by individual ambassadors such as Henry McNeal Turner, who served as black Georgians' informal representative in Washington, D.C. Swayed by these reports, national legislators had been busily prying control of Reconstruction away from a president they and most of their constituents increasingly distrusted. Since convening in late 1865, the 39th Congress passed in relatively rapid-fire order and over

Johnson's strenuous objections a series of measures that gradually shifted the initiative from former enslavers back to the formerly enslaved: a civil rights bill in April, a Fourteenth Amendment in June, and a Freedmen's Bureau bill in July that once implemented would extend the agency's life another two years. Though subject to the direct control of the president, military commanders also had been doing their best to shore up black people's freedom by neutralizing some of the most egregious aspects of white southerners' lopsided laws. In his capacity as the senior general of the U.S. Army, Ulysses S. Grant, for instance, in January ordered his subordinates to shield former slaves from discriminatory criminal punishments, and in July followed up by ordering military authorities to apprehend and confine everyone who had been charged with crimes but against whom civil authorities had failed to act. Unfortunately, as Davis Tillson pointed out in his annual report, given that such "outlaws" usually had the advantage of speedy horses, thickets of sympathetic friends, and a keen sense of the local geography, they generally made their escape.[31]

Despite the recent and overwhelming repudiation of the Fourteenth Amendment by southern legislatures, these were unsettling turns of events from former slaveholders' perspectives. Increasingly doubtful of their ability to operate their plantations in the upcoming year on the coercive principles of previous seasons, and disappointed by a harvest that left many burdened with debt, some planters contemplated once again new means by which to control or acquire black workers. In southwest Georgia, talk circulated, for instance, about how best to "regulate the price of Freedmen." A few urged more draconian applications of the state's vagrancy laws, using them to push black people back into the fields. Others revived talk about bringing in "European agriculturalists to supply the place of negro laborers," and the

Dougherty County grand jury proposed restoring an older—and for ex-slaveholders more satisfactory—balance of power by giving "prompt attention to the Education of the entire white population of the County." One even thought the time might have come for planters to reevaluate their earlier decisions to rid their estates of black women. "It is probable," a correspondent to a Macon newspaper wrote, that some in "middle and south-west Georgia" had "made a mistake in excluding women, to too great an extent, from their hired force." While stopping short of recommending the employment of black women on a wage basis, he did suggest that welcoming "the 'gentler sex'" back onto cotton's plantations would pay a dividend in labor relations. The company of women "is as essential to Sambo as to his employer; and though it may be sound economy to feed none but the most effective hands . . . sound economy may be lost sight of by a too rigid adherence of this practice if it results in discontent." "Cheerfulness and contentment among the hands," the writer commented with reference to planters' favored black male workers, "is an essential element of success."[32]

Not much came of these suggestions in southwest Georgia. No European immigrants answered planters' hesitant calls, none offered any indication that they might readjust the gender composition of their plantation labor forces, and very few even bothered to attend the meetings called to discuss how best to cap the price of black labor. After loitering away most of the morning, waiting for his neighbors to answer such a call, former slaveholder Shadrack Dickey left town in disgust. "I came home to dinner," he confessed to his diary, "not enough to do anything." Instead, sharing Oliver H. Prince's rather cheerless computation that those who insisted in growing cotton with black people's labor would likely not last out the spring, many of Dickey's neighbors and colleagues began to act on an earlier conversation: selling out and starting over. Farmland flooded the market in late 1866. So too did the mules that traditionally powered local gins and pulled planters' wagons. Indeed, in just one day, fifty went under the hammer at an Albany auction. Announcing that he had "never been more depressed in [his] life," Benjamin Yancey—longtime absentee planter, the owner of multiple estates in multiple states, and kin to one of South Carolina's most devout secessionists—resolved to chuck his Dougherty County plantations even before his workers had wrapped up and shipped away the 1866 harvest. Within the space of just a few days, "two or three" of his landowning neighbors approached Thomas Willingham about buying their estates, promising him he could have them "on as long time as I wanted without any cash payment." When planters failed to find buyers, they turned to tenants or renters. A few simply threw up their hands in frustration, abandoning their once promising estates to whoever might have them. Even phosphate dealers suffered from what Willingham named as a generalized fear of "[black] *labour.*" "Of all the planter[s] who at one time" might have been expected to order a year's supply from David Barrow's agent at Albany, "there [was] not a single one" who by the close of 1866 seemed certain to stay.[33]

The new year brought little relief to cotton's unhappy planters. The 39th Congress, frustrated since it convened in December 1865 by the intransigence of ex-Rebels but more recently buoyed by mid-term elections that gave Republicans a veto-proof majority, at last took matters fully into its own hands. On March 2, 1867, both houses overrode Johnson's veto to pass the first Reconstruction Act. Within weeks, Congress had divided most of the former Confederacy into five military districts, replaced civil with military governors, and set into motion the processes by which formerly enslaved men would become fully vested participants in national political life. Almost simultaneously, black southwest Georgians stepped up their own processes of mobilization, adapting to revolutionary new circumstances the habits of collective action they had constructed on slavery's gendered terrain. Long before General John Pope, the commander of the Third Military District (which included Alabama and Florida as well as Georgia), deployed teams across the state to register hundreds of thousands of new voters and to prepare for the election of delegates to a new constitutional convention, and long before the national Republican Party embarked on its own membership drive, black people drew on long-established networks of friendship and defense—informal institutions that in southwest Georgia found their origins largely in the fields, the roads, and the plantation quarters—to call meeting after "glorious" meeting of their own. Gathering in excited and anticipatory crowds in Thomasville, Newton, and Albany, on outlying estates, and in sheltered interstitial locations, they knew—or so groused fretful former slaveholders to whoever would listen—"that the time [was] near at hand" when black people would at last take their place in the state.[34]

But as the reality of pending enfranchisement sank in, and the Confederacy's former slaves began to think systematically about the purposes to which those ballots could be put, competing visions of what it meant in practical terms to "take possession" of the government under which they all lived came into sharper focus. Farmworkers and their families, unpropertied people who were almost wholly dependent on former masters and landowners for the roofs over their heads, the beds on which they slept, the food they ate, the wood they burned, sometimes the clothes they wore as well as the medicine they took, saw in the prospect of suffrage a chance to address the inequities that constricted their lives. Guided by ex-slaves such as Dougherty

County's Philip Joiner, a self-taught son of Virginia soon to be elevated to the presidency of the local chapter of the Union League, and Simon Harris, one of the original members of the Wilkes contingent, and encouraged by the likes of Aaron Bradley—a northern-trained black lawyer with a reputation for fiercely defending black settlers' claims to the Sherman Reserve and who visited Thomasville in May—southwest Georgia's black workers revived a good many of their old dreams. Marching nightly through their plantation quarters with "guns and sticks" propped over their shoulders and drums thumping out an accompaniment, workers announced that not just an ambiguous "authority . . . to do as they please" (which was ex-slaveholders' chronic and querulous complaint) was back on the political agenda, but the removal of land from white ownership to black as well. "They ha[ve] conceived that the day for the general distribution of the lands of the country ha[s] arrived, and that the last meeting to decide the matter was to be held in Albany on the 4th or 5th Saturday in June, at which place they were ordered to be present with arms and equipment," snarled one of their more spiteful former masters.[35]

But other political ambitions besides those embraced by black workers circulated through southwest Georgia's black communities. Among the more prominent was the fairly conventional gospel favored by native sons such as William Colquitt of Newton, Tucker Tarver of Albany, and Giles Price and McCallister Davis of Thomasville. Predominantly highly skilled and educated proprietors of small businesses, farms, and shops, and many of them having been liberated long before the outbreak of war, these men preached what planters and their spokesmen usually judged to be a pleasingly "temperate" alternative to plantation laborers' more radical initiatives, notions one editorialist roundly condemned as "malignant." While certainly protective of former slaves—Davis, for instance, leaned on Thomas County civil officials to make public relief more readily available to the black poor, and Price publicly endorsed the Reconstruction amendments—southwest Georgia's black moderates and their acolytes fully embraced the same principles of industriousness, frugality, and self-perfectibility that animated so many of the northerners on duty in the post–Civil War South. As respectful of the rights of capital and as committed to a laissez-faire system as were the white patrons on whom their livelihoods often depended, theirs was a generally middle-class and mainstream position that privileged "harmonious action and cordial co-operation" over conflict and "mutual forgiveness" over vengeance. Radicalism of the redistributive sort that was galvanizing the impoverished and subordinate denizens of the cotton plantations lay far beyond such individuals' fields of political and productive vision. Indeed, when accusations surfaced against Davis that he harbored secret plans to give away privately held land, he responded with a scathing and public denouncement. Never would he "want any body's land without paying for it," he exclaimed in a Thomasville speech that won approval from an unrelentingly conservative local press. Distancing himself from those former slaves who continued to yearn for a confiscatory scheme on the scale of the one that had peopled the Sherman Reserve and that had generated widespread excitement during the first months of freedom, Davis went on to explain in no uncertain terms that he was "behind the time to be a Radical, for he had already bought himself a homestead." Equal rights before the law, Union, forgiveness, harmony, contract, and compromises—not the subversion of traditional order—were his guiding principles, just as they were for the half dozen or so black and white men who shared the podium with Davis that day.[36]

White men generally appreciated the cautious Republicanism

of men like Price and Davis, and some went so far as to reward them with new business and gifts of patronage. But the majority of black workers all but ignored the Davises among them. Not finding the answers they needed in the propertied men who presumed to speak in their behalf, rural workers accelerated their own efforts to conduct their lives on terms of their own choosing. Much to the annoyance of both Freedmen's Bureau and civil authorities, these efforts often revolved around seizing control over peacekeeping and judicial apparatus and investigating and resolving all cases of "injustice and ill treatment." Reports of such activities emanated from all corners of the region. Along the banks of the Chattahoochee River, near where a Confederate shipbuilding facility had stood during the war, "a small number of the boys Belong[ing] to the U.L. Society of Fort Gaines," guns and "pistles" in hand, assembled in a show of masculine force aimed to halt threats made by white Alabamians on the life of their society's president. In Cuthbert, black residents charged the Freedmen's Bureau subassistant commissioner with a series of transgressions against the people he had been assigned to assist, prompting the assistant commissioner to order a formal investigation. In the same town, when the city marshal arrested a black man on suspicion of theft, leading the prisoner into town with a rope festooning his neck, he provoked an inquiry by black teacher J. A. Jackson "in behalf of" yet another "freedmans committee." When civil authorities jailed freedmen on charges of drinking too much, other freedpeople broke them out, declaring in one instance that "as [white authorities failed to] arrest white drunkards, they shall not arrest and keep the colored." In rural Clay County, black men poured out of a church meeting to rescue John Dawson from the custody of Washington Wilcox, an Alabama man for whom Dawson had once worked and who had crossed the river into Georgia with murder in mind. Not satisfied with simply releasing Dawson from custody, the self-appointed posse pursued Wilcox back toward the border, pinning him against the river, which he finally dove into in an effort to make an escape. Unfortunately for Dawson, Wilcox returned with reinforcements to finish the job he had already started.[37]

Black people's attempts to neutralize or circumvent the civil judicial system were conceptually and practically inseparable from workers' initiatives on the region's plantations. Having helped weed out the civilian Bureau officials who had sided too openly with planters, and believing that the day fast approached when black men would assume legitimate places in jury boxes and legislative halls, laborers by the "thousands" aggressively confronted their employers head-on and, with weapons often in hand, demanded more liberal terms of work. Beginning in April and picking up speed thereafter, freedpeople walked out of the fields and off of their jobs. Moving in groups that varied considerably in size, but commonly included two or three or more people, some entered into new contract agreements, jobs they had often lined up before leaving their previous employer. Some took to the streets, awarding themselves impromptu "holliday[s]" that they gleefully filled with dancing, drink, and, to the consternation of former slaveholders, marksmanship practice. Others kept on moving, leaving the region entirely in hopes of finding better conditions elsewhere. Most workers stayed, but on terms better tailored to their own needs. Drawing imaginary lines in the dust of the plantations they served, they imposed new limits on employers' power to command, enlarged laborers' rights of refusal, scared off with threats of violence civil authorities and private citizens who tried to call them to heel, and as a result of their ferocity, drove incidents of white-on-black violence down to their lowest regional levels since freedom. "No white man should control them," vowed co-workers George Morrow, Livey Morrow, and Sandy Anderson to any who asked. They said that the crop they cultivated "was theirs and that they would manage it as they please." On J. B. Vanover's plantation, "Eight or Tenn of the hands" laid down their tools and walked off the job, explaining to their astonished employer that if he wished them to come back, he "must pay them before they work—Every man—& that I was to pay Every four months."[38]

While the political mobilization tended to be overwhelmingly masculine, a result of the same gendered experiences in slavery that had better fitted men to broker and enforce wage-labor arrangements, women grew increasingly bolder and more open in their critiques of the system that threatened to poison black people's freedom. Although rarely sighted at the Union League and Republican meetings that had been proliferating since spring, evidently preferring to limit their public exposure to community-based holiday and religious celebrations—assemblages that often attracted white participants as well as former slaves—freedwomen, like freedmen, intensified their domestic and workplace assaults on planters' free-labor system. Always ready to parry ex-slaveholders' blows with fast words and quick wits, black women's responses grew edgier and more physical as Reconstruction turned a radical corner. Influenced perhaps by the bristling arsenals of guns, pistols, knives, sticks, and axes that black men had taken to toting whether at work or at play, and as exhausted by employers' demands as were their husbands and brothers, women expanded and in some cases militarized their range of responses. Too bad she had no pistol, Mary mused aloud after the white woman for whom she churned found fault yet again with the butter Mary had made. If she had one, Mary told her tormentor, she would "blow her off or something to that effect." Other women staged solo and spontaneous strikes, refusing to perform the more onerous chores, or stopping work altogether when the time, in their eyes, seemed right. Nothing, howled their employers, seemed capable of scaring such single-minded women back into the fields when they "kicked up . . . and refused" to work as Amanda and her children did one morning on Daniel Horn's plantation. Indeed, one of G. M. Byne's female employees flatly told her male co-workers that she would "rather lay in jale than" spend her days in Byne's fields.[39]

By June, planters were nearing their wits' end. "Equal Rights," "military drill," "Eberhart & Co." (a not-so-veiled reference to a speech made in June by the Freedmen's Bureau superintendent of education to the freedpeople of Randolph County regarding the benefits of schooling), and visitations by "those evil disposed hirelings of a blood thirsty party," they fumed, "don't suit in this section." Landowners resented laborers' trips abroad from their plantations, muttering that unsupervised sojourns into the region's villages and small towns—locations where talk of registration, of politics, and of the possibilities therein circulated at an especially fast rate—"puts [laborers'] minds unsettled." Such talk also diverted workers' attention from the crops in the fields, and given the "tender" nature of cotton, a "day lost now," groaned planters in summer, "may work very serious mischief" come fall. Hoping to forestall that mischief, and not incidentally shore up their eroding power, employers heightened their surveillance. Some resorted to stalking, following their workers around on their days off and eavesdropping on even the most benign of black people's conversations. When a black man appeared at his door to collect a "dose of oil or something for chills" for someone "most dead," reported the Bureau's physician at Albany, "Massa John" would lurk on the street out front, keeping a watchful eye (and presumably an attentive ear) to ensure that the exchange involved only medical care and nothing as toxic as political advice. Courts cracked down on workers as well, packing black suspects into jail in the summer of 1867 on the "slight[est] suspicion of Guilt." Some were released immediately, not into freedom but into the ranks of newly devised "Chain Gang[s]," a solution favored and enforced by Stewart County's Judge Gillis until military authorities cautioned him that such usage of inmates exceeded the limits of law. Other tribunals, such as Thomas County's Superior Court, suspended operations entirely, leaving black prisoners penned up in the dank of the jail, their trials put on indefinite hold.[40]

While Bureau agents sympathized with and in many cases facilitated the mobilization of the region's ex-slaves, they too worried that an excess of political excitement would have a regrettable impact on production and labor. Concerned not only about workers violating the terms of their contracts by leaving at odd hours, disobeying instructions, and drilling in the quarters by night, but also about rumors of weapons to be distributed from government stores and of mandatory meetings in town, the Bureau's agent at Albany drafted an address to the freedpeople themselves. Scotching talk of gifts of guns and farms, he counseled them to return to their places of employment, reminding them that for six days of the week their time belonged not to them but to the person who employed them. Certainly all who were eligible should register and go to the polls and vote, he admitted. But remember, the agent continued in language that pleased the employers of those to whom he directed his words, "your success in life depends upon yourselves, upon your own conduct, your industry, your honesty, truthfulness and frugality, and that he among you who is the most industrious, the most honest, truthful and frugal, will have the greatest measure of success."[41]

Planters' threats and Bureau scolds did nothing to dampen freedpeople's enthusiasm or to slow the mobilization under way. By the time Republican Party organizers began to fan out across the countryside, they found a receptive and organized foundation on which they could graft the formal structures of partisan politics. Although wont to take credit himself for "republicanizing" the state, Henry McNeal Turner, the Macon-based party functionary and Methodist preacher, recognized the value of taking advantage especially of black Georgians' preexisting networks of communication and community. Rather than start from scratch, he advised his fleet of subordinate organizers to seek out "country churches; societies, leagues, clubs, balls, picknics and all other gatherings," transforming them into political classrooms where itinerate Republican spokesmen could preach the "radical gospel" and where "colored citizens [could] learn their rights." To ensure that those audiences appeared, Turner also directed his lieutenants to tap into and avail themselves of the cotton South's ready-made conduit for the movement of ideas as well as the movement of goods: that fleet of semiautonomous black teamsters whose ubiquitous but shadowy presence had belied their centrality in making communities of slaves, markets of labor, and now parties of people. Expanding their presence into a new realm of action, teamsters rumbled along the roads on a wholly new mission, delivering political posters, Republican messages, and sometimes radical speakers as they rolled over routes scouted out under slavery and expanded in freedom.[42]

National and state organizers also discovered a homegrown cadre of leaders with whom they could scarcely compete. Black southwest Georgians may have readily adopted the structure of the national party, but they were much more cautious about adopting its leaders and the political agendas they offered. Captains of local committees, scattered remnants of the now disbanded Wilkes Society, indigenous Union League officials, neighborhood spokesmen, and a handful of lettered men quickly rose to the top of the local Republican order. Holding the trust of their constituent communities to an extent no outsider could hope to command, men like Simon Harris of the by-then defunct Whitlock community, Philip Joiner, and Baker County's W. R. Elerson—who considered it his personal duty to escort friends and neighbors to Republican rallies—took over much of the day-to-day responsibility for "inlightin the minds of the" people. It was men drawn from local wage-working communities, rather than propertied men, itinerant strangers, or professional partisan spokesmen, who tended to lead the call-and-response catechisms by which black men absorbed Republican and Union League principles. Of the thirty-five black men elected from the region to serve as delegates to the constitutional convention, or later to political office, slightly more than 40 percent were literate, but like Philip Joiner most seemed to have made their acquaintance with letters in the months following freedom. Of the five whose antebellum background is known, all five had been enslaved, and only five of the entire thirty-five listed property of any quantity or kind in the census of 1870. It was the last characteristic that hampered the chances of McCallister Davis. An avowed Republican, but one of a different brand than the people for whom he hoped to speak, Davis had lost their support for good the day he publicly and vehemently dismissed as unseemly plans to give away land. Giles Price, a teacher, Baptist official, blacksmith, and former free man of color, lost his bid to represent Thomas County when voters reminded one another of his financial contributions to the Confederate cause. Likewise, very few registrars—usually strangers selected and appointed by northern authorities—made the transition to elected official. Most came and then left, vanishing from southwest Georgia's public life when their jobs had been done.[43]

Especially scarce were preachers sent down from the North on missions as political as they were ecclesiastical. Confident in the harmonious relation between labor and capital, and firm apostles of the power of industry and thrift to elevate people from poverty to property, men like Macon's Henry McNeal Turner and New Jersey native Theophilus Steward had little to offer poorly paid, wage-working black men and black women whose lives were punctuated by violence, terror, and fraud. For instance, Turner's belief in the sanctity of private property hardly accorded with freedpeople whose grapevines continued to vibrate with wistful reports of free soil. Dispatched to organize churches, schools, and a political movement in Stewart County, the articulate, educated, and middle-class Steward likewise failed to connect with a people whose world included mobs that called themselves cavalry and judges who rode by night in disguise. Indeed, he found himself elbowed aside by former slave Thomas Crayton. Though curtly dismissed by Steward as an untrained, "poorly equipped," "native minister," Crayton survived his critic to represent his county at several conventions (including the constitutional convention) and to hold a seat in the state senate.[44]

Voter registration commenced in late June and continued into August. Teams of three (usually two white men and one black man) moved from precinct to precinct, opening their books for business at country crossroads, county seats, and places in between in an effort to allow eligible black and white men ample opportunity to put down their names. Against a background hum of discouragement that issued forth from conservative writers, like the anti-Yankee fulminations of Thomas County's "Uncle Ben," and in defiance of wrathful employers, black men lined up at Cotton Hill and McElroy Mills in Clay County, at Chickasawhatchee and Brown's Station in Terrell County, at Davidson's Mills, Tallow Town, and Nathan Barwick's place in Sumter County, and at a host of other locations. Those who did not know where to find registrars sent "deputations" to the nearest Bureau official to ask.[45]

For many hopeful black men, the larger challenge was to register without losing their livelihoods (and that of their families) or their lives. Planters fabricated fanciful stories about how registering really served as a cover for a federal effort to get up an army in preparation for "a pending war, with somebody." Others threatened their employees with dismissal, offered to dock by as much as five dollars per day the wages of those who left the fields to sign up to vote, and leveled their pistols at workers who scoffed at the idea of fines.[46] Obediah Stevens, after issuing verbal warnings to the black men employed on his Terrell County plantation to forgo registering to vote, drove the point home with a midnight visit to one of their homes. Bursting into the cabin of elderly Prister Newkirk, Stevens managed to get two shots off, one striking the old man's back. The attack had "no other purpose," Newkirk later swore, than to deprive him of his part of the crop and of the right to vote. Some of the assaults and threats served their intended purpose. Shadrick Ross gave up on politics when faced with a choice between keeping his job and going to register. In a sign of things to come, subsistence for Ross took priority over civil liberties. A small number of others drew a similar conclusion, especially in places like the Green Hill District of Sumter County, where too easy recollection of the Black Horse cavalry discouraged ex-slaves from expressing their ambitions too freely. As of August 10, only twenty freedmen from a district that was predominantly black had pushed their way through a crowd of hostile white faces to add their names to the registrar's list.[47]

More commonly, however, southwest Georgia's ex-slaves pinned their hopes on a federal government that appeared now solidly in their corner and looked forward to the day when they too would participate in local and national elections, debate and draw up the laws under which they lived, and see their cases adjudicated by black men and white. Having survived slavery, war, civilian Bureau agents, and corrupt civil officials, most were not about to turn back. In tiny Colquitt County, home in 1860 to nineteen black men of voting age, fifteen made their way to the registrars the summer of 1867. Where Union Leagues had emerged the earliest and the collective spirit expressed itself the most openly, turnout was even stonger, often matching or exceeding average proportions for the South as a whole. Better than 2,100 black men registered in Dougherty County, and nearly that number in Sumter out of an eligible population that approached, respectively, 2,300 and 2,200. In Randolph County, where freedmen played active roles in policing both Bureau and civil officials, nearly everyone who was of age to vote queued up in front of a registrar's table: 1,053 black men out of a possible population that ranged from 873 in 1860 to 1,092 a decade later.[48]

Brushing off planters' vows to evict unpaid any worker who "voted for Reconstruction," freedmen who registered in July and August headed to the polls in November. Indeed, in many precincts they were the only men who turned out to vote, putting to rest Bureau officials' predictions of bloody election-day clashes. The poor white men of Sumter County, who for reasons of debt relief had in August expressed an interest in a Republican government, stayed away from the polls in November, "afraid," one of their number announced, "of being called Radicals." Small numbers of conservative voters also arrived at the polls. Traveling in groups of two or three or four, they hoped by voting to register their resounding disapproval of the revolutionary direction in which Reconstruction had swung. Most white Southerners, however, chose to hole up at home. Still sulking over

Congress's usurpation of what had initially been the president's business, and smarting from daily confrontations with black women and black men who refused to back down, former Confederates generally withheld their votes altogether, abandoning the polling places and courthouse squares to encampments of the occasional white Republican and large crowds of armed and eager ex-slaves. Officials counted 1,390 ballots in Sumter County, "all blacks; not a single white vote cast." Similar reports issued from Randolph County. "The negroes are having it all their own way; but few whites voting." "We white are not voting at all," confirmed a planter from Dougherty; "only 2 have voted here, none in Macon Ga. none in Columbus."[49]

With the exception of Terrell and Baker counties, where conservatives turned out in the hundreds to support two of the few opposition tickets fielded in southwest Georgia, William Smith was correct, and the polling results showed it. Republicans swept the three-day election, and black candidates led the way. The freedmen of Clay County, who fiercely patrolled the banks of the Chattahoochee and poured out of church to save the life of John Dawson, joined with those of Randolph and Terrell counties to send to the constitutional convention former slave Robert Alexander; James Jackson (the man who spearheaded regular investigations into civil and federal treatment of former slaves); the impoverished, illiterate man of the cloth William H. Noble; and carpenter-minister John Whitaker. Voters in Dougherty, Lee, and Worth counties elected former slave and president of the Dougherty chapter of the Union League, Philip Joiner, and the unlettered farm laborer Benjamin Sikes. Stewart voters, though bruised after months of assaults by night-riding mobs, favored two former slaves as well: the much-disparaged minister Thomas Crayton, and the Union League official George W. Chatters. The radical edge dulled somewhat in Thomas County, blunted by the intervention of moderate McCallister Davis and his political ally, former free person of color and blacksmith Giles Price, who together continued to emphasize cooperation and "concilia-tion" over conflict. Thus in October, when Republicans met in Thomasville to select candidates to represent their interests at the constitutional convention, they chose a full slate of white men, one of whom the local newspaper praised as a "thoroughly Southern man." More generally, however, the November election revealed just how deep the divide ran along a different axis. Aside from the scattered pockets of black people who champi-oned a less contentious form of Republicanism, southwest Geor-gia's ex-slaves positioned themselves in direct opposition to those who had once owned their lives and their labor. As a corre-spondent to the *Albany News* bitterly remarked, freedpeople's "total disregard and abandonment of all the interests of the land owners of the South is too marked and distinctive to admit of any doubt as to future relations" and importantly, "profits."[50]

The correspondent had good reason to worry. The black dele-gates who made their way from southwest Georgia to Milledgeville largely kept their own counsel within the walls of the convention hall, contributing little to the debates that un-folded between new lawmakers. But the same could not be said when they circulated the countryside, gearing up for the spring election campaigns. Work, specifically strategies for readjusting relations between employers and laborers, dominated the public discussion. Standing front and center on courthouse steps and in village squares, black men gave voice to a vision of civil and po-litical equity whose lineage could be traced back into bondage. Former slaves Philip Joiner, Simon Harris, Wallace Sherman, and Peter Hines shocked white eavesdroppers and delighted an audi-ence of laborers when they took to the Albany hustings shortly after New Year's. Speaking at the height of the most contentious contracting season since freedom, and praising the power of the unity that had achieved so much already, Joiner and his lieutenants called on freedpeople to continue standing shoulder-to-shoulder: for good wages, for land, for civil justice, and—in language that could not but resonate with black women whose livelihood and that of their babies rested heavily on the labor agreements drawn up by black men—for the good of their families. "You supposed I'd let my wife and children starve when there was plenty close by?" Joiner asked to a repeated chorus of "No, never!" Securing that well-being required not only more substantial wages, but wages paid promptly and in full. The power of labor, as most of the audience believed, would carry them most of the distance. It certainly had carried the Irish railroad workers whose strike had rocked planters' equilibrium and captured the attention of the region's slaves more than twenty years earlier. Indeed, as Peter Hines insisted in recalling the story of a late-night dash west by militia to put down the Irishmen's uprising, "The white man must have your labor—his mules cannot stand idle in the lot." But Hines and his colleagues also knew that without justice before the bar, labor would ultimately fall short. The time was coming though, Sherman promised as he took his place on the podium, "when these things will stop" and when "Poor Right" would no longer weep as she descended courthouse steps. Black jurists and black lawyers would soon take their places in jury boxes and on judges' benches, diving along with their old masters "into the mysteries of the law, and say[ing] who shall be hanged and who shall go to the penitentiary." Stand firm, the veteran of the Wilkes experiment insisted. "Let Union and unity be your words; and when you vote stand together, and all will be well."[51]

Or so black women and black men desperately hoped. Events

of the late fall and early winter, while encouraging unity of action, were giving rise to renewed concern. Freedom, it seemed, insisted on throwing more obstacles in black people's way. Poor crop yields, declining prices for cotton, and a legal structure that gave prior lien to the merchants from whom planters borrowed rather than to the workers whom those planters owed, had brought the settlement of the previous year's contracts to an agonizingly slow crawl. For a short time, while John Pope remained in command of the Third Military District, Bureau agents had been able to force payment from planters by seizing their crops and other assets, either to sell or to hold as collateral until workers' wages had been met. But General George Meade, a man who admitted being "personally opposed in principle to any laws interfering with the rights of creditors," replaced Pope in December 1867 and those seizures ceased. As a consequence, not only did freedpeople go increasingly unpaid or underpaid, many came out once again deeply in debt to the planters who employed them. To take a planter's money, the Bureau agent of Bainbridge grumbled, "is like drawing their teeth." Prospects for the ensuing year were no better. The same factors that stifled prompt payment of wages combined with landowners' "uncertainty of negro supremacy" to cause planters to balk at betting on a system they no longer fully controlled. Thus, even as black delegates sat down with white to codify a new civil and productive vision, the economic doldrums that had begun to creep across much of the South the previous season at last arrived in southwestern Georgia. In many neighborhoods, the best wages planters were willing to give hovered between five and seven dollars per month, half what workers had commanded in previous seasons.[52] It was a collapse of economy that would undermine the political effectiveness, and in some cases the political resolve, of black workers whose slavery had left them with only the most skeletal of material and institutional resources from which to draw.

Unsure what lay ahead, and preferring to pin their future on the state's new constitution, black workers refused to rush headlong into new labor agreements, particularly if in so doing they might forfeit the land some hoped a more radical government would make available. Gathering instead in small groups on town streets, plantation quarters, and elsewhere, their momentary idleness and unemployment gave rise to a whole new spate of rumors. Insurrection was just around the next corner, landowners whispered urgently to one another and to any Bureau official they thought sympathetic. Reports multiplied from Thomas to Terrell counties of suspicious fires, of black men drilling, of renewed and wild displays of nighttime shooting, and of the growing appearance of bayonet-tipped muskets in the hands of ex-slaves. Little that black people did eased old slaveholders' fears. At Newton, the small town that served as the seat of Baker County, members of the Union League rallied to the defense of one of their own after a white man attacked him. The Dougherty County Union League assembled for a similar purpose when the local police arrested a black teamster for careening through town in his wagon. With black men squaring off against white men, Bureau agents beseeched higher headquarters for reinforcements. But with the exception of two suspicious fires that broke out in Americus, and a party of several hundred heavily armed freedmen who rode to the rescue of a black man after his arrest on charges of public drunkenness by Albany authorities, the Christmas of 1867 passed off as quietly as that of two years before.[53]

The New Year opened as quietly as the old one ended. Grinding poverty guaranteed that. With nothing much to show for the services they had rendered during the previous season, and reserves insufficient to count on, southwest Georgia's former slaves had little choice but to make their way back onto one or another of the region's plantations. A few did so on terms that anticipated what would come to be known as sharecropping, cutting deals with capital-strapped ex-slaveholders to cultivate their fields on a self-directed basis. An even smaller number followed the lead of the angry and unhappy workers who seized control of their employer's estate. The majority, however, simply went back to work on whatever conditions planters demanded. This usually meant accepting wages as low as, and often considerably lower than, what landowners had been offering in early December. In Sumter County, for instance, the highest wage the best laborers managed to win after the start of the year was a measly ten dollars per month: two-thirds of the wage that had been recommended by Bureau officials only one year before. But most former slaves fared considerably worse. More commonly, workers drew promises of wages that closely resembled the puny compensation former slaveholders had offered to pay during the first season of freedom. Thus as of March 1868 the eleven thousand former slaves who lived and labored in Baker and Mitchell counties averaged "about four dollars pr. Month" according to a local Bureau official, a wage he judged insufficient to support "those not able to work."[54]

With the initiative seemingly back in their hands, Georgia's white conservatives began to snap out of their earlier lethargy. Galvanized by the advantage they had gained from the drought and depression, they called out to one another from their newspapers, bully pulpits, and courthouse steps that the time had come for "every man to bestir himself" to save their state (and by extension, the nation) from the "wicked designs of the negro Radical party." From Greensboro to Hawkinsville to Albany, Dawson, and Fort Gaines, white men revived local chapters of the Democratic Party. They also whetted their blades and loaded their rifles. Shattering the relative quiet of the previous year, assaults on former slaves by white men spiked, and in the weeks preceding the April constitutional referendum "unmistakable signs of disorder" swept across Georgia. Much of the disorder was attributed by military authorities to "secret organizations," and it claimed such high-profile victims as Republican G. W. Ashburn of Columbus, who had represented his city at the constitutional convention. Southwest Georgia's white men and planters participated with gusto, shooting down or jailing men they identified as "very violent Radical[s]." In the subdistrict of Albany, a Freedmen's Bureau jurisdiction comprising sixteen counties and in which former slaves constituted the clear majority, reported incidents of white-on-black violence increased by 250 percent over the previous year, with a disproportionate part of those cases taking place in the months leading up to the spring election. Matters turned even worse in the Thomasville subdistrict. There, in eight counties that sprawled along or just above the Florida border, reports of knifings, beatings, shootings, burnings, and murder more than tripled—shooting up from 51 in 1867 to 158 before the end of the following November. Though Republicans were Democrats' primary targets, no black men—or women—could count themselves safe. A hail of bullets greeted Republican John T. Gibson as he stepped out of the Blakely post office; in Lee County, Peter Small's wife watched a gang of white men shoot her husband down in her doorway.[55]

Democrats' strategy of calculated intimidation, reinforced by strict application of election laws and outright bribery, had its desired effect in southwest Georgia. Despite marching to the polls on April 20 en masse and under arms in a state that elevated a Republican to the governorship and ratified the new constitution, radicals around Albany, Thomasville, Dawson, and

Blakely generally failed to carry the day. There, where black voters faced gun-toting mobs of white men, election managers openly opposed "Reconstruction," and Democrats extended tantalizing promises of cash rewards for voting their way, the constitution lost in nine counties, including that hotbed of night-riding gangs, Stewart. In twelve counties, Democrats elected their own gubernatorial choices. Of twenty available seats in the state legislature, just seven went to Republicans and only one of those went to a black man: Philip Joiner of Dougherty County. Having frightened away Early County's most prominent black leader, John Gibson, Democrats around Blakely swept the election, and Charles Fryer, the only freedman whose name appeared on the ballot in any capacity, received no votes at all in a county that eight years before had a black population that topped four thousand. Something similar unfolded in Randolph County where Democratic employers rested their electoral success on a strategy of starvation, withholding the means of subsistence from the radicals who worked in their crops.[56]

Not that winning made much practical difference, particularly for those who ran for local offices. Fully aware of the power exercised by sheriffs, coroners, tax collectors, and justices of peace in their day-to-day lives, southwest Georgia's Republicans, like those across the former Confederacy, had eagerly fielded full slates anticipating the happy results if they managed to dilute conservative control over local police and judicial apparatus. And in some communities, some won. In Dougherty County, they all won, including black teacher Peter Hines, who ran for county coroner. But with empty pockets and small hope of filling them as cotton prices continued to sag and rain alternated with sun to beat down the crops, none of them had the material means to pay the bonds required to take their new positions. "Before the war while negroes were property," recalled A. L.

Holliday, a white native who had allied himself with the Republican Party, "it was no trouble to execute such a bond." Not only were elected officials much better prepared financially, but bonds had been generally lower and bondsmen were available to lend successful candidates a hand. That had all vanished into the past by 1868. With bonds frequently raised to thousands of dollars by those who hoped to "arrange only for a certain class to hold office," the poorer black and white Republicans stood little chance of taking their offices. In southwest Georgia, where radicals were all poor, including the carpetbagger contingent, no Republican occupied the seat he had won. Complaining, as Holliday eventually did in a bid to reduce his bond by five or six thousand dollars, did none of them any good. Decisions regarding bonds rested with "the corte," which in Holliday's view was "very strick, being all Democrats" and determined to "through all pediments in the way of those who favor reconstruction."[57]

With local government and its police back safe in their hands, southwest Georgia's planters and Democrats commenced once again to implement their version of freedom. Cursing "bitterly with set jaws and grinding teeth" Yankees, "blue legs, radicals and negroes," former slaveholders and landowners availed themselves of all means at their disposal, deploying courts, arson, and artful disguise, to reestablish their command over labor. Young men's clubs and more informal gangs saddled up, sometimes adopting as their name colorful variations on the Ku Klux Klan. Forming themselves into mobs that numbered as many as seventy-five men and that often included elected officials, the planters, their sons, and their allies paid late-night visits to plantation quarters and the homes of Republican leaders. Some were satisfied to issue stern warnings. "Quit the radicals [or die]," "Office No 18 of the K K K" advised Philip Joiner, not once but twice, in anonymous handwritten notes. Randolph County's James Jackson received similar mail. Other mobs, clubs, and klans favored more violent means. Arsonists' fires lit Stewart County's night skies, and a fire took the lives of Jack Ballard's babies when a mob burned his Worth County home while he was away at a Republican meeting. Increasingly, those whom Democrats and conservatives did not burn out or scare out were thrown out. For the first time since the end of the war, evictions affected more freedmen than freedwomen, as planters, with a growing surplus of labor on their hands, deemed it expedient to measure their laborers on a partisan rather than a productive basis. "Get another place, go to your Yankee friends" and "No Radical negro [can] stay here" became common refrains as planters dismissed on the flimsiest excuses those who supported (or were supposed to support) the radical cause. "It is mortifying to the extreme," a Bureau agent later admitted, "to have thes men come down driven from home, their years wages gone & [know that] I cant do a thing."[58]

Once again, freedmen and freedwomen closed ranks. Frightened of losing what little they had made for themselves since freedom, they intensified their military drill, as well as the policing of their local communities. Under the auspices of Union Leagues and newly conceived "Grant Clubs"—organizations assembled specifically for the November presidential campaign—black men perfected their game, interrupting the Sabbath quiet and evening stillness, day after day according to some frantic reports, with small-arms fire and political talk. The meetings were large. Transcending the plantation boundaries that had once defined the edges of mobilization, crowds of hundreds marched into or around Cuthbert, Camilla, and Americus and overwhelmed in one event the tiny village of Florence. "[A] hundred voices of Freedmen," led by Benjamin Anderson, Henry

Brown, "and others colored" spoke up in protest against mob injustices from the similarly diminutive town of Lumpkin. One hundred and fifty to two hundred others, mostly men, descended on a cabin near Vienna to drill, to debate, to listen to speakers, to seek counsel from one another, and especially to work toward "the security of all their rights." Safety was a paramount concern at the meetings themselves, and as conservative pressure built up, black pickets grew fierce in their challenges, stopping traffic on public roads and turning back or gunning down anyone—black person or white—who failed to provide the requisite password. In Schley County, which lies just to the north of Sumter, workers who believed the Freedmen's Bureau had been withdrawn formed themselves into "Semi military organizations." "They say they will defend themselves," the still-available agent reported. In Early County, the Union League marshaled nearly one hundred freedmen to rescue their president from the Blakely jail. Fights erupted between stalwart Republicans and those who disrupted their tenuous communities. In Sumter County, Loyal Leaguers, happening upon a man who had abandoned their fold, "whipped him severely, one report said had killed him." Something of the same befell Harry when he beat up a neighboring black man over a pig. "Arrested" at his Thomas County home one Saturday evening by his friend Bethel or Bevel McQueen and nine others, Harry was gagged, tied, and, over his wife's frantic objections, marched to a plantation on the Florida border. There, before a "right smart" crowd of men who drilled and women who "st[oo]d around, but did not drill," Bill Hill, Ned Russell, and Green Taylor lit into Harry. The three men spent the better part of the night settling their score, "whipp[ing] him some and talk[ing] to him some," before cutting Harry loose shortly before dawn. When quizzed later about his part in the affair, Taylor explained that they had "whipped old man Harry by his consent," Harry not wanting to have his case taken before any civil authority.[59]

But holding the line became steadily more difficult as the economic and political situation soured. Ignoring the epithets diehard Republicans hurled at freedmen who wavered, interest eroded in a contest that threatened to cost southwest Georgia's black men and black women precisely what they held most dear: the families they had salvaged from slavery and access to the resources to keep them safely intact. Caving in to evictions and threats of eviction, enticed by tantalizing offers of land to be had "on very reasonable terms, and with sufficient time to make payments," or promises of patronage in the case of artisans or craftsmen, many of the region's black people began to scale back their public espousal of radical ambitions. Political power no longer seemed the most expedient means of achieving domestic contentment. One by one, Republican supporters trickled away. Among the first of the more prominent men to retreat was Sumter County's William Styles. Shortly after losing his bid for a legislative seat in the spring, the onetime president of a Union League chapter announced his intention to cooperate, not compete, with his Democratic neighbors. Others soon followed, depleting the region's radical ranks. Just days before the Georgia legislature expelled twenty-seven of the thirty-one black men who had been elected in April, including Dougherty County's Philip Joiner, Willis Crawford "Culed" of Decatur County threw in the towel, explaining in a painfully written note to General Meade the bitter choices freedom had presented to the region's ex-slaves: "Sur we dunot no what is best forus to do. [S]um sait one thing an sum sait a nother. Ples tel me what is best for us to do . . . iCant rest knight nor day the white people sait we can not live on their land if we du not [suit] them. [W]e ha no land, no[t] one out of ten hundurd and wha[t] shaull we du. [W]e are in a de[s]surte." Offers of "cold batter cake an bad whiskey" could not buy a black man's vote in 1867. In 1868, as Crawford and others were sadly concluding, the knowledge of a roof over-head and a meal to eat just might.[60]

With local offices well in hand, the state government stripped of the majority of black lawmakers, and the former slaves begin-ning to question the effectiveness of open political struggle, southwest Georgia's conservatives upped the ante. What had been a guerrilla engagement took on the appearance of some-thing more systematic when the Bureau agent at Albany received word via several freedmen that a local dry-goods merchant had taken delivery on September 10 of five cases of repeating rifles, bought and paid for by the Dougherty chapter of the "Young Men's Democratic Club." Pondering then the "whys and wherefores," the agent did not have to wait long for his answers. Nine days later, a volley of gunfire greeted a crowd of nearly 150 freedmen and maybe one or two freedwomen as they arrived at the Mitchell County village of Camilla for a Republican rally. A third of them lay dead before day's end. They had been alerted to the event earlier by printed notices (one of which ex-slave Goli-ath Kendrick proudly attested having read for himself), by mes-sages passed verbally from plantation to plantation, and by the band that had been thumping out an accompaniment since the first eighteen Republicans had departed from Albany the eve-ning before. Armed with the usual assortment of worn-out shot-guns, sticks, and unloaded pistols, if they carried any weapons at all, and made somewhat cautious by rumors about the baleful nature of Camilla's conservatives, the freedpeople and their lead-ers were nevertheless caught utterly unprepared for the recep-tion they met. Not satisfied with felling black people in the town square at point-blank range, the assailants scoured the countryside from horseback and with dogs, hunting down more. The shooting and whipping continued for days. "Mobing crowd[s]" of what one black victim denounced as "southern so called democrats" combed through thickets and cabins, quarters and swamps. Gangs swept through Newton and Blakely, seeking out not just the survivors of Camilla but Republican leaders more generally, captains of companies that drilled, and not insignificantly, "every Colord man that is farming to his self or supporting the nominee of grant and Colfax." The quick-witted, when stopped for questioning, "played off democrat & proved it by showing a Seymour badge." The rest, concluded Philip Joiner in a bitter assessment of September's events, "either have to leave his home or be killed."[61]

Camilla and its aftermath drove black radicalism in southwest Georgia to ground, nearly finishing what slavery had started. Leaders struggled to rally their troops, but to little avail. Joiner traveled to Macon to lend his powerful voice to the October inaugural meeting of the Civil and Political Rights Association of Georgia. But fiery speeches and eloquent words could not protect individuals from biased courts, trumped-up charges, and murdering scourges. "The whole coloured race is so abused and intimidated" sighed a Republican later that fall from Boston, a small town located just north of the Florida line. Republican candidates suspended their canvasses. To continue would imperil their lives "and the lives of those who assemble[d] to hear" them speak. By the time the polls closed on November 5, Early County's John Gibson sat more or less permanently in jail, charged with inciting insurrection; Dougherty County's courts were eyeing something similar to silence Philip Joiner; and Democrats were celebrating a victory of astonishing proportions. Thoroughly cowed by the wave of violence that had swept across them and their families, black men had stayed away from the polls. Only two came forward to vote in Camilla. "Scarcely a radical vote was cast in Cuthbert." In Baker, a "big row about noon" frightened away Republican voters, and election officials in Americus opened the polls half a day late. If freedmen succeeded in dropping their ballots into a box, election managers refiled them into coat pockets, kicked them beneath tables, or swapped them for Democrat tickets. Nelson Tift, the merchant founder of Albany and a lifelong Democrat, won a seat in Congress by twenty-five hundred votes, even though black voters in his district outnumbered white by more than eight thousand. Only in Thomas and Lee counties did Republicans carry the day, and then by the slimmest of margins. For southwest Georgia's black men, and the women and children whose interests they guarded, creating a freedom on workers' terms would have to wait for another day.[62]

Coda: That Strange Land of Shadows

Although staggered by the electoral and often physical savaging of the 1868 presidential contest, southwest Georgia's former slaves doggedly, if much more obliquely, pursued their efforts to cast freedom on their own terms. When the state's first "Colored Labor" convention met in Macon the next year, at least five delegates attended from the counties around Albany, entering into passionate discussions about the painful oppressions suffered by black workers, exploring new forms of state- and nation-based mobilization, and returning to the plantations to launch strikes of their own. Two months later, President Ulysses S. Grant, under pressure from national Republicans, remanded Georgia once again to military rule, and ordered, among other things, the reinstatement of the black lawmakers who had been expelled from their seats in July 1868. By January 11, 1870, Philip Joiner was once again at the state capital in Atlanta, preparing a proposal to eliminate private ownership of the bridge that linked east to west Dougherty County, a measure that would offer significant savings to people otherwise compelled to pay for delivering their crop to market or buying the supplies to grow it. Toward the end of 1870, southwest Georgians elected another nine black Republicans to government offices; the next year they sent six; and nine years later, in 1880, Ishmael Lonon, one of Camilla's survivors, assumed a seat in the Georgia House of Representatives. Black men in Decatur, Thomas, Early, and Dougherty counties organized their own militias, taking for their names such politically laden phrases as "Lincoln Guards" and electing long-standing radical spokesmen to captain their ranks. And in the years following the thrashing served up by conservatives at the 1868 election, black people, census enumerators and others observed, began to abandon wage labor for what was described as land of their own.[1]

All these political and productive developments suggested that the powerful insurgency unleashed by emancipation, and accelerated in response to freedom's unexpectedly rocky terrain, continued to unfold at breakneck speed, yanking black men and black women free of the slavery behind them. But Karl Marx a century and a half ago, and French sociologist Pierre Bourdieu, a hundred years later, got it quite right. No matter how much they yearn to do so, people can never cleanly and completely step away from their pasts. "In each one of us, in differing degrees, is contained the person we were yesterday," remarked Bourdieu, picking up on Marx's insight that women and men make their own lives "under circumstances directly found, given, and transmitted" from their pasts. Previous experiences, Bourdieu continued, can be understood as a form of "accumulated capital" that in turn imposes a degree of continuity on lives otherwise subject to unforeseen upheaval and change. Or, in the words of a Cold War scholar reflecting more recently on humans and history in language better tuned to twenty-first-century ears: our pasts—even those scarcely more than a day or two old—constitute "the only data base we have." This connection between specific histories and the futures they help to condition and inform is especially easy to detect in southwestern Georgia. There, where a gendered slavery erupted abruptly but late, and where cotton truly was an immediate king, the particular circumstances of black people's lives openly stalked their heels as they passed through a war never quite realized into a freedom they never quite owned. While never determinant, it was a history that moreover would, in very short order, help reduce their insurgency to a century-long crawl.[2]

For a while, however, especially in 1866 and 1867, when cotton appeared on the verge of resuming its profitable old momentum and planters clamored for labor, it looked like southwest Georgia's black men and black women might outrun the slavery behind them. Extracting from a bank of personal and collective experiences—as producers, parents, partners, and friends—they translated a good deal of freedom into terms of their own. They repaired and extended their battered small families. They invested in new institutions and strengthened those they had exported from slavery. Black women, whose value to planters had skidded in freedom, hauled themselves back from the outermost edges of a landowner-contrived free-labor system by constructing a system distinctly their own. And black men, whose value as workers would remain high so long as the value of cotton did too, drove exceedingly hard bargains with ex-masters who had hoped never to bargain at all. As Congress prepared to extend to ex-slaves a level of citizenship that the president would not, the traditional hierarchies of property and power appeared certain to topple as freedpeople extracted themselves from a system that had commodified laborers as well as their labor. Topple those hierarchies did, in a good many places for a good many years. They were pushed to the ground in the rice districts of South Carolina, on the sugar estates that ringed the mouth of the Mississippi, and in cities throughout the former slaveholding states. They even collapsed on the cotton plantations that had once enriched the former Confederate president, Jefferson Davis: all longer-settled regions populated by people who had emerged from bondage and war in possession of durable political, social, and productive resources.[3]

But those alliances of power and property did not fall in southwestern Georgia. Still staggering from the aftereffects of a planters' regime that had stripped them too recently out of their natal communities, greedily consumed all of their days and much of their nights, and then spat them out into freedom before they had scarcely regained an old equilibrium, emancipated southwest Georgians teetered precariously on the edge of disaster. In freedom, left deeply reliant on those who had once owned them, not only for wage-paying jobs but for the cabins they lived in, the food they ate, the wood that warmed them, and the schools attended by their small children, the potency of black southwest Georgians' intense political and productive mobilization had been compromised before it had scarcely begun. Certainly, rooting out civilian Bureau officials—those men hired by Georgia's first assistant commissioner to balance out shortfalls in agency resources—had altered the political and productive landscape in freedpeople's favor, as had, for a time, black women's efforts to deflect with their families a new and gendered form of labor exploitation. The southward spread of the northern-born Union League movement, the extension of political rights to the masculine half of the nation's former slaves, and Congress's decision to seize from the president full control of federal reunion likewise shifted considerable initiative out of old masters' hands and into the hands of black people. But no one predicted an upcoming spell of unusually dry weather or the dip in the price of cotton after planters dumped thousands of hoarded bales on the postwar market. Thus when drought swept across much of the South for two consecutive summers, baking crops in the field, and the value of cotton began what would be a half-century tumble, the terrain once again shifted under freedpeople's feet. This time, however, it moved in landowners' favor. Before the third year of freedom was out, black southwest Georgians' system of family-based wage work—the invention of black women with no place to go—had been seized by their ex-masters and turned into a club with which to beat workers back down.[4]

And what a pummeling ex-masters administered in the wake of the 1868 election. Singularly successful in preventing black people from ruling at home, the region's planters and landowners clamped down all the harder, taking back what they had thought they might lose. Thus as radical Reconstruction entered into a wholly new phase across much of the rest of the former Confederacy—with black men assuming scores of positions as magistrates, sheriffs, constables, jurors, and judges, to say nothing of the hundreds of others who occupied (and would occupy in some places for decades to come) seats in federal and state governments—it withered and came close to expiring among the plantations of southwestern Georgia. Wages plummeted and violence skyrocketed. Workplaces transformed into especially dangerous terrain as planters pulled out all stops to restore, as they bluntly and repeatedly put it, capital's reign over labor. Cheerfully gloating that the Freedmen's Bureau was a "mere nothing," foremen, overseers, and vengeful ex-masters openly toted their shotguns and pistols back into the fields. They beat, whipped, shot, and stomped—sometimes to death and always with impunity—any ex-slave bold enough to talk back, fight back, or even flee in search of a new place of employment. No longer compelled by market or political conditions to respect laborers' parental and domestic dreams, planters boarded up or burned down the schools that in previous seasons they had established on their estates in order to lure back black workers. Civil authorities swept radical spokesmen out of the streets and into jail, impounding them for months at a time on frivolous charges; and planters boasted of having the right once again to "trea[t]" black workers "just as they please[d]." Not even the U.S. mail was immune to employers' and landowners' commitment to the silencing and subjection of the ex-slaves. Postmasters brazenly tore open letters and packages, looking, complained a northerner whose own correspondence suffered a similar rough treatment, for any expressions supportive of laborers' rights.[5]

Confident in the climate they were part of creating, landowners bragged aloud that their purpose was to restore those "kindly" attachments that had prevailed when planters were masters and workers were slaves. Freedpeople, and the few allies they continued to count among the region's white faces, called the assault pure "hellish."[6]

Neither strength of numbers nor a history of mobilization offered the region's ex-slaves effective protection. Indeed, previous militancy and demographic imbalance seemed to inspire a good many white people to new levels of malice. In Dougherty County, with its overwhelmingly black majority (70 percent at secession and exceeding 80 percent a decade later), where radicalism found its start on a plantation rented and run by a community of black farmers, and which produced the first black lawmaker ever elected to state office from that corner of Georgia, planters landed their punches with particular gusto. And civil authorities helped them along. Town councils and county officials wasted no time reinstituting the chain gangs that federal authorities had banned in the first days of freedom, filling their ranks with black men picked up off the streets on charges of drinking, gaming, burglary, and battery. They also targeted black men's northern-born Republican allies, usually by smothering their business interests under an avalanche of civil litigation. As they prepared to foreclose on the mortgage that had secured the

northerner-held plantation to which freedpeople had fled after the attack at Camilla and on which stood one of the few
remaining countryside schools that admitted black children,
Dougherty County's grand jurors solemnly announced that "ret-
ribution" should "follow transgression more swiftly." By the close
of 1869, two out of three of those Yankee and Republican proprietors—Edwin Flagg and his partner, William S. Fish—had declared themselves no longer in business. A. R. Reid, another of
the county's small cadre of white Republican leaders, faced his
own set of charges. Black men, newly festooned with chains and
county-supplied clothing, resumed as prisoners the road work
that had been their lot under slavery. And ordered to testify before the county's grand jury, the black delegates to the Macon labor convention faced pressure to recant their "outrage reports."
"Let the colored people know," crowed the county's conservative victors after smashing the single small strike that had been
staged by a handful of Albany's most hopeful black workers, that
"there are two sides to the labor question, and that proprietary
interest and the capital of the county will not yield to the demands" of black labor.[7]

Southwest Georgia's black men and black women never completely yielded. The flicker of "hot anger" W. E. B. Du Bois
glimpsed in the eyes of those he passed during his end-of-the-
century tour of cotton's decaying kingdom testified to a continuing, if carefully concealed, struggle.[8] So too did the trickle of
men who continued for a time to make their way to Atlanta;
conservatives' ongoing contests over which faction might have
the advantage of the black man's vote; the whispers that made
their rounds of plantation communities in the late 1870s about
Africa and the prospects of getting there ("i think it is time for
me to get where I can get my Labor," sighed one who wanted to

go badly); and later outcroppings of support for a Jamaican Pan-Africanist and his Universal Negro Improvement Association. But as the former Confederacy more generally passed into what was arguably its most militant stage—those promising years when black legislators forged bodies of liberal law, black people on sugar and rice plantations mobilized in dramatic defense of their interests as workers, and Richmond's black women perfected their drill in city streets—Reconstruction in southwestern Georgia had already long passed its prime. Thus as radicalism crested and swept through much of the rest of the South, poverty and violence washed across that corner of Georgia once judged the "greatest cotton region of the State, and perhaps the best in the whole South."[9] Militias that borrowed their names from Confederate units loaded their rifles with bullets supplied by a newly redeemed state, while those organized by black men drilled empty-handed. Joseph Means, born a slave, sold himself back into service in order to cover a one-hundred-dollar debt. Freedpeople took their children out of school to work in the crops, drank coffee brewed out of peas, and buttoned their shirts with thorns plucked from the bushes. Most of all, public declarations of radicalism tailed away, silenced and driven underground by white men's militias and by black people's retreat into a new sharecropping system, a process that diluted their political potency by dismembering the old slaveholding quarters, communities that had so brilliantly, if briefly, served as the locus and location of powerful black solidarities. Sickened by the events she witnessed from her schoolroom door, a northern-born teacher grieved for a people whose freedom bore witness to their lives under slavery. "God pity them, and hear their cry."[10]

Notes

ABBREVIATIONS

A-*n*   Records of the Bureau of Refugees, Freedmen,
                 and Abandoned Lands, National Archives, Record
                 Group 105, Freedmen and Southern Society
                 Project, University of Maryland, document control
                 number
ABCB   Albany Baptist Church Book, GDAH
ABCM   Albany Baptist Church Minutes, GDAH
AMAr*n*   American Missionary Association archives, Georgia,
                 microfilm reel number
AN   *Albany News*
AP   *Albany Patriot*
BCY   Benjamin C. Yancey Papers, SHC
C-*n*   Records of the United States Army Continental Com-
                 mands, 1821–1920, National Archives, Record Group 393,
                 Freedmen and Southern Society Project, University of
                 Maryland, document control number
CECHS   *Collections of Early County Historical Society*
CEL   Cobb-Erwin-Lamar Collection, UGA
CHP   Curry Hill Plantation Records, GDAH
"Condition   U.S. Congress, House of Representatives, "Condition of
of Affairs in   Affairs in Georgia," *House Miscellaneous Documents,*
Georgia"   40th Congress, 3d sess., no. 52
DAH   Farm Journals, Daniel A. Horn Papers, SHC
DCB   David Crenshaw Barrow Collection, UGA

DCCO	Dougherty County Court of the Ordinary Minutes, GDAH
DCIC	Dougherty County Inferior Court Minutes, GDAH
DCPC	Dougherty County Probate Court, GDAH
DCSC	Dougherty County Superior Court Minutes, GDAH
DU	Special Collections Library, Duke University
DWJ	*Dawson Weekly Journal*
ECN	*Early County News*
ECPC	Early County Probate Court Minutes, GDAH
ES	Endorsements Sent
EU	Special Collections, Robert W. Woodruff Library, Emory University
FBCB	Friendship Baptist Church Record Books, 1839–1964, EU
GDAH	Georgia Department of Archives and History, Atlanta
GHQ	*Georgia Historical Quarterly*
GIC	Governor's Incoming Correspondence, GDAH
GJM	*Georgia Journal and Messenger* (Macon)
GWT	*Georgia Weekly Telegraph* (Macon)
HJF	Huguenin and Johnston Family Papers, SHC
House Exec. Doc., 11	U.S. Congress, House of Representatives, "Freedmen's Bureau: Message from the President of the United States, Transmitting Report of the Commissioner of the Bureau of Refugees, Freedmen, and Abandoned Lands," *House Executive Documents,* 39th Cong., 1st sess., no. 11, serial 1255
House Exec. Doc., 70	U.S. Congress, House of Representatives, "Freedmen's Bureau: Letter from the Secretary of War, in Answer to a Resolution of the House of March 8, Transmitting a Report, by the Commissioner of the Freedmen's Bureau, of All Orders Issued by Him or Any Assistant Commissioner," *House Executive Documents,* 39th Cong., 1st sess., no. 70, serial 1256
HSC	Hawthorne S. Chamberline Papers, GDAH

JEB	John Emory Bryant Papers, DU
JSwGH	*Journal of Southwest Georgia History*
JVL	John V. Lester Book, Thomasville (Georgia) Genealogical, History, and Fine Arts Library
L-*n*	Records of the Office of the Secretary of War, Record Group 107, Freedmen and Southern Society Project, University of Maryland, document control number
LR	Letters Received
LS	Letters Sent
M437r*n*	War Department Collection of Confederate Records: Letters Received by the Confederate Secretary of War, 1861–1865, National Archives, microcopy 437, reel number
M798r*n*	Records of the Bureau of Refugees, Freedmen, and Abandoned Lands, National Archives, Record Group 105, microcopy 798: Records of the Assistant Commissioner for the State of Georgia, reel number
M799r*n*	Records of the Superintendent of Education for the State of Georgia, Bureau of Refugees, Freedmen, and Abandoned Lands, 1865–1870, National Archives, Record Group 105, microcopy 799, reel number
M816r*n*	Records of the Office of the Comptroller of Currency, National Archives, Record Group 101, microcopy 816: Registers of Signatures of Depositors in Branches of the Freedman's Savings and Trust Company, 1865–1874, reel number
M1003r*n*	Case Files of Applications from Former Confederates for Presidential Pardon ("Amnesty Papers"), 1865–1827, National Archives, Record Group 94, microcopy 1003, reel number
MCP	Morgan Calloway Papers, EU
MDT	*Macon Daily Telegraph*
MFU	*Milledgeville Federal Union*
MSF	MacKay and Stiles Family Papers, SHC

NOR	U.S. War Department, *Official Records of the Union and Confederate Navies in the War of the Rebellion* (Washington, D.C., 1903)
OR	U.S. War Department, *The War of the Rebellion: A Compilation of the Official Records of the Union and Confederate Armies* (Washington, D.C., 1880–1901)
RCS	Robert C. Schenck Papers, Rutherford B. Hayes Library, Fremont, Ohio
RG105	Records of the Bureau of Refugees, Freedmen, and Abandoned Lands, National Archives, Record Group 105
RG107	Records of the Office of the Secretary of War, National Archives, Record Group 107
RG393	Records of the United States Army Continental Commands, 1821–1920, National Archives, Record Group 393
RLR	Registers of Letters Received
SC	*Southern Cultivator* (Augusta, Ga.)
SE	*Southern Enterprise* (Thomasville, Ga.)
Senate Exec. Doc., 6	U.S. Congress, Senate, "Reports of the Assistant Commissioners of Freedmen, and a Synopsis of Laws Respecting Persons of Color in the Late Slave States," *Senate Executive Documents,* 39th Cong., 2nd sess., no. 6, serial 1276
SHC	Southern Historical Collection, Wilson Library, University of North Carolina, Chapel Hill
SS-*n*	Reconstruction Military District Records, Records of the United States Army Continental Commands, 1821–1920, National Archives, Record Group 393, Freedmen and Southern Society Project, University of Maryland, document control number
Statutes at Large	U.S. Congress, *United States Statutes at Large* (Washington, D.C., 1937–)
TCIC	Thomas County Inferior Court Minutes, GDAH
TCSC	Thomas County Superior Court Minutes, GDAH

THC   Thronateeska Heritage Center, Albany, Georgia
UGA   Special Collections Division, University of Georgia Li-
            braries, Athens
ULR   Unregistered Letters Received
WHS   William Henry Stiles Papers, EU
WJD   William J. Dickey Diary, UGA
WMQ   *William and Mary Quarterly*, 3rd series

INTRODUCTION

1. See, for instance, Joan Wallach Scott, *Gender and the Politics of History* (New York, 1988), 6; Robyn Wiegman, *American Anatomies: Theorizing Race and Gender* (Durham, N.C., 1995), 5–6, 11–12; Stuart Hall, "Race, Articulation, and Societies Structured in Dominance," in *Black British Cultural Studies: A Reader*, ed. Houston A. Baker Jr., Manthia Diawara, and Ruth H. Lindeborg (Chicago, 1996), 16–60; Doreen Massey, "Power-Geometry and a Progressive Sense of Place," in *Mapping the Futures: Local Cultures, Global Exchange*, ed. Jon Bird, Barry Curtis, Tim Putnam, and George Robinson (New York, 1993), 59–69.

2. Steven Hahn, *A Nation under Our Feet: Black Political Struggles in the Rural South from Slavery to the Great Migration* (Cambridge, Mass., 2003), 408–410, 460.

3. Others share my unease with the popular tendency to overstate the ability of people to shape their lives just as they please; see, for instance, Ira Berlin, *Many Thousands Gone: The First Two Centuries of Slavery in North America* (Cambridge, Mass., 1998), 2–14; Peter A. Coclanis, "The Captivity of a Generation," *WMQ* 61 (July 2004): 544–555; Wilma A. Dunaway, *The African-American Family in Slavery and Emancipation* (Cambridge, 1998), 4–5; William Dusinberre, *Them Dark Days: Slavery in the American Rice Swamps* (Athens, Ga., 1997), vii–viii; Brian Kelly, *Race, Class and Power in the Alabama Coalfields, 1908–21* (Urbana, Ill., 2001), 4–12; Orlando Patterson, *Rituals of Blood: Consequences of Slavery in Two American Centuries* (Washington D.C., 1998), 29; Thomas Spear, "Neo-Traditionalism

and the Limits of Invention in British Colonial Africa," *Journal of African History* 44 (Mar. 2003): 3–27. Care must be taken, however, not to confuse "agency" with "self-determination." The terms are not interchangeable. *Self-determination* invokes the sense that all things are possible for all people at all times; *agency* does not. *Agency* only admits that people do things, an acknowledgment that stops short of assuming game point for the subaltern side while leaving ample space for people to do something—for better or for worse—within the limitations and restraints imposed by their particular set of historical circumstances. On the last point, see Lila Abu-Lughod, "The Romance of Resistance: Tracing Transformations of Power through Bedouin Women," *American Ethnologist* 17 (Feb. 1990): 41–55.

4. For a further elaboration, see Pierre Bourdieu, *The Logic of Practice*, trans. Richard Nice (Stanford, Calif., 1990), chap. 3.

5. Karl Marx, *The Eighteenth Brumaire of Louis Bonaparte*, in *The Marx-Engels Reader*, 2nd ed., ed. Robert C. Tucker (New York, 1978), 594–595.

6. Henry Bram et al. to O. O. Howard, [20 or 21 Oct. 1865], B-53 1865, ser. 15, [A-7335]; Steven F. Miller, Susan E. O'Donovan, John C. Rodrigue, and Leslie S. Rowland, eds., "Between Emancipation and Enfranchisement: Law and the Political Mobilization of Black Southerners, 1865–1867," *Chicago-Kent Law Review* 70, no. 3 (1995): 1069–71; contract between Ben Holmes and Fanney E. Lippitt, 12 Mar. 1867, Lippitt Papers, THC; Robert Olwell, "'Loose, Idle and Disorderly': Slave Women in the Eighteenth-Century Charleston Marketplace," in *More Than Chattel: Black Women and Slavery in the Americas*, ed. David Barry Gaspar and Darlene Clark Hine (Bloomington, Ind., 1996), 97–110; Thomas F. Armstrong, "From Task Labor to Free Labor: The Transition along Georgia's Rice Coast, 1820–1880," *GHQ* 64 (Winter 1980): 432–447; Philip D. Morgan, "Work and Culture: The Task System and the World of Lowcountry Blacks, 1700–1880," *WMQ* 39 (Oct. 1982): 563–599, and idem, "The Ownership of Property by Slaves in the Mid-Nineteenth-Century Low Country," *Journal of Southern History* 49 (Aug. 1983): 399–420.

7. Work, especially the many kinds performed by slaves for their owners, lies at the center of a new interpretation of slavery that has been

refiguring a century-old field; see, for example, Berlin, *Many Thousands Gone*, and Ira Berlin, *Generations of Captivity: A History of African American Slaves* (Cambridge, Mass., 2003); David S. Cecelski, *The Waterman's Song: Slavery and Freedom in Maritime North Carolina* (Chapel Hill, N.C., 2001); Larry E. Hudson Jr., *To Have and to Hold: Slave Work and Family Life in Antebellum South Carolina* (Athens, Ga., 1997); Peter Linebaugh and Marcus Rediker, *The Many-Headed Hydra: Sailors, Commoners, and the Hidden History of the Revolutionary Atlantic* (Boston, 2000); Philip D. Morgan, *Slave Counterpoint: Black Culture in the Eighteenth-Century Chesapeake and Lowcountry* (Chapel Hill, N.C., 1998); Lorena S. Walsh, *From Calabar to Carter's Grove: The History of a Virginia Slave Community* (Charlottesville, Va., 1997); T. Stephen Whitman, *The Price of Freedom: Slavery and Manumission in Baltimore and Early National Maryland* (Lexington, Ky., 1997); Betty Wood, *Women's Work, Men's Work: The Informal Slave Economies of Lowcountry Georgia* (Athens, Ga., 1995).

8. Midori Takagi, *"Rearing Wolves to Our Own Destruction:" Slavery in Richmond, Virginia, 1782–1865* (Charlottesville, Va., 1999), chap. 5; Elsa Barkley Brown and Gregg D. Kimball, "Mapping the Terrain of Black Richmond," *Journal of Urban History* 21 (Mar. 1995): 296–346; Suzanne Schnittman, "Black Workers in Antebellum Richmond," in *Race, Class, and Community in Southern Labor History*, ed. Gary M. Fink and Merl E. Reed (Tuscaloosa, Ala., 1994), 72–86, 250–256; James Sidbury, "Slave Artisans in Richmond, Virginia, 1780–1810," in *American Artisans: Crafting Social Identity, 1750–1850*, ed. Howard B. Rock, Paul A. Gilje, and Robert Asher (Baltimore, 1995).

9. Ira Berlin, Thavolia Glymph, Steven F. Miller, Joseph P. Reidy, Leslie S. Rowland, and Julie Saville, eds., *The Wartime Genesis of Free Labor: The Lower South* (Cambridge, 1990), 331–338; Henry Bram et al. to O. O. Howard, [20 or 21 Oct. 1865], B-53 1865, ser. 15, [A-7335]; Miller et al., "Between Emancipation and Enfranchisement," 1069–71; contract between Ben Holmes and Fanney E. Lippitt, 12 Mar. 1867, Lippitt Papers, THC; Elsa Barkley Brown, "Negotiating and Transforming the Public Sphere: African American Life in the Transition from Slavery to Freedom," *Public Culture* 7 (Fall 1994): 107–146.

10. Julie Saville, "Rites and Power: Reflections on Slavery, Freedom, and Political Ritual," in *From Slavery to Emancipation in the Atlantic World*, ed. Sylvia Frey and Betty Wood (London, 1999), 81–102; Nancy D. Bercaw, *Gendered Freedoms: Race, Rights, and the Politics of Household in the Delta, 1861–1875* (Gainesville, Fla., 2003), 46–48, 128–129; Ira Berlin, Joseph P. Reidy, and Leslie S. Rowland, eds., *The Black Military Experience* (Cambridge, 1982), 26–33.

11. See, for example, Michael W. Fitzgerald, *Urban Emancipation: Popular Politics in Reconstruction Mobile, 1860–1890* (Baton Rouge, 2002); Tera W. Hunter, *To 'Joy My Freedom: Southern Black Women's Lives and Labors after the Civil War* (Cambridge, Mass., 1997); Jeffrey R. Kerr-Ritchie, *Freedpeople in the Tobacco South: Virginia, 1860–1900* (Chapel Hill, N.C., 1999); John C. Rodrigue, *Reconstruction in the Cane Fields: From Slavery to Free Labor in Louisiana's Sugar Parishes, 1862–1880* (Baton Rouge, 2001); Julie Saville, *The Work of Reconstruction: From Slave to Wage Laborer in South Carolina, 1860–1870* (Cambridge, 1994).

12. The most famous of southwest Georgia's nineteenth-century historians is W. E. B. Du Bois, who wrote of black life in Dougherty County at the end of the century; works by other historians of this area and era include Paul A. Cimbala, "A Black Colony in Dougherty County: The Freedmen's Bureau and the Failure of Reconstruction in Southwest Georgia," *JSwGH* 4 (1986): 72–89; Edmund L. Drago, "The Black Household in Dougherty County, Georgia, 1870–1900," *Prologue* 14 (Summer 1982): 81–88; and Lee W. Formwalt, "The Camilla Massacre of 1868: Racial Violence as Political Propaganda," *GHQ* 71 (Fall 1987): 399–426, and idem, "Moving in 'That Strange Land of Shadows': African-American Mobility and Persistence in Post–Civil War Southwest Georgia," *GHQ* 82 (Fall 1998): 507–532. For a useful discussion of the geography of the Civil War, especially as it relates to slavery, slaveholding, and cotton, see the introductory essay in Steven Hahn, Steven F. Miller, Susan E. O'Donovan, John C. Rodrigue, and Leslie S. Rowland, eds., *Land and Labor, 1865* (Chapel Hill, N.C., 2007).

13. The phrase *socio-ecological order* comes from David Harvey, *Justice, Nature and the Geography of Difference* (Malden, Mass., 1996), 12. Like myself, Harvey believes it is important, "theoretically and politically, to root" a

people's sense of the possible "in the mass of constraints that derive from [their] embeddedness in nature, space-time, place and a particular kind of socio-ecological order," the latter of which "regulates the material conditions of everyday life."

1. DOING THE MASTER'S BIDDING

1. Charles Hudson, *The Southeastern Indians* (Knoxville, Tenn., 1976), chap 8; Claudio Saunt, *A New Order of Things: Property, Power, and the Transformation of the Creek Indians, 1733–1816* (Cambridge, 1999); Lynn Willoughby, *Flowing through Time: A History of the Lower Chattahoochee River* (Tuscaloosa, Ala., 1999), chaps. 2–3; Lee W. Formwalt, "Violence and Diplomacy in the Creek Country: Jack Kinnard, the Chehaw, and the U.S. Government in Late Eighteenth-Century Southwest Georgia," *JSwGH* 7 (1989–1992): 1–19; Kenneth Coleman, ed., *A History of Georgia* (Athens, Ga., 1977), chaps. 9 and 11; David F. Weiman, "Peopling the Land by Lottery? The Market in Public Land and the Regional Differentiation of Territory on the Georgia Frontier," *Journal of Economic History* 51 (Dec. 1991): 835–860; John Banks, *Diary of John Banks* (Austell, Ga., 1936), 10–16; land deed, 7 Oct. 1829, Jacob Waldburg Papers, UGA.

2. Ulrich B. Phillips, ed., *Plantation and Frontier, 1649–1863* (1910; reprint, New York, 1969), 1:176–178; John B. Lamar to Dear Sister, 21 June 1846, CEL; *SC*, Nov. 1856, pp. 334–335; Randolph B. Campbell, *An Empire for Slavery: The Peculiar Institution in Texas, 1821–1865* (Baton Rouge, 1991), chap. 3; Daniel S. Dupree, *Transforming the Cotton Frontier: Madison County, Alabama, 1800–1840* (Baton Rouge, 1997), chap. 1; Donald P. McNeilly, *The Old South Frontier: Cotton Plantations and the Formation of Arkansas Society, 1819–1861* (Fayetteville, Ark., 2000), chap. 2; Christopher Morris, *Becoming Southern: The Evolution of a Way of Life, Warren County and Vicksburg, Mississippi, 1770–1860* (New York, 1995), chaps. 1–2.

3. Charles Munnerlyn to James Shackleford, 23 Nov. 1839, James Shackleford Paper, SHC; 6 Jan. 1836, 10 Mar. 1842, [n.d.] Sept. 1860, HJF; Lewis Bond Will, 6 Oct. 1836, GDAH; application of Winborn J. Lawton, 4

July 1865, M1003r20; *Columbus Enquirer,* 17 Aug. 1837; *AP,* 2 June 1859; Banks, *Diary,* 19.

4. Susan E. O'Donovan, "Journal of Nelson Tift, 1835–1836," *JSwGH* 3 (Fall 1985): 64–100; idem, ed., "The Journal of Nelson Tift, Part II: 1836–1840," *JSwGH* 4 (Fall 1986): 90–121; idem, ed., "The Journal of Nelson Tift, Part III: January–October 1841," *JSwGH* 5 (Fall 1987): 64–75; idem, ed., "The Journal of Nelson Tift, Part IV: The 1841 Legislature," *JSwGH* 6 (Fall 1988): 21–40; idem, ed., "The Journal of Nelson Tift, Part V: 1842–1843," *JSwGH* 7 (1989–1992): 81–106; idem, ed., "The Journal of Nelson Tift, Part VI: 1844–1848," *JSwGH* 8 (Fall 1993): 47–69; idem, ed., "The Journal of Nelson Tift, Part VII: January–February 1849," *JSwGH* 10 (Fall 1995): 67–84; idem, ed., "The Journal of Nelson Tift, Part VIII: March 1849–February 1850," *JSwGH* 11 (Fall 1996): 82–102; idem, ed., "The Journal of Nelson Tift, Part IX: March 1850–November 1851," *JSwGH* 12 (Fall 1997): 65–77; Nelson Tift, "Dougherty County: Historical Address," *JSwGH* 4 (Fall 1986): 1–24; 29 April 1843, A. T. Havens Journal, UGA; John Jones to Howell Cobb, 15 Feb. 1851, CEL; Michelle Gillespie, *Free Labor in an Unfree World: White Artisans in Slaveholding Georgia, 1789–1860* (Athens, Ga., 2000), chap. 1.

5. I follow Ira Berlin's understanding of a "slave society" as a society in which slaves are central to economic production, where the relationship between owned and owners conditions all other social relations, and where slaveholders have primacy of political, economic, and social place; see Berlin, *Many Thousands Gone: The First Two Centuries of Slavery in North America* (Cambridge, Mass., 1998), 8–11.

6. 29 April and 5 May 1843, Havens Journal; Hawthorne Chamberline to Mother, 23 Jan. 1846, HSC; TCSC (1826–1835), 13–14; TCSC (1838–1842), 39–41; James Loftin et al. to William Schley, 7 Dec. 1835, GIC; George Davis to David Barrow, [3]1 July 1855, DCB; *AP,* 13 Dec. 1850, 16 Dec. 1852, 4 Nov. 1853; "Regulations for the year 1838," HJF; Mary Kendall to Lydia Hamilton, 13 Apr. 1853, Hamilton-Kendall Papers, GDAH; *Macon Telegraph,* 21 Jan. 1836, 30 June 1836; *AN,* suppl., 13 July 1876; W. H. Andrews, "Plantation Life along the River and Spring Creek: Letters from W. H. Andrews," *CECHS* 2 (1979): 126; Edward E. Baptist, *Creating an Old South: Middle Florida's Plan-*

tation Frontier before the Civil War (Chapel Hill, N.C., 2002), 35–36. Unless otherwise noted, federal census figures are taken from the Geospatial and Statistical Data Center, *Historical Census Browser,* fisher.lib.virginia.edu/collections/stats/histcensus/ (accessed 4/13/06).

7. *AP,* 12 May 1847, 3 Mar. 1854; *SC,* Nov. 1856; William Porter to David Barrow, 26 Mar. 1859, DCB; George Davis to David Barrow, 2 Sept. 1859, DCB; William Porter to David Barrow, 4 Feb. 1860, DCB; James Filey to David Barrow, 9 Dec. 1860, DCB; John Lamar to [Howell Cobb], 10 Mar. 1858, CEL; John Grant to John Lamar, 28 Dec. 1858, CEL; D. B. Dicks to Benjamin Yancey, 14 Aug. 1860, BCY; James Harris to Sarah Yancey, 1[3] Sept. 1861, BCY; 23 Aug. 1858, WJD; *The Seventh Census of the United States: 1850* (Washington, D.C., 1853), 1:377–384; *Agriculture of the United States: Compiled from the Original Returns of the Eighth Census* (Washington, D.C., 1864), 2:22–29; Lewis Cecil Gray, *History of Agriculture in the Southern United States to 1860* (New York, 1941), 1026; Coleman, *A History of Georgia,* 162–163; Robert William Fogel and Stanley L. Engerman, *Time on the Cross: The Economics of American Negro Slavery* (Boston, 1974), 89–94; Numan V. Bartley, *The Creation of Modern Georgia* (Athens, Ga., 1983), 15.

8. Hawthorne Chamberline to Mother, 23 Jan. 1846, HSC; Hawthorne Chamberline to Mother, 29 Mar. 1846, HSC; Hawthorn Chamberline to Mother & Father, 29 Jan. 1860, HSC; Alexander Allen to George Allen, 21 June 1856, George Washington Allen Papers, SHC; 10 Feb. 1840, 24 Jan. 1841, 2 Apr. 1841, 10 Aug. 1841, 11 Aug. 1842, 22 Aug. 1843, 2 Aug. 1851, 5 Aug. 1852, A. J. Swinney Diary, THC; "Directions May—1842," HJF; W. E. B. Du Bois, *The Souls of Black Folk,* ed. David Blight and Robert Gooding-Williams (Boston, 1997), 105; *AP,* 9 Dec. 1848, 9 Nov. 1849, 21 Feb. 1851, 16 May 1851, 6 Feb. 1852, 13 Jan. 1854, 13 May 1858; *Appalachicolan,* 1 Jan. 1844; *GWT,* 17 May 1867; *Report of the Commissioner of Agriculture for the Year 1866* (Washington, D.C., 1867), 571–572; Sidney Andrews, *The South since the War* (1866; reprint, New York, 1969), 318; Lynn Willoughby, *Fair to Middlin': The Antebellum Cotton Trade of the Apalachicola/Chattahoochee River Valley* (Tuscaloosa, Ala., 1993), chap. 1; Willoughby, *Flowing through Time,* 48; Sam Bowers Hilliard, *Hogmeat and Hoecake: Food Supply in the Old South, 1840–1860* (Carbondale, Ill., 1972), 18–20; Works Progress Administration [WPA],

comp., *Historical Background of Dougherty County, 1836–1940* (Atlanta, 1981), 9–11.

9. Powhattan Whittle to Lewis Whittle, 25 Jan. 1854, Lewis N. Whittle Papers, SHC; Powhattan Whittle to Lewis Whittle, 27 Mar. 1854, Lewis N. Whittle Papers; *AP,* 21 Jan. 1846, 28 Jan. 1846, 3 June 1846, 6 Dec. 1850; E. G. Ponder to W. G. Ponder, 14 Oct. 1849, William G. Ponder Papers, GDAH; Mary Kendall to Dear Father, 3 Jan. 1853, Kendall-Hamilton Papers, GDAH; John B. Lamar to [Mrs. Howell Cobb], 9 Nov. 1855, CEL; WPA, *Historical Background of Dougherty County,* 19; Peter Kolchin, *American Slavery, 1619–1877* (New York, 1993), 99–100; Robert H. Gudmestad, *A Troublesome Commerce: The Transformation of the Interstate Slave Trade* (Baton Rouge, 2003), chap. 1.

10. Powhattan Whittle to Lewis Whittle, 25 Jan. 1854, Lewis N. Whittle Papers; Powhattan Whittle to Lewis Whittle, 27 Mar. 1854, Lewis N. Whittle Papers; E. G. Ponder to W. G. Ponder, 14 Oct. 1849, William G. Ponder Papers; *AP,* 21 Jan. 1846, 28 Jan. 1846, 3 June 1846, 6 Dec. 1850, 13 Dec. 1850, 11 April 1851; WPA, *Historical Background of Dougherty County,* 19; Du Bois, *Souls of Black Folk,* 110; on the demographic dimensions of the domestic migration, see Baptist, *Creating an Old South,* 61–72; Wilma A. Dunaway, *The African-American Family in Slavery and Emancipation* (Cambridge, 2003), 62–64; Gudmestad, *A Troublesome Commerce,* 19–20; Walter Johnson, *Soul by Soul: Life inside the Antebellum Slave Market* (Cambridge, Mass., 1999), 19; Steven F. Miller, "Plantation Labor Organization and Slave Life on the Cotton Frontier: The Alabama-Mississippi Black Belt, 1851–1840," in *Cultivation and Culture: Labor and the Shaping of Slave Life in the Americas,* ed. Ira Berlin and Philip D. Morgan (Charlottesville, Va., 1993), 156–157; Brenda E. Stevenson, *Life in Black and White: Family and Community in the Slave South* (New York, 1996), 204–205, 223–225.

11. D. B. Dicks to Benjamin Yancey, 14 Aug. 1860, BCY; James Harris to Sarah Yancey, 1[3] Sept. 1861, BCY; Phillips, *Plantation and Frontier,* 1:176–178; John Hill to John G. Howell, 14 Oct. 1845, *CECHS* 2 (1979): 121–122; Plantation Book, John B. Lamar Papers, UGA; *SC,* Nov. 1856, 334–335; Henry Tarver to [Elizabeth Tarver], 21 Sept. 1854, Henry A. Tarver Papers, Private Collection, Albany, Georgia. Of the slaves Lamar dispatched in the

first group, he described thirty-three as *"full hands"* and ten as "Boys & Girls" (distinct from the "Children")—individuals capable of contributing to productive activities. Historians have long debated the number of slaves who migrated in the company of their owners. In a recent reassessment, Steven Deyle accepts Michael Tadman's calculations, suggesting that between 1820 and 1860, approximately 30 to 40 percent of the slaves who were transported traveled along with their masters. See Deyle, *Carry Me Back: The Domestic Slave Trade in American Life* (New York, 2005), 281–289.

12. George Davis to David Barrow, 11 Feb. 1857, DCB. Records of Philip Joiner, 22 Sept. 1872, no. 783; Anice Weston, 3 June 1870, no. 498; Vina Micken, 27 May 1870, no. 476; Joseph Tooke, 7 Feb. 1871, no. 125; Charlotte Hill, 2 May 1870, no. 402, all in M816r6. W. F. White to [John R. Lewis], 22 Nov. 1867, RLR, M798r12; William White to Eugene Pickett, 15 Jan. 1867, ULR, M798r30; W. F. White to W. R. Moore, 21 Aug. 1867, vol. 3, p. 116, ser. 1036, RG105; Henry Tarver to Dear Wife, 27 Sept. 1854, Henry A. Tarver Papers; Alexander Allen to G. W. Allen, 26 Sept. 1850, G. W. Allen Papers, SHC; Mary Cole, "A Transcript of Pages from the Plantation Account Book of Dr. Richard Bradley Hill, Early County, Georgia," *CECHS* 2 (1979): 85–122.

13. Ira Berlin, *Generations of Captivity: A History of African American Slaves* (Cambridge, Mass., 2003), 111–123, 177–178; John Bezis-Selfa, "A Tale of Two Ironworks: Slavery, Free Labor, Work, and Resistance in the Early Republic," *WMQ* 61 (Oct. 1999): 677–700; Lois Green Carr and Lorena S. Walsh, "Economic Diversification and Labor Organization in the Chesapeake, 1650–1820," in *Work and Labor in the Early Republic*, ed. Stephen Innes (Chapel Hill, N.C., 1988), 175–188; Barbara Jeanne Fields, *Slavery and Freedom on the Middle Ground: Maryland during the Nineteenth Century* (New Haven, Conn., 1985), chaps. 1–4; Sylvia R. Frey and Betty Wood, *Come Shouting to Zion: African American Protestantism in the American South and British Caribbean to 1830* (Chapel Hill, N.C., 1998), 163–164, 190; Steven F. Miller, Susan E. O'Donovan, John C. Rodrigue, and Leslie S. Rowland, eds., "Between Emancipation and Enfranchisement: Law and the Political Mobilization of Black Southerners during Presidential Reconstruction, 1865–1867," *Chicago-Kent Law Review* 70 (1995): 1069–71; Lynda J. Morgan, *Eman-*

cipation in Virginia's Tobacco Belt, 1850–1870 (Athens, Ga., 1992), chaps. 1–3; Elizabeth Russey, "The Right Hand of Fellowship: African-Americans and the Baptist Church, 1820–1830" (M.A. thesis, University of Maryland, 2002); John T. Schlotterbeck, "The Internal Economy of Slavery in Rural Piedmont Virginia," in *The Slaves' Economy: Independent Production by Slaves in the Americas,* ed. Ira Berlin and Philip D. Morgan (London, 1991), 170–181; Tina H. Sheller, "Freemen, Servants, and Slaves: Artisans and the Craft Structure of Revolutionary Baltimore Town," in *American Artisans: Crafting Social Identity, 1750–1850,* ed. Howard B. Rock, Paul A. Gilje, and Robert Asher (Baltimore, 1995), 17–32; James Sidbury, "Slave Artisans in Richmond, Virginia, 1780–1830," in Rock et al., *American Artisans,* 48–62; Stevenson, *Life in Black and White,* pt. 2; Midori Takagi, *"Rearing Wolves to Our Own Destruction:" Slavery in Richmond, Virginia, 1782–1865* (Charlottesville, Va., 1999), chap. 2; Lorena Walsh, *From Calabar to Carter's Grove: The History of a Virginia Slave Community* (Charlottesville, Va., 1997), 119–133, chap. 7; Lorena Walsh, "Slave Life, Slave Society, and Tobacco Production in the Tidewater Chesapeake, 1620–1820," in Berlin and Morgan, *Cultivation and Culture,* 179–199; T. Stephan Whitman, *The Price of Freedom: Slavery and Manumission in Baltimore and Early National Maryland* (Lexington, Ky., 1997); John C. Willis, "From the Dictates of Pride to the Paths of Righteousness: Slave Honor and Christianity in Antebellum Virginia," in *The Edge of the South: Life in Nineteenth-Century Virginia,* ed. Edward L. Ayers and John C. Willis (Charlottesville, Va., 1991), 38–39.

14. Josephine A. Beoku-Betts, "'She Make Funny Flat Cake She Call Saraka': Gullah Women and Food Practices Under Slavery," in *Working toward Freedom: Slave Society and Domestic Economy in the American South,* ed. Larry Hudson Jr. (Rochester, N.Y., 1994), 211–231; Berlin, *Generations of Captivity,* 210–211; Margaret Washington Creel, *"A Peculiar People:" Slave Religion and Community-Culture Among the Gullahs* (New York, 1988); Charles Joyner, *Down by the Riverside: A South Carolina Slave Community* (Urbana, Ill., 1984); Timothy James Lockley, *Lines in the Sand: Race and Class in Lowcountry Georgia, 1750–1860* (Athens, Ga., 2001); Philip D. Morgan, "Task and Gang Systems: The Organization of Labor on New World Plantations," in *Work and Labor in Early America,* ed. Stephen Innes (Cha-

pel Hill, N.C., 1988), 189–220; Morgan, "Work and Culture: The Task System and the World of Lowcountry Blacks, 1700–1880," *WMQ* 39 (Oct. 1982): 563–599; Philip D. Morgan, "The Ownership of Property by Slaves in the Mid-Nineteenth-Century Low Country," *Journal of Southern History* 49 (Aug. 1983): 399–420; Dylan Penningroth, "Slavery, Freedom, and Social Claims to Property among African Americans in Liberty County, Georgia, 1850–1880," *Journal of American History* 84 (Sept. 1997): 405–435; John Scott Strickland, "Traditional Culture and Moral Economy: Social and Economic Change in the South Carolina Low Country, 1865–1910," in *The Countryside in the Age of Capitalist Transformation,* ed. Steven Hahn and Jonathan Prude (Chapel Hill, N.C., 1985), 147–148; William S. Pollitzer, *The Gullah People and Their African Heritage* (Athens, Ga., 1999), chaps. 8–10; Julie Saville, "Rites and Power: Reflections on Slavery, Freedom, and Political Ritual," in *From Slavery to Emancipation in the Atlantic World,* ed. Sylvia R. Frey and Betty Wood (London, 1999), 81–102; Betty Wood, *Women's Work, Men's Work: The Informal Slave Economies of Lowcountry Georgia* (Athens, Ga., 1995), 64.

15. James R. Lyle and John Calvin Johnson to Davis Tillson, 13 Jan. 1866, [A-5407]; Jonathan M. Bryant, *How Curious a Land: Conflict and Change in Greene County, Georgia, 1850–1885* (Chapel Hill, N.C., 1996), chap. 1; John Campbell, "'My Constant Companion': Slaves and Their Dogs in the Ante-bellum South," in Hudson, *Working toward Freedom,* 53–76; John Campbell, "As 'A Kind of Freeman'? Slaves' Market-Related Activities in the South Carolina Upcountry," in Berlin and Morgan, *The Slaves' Economy,* 131–169; Larry E. Hudson Jr., *To Have and to Hold: Slave Work and Family Life in Antebellum South Carolina* (Athens, Ga., 1997); Clarence L. Mohr, "Slavery in Oglethorpe County, Georgia, 1773–1865," *Phylon* 33 (Spring 1972): 4–21; Joseph P. Reidy, *From Slavery to Agrarian Capitalism in the Cotton Plantation South* (Chapel Hill, N.C., 1992), 65–73; Reidy, "Obligation and Right: Patterns of Labor, Subsistence, and Exchange in the Cotton Belt of Georgia, 1790–1860," in Berlin and Morgan, *Cultivation and Culture,* 138–154.

16. John Lamar to [Howell Cobb], 10 Mar. 1858, CEL; Du Bois, *Souls of Black Folk,* 111; Hawthorn Chamberline to Mother & Father, 29 Jan. 1860, HSC; Morgan, "Task and Gang Systems," 189–220; Reidy, *From Slavery to*

Agrarian Capitalism, 40–41; Miller, "Plantation Labor Organization," 155–169; Berlin, *Generations of Captivity,* 177–179.

17. *AP,* 7 Jan. 1846, 26 Jan. 1855; Plantation Journal, p. 5, HJF.

18. Powhattan Whittle to Lewis Whittle, 31 July 1854, Lewis N. Whittle Papers; *AP,* 11 Mar. 1858; "Plantation directions," [Jan. 1836], "Regulations for the year 1838," "Sumpter County 1842," "January 1845," all in HJF; Andrews, "Plantation Life along the River and Spring Creek," 129.

19. James Lyle and John Johnson to Davis Tillson, 13 Jan. 1866, [A-5407]; U.S. Congress, *Report of the Joint Committee on Reconstruction* (Washington, D.C., 1866), pt. 3, 104, 173; TCSC (1826–1835), 186, 216; George Davis to David Barrow, 6 Jan. 1860, DCB; William Clark to Edward Smith, 19 Nov. 1867, no. 20993, AMAr3; Andrews, "Plantation Life along the River and Spring Creek," 129–131; Du Bois, *Souls of Black Folk,* 111.

20. 19 Apr. 1858, WJD; vol. 2, DAH; JVL; George Davis to David Barrow, [3]0 Mar. 1855, DCB; "Directions May—1842," HJF; *SC,* 7 June 1843, Sept. 1849; Gray, *History of Agriculture,* 701, 710, 807; R. H. Clark, T. R. R. Cobb, and D. Irwin, comp., *The Code of the State of Georgia* (Atlanta, 1861), 368.

21. 6 Mar. 1861, vol. 2, DAH; Gray, *History of Agriculture,* 700–701; U.S. Naval Observatory, *Astronomical Applications,* "Sun or Moon Rise/Set Table for One Year," aa.usno.navy.mil/data/docs/RS_OneYear.html (accessed 4/13/06).

22. 22 Apr. 1857, JVL.

23. 20 July 1857, 21 July 1857, JVL; 14 June 1858, 24 June 1858, WJD; George Davis to David Barrow, [3]1 July 1855, DCB; George Davis to David Barrow, 23 Nov. 1863, DCB.

24. J. M. Harrison to David Barrow, 19 Oct. 1851, DCB; J. M. Harrison to David Barrow, 25 Nov. 1854, DCB; George Davis to David Barrow, 2 Sept. 1859, DCB; JVL; vol. 2, DAH; 19 Oct. 1858, WJD; Phillips, *Plantation and Frontier,* 1:309–312; Henry Tarver to [Elizabeth Tarver], 21 Sept. 1854, Henry A. Tarver Papers; Hawthorne Chamberline to Clara, 11 Nov. 1846, HSC.

25. George Davis to David Barrow, 14 Dec. 1860, DCB; Wm. G. Porter & Co. Letters, folder 8, box 11, DCB; 24 Dec. 1861, 31 Dec. 1861, vol. 2, DAH; JVL; WJD; Gray, *History of Agriculture,* 702–703.

26. 3 Aug. 1857, 9 Sept. 1857, 10 Sept. 1857, 11 Sept. 1857, 14–26 Sept. 1857,

JVL; George Davis to David Barrow, 17 Mar. 1855, DCB; George Davis to David Barrow, [3]1 July 1855, DCB; George Davis to David Barrow, 6 May 1859, DCB; 21 July 1858, 22 July 1858, 19 Aug. 1858, 7 Sept. 1858, 12 Oct. 1858, 25 Oct. 1858, WJD; "Sumpter County 1842," HJF.

27. 6 Mar. 1861, 8 Mar. 1861, 26 Mar. 1861, 15 June 1861, 19–20 June 1861, 24 June 1861, 1 July 1861, 6 July 1861, 27 July 1861, 8 Aug. 1861, 16 Aug. 1861, 24 Aug. 1861, 31 Aug. 1861, 7 Sept. 1861, 12 Sept. 1861, 26 Sept. 1861, 25–27 Dec. 1861, vol. 2, DAH; 4 July 1860, Gilbert M. Richardson Diary, Wright Family Papers, UGA; 6 Apr. 1857, 6 June 1857, 4 July 1857, 18 July 1857, JVL; 2 Jan. 1858, 13 Feb. 1858, 24 Apr. 1858, 1 May 1858, 15 May 1858, 25–29 Dec. 1858, WJD; "Sumpter County, 1842," HJF; J. M. Harrison to David Barrow, 13 Feb. 1855, DCB; *AP*, 27 Dec. 1850, 29 Dec. 1854, 1 Jan. 1857, 29 Dec. 1859.

28. 6 Feb. 1857, 7 Feb. 1857, JVL; "plantation instructions," [6 Jan. 1836], HJF; *SC*, July 1853.

29. George Davis to David Barrow, 10 Aug. 1860, and George Davis to David Barrow, 7 Sept. 1860, both in DCB; 31 Aug. 1857, 28 Sept. 1857, 29 Sept. 1857, JVL; *AP*, 13 Oct. 1854, 20 Oct. 1854; "January—1837" and "Regulations for the year 1838," both in HJF; fall entries, WJD.

30. JVL; vol. 2, DAH; 16 Ju[ly?] 1850, vol. 2, Moses Wadell Linton Plantation Account Book, Bass/Linton/Lipscomb/Wyche Family Papers, UGA; 6 May 1858, WJD; J. M. Harrison to David Barrow, 25 Nov. 1854, DCB; O'Donovan, "Journal of Nelson Tift (1985)," 84–85, 87, 89; "Directions for the year 1839," HJF; May Term 1852, TCSC (1838–1842); *SC*, Sept. 1849, p. 131, Dec. 1857; Gray, *History of Agriculture*, 701–703, 795–797. This evidence complicates a long-standing and generally polarized debate about the gender dimensions of slaves' agricultural work. For a recent example of those who accept the axiom "Men plowed, women hoed," see Deborah Gray White, *Ar'n't I a Woman? Female Slaves in the Plantation South*, rev. ed. (New York, 1999), 120–121; others, including Leslie A. Schwalm, in *A Hard Fight for We: Women's Transition from Slavery to Freedom in South Carolina* (Urbana, Ill., 1997), chap. 1, draw few distinctions between men and women's labor assignments.

31. JVL; vol. 2, DAH; Cole, "Plantation Account Book," 89. Slave hire records, which indicate that women brought only half the rents offered for

slave men, confirm the extent to which southwest Georgia's free citizens valued the productive capacity of men over that of women; see DCCO, M1:71–73, 82, 88, 100, 153–154; and Keith C. Barton, "'Good Cooks and Washers': Slave Hiring, Domestic Labor, and the Market in Bourbon County, Kentucky," *Journal of American History* 84 (Sept. 1997): 436–460; Randolph B. Campbell, "Slave Hiring in Texas," *American Historical Review* 93 (Feb. 1988): 107–114; Johnson, *Soul by Soul,* chap. 5; White, *Ar'n't I a Woman?* 101.

32. James Filey to David Barrow, 4 Sept. 1860, DCB; James Filey to David Barrow, 9 Sept. 1860, DCB; WJD; JVL; vol. 2, DAH; Henry Tarver to Betty, 2 June 1850, Henry A. Tarver Papers; Henry Tarver to [Elizabeth Tarver], 21 Sept, 1854, Henry A. Tarver Papers; Charlotte Thomas Marshall, ed., "Taylor Family Letters," *CECHS* 2 (1979): 75–76; Cole, "Plantation Account Book," 100–101; O'Donovan, "Journal of Nelson Tift, Part VII," 67–84, and "Journal of Nelson Tift, Part VIII," 82–102; January term 1852, ECPC (1851–1882); TCIC (1852–1859), 4, 290; Clark et al., *Code of the State of Georgia* (1861), 122.

33. J. M. Harrison to David Barrow, 2 Feb. 1855, DCB; James Filey to David Barrow, 4 Sept. 1860, DCB; George Davis to David Barrow, 4 Feb. 1861, DCB; George Davis to David Barrow, 4 Feb. 1861, DCB; Jonas Smith to John Lamar, 5 May 1851, CEL; "Directions May—1842," HJF; Cole, "Plantation Account Book," 85–120.

34. TCSC (1826–1835), 9, 13–14, 41, 46–47, 109, 145–148, 156, 192, 228–232, 353; TCSC (1835–1840), 32–34, 51; James Loftin et al. to William Schley, 7 Dec. 1835, GIC; O'Donovan, "Journal of Nelson Tift, Part II," 90–121.

35. "Sumpter County 1842," HJF; 15 Feb. 1851, vol. 2, Linton Plantation Account Books; Hawthorne Chamberline to Clara, 11 Nov. 1846, HSC; D. M. W., "Some Local History," *CECHS* 1 (1971): 116–118; Plantation Book, John B. Lamar Papers; Jonas Smith to John Lamar, 5 May 1851, CEL; Mrs. Howell Cobb to Howell Cobb, 21 Dec. 1856, CEL; W. P. Mount to John Lamar, 17 Dec. 1858, CEL; Stancil Barwick to John Lamar, 23 Dec. 1860, CEL.

36. Eliza Peterson freedwoman vs. Harry Peterson freedman, 14 Apr. 1866, Georgia Documents, EU; Alexander Allen to G. W. Allen, 24 Dec. 1849, George W. Allen Papers, SHC; records of Philip Joiner, 22 Sept. 1872,

no. 783, M816r6; Vina Micken, 27 May 1870, no. 476, M816r6; Lavinia Perkins vs. Josh Perkins, 9 July 1868, vol. 385, p. 98, ser. 1040, RG105; Emeline Saunders vs. John Saunders, 13 June 1868, vol. 186, p. 171, ser. 785, RG105; U.S. Congress, *Report of the Joint Committee on Reconstruction*, pt. 3, 104; for two examples of the age distribution of slaves in longer-settled cotton plantation areas, see Bryant, *How Curious a Land*, chap. 1; Morris, *Becoming Southern*, chap. 4.

37. TCSC (1854–1871), 220–221; DCSC, K:542–544; [Henry Tarver] to Dear Bet, 7 Sept. 1854, Henry A. Tarver Papers; Hawthorne Chamberline to Clara, 11 Nov. 1846, HSC; 21 Oct. 1860, 16 Dec. 1860, ABCB; 2 May 18 1848, 29 Dec. 1866, A. J. Swinney Diary; 16 [July] 1850, vol. 2, Linton Plantation Account Books; 27 Dec. 1858, vol. 1, WJD; Ch. Raushenberg to O. H. Howard, 6 June 1867, ser. 700, RG105; Cole, "Plantation Account Book," 103; D. M. W., "Some Local History," 116–118; *AP*, 15 Sept. 1854, 29 Dec. 1854, 1 Jan. 1857; *SE*, 19 July 1865; U.S. Congress, *Report of the Joint Committee on Reconstruction*, pt. 3, 104–105.

38. Jonas Smith to John Lamar, 5 May 1851, CEL; L. G. Childs to David Barrow, 17 Feb. 1859, DCB; DCIC (1854–1869), 289, 320; Membership Roster, Tarver Meeting House, ABCB; 15 July 1860, ABCM; 18 Apr. 1858, 2 May 1858, 9 May 1858, 10 Oct. 1858, WJD; William Clark to Edward Smith, no. 20993, AMAr3; *AP*, 4 Apr. 1851, 8 Aug. 1851, 27 Feb. 1852, 5 Mar. 1852; Eliza Frances Andrews, *A War-Time Journal of a Georgia Girl, 1864–1865* (New York, 1908), 137–138; Frances M. Stratton, trans., "Minutes and Records of the Colored Members of Macedonia Church at Blakely, Georgia, in 1860," *CECHS* 1 (1971): 86–91; Donald G. Mathews, *Religion in the Old South* (Chicago, 1997), chap. 4; John B. Boles, ed., *Masters and Slaves in the House of the Lord: Race and Religion in the American South, 1740–1870* (Lexington, Ky., 1988), chaps. 2, 5; for examples of slaves being admitted into a new church on the basis of letters of dismissal, see Blakely Baptist Church Minutes, 5 May 1860, 2 June 1860, 1 Sept. 1860, GDAH, and 19 Apr. 1840, 19 July 1840, vol. 1, FBCB. Estimates of formal slave membership in Christian churches have been tumbling in recent years, but conditions in southwest Georgia seem to have kept the population of enslaved adult evangelicals well below even the 25 percent level calculated by John C. Willis for antebellum Vir-

ginia; see Willis, "Dictates of Pride," 37–38, 51. On the relationship between the vitality of slaves' clandestine economy and their ability to organize and maintain formal churches, see Frey and Wood, *Come Shouting to Zion,* 202–203.

39. 1 Sept. and 5 Sept. 1857, JVL; James Filey to David Barrow, 28 Feb. 1863, DCB; TCSC (1846–1854), 253–254. I am not alone in calling for a more complicated understanding of what scholars commonly call "resistance." As historian Walter Johnson observes, every aspect of slaves' existence and everything they did "cannot simply be reformatted as resistance" to "the system that enslaved them." Slaves, in other words, conducted their lives and made their decisions in relationship to numerous points of reference, of which the people who owned them were only a portion (albeit a powerful portion). In addition to Johnson, see "On Agency," *Journal of Social History* 37 Fall (2003): 113–124, see Lila Abu-Lughod, "The Romance of Resistance: Tracing Transformations of Power through Bedouin Women," *American Ethnologist* 17 (Feb. 1990): 41–55.

40. David Harvey, *Justice, Nature and the Geography of Difference* (Malden, Mass., 1996), 217; Pierre Bourdieu, *The Logic of Practice,* trans. Richard Nice (Stanford, Calif., 1990), chap. 3; Thomas Spear, "Neo-Traditionalism and the Limits of Invention in British Colonial Africa," *Journal of African History* 44 (Mar. 2003): 3–27.

41. Fontaine Wells et al. to the General Assembly of Virginia, 31 Jan. 1835, Race & Slavery Petitions Project [PAR 11683507]; Edmund Lee to the General Assembly of the Commonwealth of Virginia, 29 Jan. 1851, Race & Slavery Petitions Project [PAR 11685110]; Miller et al., "Between Emancipation and Enfranchisement," 1069–71; Elsa Barkley Brown and Gregg D. Kimball, "Mapping the Terrain of Black Richmond," *Journal of Urban History* 21 (Mar. 1995): 296–346; Stephanie M. H. Camp, *Closer to Freedom: Enslaved Women and Everyday Resistance in the Plantation South* (Chapel Hill, N.C., 2004), 30–31; Mary Beth Corrigan, "'It's a Family Affair': Buying Freedom in the District of Columbia, 1850–1860," in Hudson, *Working toward Freedom,* 163–191; Frey and Wood, *Come Shouting to Zion,* 163–164, 170–172; Lockley, *Lines in the Sand,* 62–63; James Sidbury, *Race, Rebellion, and Identity in Gabriel's Virginia, 1730–1810* (Cambridge, 1997), 244–251; Takagi,

Rearing Wolves to Our Own Destruction, 26, 28–29, 31, 33–34, 44, 48, 88, 93, 101; Walsh, "Slave Life, Slave Society," 170–199.

42. 26–27 Nov. 1858, WJD; 10–11 Aug. 1857, JVL; Jonas Smith to John B. Lamar, 5 May 1851, CEL; Mary Kendall to Lydia Hamilton, 13 Apr. 1853, and Mary Kendall to Lydia Hamilton, 5 Aug. 1854, both in Hamilton-Kendall Papers, GDAH; DCCO, M1:11, 20, 34, 51–52, 69–100, 144; 21 Oct. 1860, ABCM; *SE*, 19 July 1865; *AP*, 3 Jan. 1851, 25 Dec. 1856, 1 Jan. 1857. Among the first to recognize the gendering of Deep South spaces was Debra Gray White (*Ar'n't I a Woman?* 75–76); more recent recognitions include Camp, *Closer to Freedom*, 28–32, 35–59.

43. 25 Apr. 1843, 5 May 1843, 6 May 1843, A. T. Havens Journal, UGA; John Lamar to Mrs. Howell Cobb, 9 Nov. 1855, CEL; Hawthorne Chamberlin to Ma, 29 May 1849, HSC; Hawthorne Chamberline to Ma, 22 Jan. 1851, HSC; Hawthorn Chamberlin to Mother and Father, 29 Jan. 1860, HSC; Charles L. Munnerlyn to James Shackelford, 23 Nov. 1839, James Shackelford Papers, SHC; JVL; DAH, vol. 2; Gilbert M. Richardson Diary, Wright Family Papers, UGA; WJD; Alexander Allen to G. W. Allen, 2 Feb. 1857, G. W. Allen Papers, SHC; Alexander Allen to G. W. Allen, 24 Mar. 1857, G. W. Allen Papers, SHC; *Savannah Daily Morning News*, 17 Mar. 1859; *SC*, Nov. 1852, 331; Willoughby, *Fair to Middlin'*, 117; Willoughby, *Flowing through Time*, 70–71.

44. J. M. Harrison to David Barrow, 10 Sept. 1850, 17 Oct. 1850, and 25 Oct. 1850, DCB; "Plantation Book," 14–17, John B. Lamar Papers, UGA; *AP*, 18 Sept. 1856; Henry Tarver to Dear Bet, 17 Sept. 1854, Henry A. Tarver Papers; on the location of slaves' property, see Penningroth, "Slavery, Freedom, and Social Claims," 405–435; on the relationship between black women and slaveholders' law, see Laura F. Edwards, "Enslaved Women and the Law: Paradoxes of Subordination in the Post-Revolutionary Carolinas," *Slavery & Abolition* 26 (Aug. 2005): 305–323.

45. J. E. Huguenin to Mrs. [Lewis] Whittle and Julia, 3 Jan. 1856, Lewis B. Whittle Papers, SHC; on the politics of slaves' dress, see Shane White and Graham White, *Stylin': African American Expressive Culture from Its Beginnings to the Zoot Suit* (Ithaca, N.Y., 1998), chaps. 1–2, and White and White, "Slave Hair and African American Culture in the

Eighteenth and Nineteenth Centuries," *Journal of Southern History* 61 (Feb. 1995): 45–76.

46. 22 Oct. 1842, 16 Nov. 1844, FBCB; Stratton, "Colored Members of the Macedonia Church," 86–91; "Membership Roster," ABCB.

47. "Colored Males and Females at the Arm at Tarver's Meeting House," ABCB; the distances traveled by the enslaved Baptists have been derived from unpublished landownership data for Dougherty County, compiled and mapped by the author and Lee W. Formwalt.

48. DCSC, A:253, 267, 320, 524, 552; DCSC, K:3, 24, 38, 78, 167, 184, 188, 313, 421; DCIC (1854–1869), 43, 48, 54, 56, 194; January Term, 1852, ECPC (1851–1882); TCSC (1835–1840), 8, 30–34, 122–224; TCSC (1840–1841), 39–41, 54–57, 58–64, 104–105; TCSC (1846–1854), 28–30, 60–64, 230–231, 251–254, 261–262, 288; TCSC (1854–1871), 30, 220–221; TCSC (1858–1865), 34, 56–57, 137–138, 175, 249, 257–259; TCIC, 5:4, 162, 179, 229, 259, 266, 290, 296–297, 347, 351; Clark et al., *Code of the State of Georgia* (1861), 123; George Davis to David Barrow, 17 Mar. 1855, DCB; James Filey to David Barrow, 14 Dec. 1862, DCB; Hawthorn S. Chamberline to Mother, 10 June 1847, HSC; Hawthorn S. Chamberline to Ma, 9 May 1849, HSC; *AP,* 10 June 1846, 8 Aug. 1851, 6 Feb. 1852, 1 June 1855, 17 June 1858, 24 Feb 1859; O'Donovan, "Journal of Nelson Tift, Part VII," 75; Edward A. Mueller, *Perilous Journeys: A History of Steamboating on the Chattahoochee, Apalachicola, and Flint Rivers, 1828–1928* (Eufaula, Ala., 1990), 15, 29, 36, 68–69, 72, 79, 83, 87–88, 92, 94, 97, 102, C1–C14; Lynn Willoughby Ware, "Cotton Money: Antebellum Currency Conditions in the Apalachicola/Chattahoochee River Valley," *GHQ* 74 (Summer 1990): 215–233; Donald Todd, *The History of Clay County* (Fort Gaines, Ga., 1976), 7; Louis Schmier, "Notes and Documents on the 1862 Expulsion of Jews from Thomasville, Georgia," *American Jewish Archives* 32 (April 1980): 9–22; Louis Schmier, "A 'Jewish Missionary' among the Gentiles: Charles Wesslowsky's Georgia Years," *JSwGH* 1 (Fall 1983): 23–37.

49. DCSC, A:253, 267, 320, 524, 552; DCSC, K:3, 24, 38, 78, 167, 184, 188, 313, 421; DCIC (1854–1869), 43, 48, 54, 56, 194; January term, 1852, ECPC (1858–1881); TCSC (1835–1840), 8, 30–34, 122–124; TCSC (1840–1841), 39–41, 54–57, 58–64, 104–105; TCSC (1846–1854), 28–30, 60–64, 230–231, 251–254, 261–262, 288; TCSC (1854–1871), 30, 220–221; TCSC (1858–1865), 34, 56–57,

137–138, 175, 249, 257–259; TCIC, 5:4, 162, 179, 229, 259, 266, 290, 296–297, 347, 351; Clark et al., *Code of the State of Georgia* (1861), 123; George Davis to David Barrow, 17 Mar. 1855, DCB; James Filey to David Barrow, 14 Dec. 1862, DCB; Hawthorn Chamberline to Mother, 10 June 1847, HSC; Hawthorn Chamberline to Ma, 9 May 1849, HSC; AP, 10 June 1846, 8 Aug. 1851, 6 Feb. 1852, 1 June 1855, 17 June 1858, 24 Feb. 1859; O'Donovan, "Journal of Nelson Tift, Part VII," 75; Mueller, *Perilous Journeys*, 15, 29, 36, 68–69, 72, 79, 83, 87–88, 92, 94, 97, 102, C1–C14; Ware, "Cotton Money," 215–233; Donald Todd, *The History of Clay County* (Fort Gaines, Ga., 1976), 7; Schmier, "Notes and Documents on the 1862 Expulsion of Jews from Thomasville, Georgia," 9–22; Schmier, "A 'Jewish Missionary' Among the Gentiles," 23–37.

50. TCSC (1846–1854), 251–253; AP, 30 Aug. 1850, 17 Jan. 1851, 4 Oct. 1860; 8 Oct. 1860, Swinney Diary; Nelson Tift to Charles McDonald, 28 Oct. 1843, GIC; 7 May 1843, Havens Journal; undated newspaper clipping, [Jan. 1868], Eliza Andrews Scrapbook, Andrews Papers, SHC; O'Donovan, "Journal of Nelson Tift, Part V," 103–105; Fussell Chalker, "Irish Catholics in the Building of the Ocmulgee and Flint Railroad," *GHQ* 54 (Winter 1970): 512–513. On slave watermen in transatlantic communities, as well as the revolutionary dynamics of their global conversations, see W. Jeffery Bolster, *Black Jacks: African American Seamen in the Age of Sail* (Cambridge, Mass., 1997); David S. Celeski, *The Waterman's Song: Slavery and Freedom in Maritime North Carolina* (Chapel Hill, N.C., 2001); Peter Linebaugh and Marcus Rediker, *The Many-Headed Hydra: Sailors, Commoners, and the Hidden History of the Revolutionary Atlantic* (Boston, 2000).

51. 22 Apr. 1858, WJD; 21 Jan. 1861, 15–19 May 1861, 26 Sept.-5 Oct. 1861, vol. 2, DAH; TCSC (1846–1854), 251–253; AP, 6 June 1851, 9 Jan. 1852, 24 Feb. 1859; among the more recent to note the predominance of men among runaways, see John Hope Franklin and Loren Schweninger, *Runaway Slaves: Rebels on the Plantation* (New York, 2000), 210–223.

52. Phillips, *Plantation and Frontier*, 1:312–313.

53. George Davis to David Barrow, 30 Mar. 1860, DCB.

54. "Tobacco accounts with slaves," [1859], WJD; Plantation Book, pp. 14–17, John B. Lamar Papers; 20 Oct. 1860, 9 Nov. 1860, 4 Dec. 1860, Gilbert M. Richardson Diary, Wright Family Papers; Hawthorn Chamber-

line to Clara, 11 Nov. 1846, HSC; Cole, "Plantation Account Book," 85–120; George Davis to David Barrow, 11 Mar. 1859, DCB; W. S. Rackley to David Barrow, 16 Mar. 1859, DCB; George Davis to David Barrow, 25 Mar. 1859, DCB; Eliza Peterson freedwoman vs. Harry Peterson freedman, 14 Apr. 1866, Georgia Documents, EU; *AP,* 29 Dec. 1854, 1 Jan. 1857; Monday (a slave) vs. The State of Georgia, *Reports of Cases in Law and Equity, Argued and Determined in the Supreme Court of the State of Georgia* 32 (Macon, Ga., 1869), 672–680.

2. CIVIL WAR IN THE LAND OF GOSHEN

1. See, for instance, Nancy D. Bercaw, *Gendered Freedoms: Race, Rights, and the Politics of Household in the Delta* (Gainesville, Fla., 2003), chap. 1; Wayne K Durrill, *War of Another Kind: A Southern Community in the Great Rebellion* (New York, 1990), chap. 2; Drew Gilpin Faust, *Mothers of Invention: Women of the Slaveholding South in the American Civil War* (Chapel Hill, N.C., 1996); Leslie A. Schwalm, *A Hard Fight for We: Women's Transition from Slavery to Freedom in South Carolina* (Urbana, Ill., 1993), chap. 3; Noralee Frankel, *Freedom's Women: Black Women and Families in Civil War Era Mississippi* (Bloomington, Ind., 1999), chaps. 1–2; David Williams, *Rich Man's War: Class, Caste, and Confederate Defeat in the Lower Chattahoochee Valley* (Athens, Ga., 1998); Eric Foner, *Reconstruction: America's Unfinished Revolution, 1863–1877* (New York, 1988).

2. TCSC (1826–1835), 145–148, 228–232; TCSC (1835–1840), 32–34; DCIC (1856–1866), 194; Hawthorne Chamberline to Mother, 19 Oct. 1850, HSC; *AP,* 9 Aug. 1850, 30 Aug. 1850, 10 Oct. 1850, 15 Nov. 1850, 16 Sept. 1853, 27 Oct. 1854, 24 Apr. 1856, 1 May 1856, 8 May 1856, 6 May 1858, 17 June 1858, 1 Dec. 1859; James M. McPherson, *The Battle Cry of Freedom: The Civil War Era* (New York, 1988), 148–151. Unless otherwise noted, federal census figures are taken from the Geospatial and Statistical Data Center, *Historical Census Browser,* fisher.lib.virginia.edu/collections/stats/histcensus/ (accessed 4/13/06).

3. Joseph C. C. Kennedy, comp., *Population of the United States in 1860; Compiled from the Original Returns of the Eighth Census* (Washington, D.C.,

1864), 1:62–65; DCSC, K:313, 421; *AP*, 22 Dec. 1859, 4 Oct. 1860, 11 Oct. 1860, 22 Nov. 1860, 6 Dec. 1860, 13 Dec. 1860; *SE*, 13 June 1860, 7 Nov. 1860; Williams, *Rich Man's War*, 40–41.

4. 6 Nov. 1860, A. J. Swinney Diary, THC; *AP*, 22 Nov. 1860; *SE*, 7 Nov. 1860, 14 Nov. 1860; Kenneth Coleman, ed., *A History of Georgia* (Athens, Ga., 1977), 149; Eliza Frances Andrews, *The War-Time Journal of a Georgia Girl, 1864–1865* (New York, 1908), 63; Michael P. Johnson, *Toward a Patriarchal Republic: The Secession of Georgia* (Baton Rouge, 1977), 118; Williams, *Rich Man's War*, 42.

5. *SE*, 7 Nov. 1860, 21 Nov. 1860, 12 Dec. 1860, 9 Jan. 1861; *AP*, 15 Nov. 1860, 6 Dec. 1860, 13 Dec. 1860; Williams, *Rich Man's War*, 46–50.

6. *AP*, 3 Jan. 1861, 10 Jan. 1861, 24 Jan. 1861; *SE*, 9 Jan. 1861; Johnson, *Toward a Patriarchal Republic*, 60, chap. 6; Williams, *Rich Man's War*, 46–47.

7. "Report of the Number of Members in Uniform in Each Volunteer Corps of Ga.," 1860, GIC; A. Hood to Joseph Brown, 6 May 1861, GIC; D. A. Vason to Joseph Brown, 6 June 1861, GIC; W. L. Lawton to L. Pope Walker, 4 Mar. 1861, M437r1; John Lyon to R. To[wl], 15 Mar. 1861, M437r1; early May 1861, A. J. Swinney Diary; *AP*, 14 Mar., 21 Mar., 2 May 1861; Williams, *Rich Man's War*, 52–55.

8. D. J. Brandon to President Davis, 24 Apr. 1861, M437r1; Sarah Yancey to Benjamin Yancey, 8 Nov. 1861, Benjamin C. Yancey Papers, DU; Richd. Sims to Joseph Brown, [n.d.] 1861, GIC; Waltwen Kelley to Joseph Brown, 18 June 1861, GIC; J. H. Taylor to [David] Barrow, 16 June 1861, DCB; George Davis to D. C. Barrow, 21 June 1861, DCB; James Filey to David Barrow, 20 July 1861, DCB; Jos. J. Bradford to D. C. Barrow, 24 July 1861, DCB; James Filey to David Barrow, DCB; *AP*, 16 May 1861; *SE*, 10 July 1861; Williams, *Rich Man's War*, 58.

9. 1–31 Jan. 1861, 13–22 Apr. 1861, 28 July 1861, vol. 2, DAH; Ira Berlin, Barbara J. Fields, Thavolia Glymph, Joseph P. Reidy, and Leslie S. Rowland, eds., *The Destruction of Slavery* (Cambridge, 1985), 347.

10. George Davis to David Barrow, 21 May 1861, DCB; George Davis to David Barrow, 21 June 1861, DCB; G. H. Davis to David Barrow, 24 Aug. 1861, DCB; James Filey to David Barrow, 8 Sept. 1861, DCB; George Davis to David Barrow, 13 Sept. 1861, DCB; George Davis to David Barrow, 24 Sept.

1861, DCB; G. H. Davis to David C. Barrow, 17 Nov. 1861, DCB; G. H. Davis to David Barrow, 27 Nov. 1861, DCB; George Davis to David Barrow, 4 Jan. 1862, DCB; John Lamar to Howell Cobb, 3 Nov. 1861, CEL; Hawthorne Chamberline to Father & Mother, 14 July 1861, HSC.

11. Slaveholders' insistence on maintaining discipline through arduous labor shocked even those long accustomed to the sight of hardworking slaves. When planters later in the war lengthened the workweek to include Sundays, the editor of an Early County newspaper objected. "This is what we call 'whipping the devil 'round the stump'" (*ECN*, 4 May 1864).

12. DCCO, M1:421; *SE*, 1 May 1861; Fred Burtz to Joseph Brown, 29 Mar. 1862, GIC; R. K. Hines to Joseph Brown, 6 Mar. 1862, GIC; Richard Lyon to Joseph Brown, 9 Aug. 1862, GIC; G. B. Loyaless to Joseph Brown, 9 Sept. 1862, GIC; Williams, *Rich Man's War*, 97–101, 129; T. Conn Bryan, *Confederate Georgia* (Athens, Ga., 1953), 85–87.

13. David Barrow to George Davis, 12 Apr. 1863, DCB; G. H. Davis to David Barrow, 24 Aug. 1861, DCB; DCIC (1854–1869), 372; *MDT*, 19 July 1864; P. W. Alexander to [J. H. Wilson], 1 June 1865, ser. 16, [A-5814]; J. P. M. Epping to S. P. Chase, 4 May 1864, Miscellaneous Letters Received: K series, ser. 103, National Archives, Record Group 56, Freedmen and Southern Society Project document control no. [X-256]; Allen D. Candler, comp., *The Confederate Records of the State of Georgia* (Atlanta, Ga., 1909), 2:367; Bryan, *Confederate Georgia*, 121–122; James L. Roark, *Masters without Slaves: Southern Planters in the Civil War and Reconstruction* (New York, 1977), 42.

14. *OR*, ser. 1, 14:506–507; *NOR*, ser. 1, 17:443–444, 494–497, 856–857; B. J. Smith to Joseph Brown, 13 Aug. 1864, GIC; Columbus warehouseman quoted in Williams, *Rich Man's War*, 99–100; Sidney Andrews, *The South since the War: As Shown by Fourteen Weeks of Travel and Observation in Georgia and the Carolinas* (Boston, 1866), 318.

15. Richard Lyon to Joseph Brown, 9 Aug. 1862, GIC; Y. G. Rust & Others to Joseph Brown, 24 Apr. 1861, GIC; A. Hood to Joseph Brown, 6 May 1861, GIC; *AP*, 25 Apr. 1861, 7 Nov. 1861.

16. C. B. Calloway to Joseph Brown, GIC; DCIC (1854–1869), 194; TCSC (1858–1865), 401; TCIC (1861–1870), 81–106; *AP*, 24 Jan. 1861; U.S. Congress, *Report of the Joint Committee on Reconstruction* (Washington, D.C., 1866),

pt. 3, 108; 30 Apr. 1862, 5 July 1862, A. J. Swinney Diary; on slave women as healers, see Sharla M. Fett, *Working Cures: Healing, Health, and Power on Southern Slave Plantations* (Chapel Hill, N.C., 2002), chap. 5.

17. T. H. Taylor to David Barrow, 16 June 1861, DCB; George Davis to David Barrow, DCB; Joseph Bradford to David Barrow, DCB; C. B. Calloway to Gov. Brown, 25 Feb. 1862, GIC; *SE*, 10 July 1861.

18. Perry Curry to Duncan Curry, 20 June 1862, CHP; Archibald Curry to Duncan Curry, 2 July 1862, CHP.

19. George Davis to David Barrow, 30 Mar. 1860, DCB; George Davis to David Barrow, 2 Jan. 1862, DCB; James Filey to David Barrow, 14 Dec. 1862, DCB; Martin Curry to Duncan Curry, 19 Aug. 1862, CHP; 12 Nov. 1862, Narcissa Melissa Lawton Diary, Peeples Collection, GDAH.

20. Mary Jane Curry to Duncan Curry, 28 Aug. 1862, CHP; Mary Jane Curry to Duncan Curry, 22 Sept. 1862, CHP; Mary Jane Curry to Duncan Curry, 4 Nov. 1862, CHP; George Davis to David Barrow, 27 July 1861, DCB; George Davis to David Barrow, 18 May 1862, DCB; George Davis to David Barrow, 20 July 1862, DCB; W. B. Braswell to David Barrow, 18 Aug. 1862, DCB; George Davis to David Barrow, 9 Sept. 1862, DCB; *NOR*, ser. 1, 17:323.

21. Leila Calloway to Morgan Calloway, 30 Sept. 1862, MCP; Morgan Calloway to Leila Calloway, 16 July 1863, MCP; Mary Jane Curry to Duncan Curry, 22 Sept. 1862, CHP; TCIC (1861–1870), 86.

22. DCIC (1854–1869), 320, 333, 346; D. A. Vason to [Joseph Brown], 6 June 1861, GIC; *ECN*, 11 Nov. 1863; William G. Proctor Jr., "Slavery in Southwest Georgia," *GHQ* 49 (Mar. 1965): 10.

23. Timothy S. Huebner, "The Roots of Fairness: *State V. Caesar* and Slave Justice in Antebellum North Carolina," and Ariela Gross, "The Law and Culture of Slavery: Natchez, Mississippi," both in *Local Matters: Race, Crime, and Justice in the Nineteenth-Century South,* ed. Christopher Waldrep and Donald G. Nieman (Athens, Ga., 2001), 29–52, 92–124.

24. TCSC (1858–1865), 435, 451–453, 493–495; Monday, (a slave), *vs.* The State of Georgia (1861), Georgia Supreme Court, *Reports of Cases in Law and Equity, Argued and Determined in the Supreme Court of the State of Georgia* (Macon, Ga., 1869), 32:672–680; DCSC, L:83–84.

25. R. K. Hines to Joseph Brown, 6 Mar. 1862, GIC; William Castleberry

and Wm. J. Johnson to [Joseph Brown], 1 Aug. 1862, GIC; John O'Connor to [Joseph Brown], 10 Mar. 1862, GIC; R. K. Hines to Joseph Brown, 6 Mar. 1862, GIC; J. A. Zeigler to Joseph Brown, 19 Nov. 1862, GIC; contract between E. W. Jenkins et al., and N. Tift et al., 15 July 1864, Miscellaneous Papers, M798r36; *GWT,* 18 May 1861; *AP,* 16 May 1861; John Davis to Howell Cobb, 8 May 1863, Howell Cobb Papers, UGA; *OR,* ser. 1, 14:493–494, 506–507, 645; 9 July 1861, ECPC (1851–1882); Nelson Tift, "Dougherty County: Historical Address," *JSwGH* 4 (Fall 1986): 16; Louis Schmier, "Notes and Documents on the 1862 Expulsion of Jews from Thomasville, Georgia," *American Jewish Archives* 32 (April 1980): 9–22; Maxine Turner, *Navy Gray: A Story of the Confederate Navy on the Chattahoochee and Apalachicola Rivers* (Tuscaloosa, Ala., 1988), 76–81, 149–150; Williams, *Rich Man's War,* 65–68.

26. D. A. Vason to [Joseph Brown], 6 June 1861, GIC; G. H. Davis to David Barrow, 17 Nov. 1861, DCB; Berlin et al., *The Destruction of Slavery,* 70–72, 111, 118–120, 414–415; Clarence Mohr, *On the Threshold of Freedom: Masters and Slaves in Civil War Georgia* (Athens, Ga., 1986), chap. 3; Julie Saville, "Rights and Power: Reflections on Slavery, Freedom, and Political Ritual," in *From Slavery to Emancipation in the Atlantic World,* ed. Sylvia R. Frey and Betty Wood (London, 1999), 81–102.

27. *MDT,* 22 July 1862; Stansil Barwick to Howell Cobb, 30 July 1862, CEL; Berlin et al., *The Destruction of Slavery,* 664; Mohr, *On the Threshold of Freedom,* 122–123; Bernard H. Nelson, "Confederate Slave Impressment Legislation, 1861–1865," *Journal of Negro History* 31 (Oct. 1946): 392–410.

28. William Castleberry and William Johnson to [Joseph Brown], 1 Aug. 1862, GIC; *MDT,* 28 July 1862, 30 July 1862, 7 Aug. 1862, 22 Aug. 1862, 26 Aug. 1862.

29. Richard Lyon to Joseph Brown, 9 Aug. 1862, GIC; *MDT,* 22 July 1862, 28 July 1862, 22 Aug. 1862.

30. *GWT,* 8 Aug. 1862, 15 Aug. 1862, 22 Aug. 1862, 24 Oct. 1862; *MDT,* 7 Aug. 1862, 22 Aug. 1862, 1 Sept. 1862; George Davis to David Barrow, 1 Sept. 1862, DCB; John Cobb to Howell Cobb, 20 Dec. 1862, CEL; Benjamin C. Yancey Account Book, GDAH, p. 78; Candler, *Confederate Records of the State of Georgia,* 2:236–239; Mohr, *On the Threshold of Freedom,* 122–125.

31. John Davis to Howell Cobb, 8 May 1863, Howell Cobb Papers; Theodore Moreno to Howell Cobb, 9 May 1863, Howell Cobb Papers; B. F. White to Lamar Cobb, 14 Jan. 1865, CEL; John Boatright to David Barrow, 16 Sept. 1864, DCB; *OR*, ser. 1, 14:542–543; Mohr, *On the Threshold of Freedom*, 121, 126; Turner, *Navy Gray*, 54.

32. Alexander Allen to George W. Allen, 8 Oct. 1864, George Washington Allen Papers, SHC; John Cobb to Howell Cobb, 20 Dec. 1862, CEL; *OR*, ser. 1, 26:817; Andrews, *The South since the War*, 321; Andrews, *War-Time Journal of a Georgia Girl*, 20; Mohr, *On the Threshold of Freedom*, 99–100; Berlin et al., *The Destruction of Slavery* 675–676, Durrill, *War of Another Kind*, chap. 3.

33. N. Cruger to R. Saxton, 15 July 1865, ser. 2922, RG105; John Cobb to Howell Cobb, 20 Dec. 1862, CEL; Andrews, *The South since the War*, 289; Williams, *Rich Man's War*, 108; Mary Elizabeth Massey, *Refugee Life in the Confederacy* (Baton Rouge, 1964), 85–86; Turner, *Navy Gray*, 76; Mohr, *On the Threshold of Freedom*, 100.

34. W. H. S. to Henry [Stiles], 24 Dec. 1863, MSF; [J. H. B.] Shackleford to [Joseph Brown], 19 Sept. 1863, GIC; Wm. Henry Stiles Jr. to William Henry Stiles, 14 Jan. 1864, WHS; DCCO, M1:421.

35. Hillary Mundy to Joseph Brown, 22 July 1864, GIC; M. B. Calloway, "Recollections of Plantation Life, in the Years Following the Civil War," 3, J. F. Waring Collection, Georgia Historical Society, Savannah; Lucy Cobb to Mary, 1 Dec. 1864, CEL; Howell Cobb Jr. to Mary McKinley, 13 Dec. 1864, CEL; Pope Barrow to [David Barrow], 7 Mar. 1863, DCB; Katy [Taylor] to Nelly, 28 Jan. 1865, DCB; Susan Olivia Fleming to Eleonore Eulalie Cay, 9 Mar. 1865, Eleonore Eulalie (Cay) Fleming Papers, SHC; E. H. Bacon to the Agent of the Freedmans Bureau at Savannah Georgia, [28 Sept. 1865], ser. 1022, [A-5799]; 23 Oct. 1864, ABCM; DCIC (1854–1869), 415–417; *MFU*, 23 Nov. 1866; Andrews, *War-Time Journal of a Georgia Girl*, 62–63; Massey, *Refugee Life in the Confederacy*, 106, 246; Robert Manson Myers, ed., *The Children of Pride: A True Story of Georgia and the Civil War*, abr. ed. (New Haven, Conn., 1984), 535–541.

36. G. A. Hastings to W. W. Deane, 24 Dec. 1865, ser. 632, [A-5237]; J. P. Stevens to the Chief of the Freedmens Bureau Savannah Georgia, 19 Dec.

1865, ser. 1013, [A-5748]; C. C. Richardson to Davis Tillson, 2 Jan. 1866, ULR, M798r28; Youell Rust to Joseph Brown, 24 Apr. 1864, GIC; Richd H. Clark to Dear Gov., 8 Aug. 1864, GIC; 6 Aug. 1864, ECPC (1851–1882); Sam Bowers Hilliard, *Atlas of Antebellum Southern Agriculture* (Baton Rouge, 1984), 34.

37. C. B. Calloway to Joseph Brown, 25 Feb. 1862, GIC; Williams, *Rich Man's War*, chap. 5; for a more general statement about the impact of Confederate conscription policies on nonslaveholders, see Paul D. Escott, "'The Cry of the Sufferers': The Problem of Welfare in the Confederacy," *Civil War History* 23 (Sept. 1977): 228–240.

38. John Boatright to D. C. Barrow, 16 Sept. 1864, DCB; M. W. Scott to Howell Cobb, 30 Apr. 1863, Howell Cobb Papers; John Cobb to Howell Cobb, 20 Mar. 1863, Howell Cobb Papers; John Cobb to Howell Cobb, 15 June 1863, CEL; TCSC (1858–1865), 493–495; *OR*, ser. 4, 2:160–162, 553–554; Bryan, *Confederate Georgia*, 124.

39. Tift, "Dougherty County," 9–15. These numbers are high, but not extraordinarily so; a recent estimate suggests that one-third of all Confederate soldiers died of disease or on the battlefield, while another 40 percent were wounded. See Gary W. Gallagher, *The Confederate War* (Cambridge, Mass., 1997), 29.

40. W. H. S. to My Dear Wife, 12 Sept. 1865, MSF; Mohr, *On the Threshold of Freedom*, 110.

41. W. H. S. to Henry, 24 Dec. 1862, MSF; William Henry Stiles to Elizabeth Ann Stiles, 7 Jan. 1864, 31 Mar. 1864, 2 Apr. 1864, 28 Apr. 1864, MSF; William Henry Stiles to Robert Stiles, 16 May 1864, MSF; W. H. S. to My Dear Wife, 12 Sept. 1865, MSF; "Expenditures," 1864; "List of Negroes at Plantation in Terrell Co."; "Confederate Tax of W. H. Stiles in 1864"; all in WHS.

42. William Henry Stiles to Elizabeth Ann Stiles, 7 Jan. 1864, 28 Apr. 1864, 4 May 1864, MSF; William H. Stiles to [Eliza Stiles], 12 Sept. 1865, MSF; William H. Stiles Jr. to Father, 14 Jan. 1864, and "Expenditures," 1864, both in WHS.

43. H. Whitaker to William H. Branch, 18 Mar. 1863, Branch Family Papers, SHC; for further examples of slaves' responses to owners' wartime flight, see Durrill, *War of Another Kind*, chap. 6.

44. General affidavit of Henry Baker, 23 Feb. 1891, pension file of Peter McGee, SC 22909, Civil War Pension Files, Record Group 15, National Archives; W. B. Braswell to David Barrow, 28 June 1862, DCB; W. B. Braswell to David Barrow, 18 Aug. 1862, DCB; Wm. B. Braswell to David Barrow, 4 Dec. 1862, DCB; Wm. B. Braswell to David Barrow, 22 Dec. 1862, DCB; Alexander Allen to David Barrow, 16 Oct. 1863, DCB; W. E. Davis to [David Barrow], 16 Oct. 1863, DCB; Stancil Barwick to John Cobb, 23 Dec. 1863, DCB; L. Jacks to Baker Daniel, 26 Jan. 1864, DCB; Wm. Braswell to John Cobb, 28 Feb. 1864, DCB; James Filey to David Barrow, 20 July 186[4], DCB; *MDT,* 28 July 1864; *NOR,* ser. 1, 17:323, 493–497, 648–652; Bryan, *Confederate Georgia,* 127. According to naval enlistment records, sixteen other black men with ties to southwest Georgia followed Davis's route out of bondage; see National Park Service, *Civil War Soldiers and Sailors System,* itd.nps.gov/cwss/ sailors_index.html (accessed 29/04/06).

45. Mary Jane Curry to Duncan Curry, 8 Apr. 1862, CHP; Mary Jane Curry to Duncan Curry, 9 May 1862, CHP; Perry Curry to Duncan Curry, 10 May 1862, CHP; Mary Jane Curry to Duncan Curry, 19 May 1862, CHP; Leila Calloway to Morgan Calloway, 13 May 1862, MCP; Leila Calloway to Morgan Calloway, 30 Sept. 1862, MCP; Leila Calloway to Morgan Calloway, 7 Nov. 1862, MCP; Leila Calloway to Morgan Calloway, 19 Jan. 1863, MCP; William Henry Stiles to Elizabeth Stiles, 31 Mar. 1864, MSF; Elizabeth Stiles to William Henry Stiles, 5 Apr. 1864, MSF; William Henry Stiles to Elizabeth Stiles, 14 Apr. 1864, MSF; John Davis to Howell Cobb, Howell Cobb Papers; "Out-Work," WHS; DCCO, M1:372, 421; W. E. B. Du Bois, *The Souls of Black Folk,* ed. David W. Blight and Robert Gooding-Williams (Boston, 1997), 109.

46. Leila Calloway to Morgan Calloway, 30 Sept. 1862, MCP; Leila Calloway to Morgan Calloway, 6 Oct. 1862, MCP; John A. Davis to Howell Cobb, 8 May 1863, Howell Cobb Papers; Thomas Morrow to Howell Cobb, 9 May 1863, Howell Cobb Papers; William H. Stiles to Wife, 31 Mar. 1864, MSF; [Eliza Stiles] to William H. Stiles, 5 Apr. 1864, MSF; William H. Stiles to Wife, 14 Apr. 1864, MSF; William H. Stiles to [Eliza Stiles], 8 May 1864, 27 June 1864, MSF; 25 Jan. 1862, Dougherty County Minutes of the County Court, 1859–1866, GDAH; Juanita Whiddon, "David Saunders Johnston: The Man and His Times," *CECHS* 2 (1979): 136–146.

47. Mollie Davis to David Barrow, 13 Sept. 1864, DCB; Morgan Calloway to Leila Calloway, 27 Aug. 1864, MCP; O. H. Prince to Daughter, 25 July 1864, Jackson and Prince Family Papers, *Records of Ante-Bellum Southern Plantations from the Revolution through the Civil War*, ed. Kenneth M. Stampp (Frederick, Md., 1985–), ser. J, pt. 4; H. C. Thornton to Joseph Brown, 31 July 1864, GIC; S. S. Massey to Joseph Brown, 8 Mar. 1865, GIC; *ECN*, 6 Apr. 1864, 8 Mar. 1865; Andrews, *War-Time Journal of a Georgia Girl*, 70.

48. Hillary Mundy to Joseph Brown, 22 July 1864, GIC; Mrs. H. C. Thornton to Gov. Browne, 31 July 1864, GIC; Mrs. Mitchell Jones to Joseph Brown, 22 Aug. 1864, GIC; O. H. Prince to Daughter, 4 July 1864, Jackson and Prince Family Papers; O. H. Prince to Daughter, 25 July 1864, Jackson and Prince Family Papers; O. H. Prince to Sarah, 23 Nov. 1864, Jackson and Prince Family Papers; O. H. Prince to Sarah, 30 Nov. 1864, Jackson and Prince Family Papers; *ECN*, 6 Apr. 1864.

49. Morgan Calloway to Leila Calloway, 23 Aug. 1864, MCP.

50. George Davis to David Barrow, 18 May 1862, 23 June 1862, DCB; Wm. Braswell to David Barrow, 28 June 1863, DCB; George Davis to David Barrow, 20 July 1862, DCB; J. Bradwell to David Barrow, 27 Apr. 1863, DCB; Alexander Allen to David Barrow, 16 Oct. 1863, DCB; G. H. Davis to David Barrow, 23 Nov. 1863, DCB; W. E. Davis to [David Barrow], 16 Oct. 1863, DCB; James Filey to David Barrow, 25 Oct. 1863, DCB; Stancel Barwick to John Cobb, 23 Dec. 1863, DCB; John Cobb to David Barrow, 31 Dec. 1863, DCB; James Filey to David Barrow, 9 Apr. 1864, DCB; L. Jacks to Baker Daniel, 26 Jan. 1864, DCB; John Lamar to Howell Cobb, 3 Nov. 1861, CEL; Perry Curry to Duncan Curry, 16 Apr. 1862, CHP; Mary Jane Curry to Duncan Curry, 28 Aug. 1862, 4 Nov. 1862, 9 Dec. 1862, CHP; John A. Davis to Howell Cobb, 8 May 1863, Howell Cobb Papers.

51. Lucy Barrow Cobb to Mary [McKinley], 1 Dec. 1864, CEL; George Davis to David Barrow, 6 Jan. 1862, 1 Sept. 1862, 9 Sept. 1862, 29 Sept. 1863, DCB; Mollie Davis to David Barrow, 15 Feb. 1865, DCB; Mary Jane Curry to Duncan Curry, 3 Dec. 1862, CHP.

52. See, for instance, Ira Berlin, Thavolia Glymph, Steven F. Miller, Joseph P. Reidy, Leslie S. Rowland, and Julie Saville, eds., *The Wartime Genesis of Free Labor: The Lower South* (Cambridge, 1990), 624–627, 632–635;

Schwalm, *A Hard Fight for We,* chap. 3; Bercaw, *Gendered Freedoms,* chap. 1; Frankel, *Freedom's Women,* chaps. 1–2; Thavolia Glymph, "'This Species of Property': Female Slave Contrabands in the Civil War," in *A Woman's War: Southern Women, Civil War, and the Confederate Legacy,* ed. Edward D. C. Campbell Jr. and Kym S. Rice (Charlottesville, Va., 1996), 54–71.

53. Record of "Out-Work," WHS; William H. Stiles to Wife, 31 Mar. 1864, MSF; Leila Calloway to Morgan Calloway, 19 Jan. 1863, MCP; John Cobb to David Barrow, 31 Dec. 1863, DCB; *NOR,* ser. 1, 17:648–649.

54. Leila Calloway to Morgan Calloway, 30 Sept. 1862, MCP; John Lamar to Howell Cobb, 3 Nov. 1861, CEL; George Davis to David Barrow, 13 Sept. 1861, 4 Jan. 1862, 1 Sept. 1862, 23 Nov. 1863, DCB; Perry Curry to Duncan Curry, 10 Apr. 1862, CHP; Mary Jane Curry to Duncan Curry, 11 June 1862, 11 Aug. 1862, 15 Aug. 1862, 1 Oct. 1862, 17 Nov. 1862, CHP; Archibald Curry to Duncan Curry, [late fall] 1862, CHP; Wm. H. Stiles to Wife, 31 Mar. 1864, MSF; Laurel Thatcher Ulrich, "Wheels, Looms, and the Gender Division of Labor in Eighteenth-Century New England," *WMQ* 15 (Jan. 1998): 8–9.

55. O. H. Prince to Daughter, 4 July 1864, Jackson and Prince Family Papers.

56. Perry Curry to Duncan Curry, 20 June 1862, CHP; Archibald Curry to Duncan Curry, 2 July 1862, CHP; Leila Calloway to Morgan Calloway, 13 May 1862, 30 Sept. 1862, 7 Nov. 1862, MCP; Morgan Calloway to Leila Calloway, 18 May 1863, MCP; William H. Stiles to Elizabeth Stiles, 31 Mar. 1864, MSF; Elizabeth Stiles to William H. Stiles, 5 Apr. 1864, MSF; William H. Stiles to Elizabeth Stiles, 14 Apr. 1864, MSF.

57. George Davis to David Barrow, 9 Sept. 1862, DCB; James Filey to David Barrow, 14 Dec. 1862, DCB; L. Jacks to Baker Daniel, 26 Jan. 1864, DCB; Mollie Davis to David Barrow, 13 Sept. 1864, 15 Feb. 1865, DCB; A. J. Dollar to Joseph Brown, 29 June 1864, GIC; Mrs. Mitchell Jones to Joseph Brown, 22 Aug. 186[4], GIC; *AP,* 7 Nov. 1861; Bryan, *Confederate Georgia,* 127.

58. A. J. Dollar to Joseph Brown, 29 June 1864, GIC; TCSC (1858–1865), 536, 540–546, 564, 566, 569–574; *ECN,* 5 Oct. 1864, 12 Oct. 1864, 18 Oct. 1864.

59. Eliza Peterson vs. Henry Peterson, 14 Apr. 1866, Georgia Documents, EU; Leila Calloway to Morgan Calloway, 30 Sept. 1862, MCP; Pope Barrow

to David Barrow, 7 Mar. 1863, DCB; Mollie Davis to David Barrow, 13 Sept. 1864, 15 Feb. 1865, DCB.

60. Stancil Barwick to John Cobb, 23 Dec. 1863, DCB; William Braswell to David Barrow, 28 June 1862, DCB; George Davis to David Barrow, 1 Sept. 1862, DCB; Thomas Morrow to Howell Cobb, 9 May 1863, Howell Cobb Papers; DCCO, M1:244; Isham's master is quoted in Bryan, *Confederate Georgia*, 133.

61. Morgan Calloway to Leila Calloway, 10 Aug. 1863, MCP; TCSC (1858–1865), 540–548, 569–574.

3. FINDING FREEDOM'S EDGES

1. The period between April and December 1865 is too often subsumed under the general heading Presidential Reconstruction, obscuring a series of critical struggles that established some of the most fundamental features of freedom; important exceptions include Steven Hahn, Steven F. Miller, Susan E. O'Donovan, John C. Rodrigue, and Leslie S. Rowland, eds., *Land and Labor, 1865* (Chapel Hill, N.C., 2007); Lynda J. Morgan, *Emancipation in Virginia's Tobacco Belt, 1850–1870* (Athens, Ga., 1992); Michael W. Fitzgerald, *Urban Emancipation: Popular Politics in Reconstruction Mobile, 1860–1890* (Baton Rouge, 2002); Steven Hahn, *A Nation under Our Feet: Black Political Struggles in the Rural South from Slavery to the Great Migration* (Cambridge, Mass., 2003); Leslie A. Schwalm, *A Hard Fight for We: Women's Transition from Slavery to Freedom in South Carolina* (Urbana, Ill., 1997); Stephen V. Ash, *A Year in the South: Four Lives in 1865* (New York, 2002).

2. Mollie Davis to David Barrow, 15 Feb. 1865, DCB; George Davis to David Barrow, 14 Apr. 1865, DCB; John A. Cobb to David Barrow, 15 Apr. 1865, DCB; Tom Barrow to David Barrow, 31 July 1865, DCB; Benjamin Yancey to [Sarah Yancey], 18 July 1865, BCY; Nathan Barwick to Howell Cobb, 20 Aug. 1865, CEL; T. J. Mount to John A. Cobb, 27 Aug. 1865, CEL; [Eliza Stiles] to [William H. Stiles], 2 Mar. 1865, MSF; affidavit of George King, 5 June 1865, enclosed in J. H. Fowler to Capt. Ketchum, 7 June 1865, F-

5 1865, ser. 15, [A-5815]; A. R. Lawton to "Dear Father," 27 Nov. 1865, Alexander R. Lawton Papers, SHC; Eliza Frances Andrews, *The War-Time Journal of a Georgia Girl* (New York, 1908), chap. 3; John Banks, *Diary of John Banks* (Austell, Ga., 1936), 36–37; *Statutes at Large,* 13:507–509; *ECN,* 4 May 1864; *House Exec. Doc.,* 11, p. 30.

3. *OR,* ser. 1, vol. 49, pt. 2, pp. 943–944; *NOR,* ser. 1, 17:856–857; J. H. Wilson to W. D. Whipple, 15 June 1865, vol. 13/22 CCMDM, pp. 121–127, ser. 2460, Cavalry Corps, Mil. Div. of the MS, pt. 2, no. 151, [C-4017]; *SE,* 12 July 1865; *AP,* 27 May 1865; 8 May 1865, 13 May 1865, A. J. Swinney Diary, THC.

4. Affidavits of Tal Boid, 5 June 1865, Frank Frazier, 5 June 1865, and George King, 5 June 1865, all enclosed in J. H. Fowler to Capt. Ketchum, 7 June 1865, F-5 1865, ser. 15, [A-5815]; affidavit of Mary E. Cruel, 17 Oct. 1867, C-89 1867, ser. 1040, [A-5582]; J. S. Fullerton to O. O. Howard, 28 July 1865, F-123 1865, ser. 15, [A-7359]; [Eliza Stiles] to "children," 20 Aug. 1865, MSF; William H. Stiles to [Eliza Stiles], 12 Sept. 1865, MSF; *OR,* ser. 1, vol. 49, pt. 2, pp. 1041–42; Banks, *Diary,* 36–37; U.S. Congress, *Report of the Joint Committee on Reconstruction* (Washington, 1866), pt. 3, pp. 104–105.

5. J. H. Fowler to Capt. Ketchum, 7 June 1865, F-5 1865, ser. 15, [A-5815]; J. S. Fullerton to O. O. Howard, 23 July 1865, F-122 1865, ser. 15, [A-5836]; *Statutes at Large,* 13:507–509; *House Exec. Doc.,* 11, pp. 24–32; *House Exec. Doc.,* 70, pp. 52–53, 67–68, 70, 74–75, 194; Hahn et al., *Land and Labor, 1865,* chap. 2.

6. *House Exec. Doc.,* 70, pp. 107, 181–182; Station Book of Officers and Civilians, vols. 1–2, M798r35; "List of Assistant and Sub-Com'rs. on duty July 21, 1865," enclosed in J. S. Fullerton to O. O. Howard, 22 July 1865, F-61 1865, ser. 15, [A-7360]; *OR,* ser. 1, vol. 49, pt. 2, p. 1068; *SE,* 12 July 1865, 8 Nov. 1865, 22 Nov. 1865; *AP,* 17 June 1865; J. H. Wilson to W. D. Whipple, 15 June 1865, vol. 13/22 CCMDM, pp. 121–127, ser. 2460, Cavalry Corps, Mil. Div. of the MS, pt. 2, no. 151, [C-4017]; J. S. Fullerton to O. O. Howard, 23 July 1865, F-122 1865, ser. 15, [A-5836]; J. M. Simms to [John McC. Perkins], 25 May 1865, S-15 1865, ser. 15, [A-5371]; A. P. Ketchum to R. Saxton, 1 Sept. 1865, ser. 2929, [A-5242]; William H. Stiles to dear wife, 1 July 1865, WHS; *Joint Committee on Reconstruction,* pt. 3, pp. 45–46; Paul A. Cimbala, *Under the*

Guardianship of the Nation: The Freedmen's Bureau and the Reconstruction of Georgia, 1865–1870 (Athens, Ga., 1997), 27.

7. W. R. Stickney to Thos. W. Conway, 2 July 1865, S-28 1865, ser. 1303, [A-8590]; affidavits of Tal Boid, 5 June 1865, Frank Frazier, 5 June 1865, and George King, 5 June 1865, all enclosed in J. H. Fowler to Capt. Ketchum, 7 June 1865, F-5 1865, ser. 15, [A-5815]; Edward Hatch to W. D. Whipple, 22 June 1865, H-15 1865, ser. 15, [A-9532]; C. W. Clarke to Sam[uel] Thomas, 9 July 1865, C-18 1865, ser. 2052, [A-9010]; I. Vogdes to Q. A. Gillmore, 4 June 1865, V-37 1865, ser. 4109, Dept. of the South, pt. 1, [C-1350]; *AP,* 10 June 1865; *Joint Committee on Reconstruction,* pt. 3, pp. 104–105.

8. Affidavits of Tal Boid, 5 June 1865, Frank Frazier, 5 June 1865, and George King, 5 June 1865, all enclosed in J. H. Fowler to Capt. Ketchum, 7 June 1865, F-5 1865, ser. 15, [A-5815]; W. R. Stickney to Thos. W. Conway, 2 July 1865, S-28 1865, ser. 1303, [A-8590]; *Joint Committee on Reconstruction,* pt. 3, pp. 102–108.

9. S. M. Quincy to J. M. Wilson, [late July 1865], Q-4 1865, ser. 1757, Dept. of LA & TX, pt. 1, [C-664]; [James A. Hawley] to Samuel Thomas, 4 July 1865, H-42 1865, ser. 2052, [A-9045]; J. S. Fullerton to O. O. Howard, 28 July 1865, F-123 1865, ser. 15, [A-7359]; H. R. Brinkerhoff to O. O. Howard, 8 July 1865, filed with H-17 1865, ser. 2052, [A-9044]; *AP,* 17 June 1865, 24 June 1865, 5 Aug. 1865; *SE,* 12 July 1865; *Joint Committee on Reconstruction,* pt. 3, p. 104; for a more general statement about the absence of a mass exodus, see Hahn et al., *Land and Labor, 1865,* chap. 1.

10. Statement of [John Gunn], 21 July 1865, ser. 2660, [A-2993]; affidavit of Betsey Robinson, 3 Aug. 1865, ser. 3545, [A-6603]; contract between W. C. Penick and Asbury et al., 1 June 1865, enclosed in State of Alabama vs. Asberry Penick, 28 Sept. 1865, filed under "P," ser. 9, [A-1640]; contract between A. T. Oliver and Cummins et al., 1 July 1865, filed with Levi Jones to W. H. Sinclair, 26 Mar. 1866, J-1 1866, ser. 3620, [A-3261].

11. Henry Bram et al. to Major General O. O. Howard, [20 or 21 Oct. 1865], B-53 1865, ser. 15, [A-7335]; affidavit of George King, 5 June 1865, enclosed in J. H. Fowler to Capt. Ketchum, 7 June 1865, F-5 1865, ser. 15, [A-5815]; G. H. Davis to David Barrow, 16 July 1865, DCB; pardon application of Alfred H. Colquitt, 30 Aug. 1865, #0665, M1003r17; Thos. Barrow to David

Barrow, 30 Aug. 1866, DCB; Banks, *Diary,* 36–38; *SE,* 12 July 1865; *AP,* 3 June 1865, 10 June 1865; *Joint Committee on Reconstruction,* pt. 3, pp. 104–105.

12. Affidavit of Nancy Davis, 21 Sept. 1867, D-3, ser. 1040, [A-5583]; Sarah H. Maxwell to [James H.] Wilson, 21 May 1865, filed with A-15 1865, ser. 16, [A-5814]; William H. Stiles to [Eliza Stiles], 1 July 1865, MSF; [Eliza Stiles] to "children," 20 Aug. 1865, MSF; William H. Stiles to [Eliza Stiles], 12 Sept. 1865, 22 Sept. 1865, MSF; William H. Stiles to [Rufus] Saxton, [25 Sept. 1865], ser. 1025, [A-5793]; J. H. Wilson to W. D. Whipple, 15 June 1865, vol. 13/22 CCMDM, pp. 121–127, ser. 2460, Cavalry Corps, Military Division of the MS, pt. 2, no. 151, [C-4017]; E. H. Bacon to Agent of the Freedmans Bureau at Savannah Georgia, [28 Sept. 1865], ser. 1022, [A-5799]; George Davis to David Barrow, 16 July 1865, DCB; Nathan Barwick to Howell Cobb, 10 Aug. 1865, CEL; Benjamin Yancey to [Sarah Yancey], 18 July 1865, BCY; pardon application of Alfred H. Colquitt, 30 Aug. 1865, M1003r17; Banks, *Diary,* 8; *SE,* 12 July 1865, 19 July 1865; *AP,* 3 June 1865, 5 Aug. 1865; *GJM,* 14 June 1865.

13. *Joint Committee on Reconstruction,* pt.3, p. 105; J. H. Wilson to W. D. Whipple, 15 June 1865, vol. 13/22 CCMDM, pp. 121–127, ser. 2460, Cavalry Corps, Mil. Div. of the MS, pt. 2, no. 151, [C-4017]; Eliza Stiles to "Children," 20 Aug. 1865, MSF; Eric Foner, *Reconstruction: America's Unfinished Revolution, 1863–1877* (New York, 1988), 43–44, 177; Eric L. McKitrick, *Andrew Johnson and Reconstruction* (Chicago, 1960), 91.

14. *Statutes at Large,* 13:758–761; Foner, *Reconstruction: America's Unfinished Revolution, 1863–1877,* 187–195.

15. William H. Stiles to Eliza Stiles, 1 July 1865, 12 Sept. 1865, MSF; Georgia applications, M1003r16–24; J. H. Wilson to W. D. Whipple, 15 June 1865, vol. 13/22 CCMDM, pp. 121–127, ser. 2460, Cavalry Corps, Mil. Div. of the MS, pt. 2, no. 151, [C-4017]; Benjamin C. Yancey's loyalty oath, 4 Sept. 1865, BCY; *Joint Committee on Reconstruction,* pt.3, p. 105; *Statutes at Large,* 13:758–761; *AP,* 5 Aug. 1865, 16 Sept. 1865; *SE,* 12 July 1865, 19 July 1865, 13 Sept. 1865, 20 Sept. 1865; *MFU,* 5 Sept. 1865, 24 Oct. 1865; *House Exec. Doc.,* 70, pp. 115–116; ECPC, 11 Sept. 1865; Sidney Andrews, *The South since the War: As Shown by Fourteen Weeks of Travel and Observation in Georgia and the Carolinas* (1866; reprint, New York, 1969), 289–290, 319–321; Allen D.

Candler, comp., *The Confederate Records of the State of Georgia* (Atlanta, Ga., 1910), 4:8–17, 20–21; Foner, *Reconstruction*, 187–195.

16. M. Q. Holt to [Orlando] Brown, 5 Dec. 1865, H-4 1865, ser. 3798, [A-7664]; J. S. Fullerton to O. O. Howard, 28 July 1865, F-123 1865, ser. 15, [A-7359]; Eliza Stiles to Children, 20 Aug. 1865, WHS; *AP,* 3 June 1865, 5 Aug. 1865; *SE,* 12 July 1865; see also Hahn et al., *Land and Labor, 1865.*

17. Contract between William K. Wilkinson and Joe et al., 8 Aug. 1865, Wilkinson Family Papers, GDAH; William H. Stiles to [Eliza Stiles], 22 Sept. 1865, MSF; contract between Benjamin C. Yancey and Edward et al., 22 July 1865, BCY; contract between J. McK. Gunn and Susan A. Douglas and Winston Douglas et al., 4 Aug. 1865, enclosed in J. McK. Gunn to Davis Tillson, 4 Nov. 1865, M-37 1865, ser. 631, [A-350]; DCPC, 5:162; George Davis to David Barrow, 16 July 1865, DCB; Kate Taylor to Pope Barrow, 29 Aug. 1865, DCB; T. J. Mount to John Cobb, 27 Aug. 1865, CEL; Benjamin Williams v. Nancy McKinnon, 12 Sept. 1867, vol. 385, p. 74, ser. 1044, RG105; complaint of Patsy & Archibald "Freedmen" vs. John J. Harrison, 9 Nov. 1865, vol. 385, pp. 6–7, ser. 1044, RG105; J. H. Wilson to W. D. Whipple, 15 June 1865, vol. 13/22 CCMDM, pp. 121–127, ser. 2460, Cavalry Corps, Mil. Div. of the MS, pt. 2, no. 151, [C-4017]; *OR,* ser. 1, vol. 49, pt. 2, p. 1068; Andrews, *The South since the War,* 322–323.

18. Contract between David S. Johnston and Joe et al., 15 July 1865, enclosed in F. C. Genth to O. H. Howard, 20 Dec. 1867, ser. 973, [A-5602]; contract between McQueen McIntosh and Jack et al., 8 July 1865, ser. 784, [A-5604]; contract between J. McK. Gunn and Susan A. Douglas and Winston Douglas et al., 4 Aug. 1865, enclosed in J. McK. Gunn to Davis Tillson, 4 Nov. 1865, M-37 1865, ser. 631, [A-350]; Benjamin Yancey to [Sarah Yancey], 18 July 1865, BCY; contract between Benjamin C. Yancey and Edward et al., 22 July 1865, BCY; T. J. Mount to John A. Cobb, 27 Aug. 1865, CEL; affidavit of Nancy Davis, 21 Sept. 1867, D-3, ser. 1040, [A-5583]; Davis Tillson to [Rufus] Saxton, 30 Dec. 1865, vol. 11, pp. 495–496, ser. 625, [A-5199]; O. H. Howard to A. B. Clark, 2 Sept. 1867, vol. 1, ser. 698, RG105; DCPC, *Return Book 5,* 52–57, 322; *AP,* 10 June 1865, 5 Aug. 1865; *Joint Committee on Reconstruction,* pt. 3, p. 45; Andrews, *The South since the War,* 322.

19. Benjamin Yancey to [Sarah Yancey], 24 July 1865, BCY; contract be-

tween Benjamin Yancey and Edward et al., 22 July 1865, BCY; William H. Stiles to [Eliza Stiles], 12 Sept. 1865, 22 Sept. 1865, MSF; T. J. Mount to John Cobb, 27 Aug. 1865, CEL; Tom Barrow to David Barrow, 23 July 1865, DCB; "Cousin Bessie" to Clara [Barrow?], 30 Nov. 1865, DCB; contract between William K. Wilkinson and Joe et al., 8 Aug. 1865, William K. Wilkinson Papers, GDAH; T. J. Mount to John Cobb, 27 Aug. 1865, CEL; contract between McQueen McIntosh and Jack et al., 8 July 1865, ser. 784, [A-5604]; contract between David S. Johnston and Joe et al., 15 July 1865, enclosed in F. C. Genth to O. H. Howard, 20 Dec. 1867, ser. 973, [A-5602]; William H. Stiles to [Rufus] Saxton, [25 Sept. 1865], ser. 1025, [A-5793]; affidavit of Nancy Davis, 21 Sept. 1867, D-3, ser. 1040, [A-5583]; Patsy & Archibald "Freedmen" vs. John J. Harrison, 9 Nov. 1865, vol. 385, pp. 6–7, ser. 1044, RG105; *AP,* 3 June 1865, 24 June 1865. Under certain conditions, freedpeople themselves were not averse to verbal contracts; like their ex-masters, they appreciated the inherent flexibility of oral agreements. See Hahn et al., *Land and Labor, 1865,* chap. 3.

20. Patsy & Archibald "Freedmen" vs. John J. Harrison, 9 Nov. 1865, vol. 385, pp. 6–7, ser. 1044, RG105; affidavit of Nancy Davis, 21 Sept. 1867, D-3, ser. 1040, [A-5583]; E. H. Bacon to Agent of the Freedmans Bureau at Savannah, [28 Sept. 1865], ser. 1022, [A-5799]; Kate Taylor to Pope Barrow, 29 Aug. 1865, DCB; T. J. Mount to John Cobb, 27 Aug. 1865, CEL; Benjamin Yancey to [Sarah Yancey], 18 July 1865, BCY; Benjamin Yancey to [Sarah Yancey], 24 July 1865, BCY; *AP,* 10 June 1865, 24 June 1865, 5 Aug. 1865; *Joint Committee on Reconstruction,* pt.3, p. 45; *Richmond Times,* 15 June 1865, as reprinted in the *New York Herald,* 18 June 1865.

21. Contract between McQueen McIntosh and Jack et al., 8 July 1865, ser. 784, [A-5604]; contract between William K. Wilkinson and Joe et al., 8 Aug. 1865, Wilkinson Family Papers, GDAH; contract between David S. Johnston and Joe et al., 15 July 1865, enclosed in F. C. Genth to O. H. Howard, 20 Dec. 1867, ser. 973, [A-5602]; contract between Benjamin C. Yancey and Edward et al., 22 July 1865, BCY; contract between J. McK. Gunn and Susan A. Douglass and Winston Douglas et al., 4 Aug. 1865, enclosed in J. McK. Gunn to Davis Tillson, 4 Nov. 1865, M-37 1865, ser. 631, [A-350]; Nathan Barwick to Howell Cobb, 20 Aug. 1865, CEL; T. J. Mount to John A.

Cobb, 27 Aug. 1865, CEL; George Davis to David Barrow, 16 July 1865, DCB; Tom Barrow to David Barrow, 31 July 1865, DCB; George Davis to David Barrow, 3 Aug. 1865, DCB; Kate Taylor to Pope Barrow, 29 Aug. 1865, DCB; Thos. Brown to David Barrow, 30 Aug. 1865, DCB; *SE,* 12 July 1865; *AP,* 3 June 1865, 10 June 1865, 5 Aug. 1865.

22. Testimony in the case of C. T. Humpreys vs. Ruffin Mitchell, 7 Nov. 1866, pp. 40–41, ser. 1044, RG105; contract between Benjamin C. Yancey and Edward et al., 22 July 1865, BCY; Thos. Brown to David Barrow, 30 Aug. 1865, DCB; *SE,* 12 July 1865; *AP,* 10 June 1865, 24 June 1865.

23. Contract between David S. Johnston and Joe et al., 15 July 1865, enclosed in F. C. Genth to O. H. Howard, 20 Dec. 1867, ser. 973, [A-5602]; Thos. Brown to David Barrow, 30 Aug. 1865, DCB; William H. Stiles to wife, 12 Sept. 1865, WHS; Eliza Stiles to children, 19 Sept. 1865, WHS; William H. Stiles to wife, 22 Sept. 1865, WHS; *AP,* 10 June 1865, 24 June 1865.

24. J. D. Collins to John Cobb, 31 July 1865, CEL; Nathan Barwick to Howell Cobb, 20 Aug. 1865, CEL; T. J. Mount to John Cobb, 27 Aug. 1865, CEL; George Davis to David Barrow, 16 July 1865, DCB; Tom Barrow to David Barrow, 31 July 1865, DCB; George Davis to David Barrow, 3 Aug. 1865, DCB; Kate Taylor to Pope Barrow, DCB, 29 Aug. 1865; Thos. Barrow to David Barrow, 30 Aug. 1865; George Davis to David Barrow, 6 Nov. 1865, DCB; T. G. Cooper to Benjamin Yancey, 22 Oct. 1865, BCY; William H. Stiles to Eliza Stiles, 12 Sept. 1865, 22 Sept. 1865, MSF; J. McK. Gunn to Davis Tillson, 14 Oct. 1865, ser. 632, [A-5224]; *AP,* 3 June 1865, 24 June 1865; *SE,* 19 July 1865.

25. J. S. Fullerton to O. O. Howard, 28 July 1865, F-123 1865, ser. 15, [A-7359]; Lewis Bright et al. to [Clinton B.] Fisk, 27 July 1865, B-36 1865, ser. 3379, [A-6077]; G. A. Hastings to W. W. Deane 24 Dec. 1865, ser. 632, [A-5237]; *Senate Exec. Doc.,* 6, p. 54; Cimbala, *Under the Guardianship of the Nation,* 65. On slaves and the law, see, for instance, Ariela J. Gross, *Slavery and Mastery in the Antebellum Southern Courtroom* (Princeton, N.J., 2000); Walter Johnson, *Soul by Soul: Life inside the Antebellum Slave Market* (Cambridge, Mass., 1999), 183–187, 210–213; Laura F. Edwards, "Enslaved Women and the Law: Paradoxes of Subordination in the Post-Revolutionary Carolinas," *Slavery and Abolition* 26 (August 2005): 305–326; and Timothy S. Huebner, "The Roots of Fairness: *State v. Caesar* and Slave Justice in Ante-

bellum North Carolina," Judith Kelleher Schafer, "Slaves and Crime: New Orleans, 1846–1862," and Ariela Gross, "The Law and the Culture of Slavery: Natchez, Mississippi," all in *Local Matters: Race, Crime, and Justice in the Nineteenth-Century South*, ed. Christopher Waldrep and Donald G. Nieman (Athens, Ga., 2001), 29–52, 53–91, 92–124.

26. T. G. Cooper to Benjamin Yancey, 22 Oct. 1865, BCY; William H. Stiles to Eliza Stiles, 22 Sept. 1865, WHS; Kate Taylor to Pope Barrow, 29 Aug. 1865, DCB; T. S. Hopkins to Dear Son, 1 June 1865, Elizabeth F. Hopkins Collection, GDAH; Mary Bacon to Kate, 24 Feb. 1866, WHS; Romeo v. John M. McIntosh, [mid] Nov. 1865, vol. 385, p. 7, ser. 1044, RG105; affidavit of Felix Massey, 1 Jan. 1866, vol. 385, p. 20, ser. 1044, RG105; affidavit of Frank McElroy, 14 Feb. 1866, vol. 385, p. 30, ser. 1044, RG105; C. C. Richardson to Mrs. Montgomery, 13 Nov. 1865, vol. 379, p. 10, ser. 1036, RG105; C. C. Richardson to J. J. Blackshear, 13 Nov. 1865, vol. 379, p. 12, ser. 1036, RG105; C. C. Richardson to William Stegall, 24 Nov. 1865, vol. 379, p. 15, ser. 1036, RG105; Stephen F. Dupo[r] to W. W. Deane, 23 Nov. 1865, ULR, M798r24; J. McK. Gunn to Davis Tillson, 14 Oct. 1865, ULR, M798r24; Augustus H. Hansell to Davis Tillson, 2 Dec. 1865, ULR, M798r24; Arthur Wright et al. to [Davis Tillson], 9 Sept. 1865, RLR, M798r11; B. F. White to G. A. Hastings, 16 Mar. 1866, LR, M798r13; 4 July 1865, A. J. Swinney Diary, THC; *AP*, 3 June 1865, 24 June 1865, 5 Aug. 1865; *SE*, 22 Nov. 1865.

27. United States vs. William Stringer, 27 Nov. 1865, vol. 385, pp. 7–8, ser. 1044, RG105; circular printed by Davis Tillson, [Nov. 1865], enclosed in Davis Tillson to E. M. Stanton, 15 Nov. 1865, T-1030 1865, LR, [L-76]; E. W. Gantt to J. W. Sprague, [23 Dec. 1865], G-6 1865, ser. 231, [A-2558]; C. C. Richardson to James Hayes, 24 Nov. 1865, vol. 379, p. 17, ser. 1036, [A-5216]; case of Richard "Freedman" vs. T. J. Lightfoot, 6 Nov. 1865, vol. 385, p. 1, ser. 1044, RG105; C. C. Richardson to [Davis Tillson], 6 Dec. 1865, RLR, M798r11; C. T. Watson to [C. C. Richardson], 5 Dec. 1865, vol. 385, p. 8, ser. 1044, RG105; *House Exec. Doc.*, 70, pp. 99–100; Andrews, *The South since the War*, 295.

28. William H. Stiles to Eliza Stiles, 22 Sept. 1865, WHS; Mary E. H. to Kate, 24 Feb. 1866, WHC; Nathan Barwick to Howell Cobb, 20 Aug. 1865, CEL; B. F. White to G. A. Hastings, 16 Mar. 1866, LR, M798r13; W. H. An-

drews, "Plantation Life along the River and Spring Creek," *CECHS* 2 (1979), 129, 131; Ulrich B. Phillips, ed., *Plantation and Frontier, 1649–1863* (1910; reprint, New York, 1969), 1:312–313; Andrews, *The South since the War*, 295.

29. William H. Stiles to Eliza Stiles, 22 Sept. 1865, MSF; Benjamin Yancey to Sarah Yancey, 18 July 1865, BCY; Julie Saville, *The Work of Reconstruction: From Slave to Wage Laborer in South Carolina, 1860–1870* (Cambridge, 1994), 102–110.

30. William H. Stiles to Eliza Stiles, 12 Sept. 1865, 22 Sept. 1865, MSF; William H. Stiles to Henry Stiles, 24 Oct. 1865, WHS; Benjamin Yancey to Sarah Yancey, 18 July 1865, 24 July 1865, BCY; O. H. Howard to [C. C. Sibley], 22 May 1867, RLR, M798r11; endorsement on O. H. Howard to [C. C. Sibley], 6 June 1867, ES, M798r9; J. P. Stevens to the Chief of the Freedmens Bureau Savannah Georgia, 19 Dec. 1865, ser. 1013, [A-5748]; Michael Dennis to Davis Tillson, 30 Nov. 1865, ser. 632, [A-5217]; Gideon Hastings to W. W. Deane, 24 Dec. 1865, ULR, M798r24; Andrews, *The South since the War*, 321; Saville, *The Work of Reconstruction*, 77–78. In the mountain South, a region hard hit by the domestic trade in slaves, less than 10 percent of those who emerged from slavery with dispersed families successfully put them together again in freedom; see Wilma A. Dunaway, *The African-American Family in Slavery and Emancipation* (Cambridge, 2003), 257–260.

31. Eliza Peterson vs. Harry Peterson, 14 Apr. 1866, Georgia Documents, EU; Thomas County, Court of the Ordinary, "'Colored' Record," 45–49, GDAH; Blakely Baptist Church Minutes, 2 May 1868, GDAH; 22 Oct. 1870, FBCB; 14 Oct. 1866, 17 Oct. 1866, 28 Nov. 1866, 9 Feb. 1867, 23 Feb. 1867, 27 Feb. 1867, 6 Mar. 1867, ABCB; F. A. H. Gaebel to G. L. Eberhart, 27 Mar. 1866, vol. 234, ser. 690, RG105; H. M. Turner to George Whipple, 27 Aug. 1866, no. 20056, AMAr2; John Rockwell to G. L. Eberhart, 28 Jan. 1867, LR, M799r8; E. F. Kirksey to F. A H. Gaebel, 28 May 1867, LR, M799r8; G. P. Melburn to Davis Tillson, 19 June 1866, ULR, M798r28; F. A. H. Gaebel to W. W. Deane, 29 June 1866, ULR, M798r27; G. W. Jones to W. F. White, 16 May 1867, ser. 783, RG105; C. T. Watson to C. C. Hicks, 4 Nov. 1867, ser. 700, RG105; summary of affidavit of Isaac Jones, 16 Mar. 1867, RLR, M798r11; W. F. White to [C. C. Sibley], 16 Mar. 1867, ES, M798r8; affidavit of Margaret Ann Richard-

son, 17 Apr. 1868, vol. 182, pp. 155–156, ser. 780, RG105; S. W. Stansbury to Rev. Mr. Cravath, 19 Aug. 1871, no. 24201, AMAr7; *Joint Committee on Reconstruction*, pt. 3, pp. 43–44; *SE*, 29 Nov. 1865; R. H. Clark, T. R. R. Cobb, and D. Irwin, comps., *The Code of the State of Georgia* (Atlanta, Ga., 1861), 363, and *The Code of the State of Georgia* (Atlanta, Ga., 1867), 334; William E. Montgomery, *Under Their Own Vine and Fig Tree: The African-American Church in the South, 1865–1900* (Baton Rouge, 1993), chap. 3, quote on 101; W. E. B. Du Bois, *The Negro Church: Report of a Social Study Made under the Direction of Atlanta University; Together with the Proceedings of the Eighth Conference for the Study of the Negro Problems, Held at Atlanta University, May 26th, 1903* (Atlanta, 1903), 57–63. On the practical costs of operating a church, see Sylvia R. Frey and Betty Wood, *Come Shouting to Zion: African American Protestantism in the American South and British Caribbean to 1830* (Chapel Hill, N.C., 1998), 191–202.

32. [Garrison Frazier] to E. Strieby, 2 Jan. 1865, no. 193325, AMAr1; Report of G. L. Eberhart, 15 Oct. 1866, Reports of Operations, M798r32; Peter R. Hines to Chief of Freedmen's Bureau, 1 Nov. 1865, LR, M799r8; C. C. Richardson to W. W. Deane, 9 Nov. 1865, ULR, M798r24; *Savannah Republican*, 10 Oct. 1865; Jacqueline Jones, *Soldiers of Light and Love: Northern Teachers and Georgia Blacks, 1865–1873* (Chapel Hill, N.C., 1980), 73–75.

33. William H. Stiles to Eliza Stiles, 22 Sept. 1865, WHS; E. H. Bacon to the Agent of the Freedmans Bureau at Savannah, [28 Sept. 1865], ser. 1022, [A-5799]; report by Rufus Saxton, 6 Apr. 1865, enclosed in Charles Thomas to E. M. Stanton, 24 Apr. 1865, vol. 17, pp. 282–284, ser. 16, Central Records, National Archives, Record Group 96, document control no. [Y-705]; Michael Dennis to Davis Tillson, 30 Nov. 1865, ser. 632, [A-5217]; *Joint Committee on Reconstruction*, pt. 3, p. 174; Steven F. Miller, Susan E. O'Donovan, John C. Rodrigue, and Leslie S. Rowland, eds., "Between Emancipation and Enfranchisement: Law and the Political Mobilization of Black Southerners, 1865–1867," *Chicago-Kent Law Review* 70, no. 3 (1995):1069–72; Ira Berlin, Thavolia Glymph, Steven F. Miller, Joseph P. Reidy, Leslie S. Rowland, and Julie Saville, eds., *The Wartime Genesis of Free Labor: The Lower South* (Cambridge, 1990), 331–340; Wilbert L. Jenkins, *Seizing the New Day: African Americans in Post–Civil War Charleston* (Bloomington, Ind., 1998), 51–

52; for examples of nonagricultural forms of independence, see Hahn et al., *Land and Labor, 1865,* chap. 7.

34. George Davis to David Barrow, 16 July 1865, DCB; William H. Stiles to Eliza Stiles, 12 Sept. 1865, MSF; William H. Stiles to Eliza Stiles, 22 Sept. 1865, MSF; William H. Stiles to Henry Stiles, 24 Oct. 1865, WHS; William H. Stiles to [Rufus] Saxton, [25 Sept. 1865], ser. 1025, [A-5793]; A. J. Miller to [Rufus] Saxton, [late September 1865], ser. 1025, [A-5793]; E. H. Bacon to the Agent of the Freedmans Bureau at Savannah Georgia, [28 Sept. 1865], ser. 1022, [A-5799]; C. C. Richardson to W. W. Deane, 28 Nov. 1865, ULR, M798r24; Augustus Hansell to Davis Tillson, 2 Dec. 1865, ULR, M798r24. For a more general discussion of the rumors about land, and especially their political dimensions, see Hahn, *Nation under Our Feet,* 130–142, and Steven Hahn, "'Extravagant Expectations' of Freedom: Rumour, Political Struggle, and the Christmas Insurrection Scare of 1865 in the American South," *Past and Present* 157 (Nov. 1997): 126–132.

35. *House Exec. Doc.,* 11, pp. 11–13; *House Exec. Doc.,* 70, pp. 111–112, 115–116; *Senate Exec. Doc.,* 6, pp. 52–54; *Statutes at Large,* 13:758–759; Paul A. Cimbala, "The 'Talisman of Power': Davis Tillson, the Freedmen's Bureau, and Free Labor in Reconstruction Georgia, 1865–1866," *Civil War History* 28 (June 1982): 153; Hahn et al., *Land and Labor, 1865,* chaps. 3, 7; Eric Foner, *Politics and Ideology in the Age of the Civil War* (New York, 1980), chap. 7; William S. McFeely, *Yankee Stepfather: General O. O. Howard and the Freedmen* (New Haven, Conn., 1968), chaps. 3, 6, 7.

36. Affidavit of William Wells, 3 Dec. 1866, ser. 1043, [A-5576]; H. L. O'Neal to Davis Tillson, 25 Jan. 1867, ULR, M798r30; John Dickenson, M. Rambo, and James Gates to J. T. Wimberly, 30 Jan. 1867, ULR, M798r30; James Beecher to Stewart Taylor, 6 Oct. 1865, ser. 2922, [A-7069]; McQueen McIntosh to Davis Tillson, 6 Dec. 1865, enclosed in McQueen McIntosh to Davis Tillson 4 Dec. 1865, ser. 632, [A-5248]; *AP,* 25 Nov. 1865; Saville, *The Work of Reconstruction,* 76–77.

37. John J. Robertson et al. to James B. Steedman, [27 Sept. 1865], ser. 653, [A-5166]; Simon Harris to Davis Tillson, 20 Nov. 1865, enclosed in John Heard to Davis Tillson, 21 Nov. 1865, ser. 632, [A-5231]; N. M. Reeve to Davis Tillson, 27 Nov. 1865, filed as G-37 1865, ser. 15, [A-5197]; Lewis Williams et

al. to Davis Tillson, [23? Dec. 1865], ser. 632, [A-5287]; Brien Maguire to W. W. Deane, 2 Apr. 1866, ser. 632, [A-5419]; Kenneth Coleman, ed., *A History of Georgia* (Athens, Ga., 1977), 83. On black Southerners' efforts to establish themselves as freeholders in the early Reconstruction period, see Hahn et al., *Land and Labor, 1865*, chap. 7.

38. Davis Tillson to G. A. Hastings, 15 Nov. 1865, vol. 11, pp. 122–123, ser. 625, [A-5196]; G. A. Hastings to Davis Tillson, 25 Nov. 1865, ULR, M798r24; Davis Tillson to O. O. Howard, 28 Nov. 1865, G-37 1865, ser. 15, [A-5196]; Davis Tillson to O. O. Howard, G-41 1865, 2 Dec. 1865, ser. 15, [A-5196]; Davis Tillson to Lewis Williams et al., 26 Dec. 1865, vol. 11, pp. 423–424, ser. 625, [A-5196]; Thomas G. Cooper to Benjamin Yancey, 27 Jan. 1866, BCY; Cimbala, "The 'Talisman of Power,'" 165–167, and Paul A. Cimbala, "A Black Colony in Dougherty County: The Freedmen's Bureau and the Failure of Reconstruction in Southwest Georgia," *JSwGH* 4 (Fall 1986): 77–80.

39. R. R. Porter to David Barrow, 8 Oct. 1865, DCB; George Davis to David Barrow, 6 Nov. 1865, DCB; *AP*, 16 Sept. 1865.

40. C. J. Gaulden to C. C. Richardson, 19 Dec. 1865, vol. 375, p. 21, ser. 1039, RG105; W. W. Woodruff to Davis Tillson, 3 Nov. 1865, ser. 632, [A-5279]; Howell Cobb to "Dear Wife," 5 Nov. 1865, CEL; C. N. Chamberline to Sister, 30 Dec. 1865, HSC; William H. Stiles to Henry Stiles, 24 Oct. 1865, WHS; Mary A. Huger to Kate, 8 Dec. 1865, WHS; Mary Huger to Kate, 24 Feb. 1866, WHS; R. C. Moses to Iverson D. Graves, 13 Feb. 1867, Graves Family Papers, EU; Mother to My Dear Children, 25 Aug. 1867, William E. Smith Papers, UGA; *AP*, 16 Dec. 1865, 25 Apr. 1866; *SE*, 25 Oct. 1865, 22 Nov. 1865; *Albany Tri-Weekly News*, 2 July 1867; *GWT*, 7 May 1866; Foner, *Reconstruction*, 213–214; Lucy M. Cohen, *Chinese in the Post–Civil War South: A People without a History* (Baton Rouge, 1984), chap. 4. The average monthly wages paid to farm laborers in Pennsylvania, California, and Colorado, respectively and without board, in 1866 were $29.91, $45.71, and $67.50; see U.S. Department of Agriculture, *Wages of Farm Labor in the United States: Results of Nine Statistical Investigations, from 1866 to 1892, with Extensive Inquiries Concerning Wages from 1840–1865* (Washington, D.C., 1892), 16–17.

41. Michael Dennis to Davis Tillson, 30 Nov. 1865, ser. 632, [A-5217]; *MFU*, 26 Dec. 1865; on the ritualistic aspect of Christmas in the slave-

holding South, and its meaning for the first Christmas of freedom, see Hahn, "'Extravagant Expectations,'" 138–140.

42. Samuel Thomas to O. O. Howard, 2 Nov. 1865, M-65 1865, ser. 15, [A-9219]; McQueen McIntosh to Davis Tillson, 4 Dec. 1865, ser. 632, [A-5248]; speech by Davis Tillson, 27 Oct. 1865, enclosed in Davis Tillson to E. M. Stanton, 15 Nov. 1865, T-1030 1865, LR, [L-76]; F. A. H. Gaebel to W. W. Deane, 14 Apr. 1866, ULR, M798r27; *SE*, 20 Sept. 1865; *Joint Committee on Reconstruction*, pt. 3, p. 173.

43. *MFU*, 24 Oct. 1865, 12 Dec. 1865, 26 Dec. 1865, 23 Jan. 1866; *SE*, 8 Nov. 1865, 20 Dec. 1865; Candler, *Confederate Records of the State of Georgia*, 4:414–415; *Senate Exec. Doc.*, 6, pp. 190–197, 202–220; Dan T. Carter, *When the War Was Over: The Failure of Self-Reconstruction in the South, 1865–1867* (Baton Rouge, 1985), 25. The general assembly passed the labor bill but the governor did not sign it before the legislators recessed for the holiday. On their return and in the wake of the uproar the South Carolina and Mississippi's black codes ignited among northerners, Georgia lawmakers softened the laws pertaining to ex-slaves. The "Amended Report of the Commissioners of Freedmen," which appeared shortly after the first of the year, extended to black people the same rights of contract exercised by white citizens, protected the illiterate from fraud, guaranteed wages by placing a lien against the employer's property, and returned all decisions regarding the specific conditions of work to the contracting parties. But even these provisions gave way to the final version, which its authors claimed had been "divested of all lingering prejudices." That version extended to black people the same privileges to "make and enforce contracts, sue and be sued . . . to inherit, to purchase, lease, sell, hold" and so on, as prescribed under state law for white persons, and left all decisions regarding terms of employment to the contracting parties. See *MFU*, 23 Jan. 1866; *SE*, 20 Dec. 1865; R. H. Clark, T. R. R. Cobb, and D. Irwin, *The Code of the State of Georgia* (Atlanta, Ga., 1867), 334; Candler, *Confederate Records of the State of Georgia*, 4:451–452; Donald G. Nieman, *To Set the Law in Motion: The Freedmen's Bureau and the Legal Rights of Blacks, 1865–1868* (Millwood, N.Y., 1979), 94–95.

44. Augustus H. Hansell to Davis Tillson, 2 Dec. 1865, ULR, M798r24; Nelson Tift to Davis Tillson, 9 Dec. 1865, ULR, M798r24; James Enwistle to

W. W. Deane, 30 Dec. 1865, ULR, M798r24; affidavit of Samuel Green, 9 Feb. 1866, RLR, M798r11; C. C. Richardson to [Davis Tillson], 8 Jan. 1866, RLR, M798r11; C. C. Richardson to [Davis Tillson], 14 Feb, 1866, RLR, M798r11; C. J. Gaulden to C. C. Richardson, 19 Dec. 1865, vol. 375, p. 21, ser. 1039, RG105; W. W. Woodruff to Davis Tillson, 3 Nov. 1865, ser. 632, [A-5279]; A. C. Bardwells to H. F. Sickles, 14 Dec. 1865, ser. 1013, [A-5022]; J. S. Lamar to Davis Tillson, 21 Nov. 1865, ser. 632, [A-5243]; Michael Dennis to Davis Tillson, 30 Nov. 1865, ser. 632, [A-5217]; C. C. Richardson to [Davis Tillson], 14 Feb. 1866, RLR, M798r11; Wm. Henry Stiles to [Eliza Stiles], 1 Oct. 1865, MSF; Louis Upson to David Barrow, 14 Dec. 1865, DCB; testimony in the case of Frank McElroy, 14 Feb. 1866, vol. 385, pp. 30–34, ser. 1044, RG105; case of July, 13 Nov. 1865, vol. 385, pp. 18–19, ser. 1044, RG105; case of Charles, 17 Jan. 1866, vol. 385, pp. 23–24, ser. 1044, RG105; TCSC (1858–1865), 603; *SE*, 20 Sept. 1865, 6 Dec. 1865, 20 Dec. 1865, 10 Jan. 1866; *AP*, 25 Nov. 1865, 3 Dec. 1865, 16 Dec. 1865, 23 Dec. 1865, 13 Jan. 1866; *MFU*, 26 Dec. 1865; *Joint Committee on Reconstruction*, pt. 3, pp. 46, 174–175; Candler, *Confederate Records of the State of Georgia*, 4:100–101; Andrews, *The South since the War*, 324. For the best treatments of the Christmas 1865 terror, see Hahn, *Nation under Our Feet*, chap. 3, and Hahn et al., *Land and Labor, 1865*, chap. 9.

45. McQueen McIntosh to Davis Tillson, 6 Dec. 1865, enclosed in McQueen McIntosh to Davis Tillson, 4 Dec. 1865, ser. 632, [A-5248].

46. Thomas Willingham to Davis Tillson, 6 Dec. 1865, ULR, M798r24; Thomas Willingham to Davis Tillson, 25 Dec. 1865, ULR, M798r24; G. A. Hastings to [Davis Tillson], 14 Nov. 1865, RLR, M798r11;Eliza Stiles to Dear Children, 20 Aug. 1865, WHS; William Stiles to Eliza Stiles, 12 Sept. 1865, WHS; *House Exec. Doc.*, 70, pp. 59–61. On Maryland's postemancipation wave of indentures, see Richard Paul Fuke, "Planters, Apprenticeship, and Forced Labor: The Black Family under Pressure in Post-Emancipation Maryland," *Agricultural History* 62, no. 4 (1988): 57–74, and Ira Berlin, Steven F. Miller, Joseph P. Reidy, and Leslie S. Rowland, eds., *The Wartime Genesis of Free Labor: The Upper South* (Cambridge, 1993), 494–499; see also Dunaway, *African-American Family*, 265–267, and Rebecca J. Scott, "The Battle over the Child: Child Apprenticehip and the Freedmen's Bureau in North Carolina," *Prologue* 10 (Summer 1978): 100–113.

47. Margaret Carter vs. S. W. Brooks, 31 Jan. 1866, vol. 385, pp. 25–29, ser. 1044, RG105; Thomas County, Court of the Ordinary, "'Colored' Record," 34, 51, 53, 99, 118, GDAH; Clark et al., *Code of the State of Georgia* (1867), 374–377; Dunaway, *African-American Family,* 265; Scott, "Battle over the Child," 105; Marie Jenkins Schwartz, *Born in Bondage: Growing Up Enslaved in the Antebellum South* (Cambridge, 2000), 134–148.

48. William Tony Golden et al. to H. F. Sickles, 28 Nov. 1865, ser. 1013, [A-5750]; Shelton Oliver to W. W. Deane, 21 Dec. 1865, filed under "S," ser. 632, [A-5269]; Michael Dennis to Davis Tillson, 30 Nov. 1865, ser. 632, [A-5217]; T. S. Hopkins to C. C. Richardson, 26 Dec. 1865, enclosed in C. C. Richardson to Davis Tillson, 2 Jan. 1866, ULR, M798r28.

49. Jos. W. Harris to Clinton B. Fisk, 4 Aug. 1865, H-41 1865, ser. 3379, [A-6135]; H. R. Brinkerhoff to O. O. Howard, 8 July 1865, filed with H-17 1865, ser. 2052, [A-9044]; James A. Hawley to Samuel Thomas, 4 July 1865, H-42 1865, ser. 2052, [A-9045]; McQueen McIntosh to Davis Tillson, 6 Dec. 1865, ULR, M798r24; T. S. Hopkins to C. C. Richardson, 26 Dec. 1865, enclosed in C. C. Richardson to Davis Tillson, 2 Jan. 1866, ULR, M798r28; *House Exec. Doc.,* 11, p. 39; *House Exec. Doc.,* 70, pp. 98–100; Andrews, *The South since the War,* 322–323.

50. Benjamin Yancey to Sarah Yancey, 11 Sept. 1866, Benjamin C. Yancey Papers, DU; William H. Stiles to [Eliza Stiles], 22 Sept. 1865, MSF; Michael Dennis to Davis Tillson, 30 Nov. 1865, ser. 632, [A-5217]; Junius Wingfield to Davis Tillson, 1 Dec. 1865, ser. 632, [A-5248]; Frd. Ed. Miller to E. M. Gregory, 22 Dec. 1865, ser. 3621, [A-3338]; Thos. Peacock to Davis Tillson, 16 Dec. 1865, ser. 632, [A-5255]; John Seage to Clinton B. Fisk, 4 Oct. 1865, S-73 1865, ser. 3379, [A-6197]; Wager Swayne to O. O. Howard, 5 Oct. 1865, A-20 1865, ser. 15, [A-1580]; William Tony Golden et al., to H. F. Sickles, 28 Nov. 1865, ser. 1013, [A-5750]; C. C. Richardson to James Beasley, 6 Jan. 1866, vol. 379, p. 59, ser. 1036, RG105; affidavit of Gillie Arrington, [Oct. 1866], enclosed in W. F. De Knight to O. Brown, 31 Oct. 1866, ser. 3802, [A-8289]; Noralee Frankel, *Freedom's Women: Black Women and Families in Civil War Era Mississippi* (Bloomington, Ind., 1999), 72–74; Morgan, *Emancipation in Virginia's Tobacco Belt,* 153, 174–171; Nancy D. Bercaw, *Gendered Freedoms: Race, Rights, and the Politics of the Household in the Delta, 1861–1875* (Gainesville,

Fla., 2003), 121–124; Jacqueline Jones, *Labor of Love, Labor of Sorrow: Black Women and the Family from Slavery to the Present* (New York, 1985), 53; Hahn et al., *Land and Labor, 1865,* chaps. 6, 10.

51. William H. Stiles to Elizabeth Stiles, 22 Sept. 1865, MSF; "List of Negroes at Plantation in Terrell County," 1864, WHS; William H. Stiles to Henry Stiles, 24 Oct. 1865, WHS; T. C. Clay to C. C. Richardson, mid-Nov. 1865, vol. 375, p. 13, ser. 1039, RG105; decision in case of Sidney Burdon, 3 Jan. 1866, vol. 385, p. 21, ser. 1044, RG105; C. C. Richardson to Washington Heath, 13 Nov. 1865, vol. 379, p. 10, ser. 1036, RG105; C. C. Richardson to James Beasley, 6 Jan. 1866, vol. 379, p. 59, ser. 1036, RG105; C. C. Richardson to Martha Hayes, 20 Jan. 1866, vol. 379, p. 72, ser. 1036, RG105; S. A. McLendon to F. A. H. Gaebel, 24 Apr. 1866, ser. 694, RG105; F. A. H. Gaebel to W. W. Deane, 5 Mar. 1866, vol. 234, ser. 690, RG105; F. A. H. Gaebel to W. W. Deane, 5 Mar. 1866, ULR, M798r27; *GJM,* 30 Jan. 1867.

4. BLACK WOMEN AND THE DOMESTICATION OF FREE LABOR

1. Statement of Gillie Arrington, [Oct. 1866], enclosed in W. F. De Knight to O. Brown, 31 Oct. 1866, ser. 3802, [A-8289].

2. Oliver H. Prince, *A Digest of the Laws of the State of Georgia,* 2nd ed. (Athens, Ga., 1837), 791, 806–808; Sharla M. Fett, *Working Cures: Healing, Health, and Power on Southern Slave Plantations* (Chapel Hill, N.C., 2002), 25–26; Stacey K. Close, *Elderly Slaves of the Plantation South* (New York, 1997), 46–59, 87–89; James W. Ely Jr., "'There Are Few Subjects in Political Economy of Greater Difficulty': The Poor Laws of the Antebellum South," *American Bar Foundation Research Journal* 10 (Autumn 1985): 849–879; Barbara L. Bellows, *Benevolence among Slaveholders: Assisting the Poor in Charleston, 1670–1860* (Baton Rouge, 1993), 177–181; Peter Wallenstein, *From Slave South to New South: Public Policy in Nineteenth-Century Georgia* (Chapel Hill, N.C., 1987), 47–48, 74–85; David Williams, *Rich Man's War: Class, Caste, and Confederate Defeat in the Lower Chattahoochee Valley* (Athens, Ga., 1998), 81–115; Paul D. Escott, "Joseph E. Brown, Jefferson Davis, and the Problem of Poverty in the Confederacy," *GHQ* 61

(Spring 1977): 59–71; Paul D. Escott, "'The Cry of the Sufferers': The Problem of Welfare in the Confederacy," *Civil War History* 23 (September 1977): 228–240.

3. Junius Wingfield to Davis Tillson, 1 Dec. 1865, ser. 636, [A-5284]; Joshua Elder to Clinton B. Fisk, [early] Sept. 1865, E-17 1865, ser. 3379, [A-6112]; Clinton B. Fisk to John Seage, 7 Oct. 1865, vol. 7, pp. 32–33, ser. 3373, [A-6197]; Circular 5, 22 Dec. 1865, ser. 636, [A-481]; *House Exec. Doc.,* 70, pp. 197–198; *Senate Exec. Doc.,* 6, pp. 58, 170–179, 181–230.

4. C. C. Richardson to [Davis Tillson], 2 Jan. 1866, ULR, M798r28; Joseph O'Neil to W. W. Deane, 24 May 1866, ULR, M798r28; Ch. Raushenberg to M. Frank Gallagher, 19 Nov. 1867, LR, M798r19; O. H. Howard to Agents, 14 Nov. 1867, vol. 120, ser. 690, RG105; William Pierce to [C. C. Sibley], 8 July 1868, vol. 4, ULR, M798r12; Willis Sessions vs. Amorine Dillard, 17 Nov. 1868, vol. 324, pp. 28–29, ser. 975, RG105; "Inferior Court Minutes and Apprenticeship, 1867–1871," Sumter County Inferior Court Records, GDAH; 27 Apr. 1866, Early County Inferior Court Minutes, 1866–1882, GDAH; TCIC (1861–1870), 240, 244, 249, 251–252, 254; Prince, *Digest of the Laws,* 791; R. H. Clark, T. R. R. Cobb, and D. Irwin, comps., *The Code of the State of Georgia* (Atlanta, 1861), 368; R. H. Clark, T. R. R. Cobb, and D. Irwin, comps., *The Code of the State of Georgia* (Atlanta, 1867), 155–158; Allen D. Candler, comp., *The Confederate Records of the State of Georgia* (Atlanta, 1910), 4:472–474, 513, 524–525, 534–537, 580–581; Wallenstein, *From Slave South to New South,* 88, 137–138; Paul A. Cimbala, *Under the Guardianship of the Nation: The Freedmen's Bureau and the Reconstruction of Georgia, 1865–1870* (Athens, Ga., 1997), 90–92.

5. O. Brown to O. O. Howard, 16 July 1865, vol. 18, pp. 38–40, ser. 3793, [A-7783]; *House Exec. Doc.,* 70, pp. 92–93, 94–95, 100–103; Ira Berlin, Steven Hahn, Steven F. Miller, Joseph P. Reidy, and Leslie S. Rowland, "The Terrain of Freedom: The Struggle over the Meaning of Free Labor in the U.S. South," *History Workshop* 10 (Autumn 1986): 120–123; David J. Rothman, *The Discovery of the Asylum: Social Order and Disorder in the New Republic,* rev. ed. (New York, 2002), 155–179; Jonathan A. Glickstein, *Concepts of Free Labor in Antebellum America* (New Haven, Conn., 1991), 40, 278–279; Amy Dru Stanley, *From Bondage to Contract: Wage Labor, Marriage, and the Mar-*

ket in the Age of Slave Emancipation (Cambridge, 1998), 122–128; Alexander Keyssar, *The Right to Vote: The Contested History of Democracy in the United States* (New York, 2000), 61–62, 134–136, 355–357.

6. *House Exec. Doc.,* 70, pp. 57–59; *Proceedings of the Freedmen's Convention of Georgia, Assembled at Augusta, January 10th, 1866* (Augusta, Ga., 1866), 7–17.

7. George Curkendall to [William] Gray, 7 Dec. 1865, ser. 632, [A-5211]; Wm Gray to Geo. Curkendall, 9 Dec. 1865, ser. 732, [A-5211]; W. W. Deane to Geo. Curkendall, 9 Dec. 1865, ser. 732, [A-5211]; O. O. Howard to Davis Tillson, 25 Jan. 1866, ser. 632, [A-5293]; Joseph Taylor to [Davis Tillson], 7 Apr. 1866, vol. 1, RLR, M798r11; George Wagner to Eugene Pickett, 5 Dec. 1866, ULR, M798r29; F. A. H. Gaebel to E. Pickett, 4 May 1867, LR, M798r14; F. A. H. Gaebel to E. Pickett, 25 May 1867, LR, M798r14; C. C. Sibley to O. O. Howard, 8 Feb. 1867, Operations Reports, M798r32; Clinton B. Fisk to John Seage, 7 Oct. 1865, vol. 7, pp. 32–33, ser. 3373, [A-6197]; *DWJ,* 14 Jan. 1869; *House Exec. Doc.,* 70, pp. 64–65.

8. O. H. Howard to C. C. Sibley, 23 Apr. 1867, LR, M798r15; Andrew Clark to W. F. White, 7 May 1867, ser. 1040, RG105; Wm. D. Luckie to Louis to Lambert, 23 Dec. 1865, ser. 632, [A-5245]; Cimbala, *Under the Guardianship of the Nation,* 85, 87.

9. Return of James T. Whitehead, DCPC, 5:162; return of Joseph A. Davis, DCPC, 5:52–57; return of Alfred A. Colquitt, DCPC, 5:322; contract between McQueen McIntosh and Jack et al., 8 July 1865, ser. 784, [A-5604]; G. A. Hastings to W. W. Deane, 24 Dec. 1865, ser. 632, [A-5237]; Davis Tillson to Rufus Saxton, 30 Dec. 1865, vol. 11, pp. 495–496, ser. 625, [A-5199]; Davis Tillson to [O. O. Howard], 1 Nov. 1866, Operations Reports Sent to Commissioner Howard, M798r32; O. H. Howard to A. B. Clark, 2 Sept. 1867, vol. 127, ser. 698, RG105; F. A. H. Gaebel to J. D. Stapleton, 16 Apr. 1867, vol. 120, ser. 690, RG105; affidavit of Nancy Davis, 21 Sept. 1867, ser. 1040, [A-5583]; Freedman vs. John H. Lowrie, vol. 384, p. 14, ser. 1044, RG105; Benjamin Williams &c. vs. Nancy McKinnon, 12 Sept. 1867, vol. 385, pp. 74–75, ser. 1044, RG105; Edward Morris &c. vs. Nancy McKinnon, 16 Sept. 1867, vol. 385, pp. 74–75, ser. 1044, RG105; Joseph Brown vs. R. F. Dozier, 13 Aug. 1868, vol. 324, pp. 8–9, ser. 975, RG105; Harrison Doudy vs. Mrs. Leonard, 23 Nov.

1868, vol. 324, pp. 32–33, ser. 975, RG105; W. L. Clark to J. R. Lewis, 3 Apr. 1868, LR, M799r10; 30 Dec. 1866, A. J. Swinney Diary, THF.

10. Ralph Ely to Rufus Saxton, 31 Aug. 1865, E-8 1865, ser. 2922, [A-7077]; John Seage to Clinton B. Fisk, 16 Dec. 1865, S-125 1865, ser. 3379, [A-6197]; Geo. D. Dalton to J. V. DeHanne, 1 Feb. 1867, ser. 680, RG105; A. B. Clark to W. F. White, 27 May 1867, ser. 1040, RG105; complaint of Peter Daniels, 4 July 1867, vol. 185, p. 175, ser. 785, RG105; affidavit of Charles Mitchell, 8 Oct. 1867, ser. 1040, RG105; C. C. Sibley to O. O. Howard, 8 Feb. 1868, Operations Reports, M798r32; Hawkins, Brown & Smith Attys for Aggie Crawford, Colored, to [Caleb Sibley], 3 July 1868, vol. 4, RLR, M798r12; Ch. Raushenberg to M. Frank Gallagher, 4 Aug. 1868, vol. 124, ser. 697, RG105; Willis Sessions vs. Amorine Dillard, 17 Nov. 1868, vol. 324, pp. 28–29, ser. 975, RG105; DCSC, L:416–417; DCSC, N:171–174; TCSC (1866–1869), 450–451, 468–474. For examples of black people's benevolent activities during and immediately following the war, see Wilbert L. Jenkins, *Seizing the New Day: African Americans in Post–Civil War Charleston* (Bloomington, Ind., 1998), 49–50; Elsa Barkley Brown, "To Catch the Vision of Freedom: Reconstructing Southern Black Women's Political History," in *African American Women and the Vote, 1837–1965*, ed. Ann D. Gordon, Bettye Collier-Thomas, John H. Bracey, Arlene Voski Avakian, and Joyce Avrech Berkman (Amherst, Mass., 1997), 67–70; Julie Saville, *The Work of Reconstruction: From Slave to Wage Laborer in South Carolina, 1860–1870* (Cambridge, 1994), 89; Ira Berlin, Steven F. Miller, Joseph P. Reidy, Leslie S. Rowland, eds., *The Wartime Genesis of Free Labor: The Upper South* (Cambridge, 1993), 357–358; Michael W. Fitzgerald, *Urban Emancipation: Popular Politics in Reconstruction Mobile, 1860–1890* (Baton Rouge, 2002), 52–53.

11. F. A. H. Gaebel to S. A. McLendon, 11 Mar. 1866, vol. 234, ser. 690, RG105; S. A. McLendon to F. A. H. Gaebel, 16 Apr. 1866, ser. 694, RG105; Nelson Tift to Davis Tillson, 10 May 1866, ULR, M798r29; affidavit of Joseph Taylor, 16 June 1866, vol. 240, pp. 5–6, ser. 695, RG105; O. H. Howard to Kolaski, 22 Apr. 1867, vol. 121, ser. 697, RG105; O. H. Howard to Mr. Josey, 1 May 1867, vol. 121, ser. 697, RG105; O. H. Howard to Riley Watson, 13 May 1867, vol. 121, ser. 697, RG105; D. F. McCollum to [O. H. Howard], 15 May 1867, vol. 116, ser. 700, RG105; affidavit of Isham Crowll, enclosed in Ch.

Raushenberg to O. H. Howard, 6 June 1867, ser. 700, RG105; O. H. Howard to John Neal, 5 Sept. 1867, vol. 122, ser. 697, RG105; O. H. Howard to Jeff Rigsby, 13 Sept. 1867, vol. 122, ser. 697, RG105; estate of Perry Duncan, accounts due, 1867, ser. 701, RG105; affidavit of Eliza Butler, 1 Jan. 1868, vol. 122, ser. 697, RG105; account of estate of Perry E. Duncan, [early?] 1868, ser. 701, RG105; C. C. Hicks to Wm. H. Gilbert, 16 Jan. 1868, vol. 122, ser. 697, RG105; O. H. Howard to R. E. A. Crofton, 8 May 1868, vol. 123, ser. 690, RG105; O. H. Howard to James Ulio, 19 May 1868, vol. 123, ser. 690, RG105; O. H. Howard to James Ulio, 17 June 1868, vol. 123, ser. 690, RG105; M. L. Fort to My Dear Son, [Jan.], 1866, HJF; draft of contract between M. M. Linton and Ellafarow Rachels, 23 Dec. 1866, Bass/Linton/Lipscomb/Wyche Family Papers, UGA. White and black women combined constituted 3.5 percent of the region's 1,275-strong industrial workforce in 1870; Francis A. Walker, comp., *The Statistics of Wealth and Industry of the United States . . . Compiled from the Original Returns of the Ninth Census* (Washington, D.C., 1872), 3:816–818.

12. Martha Mitchell vs. Shas. Dekle, 15 June 1868, vol. 385, p. 96, ser. 1044, RG105; affidavit of Eliza Butler, 1 Jan. 1868, vol. 122, ser. 697, RG105; M[other] to May, Oct. 18[67], William E. Smith Papers, UGA; draft of contract between M. M. Linton and Ellafarow Rachels, 23 Dec. 1866, Bass/Linton/Lipscomb/Wyche Family Papers, UGA; M. L. Fort to My Dear Son, [Jan.] 1866, HJF; Sarah [Bryan] to Annie Lawton, 27 Dec. 1865, Bryan/Willingham/Lawton Family Papers, GDAH; Mary E. H. Stiles to Kate, 24 Feb. 1866, WHS; "classification of laborers for 1866 on Dougherty plantations," [10] Jan. 1866, BCY; Tera W. Hunter, *To 'Joy My Freedom: Southern Black Women's Lives and Labors after the Civil War* (Cambridge, Mass., 1997), 21–23, 50–65, 241–243; Jacqueline Jones, *Labor of Sorrow, Labor of Love: Black Women, Work and the Family, from Slavery to the Present* (New York, 1985), 108–142.

13. TCIC (1861–1870), 204; affidavit of Isham Crowll, enclosed in Ch. Raushenberg to O. H. Howard, 6 June 1867, ser. 700, RG105; complaint of Angie Brown v. Jos[h]ua Carrol, 9 July [1868], vol. 385, p. 98, ser. 1044, RG105; W. H. S. to My Dear Wife, 22 Sept. 1865, MSF. I am indebted to the hand spinners at Harrisville Designs, Harrisville, New Hampshire, who explained that depending on several variables, including the quality of the

fleece and the desired gauge, a competent spinner could produce three to ten pounds of wool yarn in a day.

14. F. A. H. Gaebel to [W. W. Deane], early Mar. 1866, vol. 234, ser. 690, RG105; S. A. McClendon to F. A. H. Gaebel, 9 Mar. 1866, ser. 694, RG105; F. A. H. Gaebel to S. A. McLendon, 11 Mar. 1866, vol. 234, ser. 690, RG105; W. E. Griffin to F. A. H. Gaebel, 13 June 1866, ser. 694, RG105; Geo. D. Dalton to J. V. DeHanne, 1 Feb. 1867, ser. 680, RG105; O. H. Howard to Kolaski, 22 Apr. 1867, vol. 121, ser. 697, RG105; O. H. Howard to Mr. Josey, 1 May 1867, vol. 121, ser. 697, RG105; O. H. Howard to Riley Watson, 13 May 1867, vol. 121, ser. 697, RG105; D. F. McCollum to [O. H. Howard], 15 May 1867, vol. 116, ser. 700, RG105; O. H. Howard to John Neal, 5 Sept. 1867, vol. 122, ser. 697, RG105; O. H. Howard to Jeff Rigsby, 13 Sept. 1867, vol. 122, ser. 697, RG105; estate of Perry Duncan, accounts due, 1867, ser. 701, RG105; Martha Mitchell vs. Shas. Dekle, 15 June 1868, vol. 385, p. 96, ser. 1044, RG105; Tabitha Slater v. Phil Mitchell, 6 July 1868, vol. 385, p. 98, ser. 1044, RG105; complaint of Angie Brown v. Jos[h]ua Carrol, 9 July [1868], vol. 385, p. 98, ser. 1044, RG105; Jane Walker vs. Jas. Sheardon, 22 June 1868, vol. 185, pp. 157–158, ser. 785, RG105; Ailsey Martin vs. Wm. Jones, 27 June 1867, vol. 185, p. 165, ser. 785, RG105; Amy Hammonds vs. Chas. Worn, Wm. Worn, and Wm. Brenen, 2 Sept. 1867, vol. 185, pp. 11–12, ser. 785, RG105; Catherine Sutton vs. Bill Smith, 29 Nov. 1867, pp. 36–37, vol. 260½, ser. 885, RG105; Fany Monroe vs. Cato Isaac, 23 Nov. 1868, vol. 324, pp. 36–37, ser. 975, RG105; affidavit of Martha Ann Turner, 22 Aug. 1867, ser. 782, RG105.

15. F. A. H. Gaebel to W. W. Deane, 16 July 1866, ULR, M798r27; D. F. McCollum to [O. H. Howard], 15 May 1867, vol. 116, ser. 700, RG105; "To the Freedmen of Dougherty, Lee and Terrell Cos.," 10 June 1867, Orders & Circulars Issued & Rec'd, M798r34; Ch. Raushenberg to Wm. P. Pierce, 3 Apr. 1868, vol. 127, ser. 698, RG105; [J.] P. Tison to William Pierce, 22 June 1868, vol. 127, ser. 693, RG105; F. A. H. Gaebel to O. H. Howard, 10 Mar. 1867, vol. 120, ser. 690, RG105; O. H. Howard to Mr. Josey, 1 May 1867, vol. 121, ser. 697, RG105; O. H. Howard to Riley Watson, 13 May 1867, vol. 121, ser. 697, RG105; complaint of Angie Brown v. Jos[h]ua Carrol, 9 July [1868], vol. 385, p. 98, ser. 1044, RG105; Catherine Sutton vs. Bill Smith, 29 Nov. 1867, pp. 36–37,

vol. 260½, ser. 885, RG105; Fany Monroe vs. Cato Isaac, 23 Nov. 1868, vol. 324, pp. 36–37, ser. 975, RG105; *MFU*, 12 Dec. 1865; *AP*, 17 June 1865; *House Exec. Doc.*, 70, pp. 57–59, 64–65, 89–91, 95–96, 99–100, 105–106; *Senate Exec. Doc.*, 6, pp. 50–52

16. Contract between J. C. McGehee and Dawson et al., 1 Jan. 1866, filed with W. E. Wiggins to Eugene Pickett, 25 May 1867, ser. 700, RG 105; S. A. McClendon to F. A. H. Gaebel, 9 Mar. 1866, ser. 694, RG105; J. H. Taylor to W. W. Deane, 13 Apr. 1866, ULR, M798r29; F. A. H. Gaebel to Ira Ayers, 8 June 1866, vol. 234, ser. 690, RG105; F. A. H. Gaebel to W. W. Deane, 11 June 1866, vol. 234, ser. 690, RG105; F. A. H. Gaebel to W. W. Deane, 15 June 1866, vol. 234, ser. 690, RG105; F. A. H. Gaebel to W. W. Deane, 7 July 1866, ULR, M798r27; F. A. H. Gaebel to [C. C. Sibley], 8 Mar. 1867, vol. 2, RLR, M798r11; J. M. Robinson to Eugene Pickett, 11 July 1867, LR, M798r19; Ch. Raushenberg to F. A. H. Gaebel, 27 July 1867, vol. 118, ser. 693, RG105; Emiline Roberts vs. Dr. Sanders, 9 Sept. 1868, vol. 324, pp. 4–5, ser. 975, RG105; Ch. Raushenberg to Wm Oliver, 30 Oct. 1868, vol. 124, ser. 697, RG105; Mariah Bonds vs. Mark Huston, 1 Dec. 1868, vol. 324, pp. 38–39, ser. 975, RG105; contract between Wm. H. Branch and L. L. Lea and Thomas et al., 1 Jan. 1866, box 5, folder 68, Branch Family Papers, SHC; contract between Benjamin Yancey and Sam et al., [late] Dec. 1865, BCY; Cimbala, *Under the Guardianship of the Nation*, 30–35.

17. C. C. Richardson to Martha Hayes, 20 Jan. 1866, vol. 379, p. 72, ser. 1036, RG105; F. A. H. Gaebel to W. W. Deane, 23 May 1866, ULR, M798r27; F. A. H. Gaebel to Ira Ayer, 9 June 1866, ULR, M798r27; Dollie Lester vs. William Baker, 27 Jan. 1867, vol. 185, pp. 35–36, ser. 785, RG105; F. A. H. Gaebel to Eugene Pickett, 13 Apr. 1867, vol. 120, ser. 690, RG105; O. H. Howard to James Orr, 11 May 1867, vol. 121, ser. 697, RG105; Maria Wilson vs. Thos. W. Jones, early Aug. 1867, vol. 385, pp. 68–69, ser. 1044, RG105; Ch. Raushenberg to F. A. H. Gaebel, 15 Aug. 1867, ser. 693, RG105; O. H. Howard to George Beall, 6 Sept. 1867, vol. 122, ser. 697, RG105; William Clark to [C. C. Sibley], 28 Apr. 1868, vol. 4, RLR, M798r12; William L. Clark to [C. C. Sibley], 16 June 1868, vol. 5, ES, M798r10; Dinah Speight vs. Mr. Harvey, 8 July 1868, vol. 18, p. 179, ser. 785, RG105; Ch. Raushenberg to Mrs. E. Ingram, 2 Sept. 1868, vol. 124, ser. 697, RG105; Ch. Raushenberg to Wm Oliver, 30

Oct. 1868, vol. 124, ser. 697, RG105; M. L. Root to E. P. Smith, 15 May 1867, no. 20700, AMAr3; contract between Wm. H. Branch and L. L. Lea and Thomas et al., 1 Jan. 1866, box 5, folder 68, Branch Family Papers, SHC; Benjamin Yancey to Sarah Yancey, 11 Sept. 1866, Benjamin C. Yancey Papers, DU; William McKay, *Facts, Incidents and Opinions in the Life of an Ordinary Man: An Autobiography,* ed. Leila Burke Holmes, Mary McKay Stephan, and John McKay Sheftall (St. Petersburg, Fla., 1988), 96; Marie Jenkins Schwartz, *Born in Bondage: Growing Up Enslaved in the Antebellum South* (Cambridge, Mass., 2000), 60–69; Noralee Frankel, *Freedom's Women: Black Women and Families in Civil War Era Mississippi* (Bloomington, Ind., 1999), 72–73.

18. Contract between Jefferson L. Banks and Larking Street et al., 5 Dec. 1865, filed with O. H. Howard to C. C. Sibley, 15 Apr. 1867, ser. 700, RG105; F. A. H. Gaebel to S. A. McLendon, 11 Mar. 1866, vol. 234, ser. 690, RG105; Dollie Lester vs. William Baker, 27 Jan. 1867, vol. 185, pp. 35–36, ser. 785, RG105; TCSC (1866–1869), 463–468; William Warren Rogers, *Thomas County, 1865–1900* (Tallahassee, Fla., 1973), 20–21, 408, 416; Jones, *Labor of Love, Labor of Sorrow,* 53.

19. TCIC (1861–1870), 192, 201, 202, 208, 210, 212, 232, 244; TCSC (1866–1869), 463–468; U.S. Federal Manuscript Census, Schedule 1, Thomas County, 1850, p. 24b, National Archives, microcopy 432, reel 83; Rogers, *Thomas County,* 416.

20. This was a fast-moving shift of paradigmatic proportions, and only as scholars have begun to focus more closely on the era known as Presidential Reconstruction has the transition from gang to individual to family-based labor begun to come into view. One of the first works to recognize the analytical reward of looking long at this particular moment is Nancy Bercaw's *Gendered Freedoms: Race, Rights, and the Politics of Household in the Delta, 1861–1875* (Gainesville, Fla., 2003), 123–126.

21. Contract between Benjamin Yancey and Sam et al., [late] Dec. 1866, BCY; contract between Thos. K. Slaughter and Elliot Crawford et al., 25 Dec. 1865, LR, M798r13; contract between John Blocker and Stephen Blocker and Henry Thomas et al., [Jan.] 1866, enclosed in S. A. McLendon to F. A. H. Gaebel, 24 Apr. 1866, ser. 694, RG105; contract between Daniel

Palmer and Peter Gibbon et al., [Jan.] 1866, enclosed in O. H. Howard to
C. C. Sibley, 29 Apr. 1867, ser. 700, RG105; contract between W. H. Clark and
Perry et al., 29 Dec. 1865, enclosed in Ch. Raushenberg to O. H. Howard, 6
June 1868, ser. 700, RG105; contract between A. B. Duncan and Simon John-
son and Alex Jackson et al., [Jan. 1866], enclosed in O. H. Howard to C. C.
Sibley, 18 Apr. 1867, ser. 700, RG105; affidavit of Samuel Pendry, 2 Mar. 1866,
RLR, M798r11; F. A. H. Gaebel to W. W. Dean, 22 May 1866, vol. 234, ser. 690,
RG105; O. H. Howard to [Wm. P.] Pierce, 5 Apr. 1867, vol. 121, ser. 697,
RG105; Z. B. Chatfield to George D. Reynolds, 31 Dec. 1865, ser. 2268, [A-
9447]; contract between H. C. Cleaver & Bro. and Isaac Squash et al., 26
Dec. 1865, ser. 263 [A-2493]; Jeanne Boydston, *Home and Work: Housework,
Wages, and the Ideology of Labor in the Early Republic* (New York, 1990), 154–
155; Stanley, *From Bondage to Contract,* 151–152, 165–166. On military officials' early formulations of appropriate gender conventions, see, for example, *House Exec. Doc.,* 70, pp. 92–93; W. Storer How to O. Brown, 14 July
1865, filed under "1st District," ser. 3799, [A-7495]; Charles C. Soule to O. O.
Howard, 12 June 1865, S-17 1865, ser. 15, [A-7308]; J. Irvin Gregg to O. O.
Howard, 16 July 1865, G-36, ser. 15, [A-7468]; Davis Tillson to E. M. Stanton,
15 Nov. 1865, T-1030 1865, LR, [L-76]; *AP,* 17 June 1865.

22. Contract between John Blocker and Stephen Blocker and Henry
Thomas et al., [Jan.] 1866, enclosed in S. A. McLendon to F. A. H. Gaebel, 24
Apr. 1866, ser. 694, RG105; contract between A. C. Turner and Rufus et al., 1
Jan. 1866, ser. 694, RG105; contract between A. B. Duncan and Simon John-
son and Alex Jackson et al., [Jan. 1866], enclosed in O. H. Howard to C. C.
Sibley, 18 Apr. 1867, ser. 700, RG105; John R. Jones to O. H. Howard, 23 Apr.
1867, ser. 700, RG105; contract between J. C. McGehee and Dawson et al., 1
Jan. 1866, enclosed in W. E. Wiggins to Eugene Pickett, 25 May 1867, ser. 700,
RG105; contract between Daniel Palmer and Peter Gibbon et al., [Jan.] 1866,
enclosed in O. H. Howard to C. C. Sibley, 29 Apr. 1867, ser. 700, RG105; contract between Jefferson L. Banks and Larking Street et al., 5 Dec. 1865, filed
with O. H. Howard to C. C. Sibley, 15 Apr. 1867, ser. 700, RG105; affidavit
of Levi Steward, 13 July 1868, ser. 700, RG105; contract between W. H.
Clark and Perry et al., 29 Dec. 1865, enclosed in Ch. Raushenberg to O. H.
Howard, 6 June 1868, ser. 700, RG105; contract between J. B. Webb and Wil-

liam Frontman et al., 1 Feb. 1866, enclosed in S. A. McLendon to F. A. H. Gaebel, 28 Mar. 1866, ser. 694, RG105; contract between R. F. Chesire and Jim Snow et al., 1 Jan. 1866, ser. 693, RG105; contract between Richard M. Cheshire and Ned et al., [1] Jan. 1866, ser. 693, RG105; contract between W. A. McDowell and Dennis Hutchins et al., 5 Mar. 1866, ser. 693, RG105; contract between W. H. Branch and L. L. Lea and Thomas et al., 1 Jan. 1866, folder 68, box 5, Branch Family Papers, SHC; contract between George W. Mitchell and John Smith et al., 1 Jan. 1866, Nathaniel Raines Mitchell Family Papers, GDAH; contract between A. T. MacIntyre and William Bob et al., 30 Dec. 1865, A. T. MacIntyre Papers, GDAH; contract between Benjamin C. Yancey and Sam et al., [late] Dec. 1865, BCY; contract between H. T. Pullen and Jim May et al., 1 Jan. 1866, H. T. Pullen Papers, GDAH; examples of late-season agreements, contracts that featured relatively more unattached individuals than those made at the first of the year, include contract between Enoch G. Bass and Bill Wooten et al., 20 June 1866, ser. 701, RG105, and contract between D. F. Sapp and Berry Melton et al., 15 May 1866, ser. 693, RG105; Berlin et al., *Wartime Genesis of Free Labor: The Upper South*, 644–645. On the changing character of plantation labor forces on the Mississippi Delta in this period, see Bercaw, *Gendered Freedoms*, 31–50, 124–128; for a more general perspective on the same phenomenon, see Steven Hahn, Steven F. Miller, Susan E. O'Donovan, John C. Rodrigue, and Leslie S. Rowland, eds., *Land and Labor, 1865* (Chapel Hill, N.C., 2007), chap. 10.

23. F. C. Genth to O. H. Howard, 20 Apr. 1868, ser. 693, RG105; DCSC, L:228–230, 277–282, 283, 291–292, 457–459; TCSC (1866–1869), 87–88, 171–175; DCIC (1854–1869), 449.

24. Affidavits of Tom Tanner, Charles Alexander, Israel Bacon, and Philip Wade, 1 Nov. 1867, A-2004 1867, LR, ser. 5782, Bureau of Civil Affairs, 3rd Military Dist., pt. 1, [SS-661]; Wm. Brown, Arthur Coleman, and Henry Hood to [Ch. Raushenberg], 24 July 1867, RLR, M798r12; statement of Alick, 4 Dec. 1865, vol. 385, p. 10, ser. 1044, RG105; S. H. Champney to M. Smith, 25 Mar. 1870, no. 23340, AMAr6; Howell Cobb to My Dear Wife, Dec. 1866, CEL; [John Cobb] to My Dear Wife, 1 Jan. 1867, CEL; 21–25 Jan. 1867, vol. 3, DAH; TCSC (1866–1869), 468–474; *GWT,* 29 Jan. 1866, 30 Aug. 1867, 31 July 1868, 9 Oct. 1868, 12 Feb. 1869; Kenneth Coleman, ed., *A History of Georgia*

(Athens, Ga., 1977), 159–161, 232; Lynn Willoughby, *Flowing through Time: A History of the Lower Chattahoochee River* (Tuscaloosa, Ala., 1999), 117–146.

25. Howell Cobb to My Dear Wife, Dec. 1866, CEL; [John Cobb] to My Dear Wife, 1 Jan. 1867, CEL; Howell Cobb to his wife, Dec. 1866, CEL; [John Cobb] to My Dear Wife, 1 Jan. 1867, CEL; John Cobb to My Dear Wife, 4 Jan. 1867, CEL; TCSC (1866–1869), 168–175, 468–474; DCSC, L:228–230, 277–282, 283, 457–459, 949–950; statement of Alick, 4 Dec. 1865, vol. 385, p. 10, ser. 1044, RG105; McQueen McIntosh to Davis Tillson, 6 Dec. 1865, ULR, M798r24; Lewis Williams, M. Wilkinson, and Lewis Marien to Genl. Tillson, [23? Dec. 1865], ser. 632, [A-5287]; J. P. Stevens to the Chief of the Freedmen's Bureau Savannah, Georgia, 19 Dec. 1865, ser. 1013, [A-5748]; contract between B. L. Kimbrough and Ransom Brown et al., [1867], ser. 857, [A-5559]; C. C. Richardson to W. W. Deane, 6 Feb. 1866, ULR, M798r28; Joseph H. Taylor to W. W. Deane, 12 Feb. 1866, ULR, M798r29; F. A. H. Gaebel to W. W. Deane, 23 May 1866, ULR, M798r27; *GWT*, 29 Jan. 1866.

26. Contract between Jefferson L. Banks and Larking Street et al., 5 Dec. 1865, filed with O. H. Howard to C. C. Sibley, 15 Apr. 1867, ser. 700, RG105; McQueen McIntosh to Davis Tillson, 6 Dec. 1865, ULR, M798r24; J. P. Stevens to the Chief of the Freedmen's Bureau Savannah, Georgia, 19 Dec. 1865, ser. 1013, [A-5748]; G. A. Hastings to W. W. Deane, 24 Dec. 1865, ser. 632, [A-5237]; contract between Wm. H. Clark to Perry et al., 29 Dec. 1865, filed with C. Raushenberg to O. H. Howard, 6 June 1868, ser. 700, RG105; contract between A. T. MacIntrye and William Bob et al., 30 Dec. 1865, A. T. MacIntyre Papers, GDAH; contract between A. C. Turner and Rufus More et al., 1 Jan. 1866, ser. 694, RG105; contract between R. F. Cheshire and Jim Snow et al., 1 Jan. 1866, ser. 693, RG105; contract between Richard M. Cheshire and Ned et al., [1?] Jan. 1866, ser. 693, RG105; contract between J. C. McGehee and Dawson et al., 1 Jan. 1866, filed with W. E. Wiggins to Eugene Pickett, 25 May 1867, ser. 700, RG105; contract between Daniel Palmer and Peter Gibbon et al., [Jan.?] 1866, filed with O. H. Howard to C. C. Sibley, 29 Apr. 1867, ser. 700, RG105; Joseph H. Taylor to W. W. Deane, 12 Feb. 1866, ULR, M798r29; contract between W. A. McDowell and Peter Blocker et al., 5 Mar. 1866, ser. 693, RG105; contract between W. A.

McDowell and Dennis Hutchins, 5 Mar. 1866, ser. 693, RG105; S. A. McLendon to F. A. H. Gaebel, 24 Apr. 1866, ser. 694, RG105; contract between E. G. Bass and Bill Wooten et al., 20 June 1866, ser. 701, RG105; John R. Jones to O. H. Howard, 23 Apr. 1867, ser. 700, RG105; contract between B. L. Kimbrough and Ransom Brown et al., [1867], ser. 857, [A-5559]; O. H. Howard to G. L. Eberhart, 24 Apr. 1867, vol. 121, ser. 697, RG105; F. A. H. Gaebel to E. A. Ware, 30 Aug. 1867, LR, M799r9; contract between Wm. H. Branch and L. L. Lea and Thomas et al., 1 Jan. 1866, box 5, folder 68, Branch Family Papers, SHC; contract between Geo. W. Mitchell and John Smith et al., 1 Jan. 1866, Nathaniel Raines Mitchell Family Papers, GDAH; Benjamin Yancey to My Dear Wife, 23 Dec. 1865, BCY; contract between Benjamin Yancey and Sam et al., Dec. 1865, BCY; Benjamin Yancey to My Dear Wife, 2 Jan. 1866, BCY; contract between H. T. Pullen and Jim May et al., 1 Jan. 1866, H. T. Pullen Papers, GDAH; Howell Cobb Jr. to Dear Father, 3 Jan. 1866, CEL; *SE*, 31 Jan. 1866; *GWT*, 10 May 1867.

27. These are terms that are frequently, and in some circles inappropriately, allowed to operate outside of history. See, among others, Michel-Rolph Trouillot, *Global Transformation: Anthropology and the Modern World* (New York, 2003), 97–116; Rogers Brubaker and Frederick Cooper, "Beyond Identity," *Theory and Society* 29 (2000): 1–47.

28. G. A. Hastings to W. W. Deane, 24 Dec. 1865, ser. 632, [A-5237]; Francis A. Billingslea to Davis Tillson, 22 Jan. 1866, ULR, M798r25; William Serrine to Davis Tillson, 1 Mar. 1866, ULR, M798r29; S. F. Dupor to C. C. Richardson, 10 Mar. 1866, vol. 375, p. 55, ser. 1039, RG105; Henry Fallabbott to Gen. Tillson, 15 Jan. 1867, ULR, M798r30; Benjamin Yancey to My Dear Wife, 23 Dec. 1865, BCY; Benjamin Yancey to Sarah, 2 Jan. 1866, BCY; Mrs. Howell Cobb to John Cobb, 19 Feb. 1867, CEL.

29. 2 Jan., 12 Jan., 11 Mar., 20 June, 23 July, 4–5 Nov., 7–8 Nov., 19 Nov, 25 Nov., 5 Dec. 1867, vol. 3, DAH.

30. I am hardly the first to recognize this possibility; see Lila Abu-Lughod, "The Romance of Resistance: Tracing Transformations of Power through Bedouin Women," *American Ethnologist* 17 (Feb. 1990): 41–55.

31. Contract between A. C. Turner and Rufus Moore et al., 1 Jan. 1866, ser. 694, RG105; contract between Daniel Palmer and Peter Gibbon et al.,

[Jan?] 1866, filed with O. H. Howard to C. C. Sibly 29 Apr. 1867, ser. 700, RG105; contract between James Miller and Tony Fondering et al., 15 Jan. 1866, ser. 1043, RG105; F. A. H. Gaebel to W. W. Deane, 26 Mar. 1866, LR, M798r13; F. A. H. Gaebel to W. W. Deane, 31 Mar. 1866, ULR, M798r27; James W. Alexander to F. A. H. Gaebel, 14 Sept. 1867, ser. 693, RG105; J. Conr. Genth to Ch. Raushenberg, 30 Sept. 1867, ser. 693, RG105; contract between A. T. MacIntyre and William Bob et al., 30 Dec. 1865, A. T. MacIntyre Papers, GDAH; contract between Geo. W. Mitchell and John Smith et al., 1 Jan. 1866, Nathaniel Raines Mitchell Family Papers, GDAH.

32. Contract between W. A. McDowell and Peter Blocker et al., 5 Mar. 1866, ser. 693, RG105; contract between W. A. McDowell and Dennis Hutchins & Family, 5 Mar. 1866, ser. 693, RG105; O. H. Howard to Riley Scrutchins, 26 June 1867, ser. 697, RG105; *MFU*, 10 Oct. 1865, 30 Jan. 1866, 24 Feb. 1866; Clark et al., *Code of the State of Georgia* (1867), 334; *Senate Exec. Doc.*, 6, pp. 179–180. On marriage, citizenship, and power in nineteenth-century America, and the growing interest of the modern nation in governing these relationships, see, among others, Norma Basch, "Invisible Women: The Legal Fiction of Marital Unity in the Nineteenth Century," *Feminist Studies* 5 (Summer 1979): 346–366; Nancy F. Cott, *Public Vows: A History of Marriage and Nation* (New York, 2000), 88–94; Katherine M. Franke, "Becoming a Citizen: Reconstruction Era Regulation of African American Marriages," *Yale Journal of Law & the Humanities* 11 (Summer 1999): 251–309; James C. Scott, *Seeing Like a State: How Certain Schemes to Improve the Human Condition Have Failed* (New Haven, Conn., 1999); Amy Dru Stanley, "Conjugal Bonds and Wage Labor: Rights of Contract in the Age of Emancipation," *Journal of American History* 75 (Sept. 1988): 471–500.

33. Frd. Ed. Miller to E. M. Gregory, 22 Dec. 1865, ser. 2621, [A-3338]; circular letter, 17 Jan. 1866, vol. 1, p. 70, ser. 1036, RG105; F. A. H. Gaebel to E. F. Kirksey, 21 Mar. 1866, vol. 234, ser. 690, RG105; Robert T. Nesbitt to G. H. Pratt, 20 Apr. 1866, ULR, M798r28; H. C. Strong to F. A. H. Gaebel, 22 May 1866, ser. 694, RG105; Catherine Taylor v. John Taylor, 25 Mar. 1867, vol. 385, p. 42, ser. 1044, RG105; O. H. Howard to Thomas Spicer, 10 Apr. 1867, vol. 121, ser. 697, RG105; O. H. Howard to Dr. Hartwell, 17 Apr. 1867, vol. 121, ser. 697, RG105; O. H. Howard to Rueben William, 14 May 1867, vol. 121, ser. 697,

RG105; A. B. Clark to W. F. White, 27 May 1867, ser. 1040, RG105; O. H. Howard to John Chastain, 29 May 1867, vol. 121, ser. 697, RG105; F. A. H. Gaebel to Randolph County Jailor, 6 Aug. 1867, vol. 120, ser. 690, RG105; F. A. H. Gaebel to Eugene Pickett, 18 Aug. 1867, vol. 120, ser. 690, RG105; F. A. H. Gaebel to E. A. Ware, 1 Sept. 1867, LR, M799r9; Ch. Raushenberg to Judge Spicer, 18 Feb. 1868, vol. 124, ser. 697, RG105; Caroline v. Mr. Lester, 3 Mar. 1868, vol. 185, pp. 59–60, ser. 785, RG105; Celia Dixon v. Jacob Dixon, 12 Mar. 1868, vol. 185, pp. 69–70, ser. 785, RG105; Collier Clark v. Mary Clark, 8 June 1868, vol. 185, pp. 119–120, ser. 785, RG105; Maria Richardson v. Peter Ficklin, 16 June 1868, vol. 185, p. 150, ser. 785, RG105; Rhody Johnson v. Chas. Johnson, 23 June 1868, p. 155, ser. 185, vol. 785, RG105; Jane Curry v. Sandy Curry, 8 July 1868, vol. 185, p. 178, ser. 785, RG105; Ch. Raushenberg to Ephraim Tripp, 20 Oct. 1868, vol. 124, ser. 697, RG105; Ch. Raushenberg to Frank B. Lippitt, 11 Nov. 1868, vol. 124, ser. 697, RG105.

34. Joshua Cook to O. H. Howard, 18 Feb. 1867, ser. 694, RG105; Jared Irwin to O. H. Howard, 18 May 1867, vol. 116, ser. 700, RG105; O. H. Howard to B. F. Roberts, 18 July 1867, vol. 122, ser. 697, RG105; O. H. Howard to J. W. Jones, 10 Aug. 1867, vol. 122, ser. 697, RG105; Ch. Raushenberg to Andrew Clark, 28 Jan. 1868, vol. 127, ser. 698, RG105; Ch. Raushenberg to O. H. Howard, 10 July 1868, ser. 698, RG105; Antony Bibb v. Cuyler Freeman, 4 Aug. 1868, vol. 2, pp. 24–25, ser. 785, RG105.

35. Complaint of Hely Ann Mervier, 17 Jan. 1867, vol. 193, p. 19, ser. 884, RG105; O. H. Howard to W. W. Kendrick, 19 Mar. 1867, vol. 121, ser. 697, RG105; O. H. Howard to W. W. Kendrick, 10 Apr. 1867, vol. 121, ser. 697, RG105; affidavit of Jane Young, 23 Apr. 1867, vol. 121, ser. 697, RG105; O. H. Howard to Rueben William, 14 May 1867, vol. 121, ser. 697, RG105; affidavit of Sarah Oliver, 16 May 1867, vol. 121, ser. 697, RG105; O. H. Howard to Thomas Spicer, 17 June 1867, vol. 121, ser. 697, RG105; affidavit of Patsy Kendrick, 17 June 1867, ser. 700, RG105; O. H. Howard to J. W. Jones, 10 Aug. 1867, vol. 122, ser. 697, RG105; Patience Jones vs. Cato Jones, 31 Nov. 1867, pp. 34–35, vol. 206½, ser. 885, RG105; O. H. Howard to B. F. Roberts, 18 July 1867, vol. 122, ser. 697, RG105; Susann Sibles vs. Edmund Cain, 16 Jan. 1868, pp. 66–68, vol. 206½, ser. 885, RG105; Ch. Raushenberg to Andrew Clark, 28 Jan. 1868, vol. 127, ser. 698, RG105; N. A. Smith to O. H. Howard, 8 Feb. 1868,

ser. 700, RG105; Tom Arnet vs. Wife, 12 Mar. 1868, vol. 185, p. 69, ser. 785, RG105; Ch. Raushenberg to [C. C. Sibley], 19 May 1868, RLR, M798r12; Missouri Jackson v. Mary Jackson, 6 June 1868, ser. 785, RG105; Emeline Sanders v. John Sanders, 13 June 1868, vol. 185, ser. 785, RG105; W. F. White to H. McLendon, 18 June 1868, vol. 379, p. 263, ser. 1036, RG105; John Saunders vs. Emeline Ficklin, 6 July 1868, vol. 185, p. 177, ser. 785, RG105; Lavinia Perkins vs Josh Perkins, 9 July 1868, vol. 385, pp. 98–99, ser. 1044, RG105; Ch. Raushenberg to O. H. Howard, 10 July 1868, ser. 698, RG105; Maria Donaldson v. Burgess Hill, 11 July 1868, vol. 185, p. 183, ser. 785, RG105; Antony Bibb v. Cuyler Freeman, 4 Aug. 1868, vol. 2, pp. 24–25, ser. 785, RG105; Ch. Raushenberg to Peter Daniel, 31 Aug. 1868, vol. 124, ser. 697, RG105; Ch. Raushenberg to William Oliver, 26 Oct. 1868, vol. 124, ser. 697, RG105.

36. Mary (Freedwoman) to [S. A. McLendon], 24 Feb. 1866, RLR, M798r11; W. E. Griffin to [F. A. H. Gaebel], 6 Mar. 1866, ser. 694, RG105; affidavit of Mary Jane Hyman, 15 Apr. 1867, ser. 701, RG105; affidavit of Cipio and Sarah Stafford, 11 June 1867, ser. 701, RG105; F. A. H. Gaebel to County Judge, 8 May 1867, vol. 120, ser. 690, RG105; affidavit of Nancy Houston, 12 July 1867, vol. 116, ser. 700, RG105; Andrew Clark to O. H. Howard, 3 Feb. 1868, ser. 693, RG105; O. H. Howard to M. Frank Gallagher, 24 Mar. 1868, LR, M798r20; O. H. Howard, "Report of Assaults Committed upon Freedpeople with Intent to Kill," 23 May 1868, LR, M798r21; affidavit of Mary Ballard, 1 July 1868, GIC; affidavit of Maria Jones, 5 Oct. 1868, LR, M798r22. Additional information on the complaints brought by freedwomen (and freedmen) can be found in a database compiled by the author from the following registers: vol. 385, ser. 1044; vol. 240, ser. 695; vol. 193, ser. 884; vol. 260½, ser. 885; vol. 185, ser. 785; vol. 324, ser. 975, all in RG105.

37. Contract between Jefferson L. Banks and Larking Street et al., 5 Dec. 1865, filed with O. H. Howard to C. C. Sibley, ser. 700, RG105; Circular no. 5, 22 Dec. 1865, pp. 333–335, ser. 636, [A-418]; contract between Wm H. Clark and Perry et al., 29 Dec. 1865, filed with Ch. Raushenberg to O. H. Howard, 6 June 1868, ser. 700, RG105; contract between A. B. Duncan and Simon Johnson and Alex Jackson et al., [Dec. 1865 or Jan. 1866?], enclosed in O. H. Howard to C. C. Sibley, 18 Apr. 1867, ser. 700, RG105; contract between Richard M. Cheshire and Ned et al., [1?] Jan. 1866, ser. 693, RG105; contract be-

tween J. C. McGehee and Dawon et al., 1 Jan. 1866, filed with W. E. Wiggins
to Eugene Pickett, 25 May 1867, ser. 700, RG105; contract between L. H. Durham and Solomen Perry et al., 12 Jan. 1866, vol. 116, ser. 700, RG105; contract
between W. A. McDowell and Peter Blocker et al., 5 Mar. 1865, ser. 693,
RG105; S. A. McLendon to F. A. H. Gaebel, 28 Mar. 1866, ser. 694, RG105;
contract between D. F. Sapp and Berry Melton et al., 15 May 1866, ser. 693,
RG105; contract between Fanney E. Lippitt and Ben Homes, 12 Mar. 1867,
Lippett Papers, THC; affidavit of James Whaley, 6 Apr. 1867, ser. 693, RG105;
O. H. Howard to C. C. Sibley, 15 Apr. 1867, vol. 121, ser. 697, RG105; J. M.
Robinson to [C. C. Sibley], 11 July 1867, RLR, M798r12; C. C. Hicks to O. H.
Howard, 11 Oct. 1867, vol. 127, ser. 698, RG105; affidavit of Levi Steward, 13
July 1868, ser. 700, RG105.

    38. Contract between W. A. McDowell and Peter Blocker et al., 5 Mar.
1866, ser. 693, RG105; George Wagner to W. W. Deane, 27 July 1866, ULR,
M798r29; John R. Jones to O. H. Howard, 23 Apr. 1867, ser. 700, RG105; S. A.
McClendon to F. A. H. Gaebel, 24 Apr. 1866, ser. 694, RG105; affidavit of
James Whaley, 6 Apr. 1867, ser. 693, RG105.

    39. Contract between A. C. Turner and Rufus Moore et al., 1 Jan. 1866,
ser. 694, RG105; F. A. H. Gaebel to David S. McCoy, 19 Mar. 1866, vol. 234,
ser. 690, RG105; H. C. Strong to F. A. H. Gaebel, 22 May 1866, ser. 694,
RG105; 5 Sept. 1866, Shadrick A. Dickey Diary, GDAH; Ch. Raushenberg to
O. H. Howard, 6 June 1867, vol. 124, ser. 697, RG105; John H. Pope to O. H.
Howard, 7 June 1867, vol. 116, ser. 700, RG105; C. C. Hicks to M. F. Gallagher,
30 Sept. 1867, vol. 127, ser. 698, RG105; account of Adam Jefferson, [1868],
vol. 127, ser. 698, RG105; "Accounts Due, Estate of Perry E. Duncan," 1867,
ser. 701, RG105; C. C. Hicks to William Gilbert, 16 Jan. 1868, vol. 122, ser. 697,
RG105; Ch. Raushenberg to O. H. Howard, 25 May 1868, ser. 694, RG105; Ch.
Raushenberg to [C. C. Sibley], 6 June 1868, RLR, M798r12; 30 July 1868, vol.
4, DAH; 5 Apr. 1869, 18 July 1869, vol. 5, DAH.

    40. Contract between Benjamin C. Yancey and Sam et al., Dec. 1865,
BCY; contract between Wm. H. Clark and Perry et al., 29 Dec. 1865, filed
with Ch. Raushenberg to O. H. Howard, 6 June 1868, ser. 700, RG105; contract between A. B. Duncan and Simon Johnson and Alex Jackson et al.,
[Dec. 1865 or Jan. 1866?], enclosed in O. H. Howard to C. C. Sibley, 18 Apr.

1867, ser. 700, RG105; contract between A. C. Turner and Rufus Moore et al., 1 Jan. 1866, ser. 694, RG105; contract between John Blocker and Stephen Blocker and Henry Thomas et al., [Jan. 1866], enclosed in S. A. McLendon to F. A. H. Gaebel, 24 Apr. 1866, ser. 694, RG105; contract between J. C. McGhee and Dawson et al., 1 Jan. 1866, filed with W. E. Wiggins to Eugene Pickett, 25 May 1867, ser. 700, RG105; M. Timmerman to B. C. Yancey, 30 Jan. 1866, BCY; contract between W. A. McDowell and Peter Blocker et al., 5 Mar. 1855, ser. 693, RG105; contract between D. F. Sapp and Berry Melton et al., 15 May 1866, ser. 693, RG105; contract between Enoch G. Bass and Bill Wooten et al., 20 June 1866, ser. 701 RG105; George Kaigler to O. H. Howard, 8 July 1867, vol. 116, ser. 700, RG105.

41. See, for example, F. A. H. Gaebel to W. W. Deane, 29 Apr. 1866, ULR, M798r27; Joseph H. Taylor to F. A. H. Gaebel, 18 July 1866, ser. 694, RG105; affidavit of Richard Baker, 15 Mar. 1867, ser. 1040, RG105; O. H. Howard to C. C. Sibley, 15 Apr. 1867, vol. 127, ser. 698, RG105; affidavit of Cipio and Sarah Stafford, 11 June 1867, ser. 701, RG105; O. H. Howard to John P. Thomas, 24 June 1867, vol. 121, ser. 697, RG105; Stephen H. Williams to [Starkville, Georgia, Post Commander], 1 July 1867, ser. 700, RG105; O. H. Howard to Wm. Newson, 5 July 1867, vol. 122, ser. 697, RG105; Gabriel Shackleford vs. A. P. Hays, 8 July 1867, pp. 4–5, vol. 206½, ser. 885, RG105; Augustus Alexander vs. Abdallah Smith, 10 July 1867, pp. 6–7, vol. 206½, ser. 885, RG105; James Alexander v. Andrew Floyd, 15 July 1867, pp. 8–9, vol. 206½, ser. 885, RG105; E. W. Jeter vs. Russell Patterson, 2 Aug. 1867, pp. 14–15, vol. 206½, ser. 885, RG105; Ch. Raushenberg to F. A. H. Gaebel, 16 Aug. 1867, vol. 116, ser. 700, RG105; Henry A. Smith to Jacob Daniel, 20 Aug. 1867, pp. 18–19, vol. 206½, ser. 885, RG105; Wm. L. Worn to Capt. White, 20 Aug. 1867, ser. 782, RG105; Ch. Raushenberg to M. Frank Gallagher, 25 Sept. 1867, ser. 693, RG105; Betsy Slaten vs. A. Slaten, 26 Sept. 1867, pp. 26–28, vol. 206½, ser. 885, RG105; Maj. Gilbert vs. Ben Collins, 27 Oct. 1868, vol. 324, pp. 18–19, ser. 975, RG105; George Morgan vs. D. L. Johnson, 16 Dec. 1867, pp. 44–47, vol. 206½, ser. 885, RG105; affidavit of Jack Wright, 31 Jan. 1868, ser. 1041, RG105; see also complaint database in author's possession.

42. Contract between L. P. Durham and Charles Perry Sr. et al., 12 Jan. 1866, ser. 700, RG105; J. C. McCoy to H. C. Strong, 26 May 1866, ULR,

M798r28; W. P. Jordan to F. A. H. Gaebel, 18 Dec. 1866, ser. 694, RG105; affidavit of Samuel Jones, 1 Apr. 1867, ser. 701, RG105; affidavit of Hampton Jones, 6 Apr. 1867, ser. 701, RG105; O. H. Howard to John Thomas, 9 Apr. 1867, vol. 121, ser. 697, RG105; O. H. Howard to A. B. Duncan, 9 Apr. 1867, vol. 121, ser. 697, RG105; O. H. Howard to G. M. By[um], 10 Apr. 1867, vol. 121, ser. 697, RG105; O. H. Howard to C. C. Sibley, 12 Apr. 1867, vol. 121, ser. 697, RG105; F. A. H. Gaebel to S. E. Lassiter, 15 Apr. 1867, vol. 120, ser. 690, RG105; O. H. Howard to B. P. Roberts, 17 Apr. 1867, vol. 121, ser. 697, RG105; O. H. Howard to Mrs. McLaren, 23 Apr. 1867, vol. 121, ser. 697, RG105; O. H. Howard to F. A. H. Gaebel, 25 Apr. 1867, vol. 121, ser. 697, RG105; O. H. Howard to H. [P.] Calloway, 7 May 1867, vol. 121, ser. 697, RG105; affidavit of John Dawson, 27 May 1867, ser. 701, RG105; C. C. Hicks to L. H. Durham, [5] Nov. 1867, ser. 697, RG105.

43. W. W. Deane to E. F. Kinksey, 19 Mar. 1866, LS, M798r2; F. A. H. Gaebel, 29 Apr. 1866, ULR, M798r27; Joseph O'Neil to Eugene Pickett, 16 Nov. 1866, ULR, M798r28; W. P. Jordan to F. A. H. Gaebel, 18 Dec. 1866, ser. 694, RG105; O. H. Howard to C. C. Sibley, 17 Apr. 1867, vol. 121, ser. 697, RG105; O. H. Howard to C. C. Sibley, 19 Apr. 1867, vol. 121, ser. 697, RG105; Ch. Raushenberg to Eugene Pickett, 20 Aug. 1867, ser. 693, RG105; C. C. Hicks to Wm. H. Cooper, 29 Nov. 1867, ser. 697, RG105; O. H. Howard to Agents, 7 Dec. 1867, vol. 123, ser. 690, RG105; *MFU,* 16 Jan. 1866, 13 Mar. 1866; Williams & Wellborn, comp., *Williams & Wellborn's Pamphlet of the Public Laws of Georgia, Passed at the Regular Session Held at Milledgeville, in November and December 1866, Together with All the Amendments of the Code, since Its Adoption, to the Close of the Late Session of the Legislature, a Revised Court Calendar, and Tables of the Congressional, Judicial and Senatorial Districts* (Milledgeville, Ga., 1866), 58–59; Clark et al., *The Code of the State of Georgia* (1867), 523–534; Cimbala, *Under the Guardianship of the Nation,* 143–144.

5. TO MAKE A LABORERS' STATE

1. This is a conceptualization of Reconstruction-era black politics that has only recently begun to come back into historical fashion; see Michael

W. Fitzgerald, *Urban Emancipation: Popular Politics in Reconstruction Mobile, 1860–1890* (Baton Rouge, 2002), 1–8; Brian Kelly, "Black Laborers, the Republican Party, and the Crisis of Reconstruction in Lowcountry South Carolina," *International Review of Social History* 51 (Dec. 2006): 375–414.

2. *Statutes at Large*, 13:758–761; *Senate Exec. Doc.*, 6, pp. 190–197, 202–220; Eric Foner, *Reconstruction: America's Unfinished Revolution, 1863–1877* (New York, 1988), 112–118; Steven F. Miller, Susan E. O'Donovan, John C. Rodrigue, and Leslie S. Rowland, eds., "Between Emancipation and Enfranchisement: Law and the Political Mobilization of Black Southerners during Presidential Reconstruction, 1865–1867," *Chicago-Kent Law Review* 70, no. 3 (1995): 1059–77; Steven Hahn, "'Extravagant Expectations' of Freedom: Rumour, Political Struggle, and the Christmas Insurrection Scare of 1865 in the American South," *Past and Present* 157 (Nov. 1977): 122–158.

3. R. H. Clark, T. R. R. Cobb, and D. Irwin, *The Code of the State of Georgia* (Atlanta, Ga., 1867), 330–335; *Senate Exec. Doc.*, 6, pp. 179–181; U.S. Congress, *Report of the Joint Committee on Reconstruction* (Washington, D.C., 1866), pt. 3, p. 187; *GJM*, 30 May 1866; *MFU*, 12 Dec. 1865, 23 Jan. 1866, 30 Jan.1866, 6 Feb. 1866, 13 Feb. 1866, 20 Feb. 1866, 27 Feb. 1866, 13 Mar. 1866.

4. *Proceedings of the Freedmen's Convention of Georgia, Assembled at Augusta, January 10th, 1866; Containing the Speeches of Gen'l Tillson, Capt. J. E. Bryant, and Others* (Augusta, Ga., 1866), 3–4, Pamphlet Collection, DU; *SE*, 31 Jan. 1866; Philip S. Foner and George E. Walker, eds., *Proceedings of the Black National and State Conventions, 1865–1900* (Philadelphia, 1986).

5. *Freedmen's Convention . . . January 10th, 1866*, 4; *SE*, 20 Dec. 1865; Lewis Williams et al. to Gen. Tillson, [23?] Dec. 1865, ser. 632, [A-5287]; Eric Foner, *Freedom's Lawmakers: A Directory of Black Officeholders during Reconstruction*, rev. ed. (Baton Rouge, 1996), and *Reconstruction*, 112–117; Joseph P. Reidy, "Aaron A. Bradley: Voice of Black Labor in the Georgia Lowcountry," in *Southern Black Leaders of the Reconstruction Era*, ed. Howard N. Rabinowitz (Urbana, Ill., 1982), 281–308.

6. *Freedmen's Convention . . . January 10th, 1866*, 7–31; Foner and Walker, *Proceedings*, 234; *SE*, 31 Jan. 1866; *Augusta Colored American*, 6 Jan. 1866, 13 Jan. 1866.

7. *Freedmen's Convention . . . January 10th, 1866*, 32–40; *Proceedings of*

the Council of the Georgia Equal Rights Association; Assembled at Augusta, Ga. April 4th, 1866; Containing the Address of the President, Captain J. E. Bryant, and Resolutions Adopted by the Council (Augusta, Ga., 1866), JEB.

8. Walter L. Fleming, ed., *Union League Documents* (Morgantown, W. Va., 1904), 3–4; *Georgia Equal Rights Association . . . April 4th, 1866,* JEB; *Proceedings of the Convention of the Equal Rights and Educational Association of Georgia, Assembled at Macon, October 29th, 1866; Containing the Annual Address of Captain J. E. Bryant* (Augusta, Ga., 1866), 5, Pamphlet Collection, DU; address by J. E. Bryant, [early January] 1867, no. 20409, AMAr2; Michael W. Fitzgerald, *The Union League Movement in the Deep South: Politics and Agricultural Change during Reconstruction* (Baton Rouge, 1989), 2.

9. F. A. H. Gaebel to W. W. Deane, 22 May 1866, vol. 234, ser. 690, RG105; F. A. H. Gaebel to W. W. Deane, 23 May 1866, ULR, M798r27; Circular letter, 17 Jan. 1866, vol. 1, p. 70, ser. 1036, RG105; S. F. Dupor to C. C. Richardson, 10 Mar. 1866, vol. 375, p. 55, ser. 1039, RG105; T. G. Cooper to B. C. Yancey, 4 Apr. 1866, BCY; John Cobb to Howell Cobb, 27 Apr. 1866, CEL; Mary E. H. Stiles to Kate, 24 Feb. 1866, WHS; *GJM,* 30 May 1866.

10. Thos. G. Cooper to B. C. Yancey, 27 Jan. 1866, BCY; M. Timmerman to B. C. Yancey, 30 Jan. 1866, 25 Feb. 1866, 18 Mar. 1866, BCY; *GWT,* 29 Jan. 1866, 30 Apr. 1866; *DWJ,* 18 May 1866.

11. T. G. Cooper to B. C. Yancey, 4 Apr. 1866, BCY; F. A. H. Gaebel to W. W. Deane, 23 May 1866, ULR, M798r27; *DWJ,* 18 May 1866.

12. M. Timmerman to B. C. Yancey, 1 Nov. 1866, BCY; F. A. H. Gaebel to David McCoy, 23 Mar. 1866, vol. 234, ser. 690, RG105; F. A. H. Gaebel to W. W. Deane, 27 July 1866, ULR, M798r27; F. A. H. Gaebel to the Adjutant General of the Department of the Chattahochee, 2 Aug. 1866, ULR, M798r27; "Condition of Affairs in Georgia," 92.

13. Affidavit of Samuel Green, 2 Feb. 1866, LR, M798r13; F. A. H. Gaebel to W. W. Deane, 1 Mar. 1866, vol. 234, ser. 690, RG105; F. A. H. Gaebel to W. W. Deane, 6 Mar. 1866, 22 Apr. 1866, ULR, M798r27; F. A. H. Gaebel to W. W. Deane, 7 June 1866, vol. 234, ser. 690, RG105; F. A. H. Gaebel to W. W. Deane, 8 June 1866, ULR, M798r27; F. A. H. Gaebel to W. W. Deane, 11 June 1866, vol. 234, ser. 690, RG105; F. A. H. Gaebel to W. W. Deane, 14 June 1866,

20 June 1866, ULR, M798r27; F. A. H. Gaebel to W. W. Deane, 2 July 1866, LR, M798r13; J. C. Simmons to H. M. Turner, 2 July 1866, ULR, M798r29; F. A. H. Gaebel to W. W. Deane, 10 July 1866, LR, M798r13; Thomas Slaughter to Davis Tillson, 14 July 1866, LR, M798r13; F. A. H. Gaebel to N. L. Hill, 23 July 1866, vol. 234, ser. 690, RG105; E. F. Kirksey to F. A. H. Gaebel, 28 July 1866, ser. 694, RG105; F. A. H. Gaebel to W. W. Deane, 27 Aug. 1866, 28 Aug. 1866, ULR, M798r27; F. A. H. Gaebel to [W. W. Deane], 25 Dec. 1866, RLR, M798r11.

14. C. C. Richardson to [Davis Tillson], 8 Jan. 1866, RLR, M798r11; affidavit of Henry Smith, 26 Feb. 1866, vol. 385, p. 35, ser. 1044, RG105; F. A. H. Gaebel to W. W. Deane, 31 Mar. 1866, ULR, M798r27; Joseph O'Neil to W. W. Deane, 16 Apr. 1866, LR, M798r13; F. A. H. Gaebel to W. W. Deane, 23 May 1866, ULR, M798r27; Joseph O'Neil to W. W. Deane, 5 June 1855, 6 Aug. 1866, ULR, M798r28; J. C. DeGraffenried to W. W. Dean, 14 Aug. 1866, ULR, M798r26; S. A. McLendon to Davis Tillson, 1 Sept. 1866, ULR, M798r28; F. A. H. Gaebel to T. F. Forbes, 14 Sept. 1866, vol. 234, ser. 690, RG105; Davis Tillson to O. O. Howard, 1 Nov. 1866, Reports Relating to Operations, M798r32; F. A. H. Gaebel to W. Mills, 30 Aug. 1867, vol. 120, ser. 690, RG105; Donald G. Nieman, *To Set the Law in Motion: The Freedmen's Bureau and the Legal Rights of Blacks, 1865–1868* (Millwood, N.Y., 1979), 96; Paul A. Cimbala, *Under the Guardianship of the Nation: The Freedmen's Bureau and the Reconstruction of Georgia, 1865–1870* (Athens, Ga., 1997), 37–38.

15. F. A. H. Gaebel to W. W. Dean, 1 Mar. 1866, vol. 234, ser. 690, RG105; F. A. H. Gaebel to W. W. Deane, 6 Mar. 1866, ULR, M798r27; F. A. H. Gaebel to W. W. Deane, 17 Apr. 1866, vol. 234, ser. 690, RG105; Joseph Taylor to W. W. Deane, 21 Apr. 1866, ULR, M798r29; F. A. H. Gaebel to W. W. Deane, 22 May 1866, 25 May 1866, 16 June 1866, 20 June 1866, 17 July 1866, ULR, M798r27; E. F. Kirksey to F. A. H. Gaebel, 28 July 1866, ser. 694, RG105; Joseph Taylor to W. W. Deane, 21 Apr. 1866, ULR, M798r29; F. A. H. Gaebel to Eugene Pickett, 1 Aug. 1867, LR, M798r18; F. A. H. Gaebel to W. Mills, 30 Aug. 1867, vol. 120, ser. 690, RG105.

16. F. A. H. Gaebel to W. W. Deane, 29 Apr. 1866, ULR, M798r27; F. A. H. Gaebel to W. W. Deane, 22 May 1866, vol. 234, ser. 690, RG105; F. A. H. Gaebel to T. F. Forbes, 16 Sept. 1866, vol. 234, ser. 690, RG105; J. C.

McCoy to H. C. Strong, 26 May 1866, ULR, M798r28; David Harper to O. O. Howard, 10 Mar. 1866, Ltrs Rec'd Relating to Appointments, M798r31; *House Exec. Doc.,* 70, pp. 40–41, 86–87.

17. Wm. Gray to S. A. McLendon, 25 Jan. 1866, LS, M798r11; Geo. H. Pratt to J. A. Parks, 13 Mar. 1866, LS, M798r2; Geo. H. Pratt to F. A. Billingslea, 24 Mar. 1866, LS, M798r2; Geo. H. Pratt to Dan S. McCoy, 26 Mar. 1866, LS, M798r2; F. A. H. Gaebel to W. W. Deane, 27 Mar. 1866, vol. 234, ser. 690, RG105; F. A. H. Gaebel to Stenton McLendon, 12 Apr. 1866, vol. 234, ser. 690, RG105; F. A. H. Gaebel to W. W. Deane, 22 May 1866, 11 June 1866, vol. 234, ser. 690, RG105; S. A. McClendon to F. A. H. Gaebel, 12 June 1866, ser. 694, RG105; F. A. H. Gaebel to W. W. Deane, 15 June 1866, vol. 234, ser. 690, RG105; J. H. Wade to F. A. H. Gaebel, 9 July 1866, ser. 694, RG105; F. A. H. Gaebel to W. W. Deane, 16 July 1866, ULR, M798r27; Joseph O'Neil to W. W. Deane, 15 Oct. 1866, LR, M798r3; "Condition of Affairs in Georgia," 92; *Equal Rights and Educational Association . . . October 29th, 1866,* 19; Nieman, *To Set the Law in Motion,* 27.

18. S. A. McLendon to Davis Tillson, 1 Sept. 1866, ULR, M798r28; Augustus Clark to Davis Tillson, 1 Oct. 1866, vol. 375, p. 93, ser. 1039, RG105; M. V. Jordan to Davis Tillson, 27 Oct. 1866, vol. 375, pp. 103–105, ser. 1039, RG105.

19. George Pratt to S. A. McLendon, 5 Feb. 1866, LS, M798r11; S. A. McLendon, 14 Mar. 1866, ser. 694, RG105; F. A. H. Gaebel to W. W. Deane, 23 May 1866, ULR, M798r27; M. Timmerman to B. C. Yancey, 25 Feb. 1866, BCY; S. A. McLendon to F. A. H. Gaebel, 12 June 1866, ser. 694, RG105; F. A. H. Gaebel to W. W. Deane, 1 Mar. 1866, vol. 234, ser. 690, RG105; S. A. McLendon to F. A. H. Gaebel, 14 Mar. 1866, ser. 694, RG105; TCSC (1866–1869), 229–230; DCSC, L:432–440; "Condition of Affairs in Georgia," 92; Miller et al., "Between Emancipation and Enfranchisement," 1063.

20. Jeremiah Walters to [Davis Tillson], 15 Mar. 1866, RLR, M798r11; F. A. H. Gaebel to W. W. Deane, 1 Mar. 1866, vol. 234, ser. 690, RG105; *SE,* 13 June 1866.

21. H. C. Strong to [Davis Tillson], 12 July 1866, RLR, M798r11; endorsement by T. F. Forbes, 21 July 1866, ES, M798r8; *SE,* 9 May 1866, 13 June 1866.

22. F. A. H. Gaebel to Eugene Pickett, 20 Dec. 1866, vol. 235, ser. 690, RG105.

23. Wm. C. Watson et al. to H. C. Strong, 17 July 1866, ULR, M798r26; F. A. H. Gaebel to W. W. Deane, 23 May 1866, ULR, M798r27; Ch. Raushenberg to F. A. H. Gaebel, 22 July 1866, ser. 694, RG105; *DWJ*, 18 May 1866; *GWT*, 21 May 1866; 23 July 1866.

24. G. A. Hastings to Davis Tillson, 25 Nov. 1865, ULR, M798r24; Davis Tillson to O. O. Howard, 28 Nov. 1865, enclosing N. M. Reeve to Gen. Tillson, 27 Nov. 1865, G-37 1865, ser. 15, [A-5197]; Samuel Brown and Squire Sherman to George Eberhart, 5 Dec. 1866, LR, M799r8; G. A. Hastings to Davis Tillson, 7 Jan. 1866, ULR, M798r27; Florence Speed to Davis Tillson, 8 Mar. 1866, ULR, M798r29; Brien Maguire to W. W. Deane, 2 Apr. 1866, ser. 632, [A-5419]; Lawrence Speed to Davis Tillson, 4 Apr. 1866, ULR, M798r29; Samuel Brown and Squire Sherman to T. F. Forbes, 10 Aug. 1866, ULR, M798r29; Brien Maguire to T. F. Forbes, 12 Oct. 1866, ser. 632, [A-5419]; affidavit of John Griffin, 25 July 1867, ser. 1040, [A-5584]; Thomas Cooper to Benjamin Yancey, 27 Jan. 1866, BCY; *Freedmen's Convention . . . January 10th, 1866*, 4, 6; *Equal Rights Association . . . April 4th, 1866*, 8.

25. Wm. C. Watson to H. C. Strong, 17 July 1866, ULR, M798r26; *Freedmen's Convention . . . January 10th, 1866*, 36–39.

26. Wm. C. Watson to H. C. Strong, 17 July 1866, ULR, M798r26; M. Timmerman to B. C. Yancey, 1 Nov. 1866, BCY; Benjamin Yancey to My Dear Wife, 11 Sept. 1866, Benjamin C. Yancey Papers, DU; *Equal Rights and Educational Association . . . October 29th, 1866*, 9–12, 17; Miller et al., "Between Emancipation and Enfranchisement," 1060.

27. Ch. Raushenburg to F. A. H. Gaebel, 22 July 1866, ser. 694, RG105; *Equal Rights and Educational Association . . . October 29th, 1866*, 1–2; Lemuel Brown and Squire Sherman to Theodore Forbes, 16 Sept. 1866, ULR, M798r29; *GWT*, 1 Oct. 1866; *AP*, 21 July 1866; *SE*, 9 May 1866; *GJM*, 19 Sept. 1866.

28. Wm. C. Watson to H. C. Strong, 17 July 1866, ULR, M798r26; H. C. Strong to W. W. Deane, 2 July 1866, ULR, M798r29.

29. Brien Maguire to W. W. Deane, 2 Apr. 1866, ser. 632, [A-5419]; W. W. Deane to Ira Ayers, 5 Apr. 1866, LS, M798r2; Davis Tillson to Ira Ayers,

25 Apr. 1866, LS, M798r2; Theodore Forbes to W. J. Vason, 7 Aug. 1866, LS, M798r3; Samuel Brown and Squire Sherman to Theodore Forbes, 10 Aug. 1866, ULR, M798r29; Theodore Forbes to Samuel Brown and Squire Sherman, 17 Aug. 1866, LS, M798r3.

30. F. A. H. Gaebel to W. W. Deane, 15 July 1866, ULR, M798r27; S. A. McLendon to W. W. Deane, 6 Aug. 1866, ULR, M798r28; Augustus Clark to Davis Tillson, 1 Oct. 1866, vol. 375, p. 93, ser. 1039, RG105; Joseph O'Neil to W. W. Deane, 15 Oct. 1866, LR, M798r3; Registers of Civilian Agents on Duty in Georgia, ser. 646, RG105; Special Order no. 115, 25 Oct. 1866, vol. 384, p. 21, ser. 1042, RG105; Joseph Taylor to W. W. Deane, 28 Oct. 1866, ULR, M798r29; Davis Tillson to O. O. Howard, 1 Nov. 1866, Reports Relating to Operations, M798r32; Joseph O'Neil to Eugene Pickett, 16 Nov. 1866, ULR, M798r28; Lawrence Speed to G. L. Eberhart, 27 Nov. 1866, LR, M798r16; Gideon Hastings to Davis Tillson, 7 Dec. 1866, ULR, M798r27; Geo. R. Dalton to J. V. DeHanne, 2 Feb. 1867, ser. 680, RG105; Special Order no. 61, 5 Apr. 1866, ser. 694, RG105; O. H. Howard to G. L. Eberhart, 8 Apr. 1867, vol. 121, ser. 697, RG105; Howell Cobb to My Dear Wife, Dec. 1866, CEL; John Cobb to My Dear Wife, 1 Jan. 1867, 4 Jan. 1867, CEL; *SE*, 25 Jan. 1867; *GWT*, 15 Feb. 1867; *DWJ*, 23 Nov. 1866, 4 Jan. 1867, 13 January 1867; *Cuthbert Appeal*, 2 November 1866; *Statutes at Large*, 4:66–67; "Condition of Affairs in Georgia," 92.

31. H. M. Turner to J. E. Bryant, 12 Apr. 1866, JEB; H. M. Turner to J. E. Bryant, [mid-April] 1866, JEB; *Equal Rights and Educational Association . . . October 29th, 1866*, 6–9, 15–17; *Senate Exec. Doc.*, 6, p. 55; Nieman, *To Set the Law in Motion*, 196–197; Edward McPherson, *The Political History of the United States of America during the Period of Reconstruction . . .* , 2nd ed. (Washington, D.C., 1875), 102, 124, 323–324, 357.

32. *GJM*, 30 Jan. 1867; *SE*, 15 Feb. 1867; DCSC, L:392–393, 416–417; *AN*, 28 Feb. 1867; Foner, *Reconstruction*, 268–269.

33. 7 Dec. 1866 and 15 Dec. 1866, Shadrack A. Dickey Diary, GDAH; Thomas Willingham to Benjamin Yancey, 21 Nov. 1866, BCY; Benjamin Yancey to My Dear Wife, 22 Nov. 1866, BCY; Benjamin Yancey to [Sarah Yancey], 28 Nov. 1866, BCY; Malachai Timmerman to Benjamin Yancey, 12 Dec. 1866, BCY; O. H. Prince to David Barrow, 25 Feb. 1867, DCB; Howell

Cobb to My Dear Wife, Dec. 1866, CEL; John Cobb to My Dear Wife, 4 Jan. 1867, CEL; *Cuthbert Appeal*, 2 Nov. 1866, 16 Nov. 1866, 7 Dec. 1866, 4 Jan. 1867; *GWT*, 22 Feb. 1867; *SE*, 2 Jan. 1867; *GJM*, 23 Jan. 1867; *DWJ*, 1 Mar. 1867.

34. F. A. H. Gaebel to Eugene Pickett, 3 Apr. 1867, vol. 120, ser. 690, RG105; Simon Harris to J. E. Bryant, 15 Apr. 1867, JEB; A. H. Colquitt to O. H. Howard, 29 May 1867, ser. 700, RG105; Nelson Tift, T. H. Johnston, and John Davis to O. H. Howard, 11 June 1867, ser. 700, RG105; John Pope to [Robert C. Schenck], 20 May 1867, RCS; extract of letter of Henry M. Turner, 23 July 1867, enclosed in T. L. Tullock to Robert C. Schenck, 4 Aug. 1867, RCS; *Cuthbert Appeal*, 19 Apr. 1867; *GWT*, 19 Apr. 1867, 26 Apr. 1867, 10 May 1867, 31 May 1867; *SE*, 19 Apr. 1867, 24 May 1867, 28 May 1867; McPherson, *Political History of the United States*, 166–173; Foner, *Reconstruction*, 276–277; Joseph P. Reidy, *From Slavery to Agrarian Capitalism in the Cotton Plantation South: Central Georgia, 1800–1880* (Chapel Hill, N.C., 1992), 185, 191.

35. A. H. Colquitt to O. H. Howard, 29 May 1867, 30 May 1867, ser. 700, RG105; Simon Harris to J. E. Bryant, 15 Apr. 1867, JEB; *GWT*, 19 Apr. 1867; *SE*, 24 May 1867; Reidy, "Aaron A. Bradley," 281–308.

36. "Names of Speakers & Organizers Employed or Aided by the Union Republican Congressional Committee," 12 Sept. 1867, RCS; T. G. Steward to J. A. Rockwell, 6 Nov. 1867, no. 20929, AMAr3; John Rockwell to Edward Smith, 13 Nov. 1867, no. 20943, AMAr3; *SE*, 2 Apr. 1867, 19 Apr. 1867, 17 May 1867, 28 May 1867, 15 Nov. 1867; *GWT*, 22 Mar. 1867, 19 Apr. 1867, 26 Apr. 1867, 10 May 1867; *DWJ*, 26 Apr. 1867; Foner, *Freedom's Lawmakers*, 203–204.

37. George Wallbridge to C. C. Sibley, 12 June 1867, LR, M798r16; F. A. H. Gaebel to G. L. Eberhart, 27 May 1867, LR, M799r8; endorsements on Ch. Raushenberg to F. A. H. Gabel, 21 June 1867, ES, M798r9; D. Jackson to Genl Pope, 13 Sept. 1867, A-1616 1867, ser. 5782, Bureau of Civil Affairs, 3rd Military Dist., RG393, pt. 1, [SS-675]; Ch. Raushenberg to M. Frank Gallagher, 4 Oct. 1867, vol. 120, ser. 690, RG105.

38. A. B. Sibley to O. H. Howard, 15 Apr. 1867, ser. 700, RG105; T. J. Boynton to O. H. Howard, 28 Apr. 1867, ser. 700, RG105; J. J. Harral to O. H. Howard, 6 May 1867, ser. 700, RG105; M. Gormby to F. A. H. Gaebel, 7 May 1867, ser. 693, RG105; Geo. C. Edwards to O. H. Howard, 20 May 1867, ser.

700, RG105; F. A. H. Gaebel to Eugene Pickett, 24 May 1867, vol. 120, ser. 690, RG105; J. J. Jones to O. H. Howard, 29 May 1867, ser. 700, RG105; J. B. Vanover to O. H. Howard, 31 May 1867, ser. 700, RG105; C. M. Byne to O. H. Howard, 3 June 1867, ser. 700, RG105; John Pope to O. H. Howard, 7 June 1867, ser. 700, RG105; Nelson Tift, T. H. Johnston, and John Davis to O. H. Howard, 11 June 1867, ser. 700, RG105; Elbert Darden to O. H. Howard, 19 June 1867, ser. 700, RG105; G. A. Burton to C. C. Sibley, 1 July 1867, LR, M798r17; J. Davis Tonge to H. G. Crawford, 4 July 1867, ser. 783, RG105; Geo. Kaigler to O. H. Howard, 8 July 1867, ser. 700, RG105; J. B. Chambers to Ch. Raushenberg, 21 Aug. 1867, ser. 700, RG105; Ch. Raushenberg to O. H. Howard, 27 Aug. 1867, ser. 700, RG105; *Albany Tri-Weekly News,* 15 June 1867; *AN,* 2 July 1867; "Condition of Affairs in Georgia," 92–93.

39. G. M. Byne to O. H. Howard, 3 June 1867, ser. 700, RG105; John Pope to O. H. Howard, 7 June 1867, ser. 700, RG105; F. A. H. Gaebel to Eugene Pickett, 1 Aug. 1867, LR, M798r18; W. F. White to J. R. Lewis, 27 Sept. 1867, filed under "H to R District of Georgia 1867," LR, ser. 164, Dist. of GA, RG393, pt. 3; W. L. Clark to C. C. Sibley, 24 Feb. 1868, GIC; 24 Aug. 1867, vol. 3, DAH; *SE,* 5 July 1867; *GWT,* 18 Oct. 1867.

40. Geo. O. Dalton to J. V. DeHanne, 10 June 1867, ser. 680, RG105; Nelson Tift, T. F. Johnston, and John Davis to O. H. Howard, 11 June 1867, ser. 700, RG105; William Kiddo to John Hosmer, 24 June 1867, LR, M798r18; G. L. Eberhart to C. C. Sibley, 4 July 1867, LR, M798r18; M. Gillis to John Hosmer, 3 Sept. 1867, filed under "D to G District of Georgia 1867," LR, ser. 164, Dist. of GA, RG393, pt. 3; W. F. White to J. R. Lewis, 27 Sept. 1867, filed under "H to R District of Georgia 1867," LR, ser. 164, Dist. of GA, RG393, pt. 3; Aug. H. Hansell to John J. Hosmer, 9 Oct. 1867, filed under "H to R District of Georgia 1867," LR, ser. 164, Dist. of GA, RG393, pt. 3; *DWJ,* 28 June 1867, 19 July 1867.

41. O. H. Howard to Nelson Tift, L. H. Johnston, and John Davis, [12] June 1867, vol. 121, ser. 697, RG105; "To the Freedmen of Dougherty, Lee and Terrell Cos.," 10 June 1867, Orders & Circulars Issued & Received, M798r34.

42. Extract of letter from Henry Turner, 8 July 1867; extract of letter from Henry Turner, 23 July 1867; extract of letter of John Costin, 25 July 1867; all enclosed in T. L. Tullock to Robert C. Schenck, 4 Aug. 1867, RCS.

43. W. R. Elerson to Mr. Ebly Hart, 28 July 1867, LR, M799r9; Simon Harris to J. E. Bryant, 15 Apr. 1867, JEB; *AN*, 6 Apr. 1867, 16 Apr. 1867; *SE*, 9 May 1866, 2 Apr. 1867, 19 Apr. 1867, 17 May 1867, 28 May 1867, 7 June 1867, 5 July 1867; Foner, *Freedom's Lawmakers*, 174; biographical details about southwest Georgia's black Republican leadership come from a database compiled by the author.

44. "Names of Speakers & Organizers Employed or Aided by the Union Republican Congressional Committee," [12 Sept. 1867], RCS; H. M. Turner to George Whipple, 27 Aug. 1866, no. 20056, AMAr2; T. G. Steward to J. A. Rockwell, 6 Nov. 1867, no. 20929, AMAr3; John Rockwell to Edw. P. Smith, 13 Nov. 1867, no. 20943, AMAr3; T. G. Steward to [C. C. Sibley], 16 Oct. 1867, RLR, M798r12; *GWT*, 10 May 1867; Clarence E. Walker, *A Rock in a Weary Land: The African Methodist Episcopal Church during the Civil War and Reconstruction* (Baton Rouge, 1982), 130–133; Foner, *Freedom's Lawmakers*, 53, 203–204; Theophilus G. Steward, *From 1864–1914: Fifty Years in the Gospel Ministry, Twenty-Seven Years in the Pastorate; Sixteen Years' Active Service as Chaplain in the U.S. Army; Seven Years Professor in Wilberforce University; Two Trips to Europe; A Trip to Mexico* (Philadelphia, [1921]), 82, 99, 103; William Serail, *Voice of Dissent: Theophilus Gould Steward (1843–1924) and Black America* (Brooklyn, 1991), 29.

45. J. M. Robinson to F. A. H. Gaebel, 10 July 1867, ser. 693, RG105; J. N. Hard to F. A. H. Gaebel, 11 July 1867, ser. 693, RG105; F. A. H. Gaebel to G. R. Wallbridge, 19 July 1867, vol. 120, ser. 690, RG105; *Cuthbert Appeal*, 21 June 1867; *GWT*, 2 Aug. 1867, 30 Aug. 1867; *SE*, 12 July 1867, 16 July 1867, 19 July 1867, 23 July 1867, 26 July 1867, 30 July 1867, 2 Aug. 1867, 6 Aug. 1867, 9 Aug. 1867, 13 Aug. 1867, 16 Aug. 1867, 20 Aug. 1867; *DWJ*, 19 July 1867; *AN*, 4 July 1867, 6 July 1867, 10 Aug. 1867.

46. F. A. H. Gaebel to F. C. Genth, 12 July 1867, vol. 120, ser. 690, RG105; F. A. H. Gaebel to Eugene Pickett, 12 July 1867, vol. 120, ser. 690, RG105; F. A. H. Gaebel to G. R. Wallbridge, 19 July 1867, vol. 120, ser. 690, RG105; F. A. H. Gaebel to Eugene Pickett, 10 Aug. 1867, vol. 120, ser. 690, RG105; Andrew Clark to W. F. White, 22 Aug. 1867, LR, M798r17.

47. Affidavit of Prister Newkirk, 3 Aug. 1867, vol. 237, ser. 695, RG105; F. A. H. Gaebel to Eugene Pickett, 4 Aug. 1867, vol. 120, ser. 690, RG105;

affidavit of Richard Roberts, 6 Aug. 1867, vol. 237, ser. 695, RG105; F. A. H. Gaebel to Eugene Pickett, 10 Aug. 1867, vol. 120, ser. 690, RG105; affidavit of Shadrack Ross, 17 Sept. 1867, vol. 122, ser. 697, RG105.

48. "Ma" to "Dear Absent Children," 11 Oct. 1867, William E. Smith Papers, UGA; *SE,* 26 July 1867; *GWT,* 4 Oct. 867. Basing my calculations on population figures drawn from the 1860 federal census, and the estimated 14 percent wartime increase of southwest Georgia's black population, somewhere between a low of 87 percent and an impossibly high 118 percent of the region's eligible black men swore their oaths and recorded their names during that first registration summer. Except for the extreme at the high end, this range is not out of line with a southern average of 96.3 percent computed by Lawrence N. Powell; see Fitzgerald, *Union League Movement,* 43.

49. Extract of letter from Henry Turner, 23 July 1867, enclosed in T. L. Tullock to Robert C. Schenck, 4 Aug. 1867, RCS; endorsement of W. F. White on A. B. Clark to J. R. Lewis, 12 Sept. 1867, LR, M798r17; C. C. Hicks to J. R. Lewis, 9 Oct. 1867, LR, M798r18; "W" to Sisters Sallie & Mattie, 30 Oct. 1867, William E. Smith Papers, UGA; G. S. Ch[exeur] to F. C. Genth, 6 Nov. 1867, vol. 120, ser. 690, RG105; *SE,* 29 Oct. 1867; *GWT,* 30 Aug. 1867; 1 Nov. 1867, 8 Nov. 1867; *DWJ,* 1 Nov. 1867; *AN,* 7 Nov. 1867.

50. *AN,* 1 Nov. 1867; *SE,* 15 Oct. 1867, 22 Oct. 1867; *GWT,* 8 Nov. 1867, 15 Nov. 1867; state-by-state list of election results, [January] 1868, RCS; author's database on black leaders.

51. Unidentified newspaper clipping, 4 Jan. 1868, Eliza Frances Andrews Scrapbook, Garnett Andrews Papers, SHC; Nelson Tift to Charles McDonald, 28 Oct. 1843, GIC; 7 May 1843, A. T. Havens Journal, UGA; Susan E. O'Donovan, ed., "The Journal of Nelson Tift, Part V: 1842–1843," *JSwGH* 7 (1989–1992): 103–105; Fussell M. Chalker, "Irish Catholics in the Building of the Ocmulgee and Flint Railroad," *GHQ* 54 (Winter 1970): 512–513.

52. Fr. Conr. Genth to O. H. Howard, 14 Nov. 1867, ser. 693, RG105; O. H. Howard to M. Frank Gallagher, 25 Nov. 1867, vol. 123, ser. 690, RG105; Andrew Clark to O. H. Howard, 30 Nov. 1867, ser. 694, RG105; O. H. Howard to Agents, 7 Dec. 1867, vol. 123, ser. 690, RG105; O. H. Howard to Messrs. Rust, Johnson, & Co., 2 Jan. 1868, vol. 123, ser. 690, RG105; A. B. Clark to O. H.

Howard, 3 Jan. 1868, ser. 693, RG105; William L. Clark to J. R. Lewis, 3 Apr. 1868, LR, M799r10; *AN,* 21 Dec. 1867; *DWJ,* 2 Jan. 1868, 27 Feb. 1868; unidentified newspaper clipping, 4 Jan. 1868, Eliza Frances Andrews Scrapbook, Garnett Andrews Papers, SHC; "Condition of Affairs in Georgia," 93; [Major General George G. Meade], *Report of Major General Meade's Military Operations and Administration of Civil Affairs in the Third Military District and Dept. of the South* (Atlanta, 1868), 4; Gerald D. Jaynes, *Branches without Roots: Genesis of the Black Working Class in the American South, 1862–1888* (New York, 1986), 141–144; Gavin Wright, *The Political Economy of the Cotton South: Households, Markets, and Wealth in the Nineteenth Century* (New York, 1978), 172; Gavin Wright, *Old South, New South: Revolutions in the Southern Economy since the Civil War* (New York, 1986), 56–57; Lawrence N. Powell, *New Masters: Northern Planters during the Civil War and Reconstruction* (New Haven, Conn., 1980), 146–149; Roger L. Ransom and Richard Sutch, *One Kind of Freedom: The Economic Consequences of Emancipation* (Cambridge, 1977), 64–65.

53. O. H. Howard to C. C. Sibley, 21 Dec. 1867, vol. 123, ser. 690, RG105; J. M. Robinson to O. H. Howard, 23 Dec. 1867, 25 Dec. 1867, ser. 693, RG 105; O. H. Howard to C. C. Sibley, 25 Dec. 1867, vol. 123, ser. 690, RG105; O. H. Howard to M. Frank Gallagher, 31 Dec. 1867, vol. 123, ser. 690, RG105; O. H. Howard to The Freedmen in the Sub-District of Albany, 17 Jan. 1868, LR, M798r20; *DWJ,* 19 Dec. 1867; *SE,* 22 Nov. 1867.

54. Thomas Barrow to Roole, 8 Jan. 1868, DCB; O. H. Howard to James Laing, 17 Mar. 1868, vol. 123, ser. 690, RG105; O. H. Howard to M. Frank Gallagher, 21 Nov. 1868, vol. 125, ser. 690, RG105; O. H. Howard to The Freedmen in the Sub-District of Albany, 17 Jan. 1868, LR, M798r20; J. M. Robinson to M. Frank Gallagher, 31 Jan. 1868, LR, M798r20; *DWJ,* 2 Jan. 1868, 11 Feb. 1868; W. L. Clark to W. F. White, 17 Feb. 1868, vol. 182, p. 57, ser. 780, RG105; 10 Feb. 1868, vol. 4, DAH.

55. O. H. Howard to M. Frank Gallagher, 24 Mar. 1868, LR, M798r20; "Report of W. F. White S.A. C.," [March] 1868, Reports of Outrages Committed on the Freed People in Georgia, M798r32; "Report of Outrages Committed upon Freedpeople State of Ga.," 1 Jan.—15 Nov. 1868, Reports of Outrages Committed on the Freed People in Georgia, M798r32; affidavit of

Elbert Lewis, 18 May 1868, ser. 693, RG105; affidavit of John T. Gibson, 3 Mar. 1866, vol. 237, pp. 35–36, ser. 695, RG105; *GWT*, 15 Nov. 1867, 7 Feb. 1868, 20 Mar. 1868, 27 Mar. 1868, 3 Apr. 1868; *Savannah Freedman's Standard,* 9 Apr. 1868; *Report of Major General Meade's Military Operations,* 10, 28–29, 97–98; "Condition of Affairs in Georgia," 93; Reidy, *From Slavery to Agrarian Capitalism,* 200; Jonathan M. Bryant, *How Curious a Land: Conflict and Change in Greene County, Georgia, 1850–1885* (Athens, Ga., 1996), 119–121.

56. Affidavit of John T. Gibson, 22 Feb. 1868, RLR, M798r12; Cass Durham to R. C. Shaw, 22 Apr. 1868, filed under "M. to R. District of Georgia 1868," LR, ser. 164, Dist. of GA, RG393, pt. 3; Cass Durham to John Hosmer, 22 Apr. 1868, LR, ser. 164, Dist. of GA, RG393, pt. 3; M. A. Cochran to John Hosmer, 29 Apr. 1868, LR, ser. 164, Dist. of GA, RG393, pt. 3; Cass Durham to John Hosmer, 28 Apr. 1868, GIC; affidavit of Moses Slaughter, 5 May 1868, GIC; affidavit of Lawrence Solomons, 4 May 1868, GIC; O. H. Howard to C. C. Sibley, 22 Apr. 1868, vol. 123, ser. 690, RG105; O. H. Howard to John Hosmer, 15 May 1868, vol. 123, ser. 690, RG105; Ch. Raushenberg to A. M. Cochran, 20 Apr. 1868, vol. 124, ser. 697, RG105; Ch. Raushenberg to Jos. Shadows, 21 Apr. 1868, vol. 124, ser. 697, RG105; *Savannah Freedman's Standard,* 9 Apr. 1868; *GWT,* 17 Apr. 1868, 1 May 1868, 8 May 1868.

57. A. L. Holliday to R. L. Hunter, 18 June 1868, GIC; *GWT,* 15 May 1868; *MFU,* 16 Jan. 1866; DCIC (1854–1869), 590, 593, 595; Edmund L. Drago, *Black Politicians and Reconstruction in Georgia: A Splendid Failure,* 2nd ed. (Athens, Ga., 1992), append. B.

58. M. A. Cochran to John Hosmer, 27 Apr. 1868, LR, ser. 164, Dist. of GA, RG393, pt. 3; Cass Durham to John Hosmer, 28 Apr. 1868, GIC; Green Gilchrist vs. J. B. Griffin, 13 May 1868, vol. 185, pp. 105, 111, 153, ser. 785, RG105; Dennis Hopkins vs. Camilla Citizens and Residents of Mitchell County, 13 June [1868], vol. 2, p. 43, ser. 785, RG105; affidavit of Alfred Felton, 20 June 1868, ser. 1040, RG105; William Clark to C. C. Sibley, 28 June 1868, LR, M798r21; affidavit of Mary Ballard, 1 July 1868, GIC; affidavit of Fanny Stovall, 1 July 1868, GIC; affidavit of Jack Ballard, 1 July 1868, GIC; J. E. Blount to Rufus B. Bullock, 31 Aug. 1868, GIC; Mego Ku Klascan to Philip Joiner, [1868], vol. 237, ser. 695, RG105; Melak Mk. Ex Lan to Philip Joiner, [1868], vol. 237, ser. 695, RG105; Benjamin Anderson, Henry Brown,

"and others," to Rufus B. Bullock, 2 Sept. 1868, GIC; affidavit of James Roberts, 6 Oct. 1868, LR, M798r23; affidavit of Henry Washington, 10 Oct. 1868, LR, M798r22; Wm. C. Morrill to [J. R. Lewis], 2 Nov. 1868, LR, M798r23; "Report of Outrages Committed upon Freedpeople State of Ga.," 1 Jan.—15 Nov. 1868, Reports of Outrages Committed on the Freed People in Georgia, M798r32; "Condition of Affairs in Georgia," 93, 119, 121; *Report of Major General Meade's Military Operations,* 39–40.

59. Geo. R. Ballou to O. H. Howard, 27 June 1868, LR, ser. 164, Dist. of GA, RG393, pt. 3; W. C. Morrill to M. Frank Gallagher, 8 Aug. 1868, LR, M798r21; affidavit of George Washington, 10 July 1868, ser. 695, RG105; O. H. Howard to [M. Frank Gallagher], 23 May 1868, LR, M798r21; O. H. Howard to M. Frank Gallagher, 19 Sept. 1868, LR, M798r22; "Report of Outrages Committed upon Freedpeople State of Ga.," 1 Jan.–15 Nov. 1868, Reports of Outrages Committed on the Freed People in Georgia, M798r32; A. G. Ronaldson to Thomas H. Ruger, 29 May 1868, GIC; Daniel Losey to C. C. Sibley, 8 Sept. 1868, GIC; Benjamin Anderson, Henry Brown "and others," to Governor Rufus Bullock, 2 Sept. 1868, GIC; TCSC (1866–1869), 468–474; *GWT,* 14 Aug. 1868, 21 Aug. 1868, 11 Sept. 1868, 25 Sept. 1868; *GJM,* 19 Aug. 1868; *DWJ,* 27 Aug. 1868.

60. W. R. Elerson to Mr. Ebly Hart, 28 July 1867, LR, M799r9; Willis Crawford to General Meade, 12 Aug. 1868, LR, M798r21; John Cobb to Howell Cobb, 26 Sept. 1868, CEL; *DWJ,* 30 Apr. 1868; 25 June 1868, 6 Aug. 1868, 13 Aug. 1868, 31 Aug. 1868; *GWT,* 8 May 1868, 19 June 1868, 11 Sept. 1868, 18 Sept. 1868, 25 Sept. 1868; *Report of Major General Meade's Military Operations,* 11–12; Reidy, *From Slavery to Agrarian Capitalism,* 200–201.

61. O. H. Howard to J. R. Lewis, 10 Sept. 1868, LR, M798r22; affidavit of Goliath Kendrick, 23 Sept. 1868, LR, M798r22; affidavit of Peter Hines, 23 Sept. 1868, LR, M798r22; affidavit of Jackson O'Brien, 23 Sept. 1868, LR, M798r22; affidavit of Washington Jones, 23 Sept. 1867, LR, M798r22; affidavit of John Bird, 23 Sept. 1868, LR, M798r22; Ch. Raushenberg to O. H. Howard, 28 Sept. 1868, LR, M798r22; Ch. Raushenberg to M. Frank Gallagher, 30 Sept. 1868, LR, M798r23; Philip Joiner to John Bryant, 30 Sept. 1868, JEB; W. F. White to M. Frank Gallagher, 5 Oct. 1868, LR, M798r23; affidavit of Maria Jones, 5 Oct. 1868, LR, M798r22; affidavit of James Rob-

erts, 6 Oct. 1868, LR, M798r23; affidavit of Henry Washington, 10 Oct. 1868, LR, M798r22; Ch. Raushenberg to M. Frank Gallagher, 15 Oct. 1868, LR, M798r23; W. L. Clark to J. R. Lewis, 21 Oct. 1868, LR, M798r23.

62. J. L. Powell to Rufus Bullock, 27 Sept. 1868, GIC; O. H. Howard to M. Frank Gallagher, [31] Oct. 1868, LR, M798r23; Wm. C. Morrill to C. C. Sibley, 2 Nov. 1868, LR, M798r23; George Ballou to O. H. Howard, 3 Nov. 1868, LR, M798r23; Wm. C. Morrill to C. C. Sibley, 3 Nov. 1868, LR, M798r23; Andrew Clark to O. H. Howard, 3 Nov. 1868, LR, M798r23; Wm. C. Morrill to M. Frank Gallagher, 5 Nov. 1868, LR, M798r23; John Gibson to Rufus Bullock, 20 Nov. 1868, GIC; Ch. Raushenberg to O. H. Howard, 21 Nov. 1868, LR, M798r23; George Ballou to O. H. Howard, 23 Nov. 1868, LR, M798r23; O. H. Howard to J. R. Lewis, 27 Nov. 1868, LR, M798r23; DCSC, L:887; ECPC (1851–1882), 90–116; *GWT,* 9 Oct. 1868, 16 Oct. 1868, 6 Nov. 1868, 13 Nov. 1868; Russell Duncan, "A Georgia Governor Battles Racism: Rufus Bullock and the Fight for Black Legislators," in *Georgia in Black and White: Explorations in the Race Relations of a Southern State, 1865–1950,* ed. John C. Inscoe (Athens, Ga., 1994), 48.

CODA: THAT STRANGE LAND OF SHADOWS

This chapter's title is taken from the words of W. E. B. Du Bois, *The Souls of Black Folk,* ed. David Blight and Robert Gooding-Williams (Boston, 1997), 105.

1. Benj. Jestae et al. to James Smith, 29 May 1872, GIC; Chas. P. Hansel to James Smith, 13 July 1872, GIC; A. J. Nicholson et al. to James Smith, 4 Oct. 1873, GIC; P. Joiner et al. to James Smith, 15 Nov. 1873, GIC; James Jones to James Smith, 21 Aug. 1874, GIC; 1 Jan. 1869, vol. 5, DAH; Plantation Account Book, 4:6–17, 20–21, George W. Bryan Papers, SHC; *GWT,* 22 Oct. 1869, 29 Oct. 1869, 4 Jan. 1870; *AN,* 10 Jan. 1871; *Journal of the House of Representatives of the State of Georgia,* 1870, pp. 19, 185, 427, 563; Thronateeska Chapter, Daughters of the American Revolution, comp., *History and Reminiscences of Dougherty County, Georgia* (Spartanburg, S.C., 1978), 88; Russell Duncan, "A Georgia Governor Battles Racism: Rufus Bullock and the Fight

for Black Legislators," in *Georgia in Black and White: Explorations in Race Relations of a Southern State, 1865–1950*, ed. John C. Inscoe (Athens, Ga., 1994), 56–57.

2. Karl Marx, *The Eighteenth Brumaire of Louis Bonaparte*, in *The Marx-Engels Reader*, 2nd ed., ed. Robert C. Tucker (New York, 1978), 594–595; Pierre Bourdieu, *The Logic of Practice*, trans. Richard Nice (Stanford, Calif., 1980), 56; John Lewis Gaddis, *The Landscape of History: How Historians Map the Past* (New York, 2002), 9.

3. On the low country, see, for instance, Russell Duncan, *On Freedom's Shore: Tunis Campbell and the Georgia Freedmen* (Athens, Ga., 1986); Julie Saville, *The Work of Reconstruction: From Slave to Wage Laborer in South Carolina, 1860–1870* (Cambridge, 1994); John Scott Strickland, "Traditional Culture and Moral Economy: Social and Economic Change in the South Carolina Low Country, 1865–1880," in *The Countryside in the Age of Capitalist Transformation*, ed. Steven Hahn and Jonathan Prude (Chapel Hill, N.C., 1985), 141–178; Eric Foner, *Nothing but Freedom: Emancipation and Its Legacy* (Baton Rouge, 1983); on urban areas (which were often part of a larger maritime world as well), see, for instance, Michael W. Fitzgerald, *Urban Emancipation: Popular Politics in Reconstruction Mobile, 1860–1890* (Baton Rouge, 2002); David S. Cecelski, *The Waterman's Son: Slavery and Freedom in Maritime North Carolina* (Chapel Hill, N.C., 2001), chap. 7; David S. Cecelski and Timothy B. Tyson, eds., *Democracy Betrayed: The Wilmington Race Riot of 1898 and Its Legacy* (Chapel Hill, N.C., 1998), chaps. 1–2; Elsa Barkley Brown, "Negotiating and Transforming the Public Sphere: African American Political Life in the Transition from Slavery to Freedom," *Public Culture 7* (Fall 1994): 107–146; on freedom in the sugar parishes, see John C. Rodrigue, *Reconstruction in the Cane Fields: From Slavery to Free Labor in Louisiana's Sugar Parishes, 1862–1880* (Baton Rouge, 2001), and Rebecca J. Scott, "'Stubborn and Disposed to Stand Their Ground': Black Militia, Sugar Workers and the Dynamics of Collective Action in the Louisiana Sugar Bowl, 1863–87," in *From Slavery to Emancipation in the Atlantic World*, ed. Sylvia R. Frey and Betty Wood (London, 1999), 103–126; on Davis Bend, see Janet Sharp Hermann, *The Pursuit of a Dream* (New York, 1981); *House Exec. Doc.*, 11, p. 30.

4. Gerald D. Jaynes, *Branches without Roots: Genesis of the Black Working Class in the American South, 1862–1888* (New York, 1986), 141–144; Gavin Wright, *The Political Economy of the Cotton South: Households, Markets, and Wealth in the Nineteenth Century* (New York, 1978), 172; Gavin Wright, *Old South, New South: Revolutions in the Southern Economy since the Civil War* (New York, 1986), 56–57; Lawrence N. Powell, *New Masters: Northern Planters during the Civil War and Reconstruction* (New Haven, Conn., 1980), 146–149; Roger L. Ransom and Richard Sutch, *One Kind of Freedom: The Economic Consequences of Emancipation* (Cambridge, 1977), 64–65.

5. W. F. White to E. A. Ware, 13 Nov. 1868, LR, M799r12; Sarah H. Champney to E. P. Smith, 1 Dec. 1868, no. 21787, AMAr4; S. H. Champney to E. P. Smith, 30 Jan. 1869, no. 22020, AMAr4; John L. Wheeler to J. R. Lewis, 7 Feb. 1870, LR, M799r14; S. H. Champney to E. P. Smith, 29 Mar. 1869, no. 22245, AMAr5; W. L. Clark to J. R. Lewis, 8 Apr. 1869, LR, M799r12; *GWT,* 12 Feb. 1869, 16 Apr. 1869; *GJM,* 26 Oct. 1869; "Condition of Affairs in Georgia," 94; Philip S. Foner and Ronald L. Lewis, eds., *The Black Worker: A Documentary History from Colonial Times to the Present* (Philadelphia, 1978), 2:14; William McKay, *Facts, Incidents and Opinions in the Life of an Ordinary Man* (Clearwater, Fla., 1988), 114–115; Steven Hahn, *A Nation under Our Feet: Black Political Struggles in the Rural South from Slavery to the Great Migration* (Cambridge, Mass., 2003), 216–219; on Georgia specifically, see Edmund L. Drago, *Black Politicians and Reconstruction in Georgia: A Splendid Failure* (1982; repr., Athens, Ga., 1992), 78–85.

6. S. W. Stansbury to E. P. Smith, 30 Dec. 1860, no. 23064, AMAr6; *GJM,* 26 Oct. 1869; *GWT,* 15 Jan. 1869; "Condition of Affairs in Georgia," 156.

7. Putney & Flagg to E. P. Smith, 16 Nov. 1869, no. 22914, AMAr5; [Jane McNeil] to E. P. Smith, 22 Dec. 1869, no. 23043, AMAr6; Jane McNeil to E. P. Smith, [late] Dec. 1869, no. 23117, AMAr6; *AP,* 2 Nov. 1869, 14 Dec. 1869, 28 June 1870.

8. W. E. B. Du Bois, *The Souls of Black Folk,* ed. David W. Blight and Robert Gooding-Williams (Boston, 1997), 113–114. Dougherty County and its people are the subject of chapters 7 and 8 in *Souls of Black Folk.*

9. Wm. Birts to Wm. Coppinger, 2 Aug. 1878, Records of the American

Colonization Society, Library of Congress, ser. 1A, microfilm reel 117; J. F. Johnson and T. F. Green to John B. Gordon, 5 Feb. 1889, GIC; *Report of the Commissioner of Agriculture for the Year 1866* (Washington, D.C., 1867), 571–572; Hahn, *Nation under Our Feet*, 468–471; Elsa Barkley Brown and Gregg D. Kimball, "Mapping the Terrain of Black Richmond," *Journal of Urban History* 21 (Mar. 1995): 306–307; Eric Foner, *Reconstruction: America's Unfinished Revolution, 1863–1877* (New York, 1988), 346–411; Brian Kelly, "Black Laborers, the Republican Party, and the Crisis of Reconstruction in Lowcountry South Carolina," *International Review of Social History* 51 (Dec. 2006): 375–414; Rodrigue, *Reconstruction in the Cane Fields*, 120–158; Richard M. Valelly, *The Two Reconstructions: The Struggle for Black Enfranchisement* (Chicago, 2004), 79–87.

10. E. McClellan to E. P. Smith, 16 Sept. 1869, no. 22776, AMAr5; M. E. Hansen to E. M. Cravath, 24 Dec. 1870, no. 23844, AMAr7; M. E. Hansen to A.M.A., 27 Dec. 1870, no. 23848, AMAr7; M. E. Hansen to E. M. Cravath, 2 Mar. 1871, no. 23966, AMAr7; "Huguenin Plantation Sumter County Georgia," [1907], HJF; "Two Plantations Belonging to Geo. W. Bryan, Lying in Worth Co., Ga.," [1876], Plantation Account Book, vol. 4, George W. Bryan Papers, GDAH; L. P. Dickinson to E. M. Cravath, 21 May 1876, no. 26125, AMAr10; contract between W. H. Branch and freedpeople, undated, Branch Family Papers, SHC; Joseph Means to David Vason, 16 [Jan.] 1876, Callaway, Hamner, Harris, Newsom, & Vason Collection, GDAH; Duncan Curry to Jaine, 25 Jan. 1885, CHP; vols. 3, 7, 11, and 12, DAH; *DWJ*, 2 Nov. 1870, 4 Dec. 1873; *GWT*, 12 Nov. 1869, 4 Jan. 1870, 11 Jan. 1870, 25 Jan. 1870; *AN*, 9 Dec. 1870, 5 Jan. 1872; Edmund L. Drago, "The Black Household in Dougherty County, Georgia, 1870–1900," *Prologue* 14 (Summer 1982): 81–88.

Index